Microsoft 365 All-in-one Guide

Understanding and deploying Microsoft 365 applications, PowerShell, and Power Automate

---

Pranjali Vaidya Bramhe

bpb

www.bpbonline.com

First Edition 2026

Copyright © BPB Publications, India

ISBN: 978-93-65896-480

LIMITS OF LIABILITY AND DISCLAIMER OF WARRANTY

The information contained in this book is true and correct to the best of author's and publisher's knowledge. The author has made every effort to ensure the accuracy of these publications, but the publisher cannot be held responsible for any loss or damage arising from any information in this book.

All trademarks referred to in the book are acknowledged as properties of their respective owners but BPB Publications cannot guarantee the accuracy of this information.

To View Complete
BPB Publications Catalogue
Scan the QR Code:

Dedicated to

My parents who instilled in me the values of perseverance and learning.

To my family for their unwavering support.

*To every learner, educator, and changemaker around the world
who believes in the power of digital transformation.*

About the Author

Pranjali Vaidya Bramhe is a passionate advocate of digital empowerment, an eloquent and fervent change maker who believes in bringing change by learning, relearning, and unlearning. With 19 years of experience in the field, she brings a wealth of knowledge and expertise to her role. She is also the co-founder of a tech enterprise that has immensely contributed to the field of Information Science and Education Technology by imparting training to more than 40k users on Microsoft technologies. Currently, she is working on evolving technologies like Microsoft 365 Copilot. Her role involves promoting the adoption process by delivering tailored training programs to global corporations. She has been instrumental in leading digital transformation initiatives, with a focus on Microsoft 365 tools and user adoption strategies. She empowers individuals and organizations to use tools like Teams, Outlook, and Copilot for enhanced collaboration, communication, and productivity. She has independently handled various projects with many corporations like Microland, Ernst & Young, British Council(Shared Services), Microsoft Global Partners, Thyssenkrupp, NTPC, Bajaj Auto, Crayon Pvt Ltd, NIIT Ltd, UB Group, and many more, where she looked after the adoption process, change management process, and training across the globe (covering different regions like EMEIA, America, APAC, and Oceania). She has travelled through the length and breadth of the globe. She had delivered sessions for **Village Level Entrepreneurs** (**VLEs**) to enable them to use the AI-based features in Office applications under CSC and Microsoft collaboration. She obtained her M.Tech (CS) from Manav Bharati University. She holds a Master's and Bachelor's degree in computer applications from Indira Gandhi National Open University. With a strong background in educational technology and corporate learning solutions, she blends strategic insight with a hands-on approach to make technology accessible, engaging, and impactful for all.

She is an esteemed member of various Microsoft forums and has contributed extensively. She has several accreditations, like **Microsoft Certified Trainer** (**MCT**) since 2009, MCP, MCPD, and MCTS. As a Global Minecraft Trainer and Microsoft Office Specialist, she has championed game-based and ICT-driven learning in education. She had executed various technology-based programs for early career researchers and several academicians of various state and central universities. She has led key Microsoft initiatives like the Incubator, Showcase School, and MIEE Programs, driving impactful digital transformation in education. She is a reputed speaker and contributes to faculty development programs and workshops across K12 and higher education. She has conducted Education Transformation Framework workshops where principals and educators shared their digital transformation journeys.

When not engaged in writing, she enjoys simple joys that keep her grounded and connected to her roots, such as travelling to the mountains, listening to music, and spending quality time with her family.

About the Reviewers

❖ **Nandhakumar Raju** is a visionary technology leader with over 25 years of experience in digital transformation, AI/ML innovation, and large-scale enterprise modernization. As Director of Technology at a leading healthcare organization, he has played a critical role in revolutionizing health systems that impact millions of lives across the United States. His work focuses on building scalable, intelligent, and people-centric solutions that improve access, efficiency, and equity in healthcare.

He is also the co-founder of My Ayur Health and Mazo Solutions, ventures that reflect his passion for blending technology with purpose. Through these platforms, he empowers individuals and businesses with tools for wellness, automation, and operational excellence.

An award-winning innovator, published researcher, and mentor, Nandhakumar is committed to nurturing the next generation of global leaders and driving meaningful change through responsible technology.

❖ **Mudappallur Raman Venkateswaran (Venkat)** is a Senior Product Manager (PSPO certified) at Walmart Global Tech. He joined Walmart after earning his master's degree in Management Information Systems from the University at Buffalo and is now a part of the Technology Platform product team. His work focuses on managing Atlassian products and internal applications that enable intelligent workforce management powered by Generative AI, supporting Walmart associates globally.

Venkat is passionate about innovation and product excellence, with a proven track record of launching impactful digital transformation and enterprise products at Walmart and Cognizant. His experience spans leading cross-functional teams and delivering solutions that drive measurable outcomes.

As an avid reader of non-fiction, Venkat stays updated on emerging technologies and believes in the transformative potential of technology to create meaningful change. He aspires to contribute to this revolution by delivering life-changing products or serving as a technical reviewer for technology books and research papers.

Acknowledgement

I would like to express my sincere gratitude to all those who contributed to the completion of this book.

First and foremost, I extend my heartfelt appreciation to my family and friends for their unwavering support and encouragement throughout this journey. Their love and belief in me have been a constant source of strength and motivation.

A special note of appreciation to Dr Priya Vaidya for her valuable input and thoughtful contributions. Your insights and feedback have been instrumental in shaping the content and elevating the quality of this book. Thank you for your invaluable support.

A heartfelt thank you to my daughter, Ms. Siddhi Bramhe, a young author in her own right, whose creativity and passion continue to inspire me to pursue my own.

I am deeply grateful to BPB Publications for their guidance and expertise in bringing this book to life. Their professional support and assistance have been invaluable in navigating the complexities of the publishing process.

I would also like to acknowledge the efforts of reviewers, technical experts, and editors whose constructive feedback and suggestions have greatly contributed to refining the manuscript and enhancing its overall quality.

Last but not least, I want to express my gratitude to the readers who have shown interest in this book. Your support and encouragement have been deeply appreciated.

Thank you to everyone who has played a part in making this book a reality.

Preface

In today's fast-evolving digital landscape, organizations and individuals alike are constantly seeking efficient, collaborative, and scalable solutions to enhance productivity. From business and education to research and administration, Microsoft 365 (formerly Office 365) has emerged as a transformative suite of applications that caters to the diverse needs of users. Its cloud-based infrastructure, seamless integration, and powerful tools have redefined how we work, communicate, and manage data.

For students, teachers, IT specialists, and business users who want to fully utilize Microsoft 365, this book, is intended to be a thorough reference guide. This book offers organized, detailed insights into every element, regardless of your level of experience, whether you are a novice investigating these applications for the first time or an accomplished professional seeking to improve your deployment tactics. This book provides structured, step-by-step insights into each component of the Microsoft 365 ecosystem.

Although Microsoft 365 has become widely used across industries, many users still find it difficult to navigate its extensive feature set and deployment challenges. This book fills that void by providing:

- **Holistic overview**: The book methodically examines each application, beginning with the foundations of cloud computing and Microsoft 365 (Chapter 1) to guarantee that readers acquire both practical knowledge and conceptual clarity.

- **Effective deployment strategies**: The book explores user and group administration (Chapter 2), cloud storage options (Chapter 9), and collaboration tools (Chapter 8), offering administrators practical insights beyond program usage.

- **Productivity enhancement**: Readers will learn how to automate processes and optimise workflows using basic programs like Word, Excel, and PowerPoint (Chapters 4-6) and more sophisticated solutions like Power Platform (Chapter 12).

- **Collaboration and innovation**: The book highlights contemporary workplace cooperation, guaranteeing that teams remain connected and productive, with special chapters on Teams, OneDrive, SharePoint, and Viva Engage (Chapters 8–10).

- **Emerging technologies**: In order to enable users to take advantage of AI-driven and low-code solutions, the last chapters present state-of-the-art technologies such as OneNote, Sway, Whiteboard (Chapter 11), and Power BI (Chapter 12).

This book caters to an eclectic audience and offers them how Microsoft 365 improves digital learning through cloud-based assignments, interactive presentations, and collaborative writing. Business professionals could learn how data analysis and business processes can be streamlined with Excel, Power BI, and Power Automate. On the other hand, IT developers and administrators can become proficient in security regulations, third-party app integration, and the deployment and management of Microsoft 365 environments. According to these experts, advanced capabilities in Word, OneNote, and Sway can be used by researchers, educators, students, and content creators for effective documentation and digital storytelling.

This book is organised into 12 chapters, each focusing on a crucial aspect of Microsoft 365 applications and their functionalities:

Chapter 1: Overview of Microsoft 365 and Its Deployment - This chapter provides a foundational understanding of Microsoft 365 and cloud computing, including its various types. It traces the evolution from Office 365 to Microsoft 365 and explains the different licensing models. Readers will also learn about deployment strategies and the purpose of key M365 applications.

Chapter 2: Managing Office 365 Users and User Groups - This chapter explains how to configure permissions, create public/private groups, and define administrative policies. It focuses on managing users, different group types, and their memberships, while also covering key aspects like group creation, management, and expiration policies.

Chapter 3: Office 365 Tools and Their Functions - This chapter offers an overview of core Microsoft 365 tools and their key functions, highlighting how they support communication, collaboration, and productivity. The chapter emphasizes how these integrated applications streamline workflows and enhance efficiency in both individual and team settings.

Chapter 4: Creating Masterpiece Documents with MS Word - This chapter provides a comprehensive guide to mastering Microsoft Word by exploring each key tab and its functions. It covers the Home, Insert, Draw, Design, and Layout tabs for formatting and structuring content; explains the use of the References and Mailings tabs for citations and document automation; and highlights the Review and View tabs for editing and navigation. The chapter also emphasizes the importance of the Help tab as a valuable resource for ongoing support and learning, enabling users to create polished, professional documents with confidence.

Chapter 5: Sorting and Organising Data in Microsoft Excel - This chapter focuses on techniques for data organisation, formulas, functions, and data visualisation. Additionally, it explains how to organize data using tables and visually represent information through charts, enabling users to draw insights and make informed decisions with clarity and precision.

Chapter 6: Designing Professional Presentations with Microsoft PowerPoint - This chapter guides readers through the process of creating impactful and professional presentations with multimedia integration. It covers essential skills such as managing slides, exploring different presentation views, and configuring slide shows for effective delivery. Readers will also learn how to insert various objects, apply transitions, and animations to enhance visual appeal.

Chapter 7: Developing and Administering Databases Using Microsoft Access - This chapter introduces the fundamentals of relational database management, guiding readers in developing and administering efficient databases. It covers key components of RDBMS, data types, and the process of creating tables and queries. The chapter also explains normalization techniques, different types of relationships, the use of wildcards for flexible data searches, and generating reports to present data in a structured and meaningful way.

Chapter 8: Transforming Learning with Microsoft Teams - This chapter explores how Microsoft Teams serves as a powerful platform for enhancing collaboration through channels, meetings, and third-party integrations. It provides an overview of the Teams interface and explains different types of channels, standard, private, and shared, for organizing discussions and resources. The chapter covers various meeting types, such as scheduled, instant, and Webinar formats, along with different views and notification settings to enhance the user experience. It also introduces the use of Copilot in Teams for intelligent assistance and highlights the functionality of the mobile version, enabling seamless learning and collaboration on the go.

Chapter 9: OneDrive for Business and SharePoint - This chapter explains the power of OneDrive for Business and SharePoint within the Microsoft 365 ecosystem. It highlights the utilization of cloud storage, file sharing, and organisational intranet solutions. This chapter discusses SharePoint, explaining its core components and the structure of a SharePoint team site, including libraries, lists, web parts, and site pages. Together, these tools enable efficient file management, team collaboration, and information sharing across organizations.

Chapter 10: Microsoft Forms, Outlook, Planner, and Yammer - This chapter introduces a set of Microsoft 365 tools designed to streamline communication, collaboration, and task management. It includes administering surveys, managing emails, tracking tasks, and facilitating enterprise social networking, community building within the organization using Viva Engage.

Chapter 11: OneNote, Sway, Whiteboard, and To Do - This chapter explores four powerful Microsoft 365 tools, OneNote, Sway, Whiteboard, and To Do, that enhance the way individuals and teams capture ideas, express creativity, and manage tasks in a digital environment. Empowering digital productivity and engaging in digital note-taking features like handwriting, audio recording, tagging and real-time collaboration, interactive storytelling for modern presentations, visually appealing newsletters, portfolios and visual collaboration in real-time using Microsoft Whiteboard that enables brainstorming, planning and sketching ideas with teammates and effective task management tool designed to help users plan their day, track goals, and stay organized.

Chapter 12: Microsoft Power Platform - Unleashing Business Intelligence and Automation. This chapter is an introduction to Microsoft Power Platform, focusing on how Power BI, Power Apps, and Power Automate work together to transform data into insights, build custom applications, and automate workflows. It highlights practical use cases and the strategic value of integrating these tools to drive smarter decisions, improve efficiency, and empower users across all levels of an organization.

As an outcome, Microsoft 365 is a catalyst for digital transformation rather than only a software suite. To enhance productivity, teamwork, and creativity in your personal and professional pursuits, this book seeks to be your reliable guide through its many features. We hope that this tutorial will enable you to fully utilize Microsoft 365 and encourage you to experiment with new methods of working in a world that is becoming more interconnected by the day.

Coloured Images

Please follow the link to download the
Coloured Images of the book:

https://rebrand.ly/d867f4

We have code bundles from our rich catalogue of books and videos available at
https://github.com/bpbpublications. Check them out!

Errata

We take immense pride in our work at BPB Publications and follow best practices to ensure the accuracy of our content to provide with an indulging reading experience to our subscribers. Our readers are our mirrors, and we use their inputs to reflect and improve upon human errors, if any, that may have occurred during the publishing processes involved. To let us maintain the quality and help us reach out to any readers who might be having difficulties due to any unforeseen errors, please write to us at :

errata@bpbonline.com

Your support, suggestions and feedbacks are highly appreciated by the BPB Publications' Family.

At www.bpbonline.com, you can also read a collection of free technical articles, sign up for a range of free newsletters, and receive exclusive discounts and offers on BPB books and eBooks. You can check our social media handles below:

Instagram   *Facebook*   *Linkedin*   *YouTube*

Get in touch with us at: business@bpbonline.com for more details.

Piracy

If you come across any illegal copies of our works in any form on the internet, we would be grateful if you would provide us with the location address or website name. Please contact us at business@bpbonline.com with a link to the material.

If you are interested in becoming an author

If there is a topic that you have expertise in, and you are interested in either writing or contributing to a book, please visit www.bpbonline.com. We have worked with thousands of developers and tech professionals, just like you, to help them share their insights with the global tech community. You can make a general application, apply for a specific hot topic that we are recruiting an author for, or submit your own idea.

Reviews

Please leave a review. Once you have read and used this book, why not leave a review on the site that you purchased it from? Potential readers can then see and use your unbiased opinion to make purchase decisions. We at BPB can understand what you think about our products, and our authors can see your feedback on their book. Thank you!

For more information about BPB, please visit www.bpbonline.com.

Join our Discord space

Join our Discord workspace for latest updates, offers, tech happenings around the world, new releases, and sessions with the authors:

https://discord.bpbonline.com

Table of Contents

CHAPTER 1

Overview of Microsoft 365 and Its Deployment

Introduction

Technological integration and its adoption in the academic and non-academic sectors have become facile with the advent of the Internet. Due to this, it has embraced all the learning demands of the 21st century and paved the way to blended learning for all learners and educators. Microsoft and its various versions in this technological race have left no stone unturned to rule over the profit and non-profit sectors. All the cutting-edge technologies are supposed to make our lives easier and inspire us to be more aware of doing any desirable tasks. The first chapter of the book will uncover **Microsoft 365 (M365)** and its types.

Further, it would encompass various collaboration tools that are highly beneficial for all stakeholders and the student community. Moreover, the readers would learn the concept of cloud computing and its types. Ultimately, the learners and the practitioners will be able to understand the deployment of the M365 environment and why it is required to implement it.

Structure

In this chapter, the following topics will be covered:

- Understanding Microsoft 365
- Cloud computing and its types
- Evolution of M365 and O365
- Types of subscriptions or licenses
- Deployment of the M365 environment
- Overview of Microsoft 365
- Applications and their purpose

Objectives

By the end of this chapter, you will learn about M365. Along with this, you will learn about applications and services available in M365. You will be able to learn how to deploy the M365 environment along with various subscriptions and its offerings.

Understanding Microsoft 365

M365 is a cloud-based product. M365 evolved from Office 365, which offers premium Office applications like Word, Excel, PowerPoint, Outlook, OneNote, and so on, with 1 TB of **OneDrive for Business** (**ODB**) cloud storage and high-level security features. It further provides device management capabilities and many more things to help you get things done. The concept behind M365 is to use all applications and services throughout 365 days, from anywhere, anytime, on any device.

M365 comes with various plans and subscriptions. If the company has 300+ users, then the Enterprise Plan benefits the entire year. We will discuss this in more detail.

Cloud computing and its types

The creation of an environment on a computer using an online application stored on the cloud and run through a web browser is known as cloud computing. In simple terms, IT resources are delivered on-demand via the Internet with a pay-per-use model in cloud computing. By using this service, you can save time, effort, and money. Instead of getting and maintaining computer products and services, you can use cloud computing services. There are a variety of technologies used to create every cloud.

Cloud-based services

There are three types of services available, which are given as follows:

- **Software as a Service (SaaS)**
- **Platform as a Service (PaaS)**
- **Infrastructure as a Service (IaaS)**

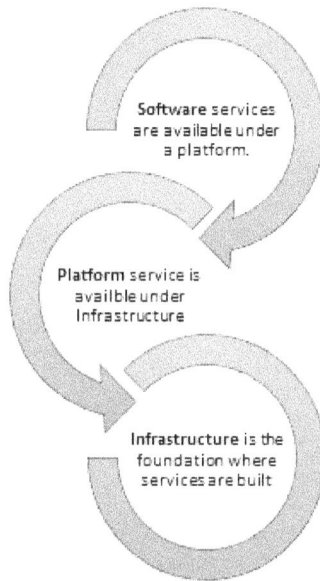

Figure 1.1: Types of cloud computing services

Software as a Service

M365 is a SaaS product where many applications can be used over the cloud. Its applications can be accessed from anywhere, anytime and with any device, with no need to store data on the computer's hard drive. It is also known as an on-demand service. Security features like SSL encryption are also available in SaaS. It can also be accessed via a web browser known as a web application that eliminates the installation of an application on the device. Microsoft Word can be used on the browser (Edge, Chrome, and so on), and data will be saved automatically. By default, the AutoSave option is turned on. Users will focus on the data, and the cloud will take care of the data by saving your file.

In a nutshell, without using any hardware or software, users can access the cloud-hosted application. For example, Gmail, Yahoo mail, Rediff mail, etc.

Platform as a Service

As the name suggests, PaaS provides a platform-like **application programming interface** (**API**) and handles the implementation. Examples are Salesforce, Microsoft Azure, and Zoho Creator.

It is a platform for developers to code using APIs and create their own SaaS applications. In the PaaS model, the user will get an operating system, database, programming language, execution environment, and a web server. Most of the time, PaaS providers render pre-built blocks that developers can plug and play to build better applications quickly.

Examples of PaaS are Microsoft Azure, CloudBees, and so on.

Infrastructure as a Service

In this model, infrastructure (hardware) manages the servers, network, virtualization, and data storage with the help of the Internet. The user has access through the API and rents the infrastructure for a limited time. Architects can work under this model. A few examples include Amazon Web Services, Microsoft Azure Virtual Machines, OpenStack, Azure Stack, etc, as shown in the following figure:

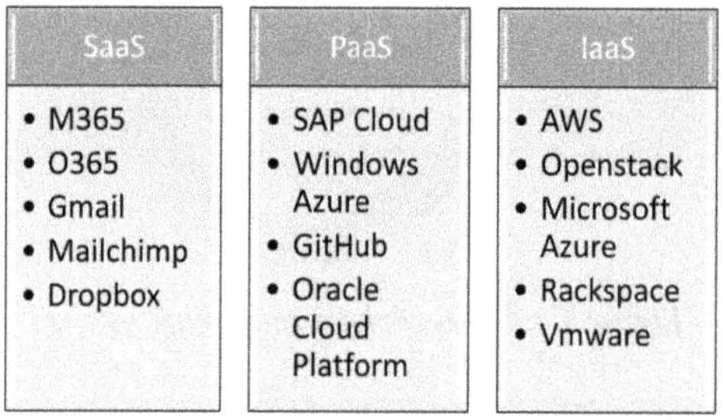

SaaS	PaaS	IaaS
• M365 • O365 • Gmail • Mailchimp • Dropbox	• SAP Cloud • Windows Azure • GitHub • Oracle Cloud Platform	• AWS • Openstack • Microsoft Azure • Rackspace • Vmware

Figure 1.2: Examples of SaaS, PaaS, IaaS

Evolution of Microsoft 365 and Office 365

As a part of the **Office 365 (O365)** subscription model, Microsoft introduced the concept of SaaS. Office 365 consists of productivity apps like MS Word, MS Excel, and so on, along with collaboration and communication services like SharePoint, Skype for Business, and Exchange. O365 is available for corporate users, academicians, and businesspeople with different subscription plans for them.

M365 is the extension of Office 365 with best-in-class productivity applications from O365 with advanced intelligent security, device management, and innovation services.

The following figure illustrates the differences between M365 and Office 365:

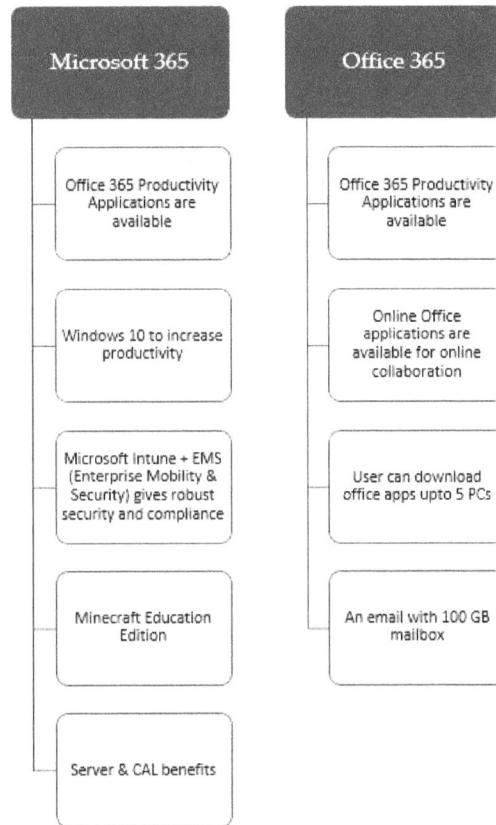

Figure 1.3: *Comparison between M365 and O365*

Types of subscriptions or licenses

M365 subscriptions are available in different types of plans. With M365, you can transform ideas into reality, stay safer, and focus on what matters most. M365 can enhance productivity with its dynamic and vibrant applications, viz., Microsoft Teams, Word, Excel, PowerPoint, and many more, all available under a single platform. These apps allow us, the learners and stakeholders, to stay connected and get things done with M365. These apps provide us with multiple options to meet our needs, like connecting with family and friends, and so on. Anyone can learn and collaborate remotely with your team, helping you stay organized and simplify your day.

On any device, stay secure and productive. You can rest assured knowing that your personal information, devices, apps, and data are protected with comprehensive, intelligent, enterprise-grade security features. Big and small organizations are digitally transforming with M365.

Embrace M365 and Microsoft Teams to reimagine productivity (Microsoft 365, 2023b). Get started with M365 with the following subscriptions:

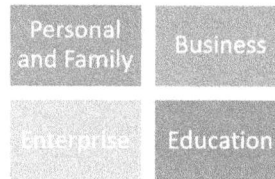

Figure 1.4 *Types of subscription/licenses*

Personal and family

In this sub-section, M365 has the app and features to help you turn ideas into reality and focus on the important points (Microsoft Store, 2023). Thus, Microsoft subscription features for personal and family are listed as follows:

- **M365 Family** (yearly plan is available):
  - For one to six people.
  - Use up to 5 devices simultaneously.
  - It works on PC, Macs, iPhones, iPads, Android phones, and Tablets.
  - Up to 6TB of cloud storage (1 TB per person).
  - Access to latest updates.
  - Ongoing technical support.
  - Microsoft Family Safety.
  - Office apps (Word, Excel, PowerPoint).
  - Microsoft Teams, Outlook, Microsoft Forms, OneNote, and Skype applications are available.
  - Access and Publisher are available only for PC. A visual representation of these features can be seen in the following figure:

Figure 1.5: *Office applications for family*

- **M365 Personal** (yearly plan is available):
  - For only one person.

o Use up to 5 devices simultaneously. (Works across multiple devices).

o It works on PC, Macs, iPhones, iPads, Android phones, and tablets.

o 1 TB of cloud storage.

o Office apps with offline access along with Access and Publisher (PC only).

o Microsoft Teams, Outlook, Microsoft Forms, OneNote, and Skype applications are available.

o Apps available are separate downloads; you must accept Clipchamp's terms of service and privacy policy. A visual representation of these features can be seen in the following figure:

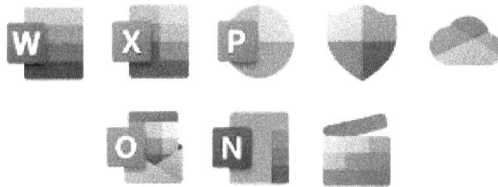

Figure 1.6: Office applications available for personal

Business

It is a subscription service that allows you to run your organization in the cloud while Microsoft takes care of the IT for you. It provides employees with access to the people, information, and content they require to perform their best work, regardless of their location (Microsoft 365 Plans, 2023).

M365 Business Basic: Best for businesses that need easy remote solutions, with Microsoft Teams, secure cloud storage, and Web and mobile versions of Office apps (desktop versions not included). The features of this plan are:

• Host email with 50 GB mailbox and custom email address.

• Work from anywhere, on any device.

• Create a hub for teamwork to connect people using Microsoft Teams.

• Office applications for the web are available, which include Outlook, Word, Excel, PowerPoint, and OneNote.

• 1 TB of OneDrive cloud storage per user to store and share files.

• Facilitate online meetings, chat, and video conferencing for up to 300 users.

With Microsoft's round-the-clock phone and web support, you can receive assistance at any time. (24/7 support included). A visual representation of these features can be seen in the following figure:

Web and Mobile only

Figure 1.7: *M365 Business Basic applications*

M365 Business Standard: Best for businesses that need full-time remote work and collaboration tools, including Microsoft Teams, secure cloud storage, business email, and premium Office applications across devices. The features of this plan are:

- Desktop versions are available for Office applications, including Outlook, Word, Excel, PowerPoint, and OneNote (plus Access and Publisher for PC only)

- Host email with 50 GB mailbox and custom email domain.

- Create a hub for teamwork to connect people using Microsoft Teams.

- Store and share files with 1 TB of OneDrive cloud storage per user.

- Work from anywhere, on any device.

- Use one license to cover fully installed Office apps on five mobile devices, five tablets, and five PCs or Macs per user.

With Microsoft's round-the-clock phone and web support, you can receive assistance at any time. (24/7 support included) A visual representation of these features can be seen in the following figure:

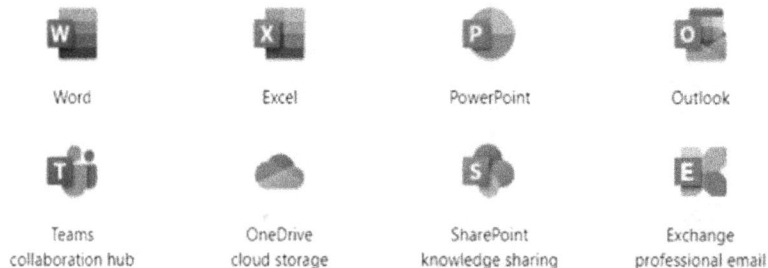

Figure 1.8: *M365 Business Standard applications*

M365 Business Premium: This is best for businesses that require secure, remote work solutions with everything included in Business Standard, plus advanced cyber threat protection and device management. This plan has the following features:

- Stay up to date with the latest versions of Word, Excel, PowerPoint, and more.
- Connect with customers and coworkers using Outlook, Exchange, and Microsoft Teams.
- Use Microsoft Teams to meet online and chat securely.
- Manage new PCs and devices quickly and easily.
- Manage your files from anywhere with 1 TB of cloud storage on OneDrive per user.
- Defend your business against advanced cyber threats with sophisticated phishing and ransomware protection.
- Control access to sensitive information using encryption to help keep data from being accidentally shared.
- Secure devices that connect you to your data and help keep iOS, Android, Windows, and MacOS devices safe and up to date. A visual representation of these features can be seen in the following figure:

Figure 1.9: M365 Business Premium applications

M365 apps for Business: Best for businesses that need Office apps across devices and cloud file storage. Business email and Microsoft Teams are not included. Anytime phone and web support.

- Web versions are available for Word, Excel, and PowerPoint.
- 1 TB of OneDrive cloud storage per user is available to store and share files.
- One license will cover fully installed Office apps on five phones, five tablets, and five PCs and Macs per user.
- Work from anywhere, on any device.
- Free 24/7 support is available.

A visual representation of these features can be seen in the following figure:

Figure 1.10: M365 apps for business

Enterprise

Powerful tools are available to support your enterprise. Office 365 and M365 apps enable you to create, share, and collaborate from anywhere on any device with a cloud-based suite of productivity apps and services (Microsoft 365 Enterprise, 2022).

- **M365 apps for enterprise**: The enterprise edition of the Office apps plus cloud-based file storage and sharing. Business email not included. A visual representation of these features can be seen in the following figure:

Figure 1.11: M365 apps for enterprise

- **Office 365 E1**: Business services include email, file storage, and sharing, as well as Office for the web, meetings, IM, and more. The Office apps are not included in this. A visual representation can be seen in the following figure:

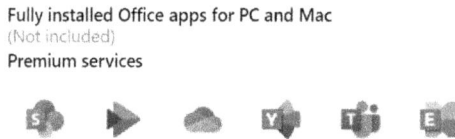

Figure 1.12: Office 365 E1

- **Office 365 E3**: All the features included in M365 apps for enterprise and Office 365 E1 plus security and compliance are shown as follows:

Figure 1.13: Office 365 E3

- **Office 365 E5**: All the features of Office 365 E3 plus advanced security, analytics, and voice capabilities:

Fully installed Office apps for PC and Mac

(PC Only)   (PC Only)

Premium services

Figure 1.14: Office 365 E5

- **M365 E3**: Get best-in-class productivity apps combined with core security and compliance capabilities for your enterprise.

- **M365 E5**: Get best-in-class productivity apps and advanced security, compliance, voice, and analytical capabilities for your enterprise.

- **M365 F3**: Formerly M365 F1, this solution is designed for frontline workers to achieve more with productivity apps and cloud services that allow them to do their best work. It is best to safeguard company assets with intelligent security that would not slow down frontline productivity. The frontline workforce is the backbone of the organization.

| Word | Excel | PowerPoint | Outlook | OneNote | Teams | Windows | Microsoft Endpoint Manager |

Figure 1.15: M365 F3 includes Office Web and mobile apps

Recommendations based on personas

Each plan is customized to meet the unique requirements of the organization. This section outlines various plans, providing a clear understanding of the different subscription options available within Microsoft offerings as follows:

- **Small business owner**: If the company prefers M365 Business Standard, it includes desktop applications, email, and collaboration tools without overloading them with enterprise-level features.

- **Remote or hybrid workforce:** If the company prefers to use M365 Business Premium, it offers secure access to data and device management for remote employees.

- **Educational institution**: If the institute prefers to use the A3 plan, it will include offline access, advanced tools for teachers, and secure student communication.

- **Large organizations**: If a company acquires E5 licenses, it integrates comprehensive security, compliance tools, and advanced analytics to manage enterprise needs.

- **Frontline worker**: If the company prefers to use an F3 license, it is designed for lightweight usage with mobile-friendly access and essential communication tools.

Education

For education purposes, the following table will provide a description of M365 educational subscriptions categorized into three groups: A1, A3, and A5 (Microsoft 365 Education, 2023; Office 365 For Education, 2023).

Table 1.1 shows how M365 apps are available on different platforms:

Microsoft 365 Apps	A1 for devices	A3	A5
Desktop client apps[1]	✓	✓	✓
Office Mobile apps[2]	✓	✓	✓
Install upto 5 Pcs/Mac	✓ (Mobile apps only)	✓	✓
Office for the web	✓	✓	✓
Visio for the web[3]	✓	✓	✓
Microsoft Editor premium features	×	✓	✓
Multilingual user interface for Office applications	✓	✓	✓

Table 1.1: *M365 Apps*

More features like email, calendar, and scheduling can be seen in the following *Table 1.2*:

Email, calendar, and scheduling			
Exchange Plan 1 (50 GB mailbox)	✓	×	×
Exchange Plan 2 (100 GB mailbox)	×	✓	✓
Calendar	✓	✓	✓
Outlook desktop client	✓	✓	✓
Exchange Online Protection	✓	✓	✓
Public folder mailboxes	✓	✓	✓
Auto-expanding email archive	×	✓	✓
Microsoft Bookings	×	✓	✓

Table 1.2: *Email, calendar, and scheduling*

About the storage, you can find mentioned in the following *Table 1.3*:

Social, intranet, and storage			
SharePoint Plan 1 (1 TB storage)	✓	×	×
SharePoint Plan 2. Microsoft provides an initial 5 TB of storage/user.	×	✓	✓

---

1. Includes Word, Excel, PowerPoint, OneNote, Outlook, Access, and Publisher (PC only)
2. Includes Word, Excel, PowerPoint, OneNote, Outlook mobile apps
3. Available beginning August – December 2021 depending upon region

Yammer Enterprise	✓	✓	✓
Microsoft Viva connections	✓	✓	✓

Table 1.3: Storage in M365 Apps

About meetings, you can find the details mentioned in the following *Table1.4*:

Meetings, calling, and chat			
Microsoft Teams	✓	✓	✓
1:1 and group online audio and video calls	✓	✓	✓
Scheduled meetings	✓	✓	✓
Recorded meetings	✓	✓	✓
Live meetings	×	✓	✓
Webinars	×	✓	✓
Phone System	×	×	✓
Audio Conferencing[4]	×	×	✓
Classroom tools			
Classroom experience in Microsoft Teams	✓	✓	✓
Microsoft Whiteboard	✓	✓	✓
OneNote Class Notebook	✓	✓	✓
Minecraft Education Edition with Code Builder	✓	✓	✓
Take a Test app (Access via Microsoft Store for Education)	✓	✓	✓
Set up School PCs app (Access via Microsoft Store for Education)	✓	✓	✓

Table 1.4: Meetings & Classroom Tools

You can find information about Microsoft tools in the following table:

Knowledge, insights, and content			
Microsoft Graph API	✓	✓	✓
Microsoft Search	✓	✓	✓
Microsoft Stream	✓	✓	✓
Microsoft Forms	✓	✓	✓
Microsoft Lists	✓	✓	✓
Delve	✓	✓	✓

Table 1.5: Microsoft tools

---

4. Check country and region availability at https://docs.microsoft.com/microsoftteams/country-and-region-availability-for-audio-conferencing-and-calling-plans

The following table discusses about task management:

Project and task management			
Microsoft Planner	✓	✓	✓
Microsoft To-Do	✓	✓	✓
Briefing Email	✓	✓	✓

Table 1.6: Task management apps

The following table discusses about analytics:

Analytics			
Compliance Management	✓	✓	✓
Viva Insights + Personal Insights	×	✓	×
Education Analytics	✓	✓	✓
PowerBI Pro	×	×	✓

Table 1.7: Analytics apps

The following table discusses about app management:

Endpoint and app management			
Microsoft Intune for Education	✓	✓	✓
Mobile Device Management (MDM)	✓	✓	✓
Microsoft Endpoint Manager (MEM)	✓	✓	✓
Mobile Application Management (MAM)	✓	✓	✓
Group Policy Support	✓	✓	✓
Shared computer activation for M365 Apps	×	✓	✓
Cortana Management	×	✓	✓
Endpoint Analytics	×	✓	✓

Table 1.8: MAM & MDM

The following table discusses about access management:

Identity and access management			
Azure Active Directory Education	✓	×	×
Azure Active Directory Premium Plan 1	×	✓	×
Azure Active Directory Premium Plan 2	×	×	✓
User Provisioning	✓	✓	✓
Self Service Password Reset	✓	✓	✓
Multi Factor Authentication (MFA)	✓	✓	✓

Microsoft 365 Groups	✓	✓	✓
Microsoft Advanced Threat Analytics	×	✓	✓
On-premises Active Directory sync for SSO	✓	✓	✓
Advanced Security Reports	×	✓	✓

Table 1.9: Access management tools

The following table discusses about chatbots and app building

Automation, app building and chatbots[5]			
PowerApps for Microsoft 365	✓	✓	✓
Power Automate for Microsoft 365	Cloud Flows only, No Desktop flows	✓	✓
Power Virtual Agent for Teams	✓	✓	✓
Dataverse for Teams	✓	✓	✓

Table 1.10: App building tools

The following table discusses all about viva learning:

Viva learning (Included with Faculty licenses only, Course recommendations and progress tracking, integration with 3rd party content providers and LMS (Learning Management Systems) and learning content surfaced across Microsoft 365 suite available with Viva Learning.			
Viva learning in Teams	✓	✓	✓
Creating learning tabs in Teams Channel	✓	✓	✓
Search, share and chat about learning content	✓	✓	✓
Microsoft Learn and Microsoft 365 Training libraries _125 top LinkedIn Learning courses	✓	✓	✓
Organization-generated content with SharePoint and Viva Learning	✓	✓	✓

Table 1.11: Viva learning

The following table discusses about protection:

Threat protection			
Microsoft Defender Antimalware	×	✓	✓
Microsoft Defender Firewall	×	✓	✓
Microsoft Defender Exploit Guard	×	✓	✓
Windows Information Protection	×	✓	✓
BitLocker and BitLocker to Go	×	✓	✓

Table 1.12: Available protection list in M365

---

5. Refer to the licensing FAQs and Licensing Guide at https://docs.microsoft.com/power-platform/admin/ powerapps-flow-licensing-faq for details including functionality limits.

Deployment for M365 apps

Here, we will discuss the deployment process in a way that explains important deployment concepts and detailed deployment procedures. Deployment is valuable information for IT decision-makers, program managers, and technical implementation leads. There are tasks and activities that are required to get ready and fully implement M365 deployment. The implementation of M365 for enterprises is a multi-phased project that requires close communication and coordination between the internal teams and any partners involved (Microsoft 365, 2023a).

A few basic things you need to keep ready while setting up your subscription are:

- **Domain**: A domain is a unique name that appears after the @ sign in email address and after www in a web address. It usually takes the form of your organization's name and a standard Internet suffix, like *abc.com* or *abuniversity.edu*.

- **Subscription plan:** According to your organization's needs, choose the right subscription plan for your business. For available plans, go to any browser and search for M365 subscriptions. It will show you the plan along with the pricing and features that are included with each subscription plan. Choose any plan to view the services and applications that are available with every plan. If you are not sure, select **Help me choose.** You will be taken to a wizard that will help you to make the right decision. Once you have decided on a subscription, click on the **Buy Now** button, as follows:

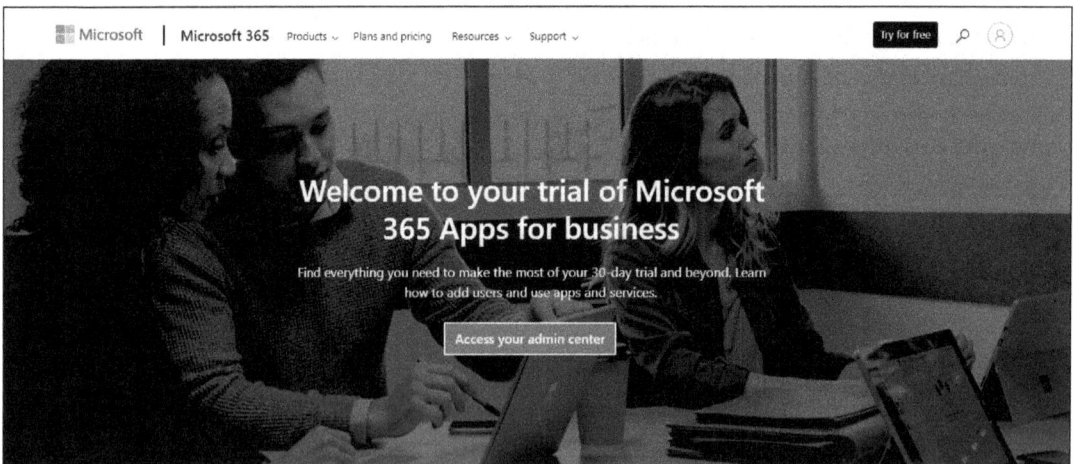

Figure 1.16: M365 for business

When you are ready to move your business to Microsoft Cloud, you will go through the following steps to set everything up:

1. Sign up for a subscription, which we have discussed in the previous section.

2. Search for M365 Business Premium Microsoft Enterprise or M365 Education on the web and go through the steps shown on the screen to set up an account. *Figure 1.17* shows the screen to set up an account:

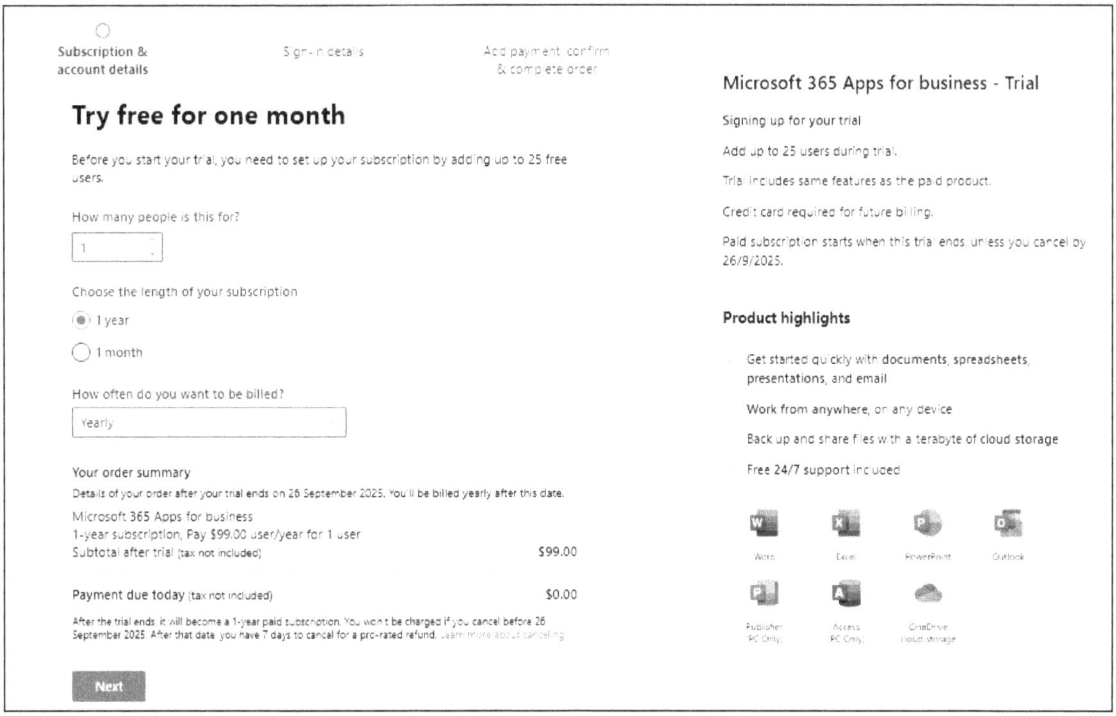

Figure 1.17: Set up an account for the first time

3. After that, you will want to add a domain name (like *xyz.com*) so that your business name appears in your email and sign-in address (optional step). Note that to add, modify, or remove domains, you must be a Global Administrator of a Business, Enterprise, or Education Plan. These changes affect the whole tenant, Customized administrators, or regular users who will not be able to make these changes. Domain names can be added from any domain connect registrar integrating with M365, like GoDaddy or Bigrock (Microsoft Learn, 2021).

4. Add your employees as users to the service and assign licenses to them so they can start using apps and services.

5. Then, enable threat protection and data loss protection in Office apps like Outlook and Word. These features help protect you and your employees from clicking links or opening files that have malicious content in them and help prevent accidental sharing of sensitive data like social security numbers outside the company.

6. Another important area is the security and management of your computers and phones. The default settings enable encryption, passcodes, and device policies that

help prevent cyber threats for all employees. To take full advantage of M365 Business Premium security, device, and app management features, you will need to upgrade all your PCs to Windows 10 Professional.

7.   The upgrade is free if you are currently running a pro version of Windows. Connect your PCs to the M365 work account to create a managed device experience.

8.   Now, you can start using productivity applications like Microsoft Teams, Microsoft Word, Microsoft Excel, and Outlook. If you have email and documents from a previous provider, you can migrate them to M365.

9.   When you install Office apps on your phones, you can also set up security so that Office app data is managed by your company, since now your business is running in the cloud with M365 Business Premium.

Here, we will talk about M365 Education deployment. With M365 Education, educators can unlock creativity, promote teamwork, and provide a simple and secure learning experience in a single, affordable solution. With the help of the following procedure will help IT administrators deploy Microsoft Education offerings from start to finish in an easy manner.

M365 Education consists of:

- Office 365 for Education

- Windows 10 for Education

- Management & Security

Deployment for M365 Education

Using the M365 Education deployment guide, you will learn how to configure the products and features of M365 Education correctly and efficiently. Make it easier for you to update your client software with the latest productivity and security enhancements by providing the infrastructure for integrating security and simplifying management. Based on M365 Education workloads and scenarios, the foundation infrastructure is organized into numbered phases that build upon each other.

For educating customers, the first step is **cloud deployment**, which includes **networking** and **identity**. These steps will enable you to deploy education workloads and scenarios, including Teams for Education, Exchange, SharePoint, and OneDrive.

It is highly recommended that you upgrade your PC to Windows 10 if you have not already done, so that you use the most current version of Office365, Office365 ProPlus, that helps you manage and secure your organization's devices with Intune for Education.

It is also recommended to visit the Microsoft Store for Education to download education apps and deploy Minecraft: Education Edition to let students know about game-based learning platforms.

There are four phases and associated steps in the guide, as shown in the following table:

Phase 1 Cloud deployment	Phase 2 Device management	Phase 3 Apps management	Phase 4 Complete your deployment
1. Create Office 365 tenant account. **https://products.office.com/en-us/academic/compare-office-365-education-plans** 2. Secure and configure network. 3. Sync with Active Directory 4. Assign licenses to users	1. Deploy Windows 10 2. Manage devices with Intune for EDU	1. Configure admin settings. 2. Configure Teams for Education 3. Install Office apps on devices. 4. Install Minecraft: Education Edition	1. Deploy Exchange Online 2. Deploy SharePoint Online and OneDrive

Table 1.2: Four phases and its steps

Pilot deployment

Sometimes, your organization may want to conduct a pilot deployment as part of its Office 365 planning and evaluation process. Developing a pilot plan is recommended to help keep the pilot on track. The pilot enables your organization to conduct its own in-house testing of Office 365 for enterprise features and functionality. It helps you identify and assess any service issues that might affect your business prior to moving a significant number of individuals to Office 365 service offerings.

Organizations normally start a pilot with a minimum of 10 users participating in the pilot. It varies from company to company.

In addition, pilot deployments can help you test migration processes against the various types of mailboxes that are found within your environment.

To launch your pilot program, your organization signed up for Office 365 in the usual manner. It is always suggested to use a test domain when signing up for the pilot deployment rather than what you plan to use in production.

When setting up M365, users may face issues that affect activation, installation, or overall performance.

The following are some of the common deployment mistakes and troubleshooting steps in M365 Setup.

- **M365 activation issues**:
  o **Mistake:** users see an error message starting that M365 is not activated.
  o **Troubleshooting:** Ensure that the subscription is active by checking *account. microsoft.com*.

- **OneDrive not syncing**:
  - o **Mistake:** Files do not sync between OneDrive and the local drive.
  - o **Troubleshooting:** Restart OneDrive by clicking the OneDrive icon | **Settings** | **Quit OneDrive**, then reopen it. Check for updates in Windows update. Sign out and sign in back into OneDrive.

Overview of M365 admin center

After deployment, the user can navigate to the M365 admin center. This center provides modern cloud management for administrators who deploy and manage M365 Apps.

The details will be discussed in the following section.

Opening Admin Center

Sign in at *portal.office.com* with your admin account. To sign into the admin center, your account must have either the global administrator, security administrator, or Office apps administrator role.

The following steps need to be taken to open the home screen of Office 365:

1. First, you need to enter your sign in details on the login page, as shown in the following figure:

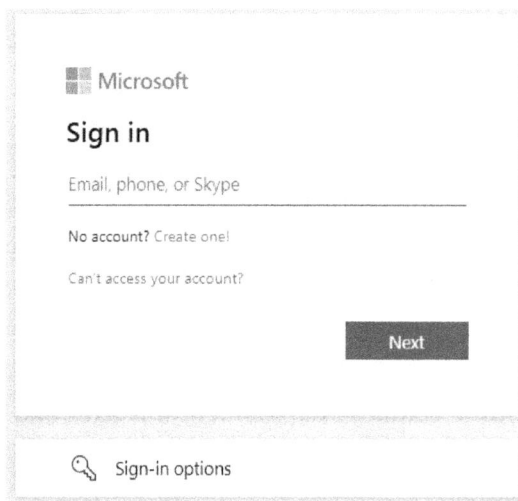

Figure 1.18: Sign-in dialog box

2. After entering the credentials, it will redirect to the home page of M365 page, as shown in the following figure:

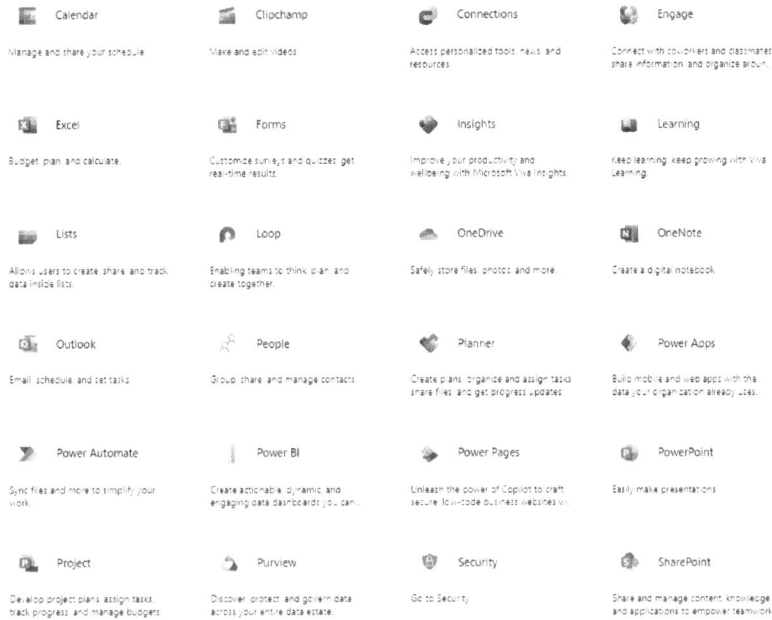

Figure 1.19: *Applications under Office 365 platform*

3. Here, the user can count **All apps** available under the subscription, as shown in the following figure:

All apps

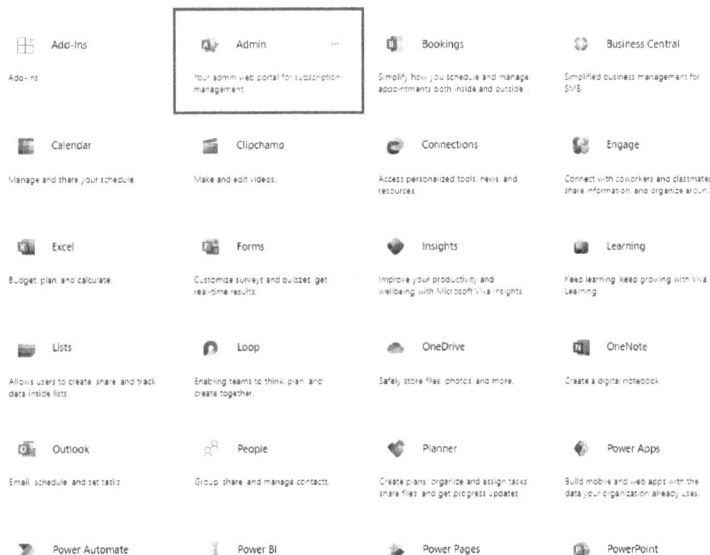

Figure 1.20: *More applications under Office 365 platform*

4. If you are the admin, then click on the **Admin** button. From here, you can navigate all the admin centers like the **Security** admin center, known as M365 Defender, Microsoft Purview **Compliance** portal, **Exchange** admin center, **SharePoint** admin center, Microsoft **Teams** admin center, and so on, as shown in the following figure:

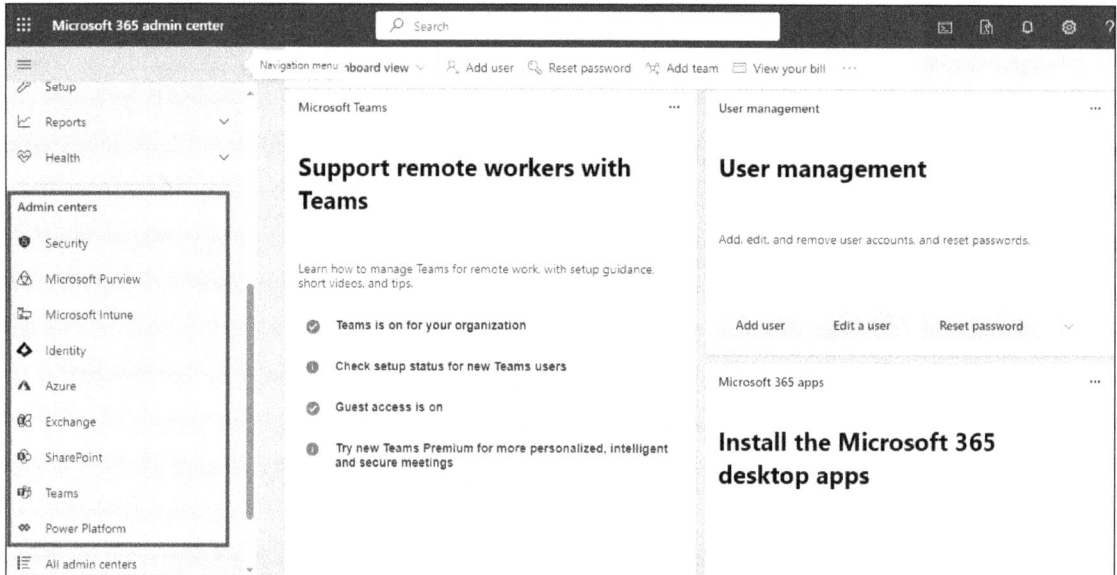

Figure 1.21: Microsoft admin center

Assigning M365 licenses to users

Licensing is important in Office 365 because users cannot use any Office 365 services or applications until their accounts have been licensed (Microsoft, 2022).

Following are the ways to assign license users:

*   **Group-based licensing**: You can configure security groups in Azure AD to automatically assign licenses from a set of subscriptions to all the members of the group. This is known as **group-based licensing**. With group-based licensing, administrators no longer have to write a complex PowerShell script. Azure AD includes group-based licensing, which allows you to assign one or more product licenses to a group. Azure AD ensures that the licenses are assigned to all members of the group. Any new members who join the group are assigned the appropriate licenses. When they leave the group, those licenses are removed. Group-based licensing is currently available only through the Azure portal.

*   **Office 365 PowerShell**: If you have more than 50 users, you can use Office 365 PowerShell to assign licenses.

- **Management portals**: If you have less than 50 users, then choose the Azure Management portal to manage the licenses.

Adding users and assigning licenses at the same time

When people join your company, they need a user account with the proper licenses. The easiest way to add a user account and assign licenses is to go to the admin center. Once you complete the step, your users have M365 licenses, sign in credentials, and M365 mailboxes. Follow these steps for the same:

Note: **You must be a global, license, or user admin to add users and assign licenses.** *Figure 1.22* **shows how to add user admin in your tenant.**

1. Whenever a new person joins your company, you need to add them to your tenant and provide licenses. From the M365 admin center, go to **User Management** and select **Add User**, as shown:

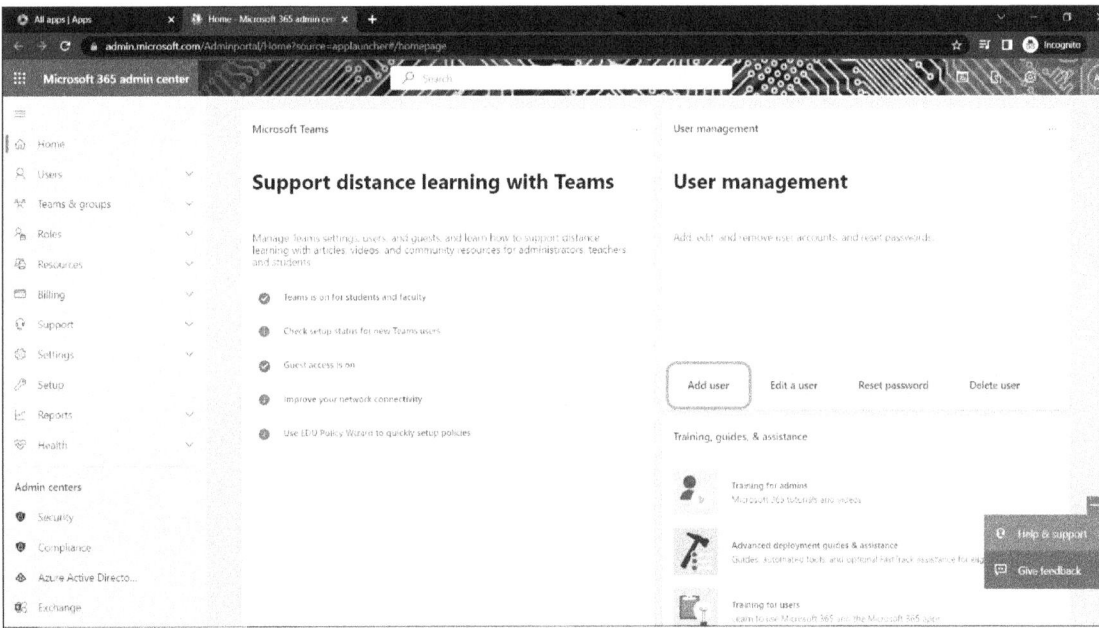

Figure 1.22: Add user

2. Enter all the details, such as **First Name** and **Last Name**. The **Display Name** fills in automatically, but you can change it according to what naming convention the company follows. Enter your **Username** (it should be unique), which will be their email address. Choose the correct domain for the organization. Select whether to **Automatically create a password** or *let me create the password*.

Figure 1.23 shows all the fields that are mandatory to fill in:

3. You can also choose the option to **require this user to create their password when they first sign in**. You can also select if you want the account details sent by email. Once you select the option, your email will automatically be added. It is always a good idea to add the new user's alternate email, so they get the account details as well.

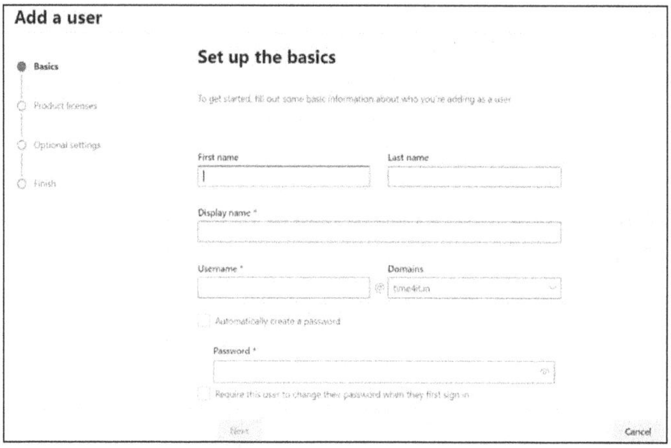

Figure 1.23: Creating user profile

4. Click the **Next** button to move to the **Assign product licenses** option. The product license listing may vary depending on the licenses loaded on your tenant. Generally, Power Automate and Power Apps licenses are provided with all plans because they work as glue to bind different products where events in one application can be used to generate some action in another application, i.e., when a Microsoft form is filled, you get the alert or details directly in email.

Figure 1.24 shows how to assign the product licenses to users:

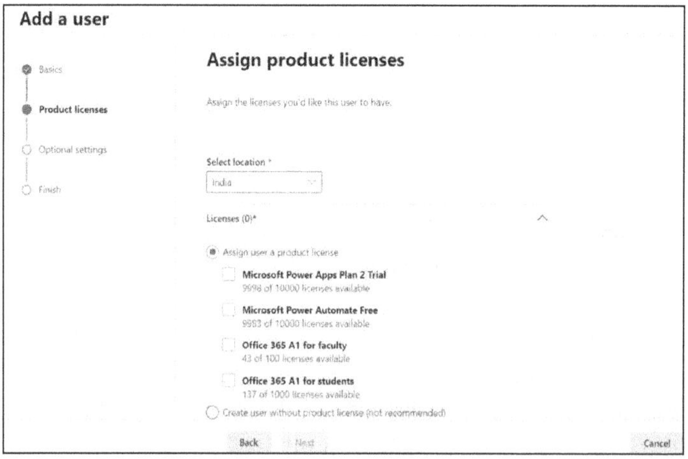

Figure 1.24: Assigning product licenses

5. After assigning the product license to the user, you need to check the optional settings wherein the user will fill in additional profile information. Click **Next**:

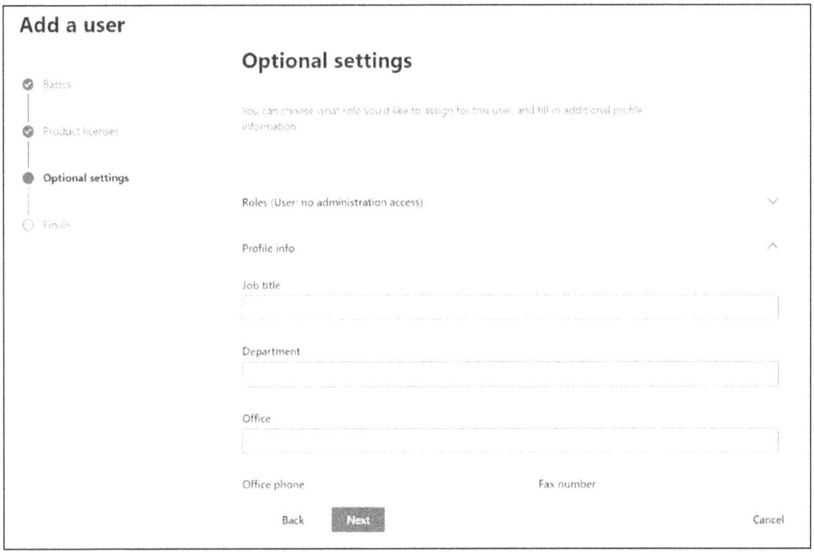

Figure 1.25: *Profile info for user*

Before finishing adding user details, check all the fields properly, like display name and username, password, and product license. Once all details are correct, click on the **Finish adding** button.

Figure 1.26 shows the final page of user creation:

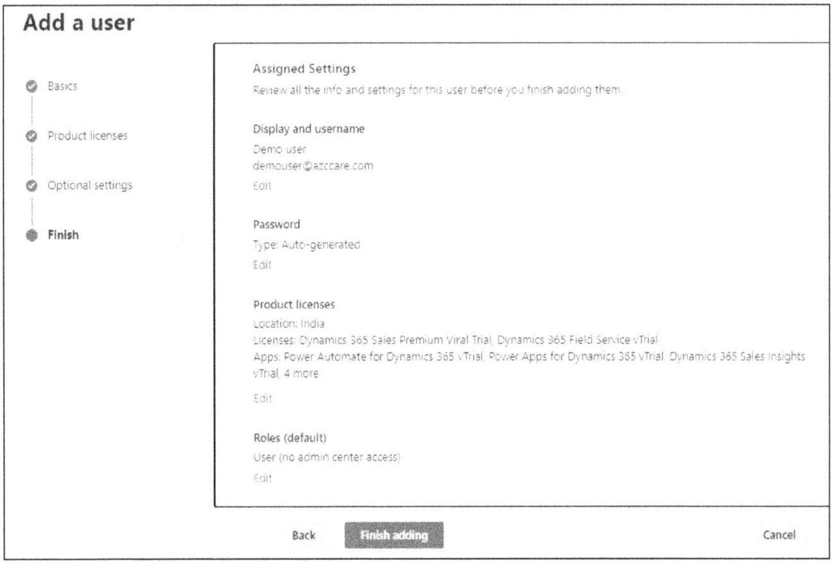

Figure 1.26: *Final interface of user creation*

Applications and their purposes

In Office 365 / M365, 20+ applications are available on the home page that can be used for different purposes. Office applications can be used for collaboration, creating beautiful documents, maintaining Excel worksheets, and many more.

The application may vary depending on your chosen subscription model. Office applications are available in almost all subscriptions (Carutasu & Pirnau, 2017). Team collaboration applications are also available. Task and project management applications are available, like Tasks, To-Do, Planner, and so on. Mailbox is available via Outlook. File storage applications are available like OneDrive, Teams SharePoint Site, and so on. Applications like MS Forms are available for collecting surveys.

These are some of the main elements included in Office 365 Suite of applications:

Admin	Admin web portal for managing the subscription
Bookings	Simplify how you schedule and manage appointments
Calendar	Manage and share your schedule
Class Notebook	Organize your lesson plans in a digital notebook
Compliance	Meet your organization's legal, regulatory and technical standards for legal security and data use
Delve	Get personal insights and relevant information based on who you work with and what application you are working on
Excel	Maintain worksheet and workbook
Forms	Customize surveys and quizzes, get real-time results.
Lists	Allows users to create, share and track data inside lists.
OneDrive	Securely store all your files on cloud.
OneNote	Create a digital notebook
Outlook	Email, schedule and set tasks
People	Group, share and manage contacts
Planner	Create plans, organize, and assign tasks

◆	PowerApps	Build mobile and web apps with the data your organization already use
➤	Power Automate	Sync files and automate the work
▣	PowerPoint	Make presentations
▣	Project	Develop project plans, assign tasks, track progress, and manage budgets
▣	Security	Manage security
▣	SharePoint	Share and manage content, knowledge, and applications to empower teamwork.
▣	Staff Notebook	Collaborate with faculty and staff to share policies, procedures and calendars
▶	Stream	Share videos, presentations and training sessions
▣	Sway	Create interactive reports and presentations
▣	Microsoft Teams	Meet, share and chat
✔	To Do	List and manage your tasks
▣	Visio	Simplify and communicate complex information visually
●	Viva Insights	Improve your productivity and well-being with Microsoft Viva Insights
▣	Whiteboard	Ideate and collaborate on a freeform canvas designed for pen, touch and keyboard
▣	Word	Manage documents and do real time collaboration
▣	Yammerx	Connect with coworkers and classmates, share information, and organize around projects

Table 1.3: Main elements included in Office 365 suite of applications

Conclusion

In this chapter, users got to know about cloud computing concepts and their types. We discussed the evolution of the M365 and O365 concepts, different types of subscriptions and plans available in M365, and the shared deployment guide for various subscription plans. Also mentioned are various applications available under the Office 365 platform. Thus, Office 365 is a cloud-based service offered by Microsoft, hosted on Microsoft's servers. Organizations can benefit from different plans and can be upgraded to premium features in every plan of Office 365. Hence, M365 comes with many features such as agreements, web support, 24/7 support for critical issues, active directory integration to easily manage user credentials and permissions, global data security, and many more.

In the next chapter, we will discuss M365 users and groups and the importance of groups in different applications.

References

- Carutasu, G., & Pirnau, M. (2017). Facilities and Changes in the Educational Process When Using Office365. *Journal of Information Systems & Operations Management*, May, 29–41. **https://www.researchgate.net/publication/317717345**

- Microsoft. (2022, August 20). *Phase 1: Cloud deployment.* **https://learn.microsoft.com/en-us/microsoft-365/education/deploy/license-users**

- Microsoft 365. (2023a). *Microsoft 365 for Business.* **https://www.microsoft.com/en-in/microsoft-365/business?ef_id=5903a8498a35112eea63cb83cde6c953:G:s&OCID=AIDcmmwf9kwzdj_SEM_5903a8498a35112eea63cb83cde6c953:G:s&lnkd=Bing_O365SMB_Brand&msclkid=5903a8498a35112eea63cb83cde6c953**

- Microsoft 365. (2023b). *Office is becoming Microsoft 365.* **https://www.microsoft.com/en-in/microsoft-365**

- Microsoft 365 Education. (2023). *Microsoft 365 Education for Schools.* **https://www.microsoft.com/en-us/education/products/microsoft-365**

- Microsoft 365 Enterprise. (2022, September 29). *Subscriptions, licenses, accounts, and tenants for Microsoft's cloud offerings.* Microsoft Learn. **https://learn.microsoft.com/en-us/microsoft-365/enterprise/subscriptions-licenses-accounts-and-tenants-for-microsoft-cloud-offerings?view=o365-worldwide**

- Microsoft 365 Plans. (2023). *Reimagine productivity with Microsoft 365 and Microsoft Teams.* **https://www.microsoft.com/en-in/microsoft-365/business/compare-all-microsoft-365-business-products**

- Microsoft Learn. (2021, August 31). *Microsoft 365 Education documentation and resources.* **https://learn.microsoft.com/en-us/microsoft-365/education/deploy/create-your-office-365-tenant**

- Microsoft Store. (2023). *Everything you need to achieve more in less time.* **https://www.microsoft.com/en-in/microsoft-365/buy/compare-all-microsoft-365-products-b**

- Office 365 For Education. (2023). *Get Office 365 free for you entire school.* **https://www.microsoft.com/en-in/microsoft-365/academic/compare-office-365-education-plans?activetab=tab:primaryr1**

CHAPTER 2
Managing Office 365 Users and Groups

Introduction

Microsoft 365 (**M365**) users and groups play a significant role. It allows you to choose a set of people with whom you want to collaborate and create a collection of resources. Adding members to the group automatically grants permission to use various things. Microsoft Teams and Yammer use M365 groups to manage their membership. Groups make your work easy. It has lots of advantages, as we will see in this chapter.

Structure

In this chapter, the following topics will be covered:

- Microsoft 365 groups
- Creating groups in various Microsoft 365 applications
- Public and private groups
- Microsoft 365 groups for administration
- Administration of Microsoft 365 groups
- Group creation and management by members
- Group expiration policy

Objectives

By the end of this chapter, you will learn how to manage M365 groups and users and the functionalities of different types of groups. Different kinds of users are available in M365.

Microsoft 365 groups

Using M365 groups, you can collaborate with your colleagues on documents and spreadsheets, plan projects, schedule meetings, or send emails. The groups in M365 allow users to select a group of people with whom they can share resources. Collaborative resources include a shared Outlook, a calendar, and a document library. When members are added to the group, they are automatically granted access to the tools your group provides (*Learn about Microsoft 365 groups*, 2022). Additionally, it provides a much better user experience than distribution lists or shared mailboxes.

Creating groups in various application of M365

M365 provides the tools to allow your teams to collaborate however they choose. The crucial point is determining whether you wish to create a public or a private group. Anyone in your organization can view the content of a public group, and anyone in your organization may join the group. A private group's content can only be considered by its members, and anyone wishing to join one must be approved by its owner.

Neither public nor private groups outside your organization may be accessed or viewed unless they have been specifically invited as guests (Learn about Microsoft 365 groups, 2022).

- **A group in Outlook:** When a team wishes to collaborate via email and needs a shared calendar, then a group is needed.
- **Create a Microsoft Team:** If a team wants to collaborate in a persistent chat environment.
- **Create a group in Yammer:** If you want to create a large, open discussion forum for your company to do some executive-level announcements and discussions.
- **A team site in SharePoint Online:** If a team wants to share files and folders via the Team site.
- **Create a plan in Microsoft Planner:** When your team creates a plan, by default a group has been made in OneDrive, SharePoint etc.

Creating a group in Microsoft Outlook

M365 group differs from a contact group (formerly known as a distribution list). A contact group is nothing but a set of email addresses.

The following steps are followed to create a group in Microsoft Outlook:

1. Open Outlook.

2. Select **Home | New Group**. (If you cannot see **New Group** in the ribbon, contact your IT department to enable Groups)

3. Enter the group information in the dialog box as shown:

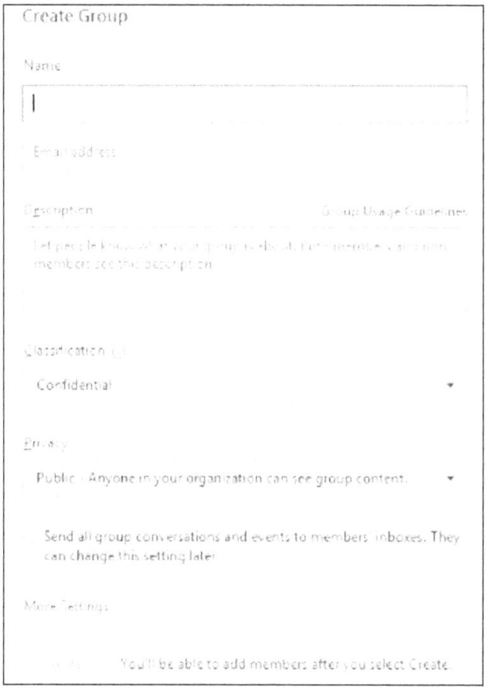

Figure 2.1: Create group in Outlook

Details about the group information box are as follows:

a. **Group name**: Choose a name that reflects the group's spirit. Once you enter a name for your group, it will suggest a unique email address. You should always try a unique name for your group. Note that it cannot be changed once you choose a group name.

b. **Description:** Optionally, enter a description to help others understand the group's purpose. The welcome email will include this description when others join the group.

c. **Classification:** Options available depending upon the organization.

d. **Privacy:** Privacy is the ability of an individual or group to seclude themselves or information related to them. We need to be careful while creating groups whether it should be public or private.

e. **Public:** A public group can be accessible by everyone in the organization without any approval from the owner and able to see the contents also.

    f.   **Private**: When you are creating a group, it will be private by default. It means that only approved members can see the files, folders, and other related data. The group is not accessible to anyone else in your organization who is not approved.

4. Select the option ✔ Send all group conversations and events to members' inboxes. This means members can see all group conversations and events in their inboxes. Members can individually change the settings for their mailboxes.

5. Select the **Create** button.

Creating a group in Microsoft Teams

The user can create a team/group using MS Teams. The steps for the same are as follows:

1. Launch Microsoft Teams and create a team.

2. Give a name to the team and add a short description.

3. By default, the team is private, and users can add people accordingly.

4. Users can change the type of team, that is, to the public (which means anyone can join the team without obtaining permission from the Owner).

5. Once you enter the members' name in the team, select **Add** and then **Close**.

6. After creating a team, a general channel is created by default.

7. To add more, select ellipses (…) and select **Add Channel** to add/create more channels specific to a subject.

8. Enter a name and description for the channel. (Channels can be created around a specific topic, project, department name, etc.).

9. Select **Automatically favourite this channel** for the whole team if you want this channel to be automatically visible in everyone's channel list.

10. Select **Add**.

Creating a group in Yammer (Viva Engage)

Yammer is a central place for conversations, files, and updates. It facilitates collaborative work on projects and events. As soon as you create a group, you automatically become its owner. Follow these steps to create a group in Yammer:

1. Open the Yammer App from M365 and click on **Create a group**, as shown in the following figure:

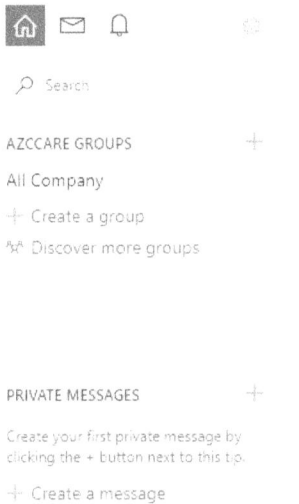

Figure 2.2: Create group in Yammer

2. It will open a dialog box. Enter the name of your group, under **Group Name**. (To make it easier for people to scan the list of groups, choose a short name. Your company may have naming conventions for its groups.)

3. For **Group Members**, enter the names or email addresses of anyone you want to add, as shown:

Figure 2.3: Naming group

4. Under **Who can view conversations and post messages**, select one of the following:

    a. **Public Access:** This group is open to anyone in your network to view and join the content posted to it.

    b. **Private Access:** If the group administrator approves the members, they can only view the content.

5. Additionally, you will see a classification section if your group is connected to M365.

6. Select **Create Group**.

Creating a team site in SharePoint

You can share information and collaborate on projects with your colleagues by creating a SharePoint team site. SharePoint site consists of a default document library and web parts that can be tailored according to specific needs.

Team site or communication site

A team site can be used to communicate with the members where they can provide content to a team site, and the data is restricted to members, whereas a communication site can be used when you transmit the information to a large audience (Waghmare, 2020).

The following figure illustrates the unique points for team sites and communication sites:

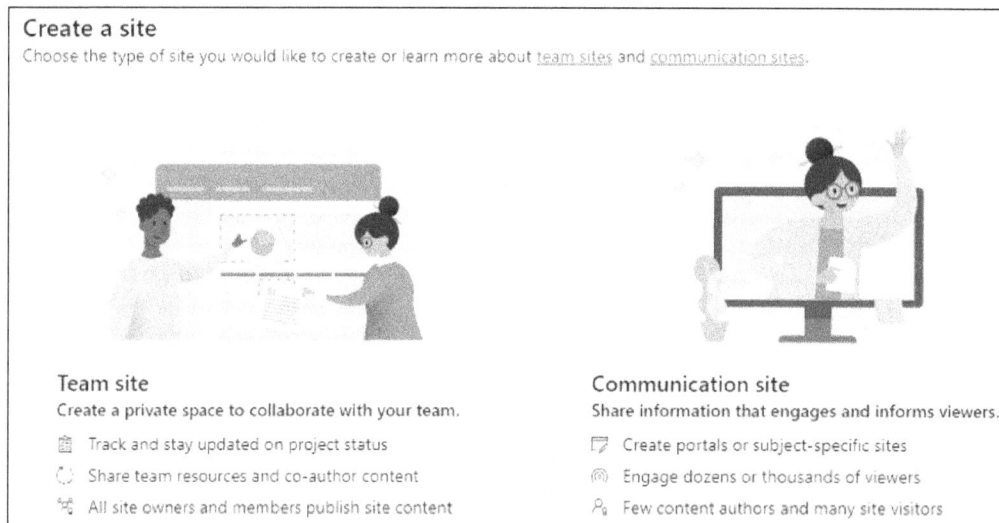

Create a site
Choose the type of site you would like to create or learn more about team sites and communication sites.

Team site
Create a private space to collaborate with your team.
- Track and stay updated on project status
- Share team resources and co-author content
- All site owners and members publish site content

Communication site
Share information that engages and informs viewers.
- Create portals or subject-specific sites
- Engage dozens or thousands of viewers
- Few content authors and many site visitors

Figure 2.4: Types of sites

To create a team site, please follow the steps as shown:

1. Sign in with your M365 credentials. Click the app launcher icon ▦ on the top left corner and select the SharePoint tile.

2. On SharePoint page, select + icon to Create Site | Choose Team site option. A wizard will open on the right-hand side of the screen, where you enter the information to create a team site along with the description. It will appear as shown in the following figure:

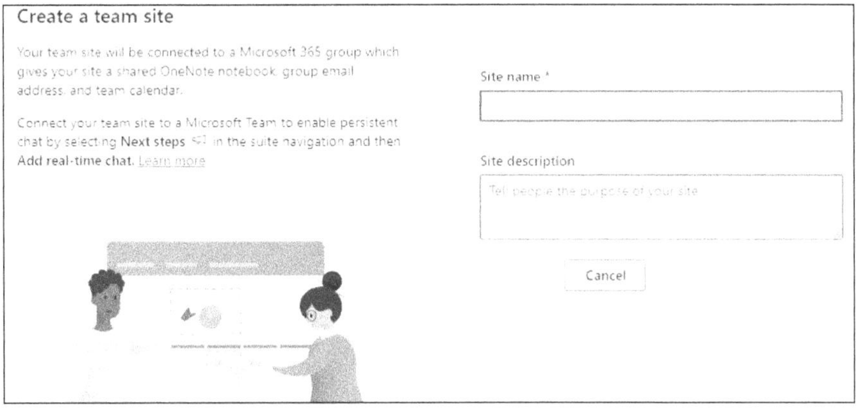

Figure 2.5: Create team site

3. Select a team site template to serve a specific scenario or create a team site from scratch.

4. As you type, you will see whether the name you entered is available. Click **Next**.

5. If asked, in the **Privacy Settings** section, choose Public or Private to control who has access to your site.

6. Select a language for your site. Click **Next** as shown:

Figure 2.6: Team site details

7. **Add members** (name or email addresses) for your site. The site creator is a member of the site owners' group. Members added to the M365 group are automatically associated with the site. Refer to the following figure for a better understanding:

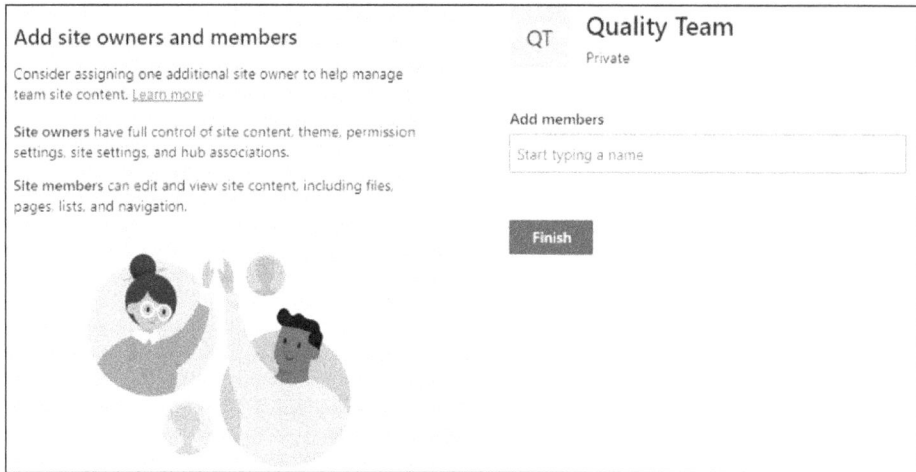

Figure 2.7: *Adding members to team site*

8. Click on **Finish**.

You can follow the site once it is created.

Creating a plan in Microsoft Planner

Once you log in to the Planner application, it will show you the plan for every M365 group. Follow the given steps to create a plan in Microsoft Planner:

1. Login with M365 credentials and go to the app launcher | Select **Planner Application**.

2. Create a **New Plan**. The following window will open:

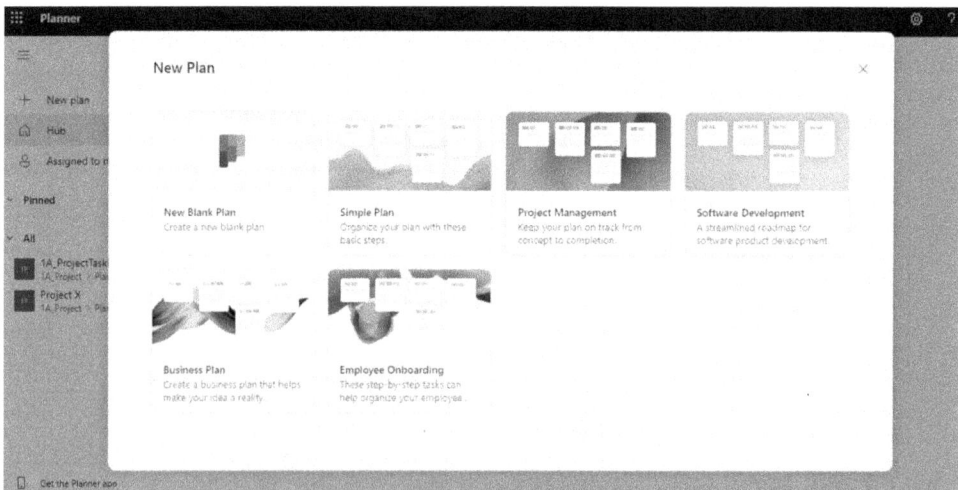

Figure 2.8: *Create new plan*

3. M365 groups are created when you create a plan. Using M365 groups, you and your team can work together on Planner, OneNote, Outlook, OneDrive, and more.

4. To create a new plan, Select **New Blank Plan** | give name to your plan and select whether you want to add your plan to an existing group (optional) or it should be a new one, as shown:

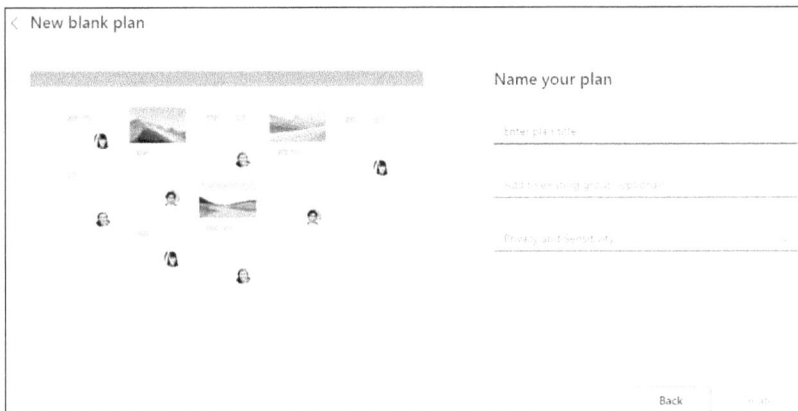

Figure 2.9: Naming a plan

5. Set the privacy level.

6. Click on the **Create** plan button.

Note: **Public plans are visible to all within the organization. Private plans are only for the people you have added to the plan. Only public plans appear when people in your organization search for plans. It is important to remember that the privacy of Office 365 Group depends upon your plan, whether it is public or private.**

Adding a plan to an existing group

The user can add a plan to the same members, document library, and other group features they are already using by following these steps:

1. Give a name to your plan and **add it to an existing Office 365 Group**.

2. Search for a group from the list.

3. Select **Choose Group** and then Create a plan.

Public or private in Microsoft 365 groups

When you want to change the policy or rights of the members, make your group either public or private. M365 groups are the replacements of Office 365 distribution lists. When you create a group, it will be created as a public group by default.

The following table summarizes the difference between public and private groups:

Public	Private
Everyone can see the group and its content.	Only approved members are allowed.
By default, the group is Public.	Users need to change the privacy level.
Everyone in the organization can join the group if it is Public.	Users need permission to join the group.
All users can invite anyone in the group.	Only the group owners can invite a user to the group.
All group members can view, edit, and share the files.	Only approved members can view, edit, and share files.

Table 2.1: Difference between public and private groups

Microsoft 365 groups for administrators

M365 groups is the foundation for all teamwork within M365. With M365 groups, you can give access to a collection of shared resources to a group of people (Overview of Microsoft 365 groups for administrators, 2023).

These resources are as follows:

- A shared calendar
- A shared Outlook inbox
- A shared document library
- A plan in Planner
- A OneNote notebook
- PowerBI
- Yammer
- A Team
- Stream etc.

With an M365 group, there is no need to assign permission manually to any of these resources. Once you add people to the group, the group automatically permits them. Anyone can create groups unless you limit group creation.

Following are some roles for the groups:

- **Owners:** A group owner can add or remove members and provide exclusive permissions, such as the ability to delete conversations from the group inbox or change the group's settings. A group owner can rename the group, update the description and change the logo of the group.

- **Members:** Members do not have permission to change group settings.
- **Guests:** Guests are not a part of your organization. (Check organization policy)

M365 admin center allows only global admins, user admins, and group admins to create and manage groups.

An administrator can do the following:

- Group creation should be restricted to certain individuals.
- Establish a naming policy for your organization's groups.
- Select your organization domain while creating a group.
- Establish guest access rights to groups.
- Maintain when to recover a deleted group (within 30 days of deletion).

An administrator can manage groups from the M365 admin center or by using PowerShell.

Group limits

The following table will give the limits that are applicable to the M365 group:

The limit of the default number of groups is 500,000.

Description	Range
Owners per group can be	100
A user can create max.	250 groups
Permission for admin to create groups	No Microsoft365 group-specific limits. It depends upon AzureAD object limit specific to each organization. An Azure AD administrator with access to manage groups in the organization may create an unlimited number of groups.
Number of members	It can be more than 1000, but only 1000 can access the group conversations concurrently.
Group mailbox size	50 GB
File storage	1 TB + 10 GB per user + any other storage purchased. An unlimited amount of storage can be purchased.

Table 2.1: M365 limits in the group

M365 admin center has a reporting tool that allows one to check the storage use, number of active groups, and how users are using the groups. If you have actionable information about using your M365 groups, you can manage them more effectively.

Sensitivity labels

Sensitivity labels serve as an effective mechanism to secure sensitive information across various sectors while also facilitating adherence to regulations such as GDPR, HIPAA, and CCPA. Organizations have the flexibility to customize these labels according to their unique requirements, thereby ensuring that essential data is adequately protected without compromising operational efficiency. An employee in the organization can set sensitivity labels when they create a M365 group.

With sensitivity labels, you can configure the following:

- Privacy (Public or Private)
- External user access
- Unmanaged device access

Suppose a user creates a label called **Highly Confidential**. You can specify that any group created with the Highly Confidential label will be private and inaccessible to external parties or users.

The following are a few enterprise-specific instances of how sensitivity labels can be applied in different scenarios:

- **Health**: Hospitals need to safeguard the patient's health records and ensure compliance with HIPAA regulations. For instance, sensitivity labels like **Protected Health Information** (**PHI**) can be applied to patient records and restrict access to authorized doctors, nurses, and administrators. Confidentially, research data can be applied to internal medical research documents, or watermarks can be added to all PDFs, and printing can be restricted to prevent data leaks.

- **Technology**: Tech companies need to protect source code by putting sensitivity labels like **Highly Confidential**, which are applied to repositories and code files in SharePoint or OneDrive. It also prevents downloads to unmanaged devices and requires MFS for access.

- **Financial sector**: The bank needs to protect customer financial data and internal budget reports from unauthorized access by implementing sensitivity labels such as **Confidential-Customer Data**, which are applied to documents like customer loan agreements, etc.

Managing Microsoft 365 groups

You can manage M365 groups depending on the configuration. User accounts can be controlled via the M365 admin center, PowerShell, **Active Directory Domain Services** (**AD DS**), or the **Azure Directory** (**Azure AD**) admin center. Depending on the identity model you choose for M365, you may be able to manage your user accounts in different ways (*Manage Microsoft 365 groups*, 2023).

The two models are given as follows:

- **Cloud-only:** You can administer groups using PowerShell, the Azure AD admin center, and the M365 admin center.

- **Hybrid:** Although groups from AD DS are synchronized with M365, you must administer these groups locally using AD DS tools.

Creating and managing groups by members

Using Azure AD, group owners rather than IT administrators may manage groups. Self-service management is a feature that enables group owners without administrative roles to create and administer security groups (Manage Microsoft 365 groups, 2023). The group owner receives the request to join a security group. Team leaders, project managers, or business owners who are familiar with the group's intended function and can oversee its membership on a daily basis can control membership.

Setting dynamic group membership

In Azure AD, you can configure some commands that will automatically add or remove user accounts from a group known as **dynamic group membership**. The rules/commands are based on user account attributes like department or country.

Rules are applied as follows:

- New users become members of a group if they meet all the requirements for membership.

- When a user account's properties are changed to the point where it satisfies all the group's requirements, it joins the group.

- A user is not added to the group if it does not match all the rules.

- A user account is no longer considered to be a member of the group if its attributes change so that it no longer complies with all the group's requirements.

To use dynamic membership, you must identify the sets of groups that have a common set of user account attributes. For instance, since the user account attribute department is set to HR, all employees in the HR department ought to be in the HR Azure Active Directory group.

Microsoft 365 group expiration policy

With the increased usage of groups in various applications of M365, in Microsoft Teams, unused groups and teams need to be cleaned up by administrators and users. M365's expiration policy will assist in removing inactive groups from the system (Microsoft 365 group expiration policy, 2023).

Note: Nearly all connected services, such as OneNote, any email, Planner, SharePoint site or team, etc., are also erased when a group expires.

Administrators can set an expiration date; however, any dormant groups that do not get renewed when they do will be destroyed. A group is soft-deleted after it expires, meaning that it can still be restored for up to 30 days.

Owners of the group will be alerted automatically before it expires so they can renew it for the following expiration date. Group expiration alerts will show up in the Teams Owners feed.

Groups that are in use are renewed automatically around 35 days before the group expires. Any of the following actions will automatically renew a group:

- **Microsoft SharePoint:** Viewing a SharePoint page does not count as an action for automatic renewal.
- **Microsoft Outlook:** Join or edit a group, read or write group messages.
- **Microsoft Teams:** Call on a team's channel.
- **Yammer:** View a post on the Yammer community or any interactive email in Outlook.
- **Microsoft Forms:** View, create, edit, or submit a response to a form.

Who can configure and use the M365 groups expiration policy?

Refer to the following table for the same:

Role of the Admin and User	Permissions granted
Office 365 Global Admin	Create, Update, Delete and Read
User	Restore an M365 group that they own

Table 2.2: Expiration policy

Setting of the expiration policy

An administrator can set the expiration policy for the groups. To set the expiration policy, navigate to Azure Active Directory, click on **Groups**, and set **Expiration**. An admin can select the default group lifespan. The group lifespan can be set to 180, 365, or a custom value you choose. It is specified in days. There must be at least 30 days in the custom value.

If the group has no owner, the expiration email will be sent to the designated email.

You can choose to specify the policy for every group you belong to, just a few of them (up to 500), or none. All active groups awaiting verification will not have an expiration date if You choose **None**. The already-expired groups, however, are unaffected.

Remember that you cannot have policies for various groups now.

Common issues related to expiration policies

The following are some of the common issues related to expiration policies:

- **Inadvertent deletion of active content:** Users may overlook renewal notifications, leading to unintended deletion of active groups, Teams, or SharePoint sites.

- **Overloading IT with manual restorations:** Frequent manual restoration of deleted groups or content creates a bottleneck for IT admin.

- **Owners ignoring notifications:** Owners may ignore renewal notifications due to email overload or unclear communication.

- **Expired resources that should have been archived:** Data retention policies may conflict with expiration policies, leading to lost historical records.

Best practices for managing expiration policies

The following are some of the best practices for managing expiration policies:

- **Test policies in a pilot environment:** Evaluate the impact of expiration policies on a limited user group or specific test site before full-scale deployment across the organization.

- **Regularly update policies:** Regularly examine and modify expiration and retention settings to align with evolving organizational requirements.

- **Ensure clear communication:** Inform all stakeholders about expiration policy changes, timelines, and the process for renewal or restoration.

- **Leverage automation:** Use tools like Power Automate or scripts to manage recurring tasks associated with expiration policies.

Conclusion

In this chapter, we learned about the importance of groups in M365. Groups can be created using various applications of M365. It has more features and benefits like restoration of deleted groups, setting up expiration policy, naming policy, group owner permission, group member permission, group label management etc.

In the next chapter, we will learn about Office 365 tools/applications functionalities and its benefits. You will also understand how all applications can be accessed online as well as offline.

References

- *Learn about Microsoft 365 groups* (2022) *Microsoft 365 Support*. Available at: **https://support.microsoft.com/en-us/office/learn-about-microsoft-365-groups-b565caa1-5c40-40ef-9915-60fdb2d97fa2** (Accessed: 10 March 2023).

- *Manage Microsoft 365 groups* (2023) *Microsoft 365 Enterprise*. Available at: **https://learn.microsoft.com/en-us/microsoft-365/enterprise/manage-microsoft-365-groups?view=o365-worldwide** (Accessed: 10 March 2023).

- *Microsoft 365 group expiration policy* (2023) *Microsoft Learn*. Available at: **https://learn.microsoft.com/en-us/microsoft-365/solutions/microsoft-365-groups-expiration-policy?view=o365-worldwide** (Accessed: 10 March 2023).

- *Overview of Microsoft 365 groups for administrators* (2023) *Microsoft 365*. Available at: **https://learn.microsoft.com/en-us/microsoft-365/admin/create-groups/office-365-groups?view=o365-worldwide** (Accessed: 10 March 2023).

- Waghmare, C. (2020) *Augmenting Customer Experience with SharePoint Online: building portals and practices to improve usability*. 1st edn, *Augmenting Customer Experience with SharePoint Online*. 1st edn. Mumbai, India: Apress Berkeley, CA. doi: 10.1007/978-1-4842-5534-6.

Join our Discord space

Join our Discord workspace for latest updates, offers, tech happenings around the world, new releases, and sessions with the authors:

https://discord.bpbonline.com

CHAPTER 3

Office 365 Tools and their Functions

Introduction

In this chapter, we will discuss Microsoft 365 (formerly known as Office 365) tools and their functions. Microsoft 365 offers a variety of applications and services that can be used by an organization to improve workplace productivity. As part of Microsoft 365, all standard Microsoft applications can be accessed online and offline (desktop mode), including Microsoft Word, Microsoft Excel, Microsoft PowerPoint, OneNote, and Outlook.

The Office 365 suite contains a variety of powerful and useful tools that can make businesses, large and small, more productive and collaborative.

Structure

In this chapter, we will discuss the following topics:

- Microsoft 365 home page
- Benefits of Microsoft 365 tools
- Productivity tools and their usage
- M365 application to use in different scenarios

Objectives

By the end of this chapter, you will learn about the Microsoft 365 home page and available applications under the M365 suite. After reading this chapter, you will become familiar with productivity tools and how to use them daily. Moreover, you will also learn how to apply it to different scenarios.

Microsoft 365 home page

Microsoft Office 365 is a subscription service that presents important business tools to enhance communication and collaboration in the workplace. To access the home page of Office 365, you must have a username and password for the same.

The following are a few steps:

1. To log in, open **portal.office.com** using any browser
2. Enter credentials of Microsoft 365 (username and password)

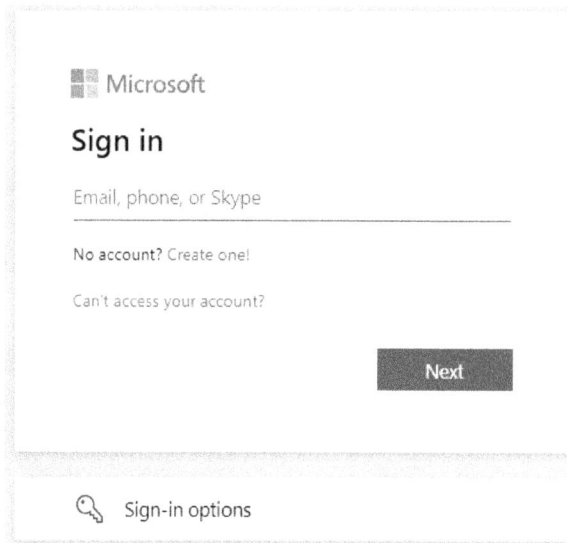

Figure 3.1: Login credentials screen

3. After using your credentials, the page will be redirected to the home page of Office 365. Click on **App Launcher (9 dots)** | Few applications are visible. To view all applications and services, click on **More Apps**, as shown in *Figure 3.2:*

All apps

Add-Ins	Admin	Bookings	Business Central
Add-ins	Your admin web portal for subscription management	Simplify how you schedule and manage appointments both inside and outside	Simplified business management for SMB
Calendar	Clipchamp	Connections	Engage
Manage and share your schedule	Make and edit videos.	Access personalized tools, news, and resources.	Connect with coworkers and classmates share information, and organize aroun...
Excel	Forms	Insights	Learning
Budget, plan and calculate	Customize surveys and quizzes, get real-time results.	Improve your productivity and wellbeing with Microsoft Viva Insights.	Keep learning, keep growing with Viva Learning.
Lists	Loop	OneDrive	OneNote
Allows users to create, share and track data inside lists.	Enabling teams to think, plan and create together.	Safely store files, photos, and more	Create a digital notebook
Outlook	People	Planner	Power Apps
Email, schedule and set tasks	Group, share and manage contacts.	Create plans, organize and assign tasks, share files and get progress updates	Build mobile and web apps with the data your organization already uses.

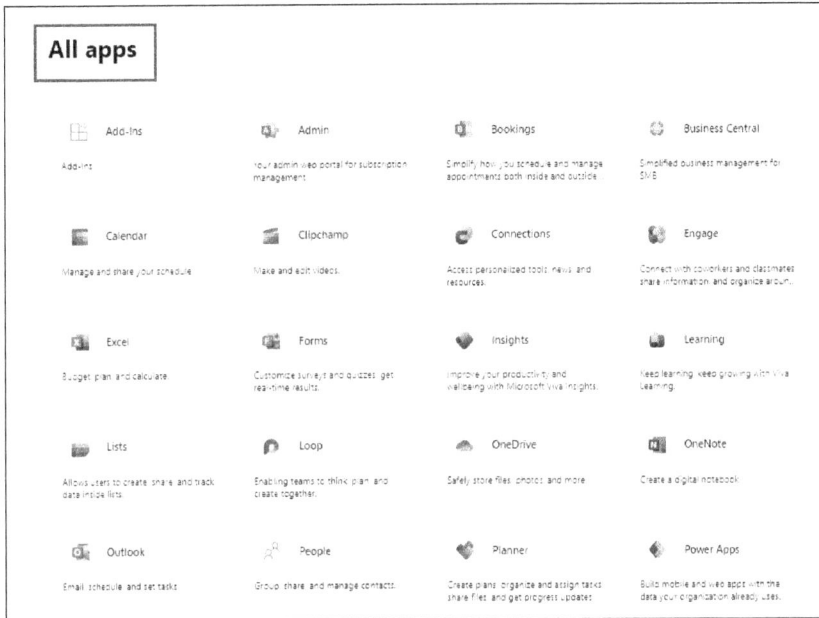

Figure 3.2: All Applications through app launcher

After you click on More Apps, another window will open will all applications available in Microsoft 365 environment, as shown in the following figure:

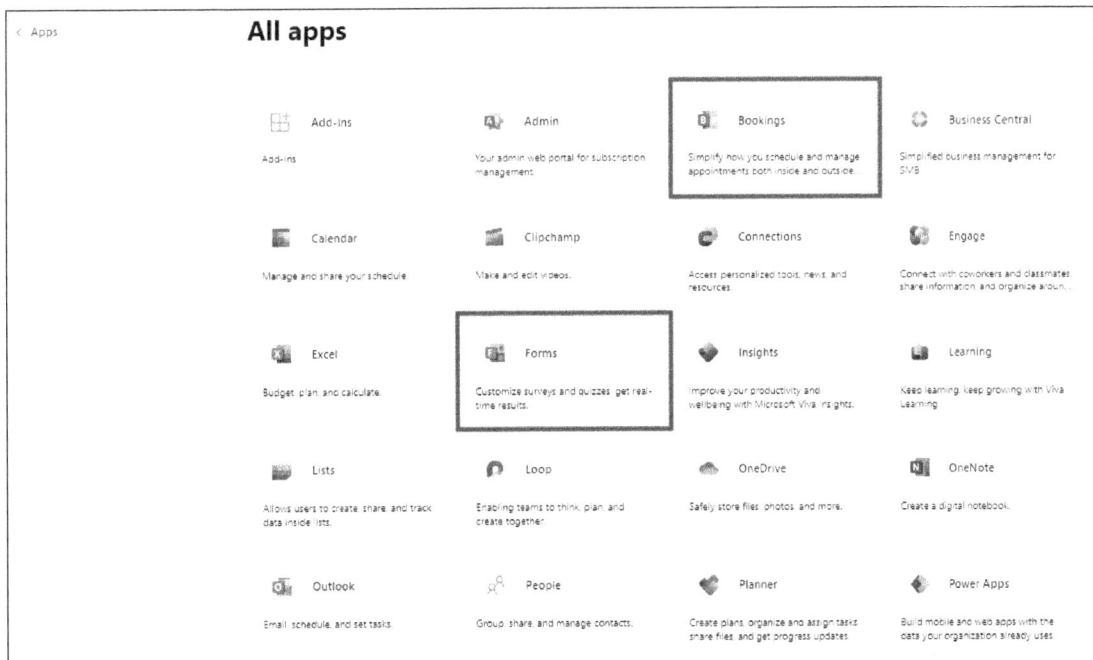

< Apps

All apps

Add-Ins	Admin	Bookings	Business Central
Add-ins	Your admin web portal for subscription management.	Simplify how you schedule and manage appointments both inside and outside.	Simplified business management for SMB
Calendar	Clipchamp	Connections	Engage
Manage and share your schedule	Make and edit videos.	Access personalized tools, news, and resources.	Connect with coworkers and classmates share information and organize aroun...
Excel	Forms	Insights	Learning
Budget, plan and calculate.	Customize surveys and quizzes, get real-time results.	Improve your productivity and wellbeing with Microsoft Viva Insights.	Keep learning, keep growing with Viva Learning
Lists	Loop	OneDrive	OneNote
Allows users to create, share and track data inside lists.	Enabling teams to think, plan, and create together	Safely store files, photos, and more.	Create a digital notebook.
Outlook	People	Planner	Power Apps
Email, schedule, and set tasks.	Group, share, and manage contacts.	Create plans, organize and assign tasks share files and get progress updates	Build mobile and web apps with the data your organization already uses

Figure 3.3: Home screen of Microsoft 365

If you are an admin, you will be able to see **Admin** section from where entire subscription of **Microsoft 365** can be controlled. In *Figure 3.3*, we will see **Booking Application, Forms** to create **surveys** and Polls which can be used in a training session or meeting.

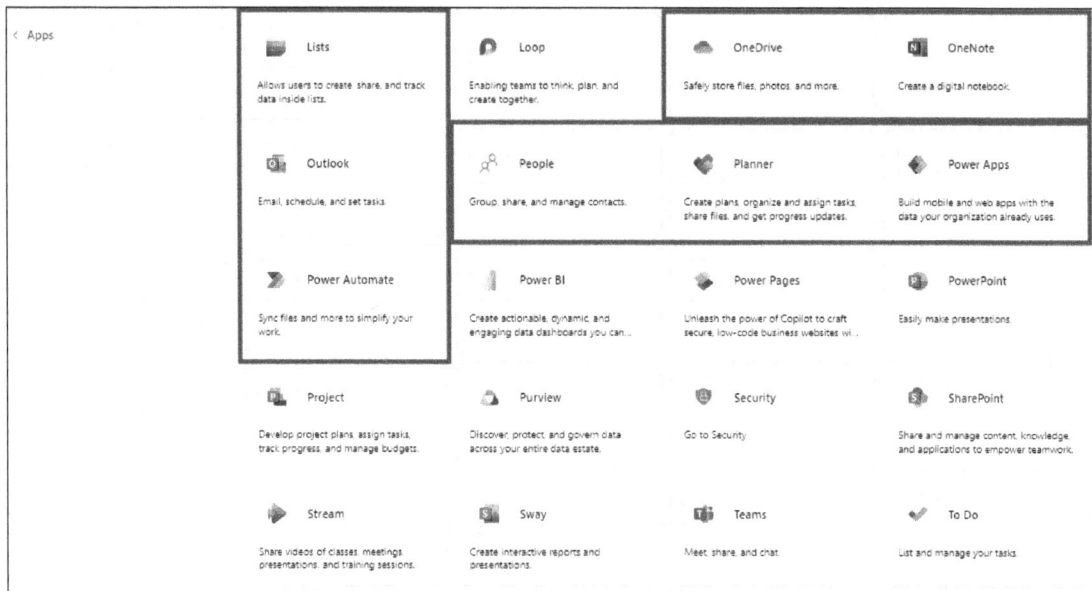

Figure 3.4: More applications on the Microsoft 365 portal

In *Figure 3.4*, more applications are visible like **Lists, OneDrive** (cloud storage), **OneNote, Outlook** (mailbox), **People, Planner, Power Apps, Power Automate** to automate the business or process flow.

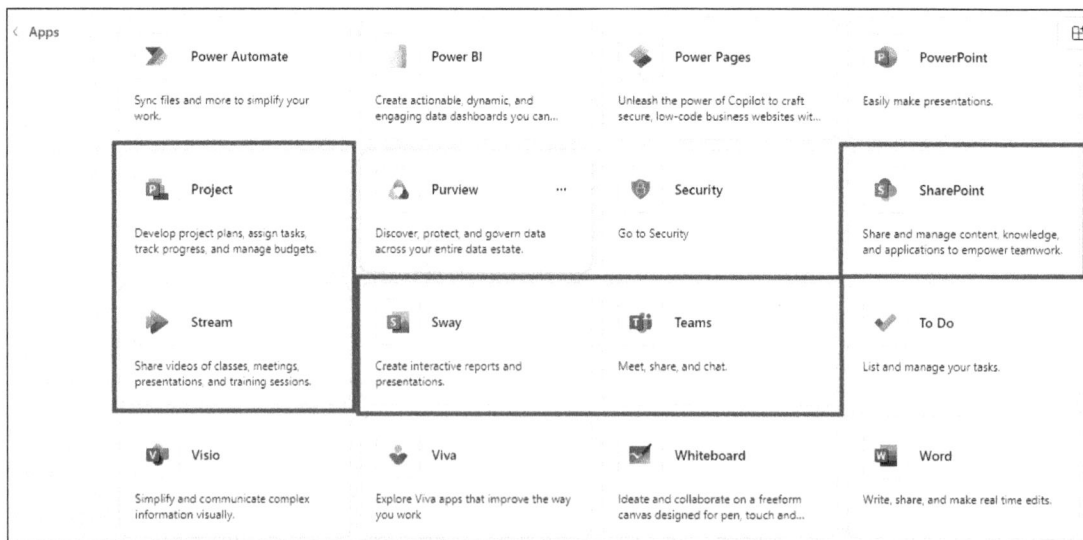

Figure 3.5: Applications under Microsoft 365

In *Figure 3.5*, applications like **Project**, **Teams**, **SharePoint**, **Stream**, and **Sway** are available as shown:

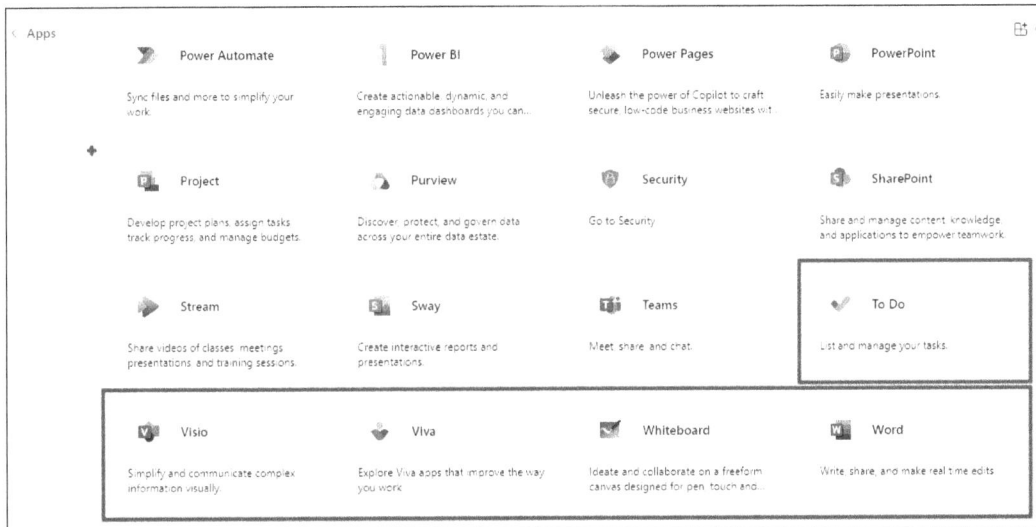

Figure 3.6: *Few more applications in Microsoft 365*

In *Figure 3.6*, applications like **To Do**, **Visio**, **Viva apps**, **Whiteboard** and **Word** are available.

Benefits of Microsoft 365 tools

There are many benefits for businesses using Microsoft Office 365 tools, including reducing costs, assisting growth, and enhancing productivity. By providing web-enabled access to email, contacts, documents, and calendars, it promotes unified collaboration among employees. Users can collaborate, edit resources in real time, and save versions for future use. In this way, employees and different departments will be able to communicate clearly, thus improving productivity and, ultimately, enhancing the success of the business. The best thing is the user can access applications from anywhere, any device and anytime using only an internet connection, while your data remains safe and secure under Microsoft lock and key (Credentials). Microsoft 365 ID is created to be used on Android smartphones and tablets, Mac devices, Windows-based laptops, and so on.

Microsoft 365's cloud-based nature, as discussed above, enables organizations to create secure and centralized cloud storage environments. Microsoft 365 offers **Single Sign On** (**SSO**) facility to every user. Cloud computing ensures that important business applications are always accessible by running the applications and storing the data. Additionally, you will benefit from business-class support and services, including robust security, geo-redundant data centers, application standards, privacy controls, disaster recovery procedures, and many more.

SharePoint provides centralized storage for all the documents, acting as a well-knitted structure for critical business information. With SharePoint's ability to integrate with other

Microsoft 365 applications such as Word and Excel, multiple users can work on the same document simultaneously. Document management and knowledge sharing require improved collaboration and secure storage. Integration of OneDrive with Microsoft Teams and Outlook allows you to create, edit, share, and manage documents based on numerous libraries, projects, teams, communities, etc. For efficient document management, SharePoint is the ideal platform.

Microsoft offers a secure environment and centralized integration with One Drive for Business that will help users work with any application of Microsoft 365. With Microsoft Teams you can schedule meetings, do individual and group chats, and integrate many more applications so that every user is on the same page.

Microsoft 365 offers multifactor authentication and multi-level permission, ensuring enterprise-level security for their accounts, documents, and information. It will allow you to work on five devices with one account. Microsoft 365 allows users to build multiple simple as well as complex automated workflows using Power Automate. It will help users cut down on time-consuming business procedures. Automatic email notification, adding document approval workflows, application status tracking, and attendance trackers become easier.

Productivity tools and their usage

When it comes to productivity tools, Microsoft 365 (Office 365) is the top priority for organizations. It comes with popular office applications like **Word**, **Excel**, **PowerPoint**, **OneNote**, and many more. Integration between Microsoft 365 applications will enhance collaboration, productivity, and data management. One of the key integrations is how Microsoft Teams connects with SharePoint and OneDrive, enabling users to share, store, and collaborate on files efficiently.

MS Teams integrates with SharePoint and OneDrive as follows:

- **Teams and SharePoint integration:**
  o When a **new team** is created in Microsoft Teams, a corresponding **SharePoint site** is automatically generated.
  o **Files shared in a Teams channel** are stored in the **SharePoint document library** associated with that team.
  o Users can access the files from both **Teams and SharePoint**, ensuring seamless document management.
  o SharePoint permissions sync with Teams, so only authorized users can view or edit files.
  o For example, a marketing team collaborates on campaign documents in Teams. These files are stored in SharePoint, where members can access, edit, or track versions.
- **Teams and OneDrive integration:**
  o **OneDrive stores personal files**, while SharePoint stores shared team files.
  o Files sent via **Teams private chats** are stored in the sender's **OneDrive** and shared with the recipient.

- o   Users can open OneDrive files directly in Teams, making it easy to collaborate without switching apps.
- o   Syncing between OneDrive and Teams allows access to cloud-stored files from any device.
- o   For example, a manager shares a confidential report via Teams chat. The document is stored in their OneDrive and is automatically shared with the recipient, ensuring security and controlled access.

These applications are available in web versions also, where collaboration is possible. We will explore other productivity applications and their usage by analyzing *Figure 3.7*:

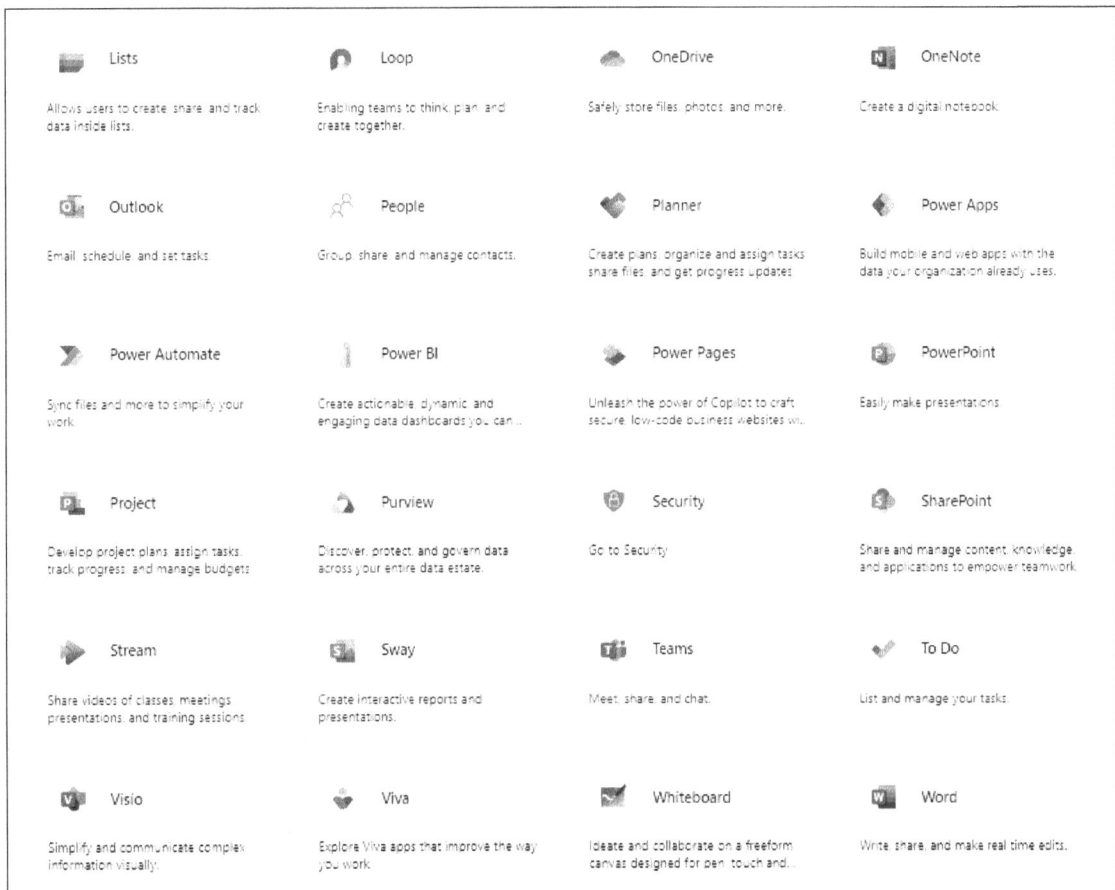

Lists Allows users to create, share, and track data inside lists.	**Loop** Enabling teams to think, plan, and create together.	**OneDrive** Safely store files, photos, and more.	**OneNote** Create a digital notebook.
Outlook Email, schedule, and set tasks.	**People** Group, share, and manage contacts.	**Planner** Create plans, organize and assign tasks, share files, and get progress updates.	**Power Apps** Build mobile and web apps with the data your organization already uses.
Power Automate Sync files and more to simplify your work.	**Power BI** Create actionable, dynamic, and engaging data dashboards you can...	**Power Pages** Unleash the power of Copilot to craft secure, low-code business websites wi...	**PowerPoint** Easily make presentations.
Project Develop project plans, assign tasks, track progress, and manage budgets.	**Purview** Discover, protect, and govern data across your entire data estate.	**Security** Go to Security.	**SharePoint** Share and manage content, knowledge, and applications to empower teamwork.
Stream Share videos of classes, meetings, presentations, and training sessions.	**Sway** Create interactive reports and presentations.	**Teams** Meet, share, and chat.	**To Do** List and manage your tasks.
Visio Simplify and communicate complex information visually.	**Viva** Explore Viva apps that improve the way you work.	**Whiteboard** Ideate and collaborate on a freeform canvas designed for pen, touch and...	**Word** Write, share, and make real time edits.

Figure 3.7: All apps in one go

There are multiple options in Microsoft 365 which can be overwhelming. The greatest advantage is its cloud-based nature. Microsoft hosts your applications and data, allowing you to save on IT expenditures and overhead while accessing Microsoft's enterprise-grade platform and security - benefit that organizations of all sizes can leverage, scale, and decrease costs.

It is especially beneficial for small and medium-sized businesses because Office 365 offers all the productivity tools for a predictable monthly fee that can be canceled at any time rather than requiring an upfront investment.

Most employees are seeking flexibility, and there is a great deal of data to show how much impact it has made when you stop thinking of work as always taking place at the same desk, in the same office. It is possible to store data in the cloud and install applications on all of your devices using Office 365. Consequently, you can work on a document in the office, review it on your mobile while riding the train to your next meeting, and finish editing it on your home PC when you return home. Since documents can be accessed via any internet-enabled device, it is not only possible but also very easy to enable a truly mobile workforce.

M365 application to use in different scenarios

All applications are divided into four categories, that is, Messaging, Collaboration, Productivity, and Discovery, as shown in *Figure 3.8*:

Figure 3.8: Four categories of Office 365

Messaging applications

When a user wants to communicate, they can use the following applications:

The details are as follows:

Skype for business

Skype for Business is a communication platform that allows users to hold online meetings, make voice and video calls, send instant messages, share files, and collaborate in real time. It is particularly useful for businesses and organizations, as it enables remote communication and collaboration between team members, regardless of their physical location.

- It enables you to schedule and hold online meetings with up to 250 participants and share files and presentations during the meeting. It also allows you to make voice and video calls to other Skype for Business users or to phone numbers, directly from your computer.

- It has a built-in instant messaging feature that allows you to send text messages, share files and collaborate in real-time.

- It is tightly integrated with other Microsoft Office products, such as Outlook, Word, and PowerPoint, making it easy to schedule meetings, share documents, and collaborate with team members.

Outlook

Outlook is an email client and personal information manager that is part of the Microsoft 365 suite of productivity tools. It is designed to help users manage their emails, contacts, calendars, and tasks all in one place. Additionally, Outlook is compatible with other Microsoft 365 applications, including Word, Excel, and PowerPoint, making it easy to collaborate with others and share documents.

- Email and data are protected by a number of security features in Outlook, such as spam filters, phishing protection, and encryption.

- Outlook allows you to manage multiple email accounts, including personal and work accounts, in one place. With the help of Outlook, you can create to-do lists, set reminders, and track your progress on projects.

- Outlook's calendar allow you to schedule and manage appointments, meetings, and events, and provide reminders to help you stay on track. It allows you to manage contacts, including names, email addresses, phone numbers, and other information, and makes it easy to send emails and schedule meetings with them.

Microsoft Teams and Yammer lie in between messaging and collaboration applications.

Microsoft Teams

It is a chat-based workspace to support team collaboration via voice and video calls and integration of Office 365 services and third-party applications. It has *ME* and *WE* space, which can be categorized by multiple Teams (on the left side), and workspace area (on the right side) is used for instant communication, announcements, sharing files, and many more. It is a collaboration app built for hybrid work, so you and your team stay informed, organized, and connected, all in one place. Microsoft Teams enables seamless collaboration across different departments by integrating tools like **SharePoint, OneDrive**, and **Outlook**. A realistic scenario demonstrating this integration is a *product launch project involving Marketing, Sales, and Product Development teams.*

The marketing manager sets up a *New Product Launch* team in Microsoft Teams. It includes members from marketing (content creation, advertising), Sales (customer outreach, pricing strategies), and product development (technical details, specifications). Each department has a dedicated channel to focus on specific tasks. The **Marketing team** uploads campaign materials (brochures, social media posts) to the *Marketing* channel. These files are stored in **SharePoint**, allowing real-time editing. The **Product Development team** shares product specifications in the *Technical Details* channel, linking OneDrive documents for easy reference. The **Sales team** accesses the latest marketing materials from **Teams** without searching multiple locations.

Yammer

It is an enterprise social networking tool like Facebook that allows users to create groups, share ideas and company updates with their network, post questions that do not necessarily require instant response, and provide feedback. Yammer's primary role is to facilitate communication and collaboration within an organization and to create a sense of community among employees.

- It connects employees with each other regardless of their physical location, job title, or department. Yammer makes it easy for everyone to share documents and work together in real time.

- It also helps to create a sense of community where employees can share their interests, hobbies, personal experiences, and best practices. By fostering a culture of collaboration and sharing, Yammer can help organizations to become more productive, innovative, and successful.

Collaboration applications

When a user wants to communicate/share, they can use the following applications:

The details are as follows:

OneDrive for Business

OneDrive for Business (ODB) is a cloud-based storage service used to provide a secure online space for organizations to store, share, and collaborate on files and documents. By providing secure, online storage and collaboration features, ODB can help organizations to become more productive and efficient across teams and departments.

- It provides 1 TB of space on the cloud, which can be increased up to 5 TB (depending on company policy). It allows users to share files with others, within the organization and provides a wide range of permission levels to control access to files.

- ODB makes it easy for users to collaborate on files either in real-time or asynchronously and provides features such as co-authoring and version control to manage changes.

- ODB is tightly integrated with other Microsoft 365 apps, such as Word, Excel, and PowerPoint, making it easy to create, edit, and save documents directly in OneDrive. It also provides a range of security features, such as encryption, data loss prevention, and multi-factor authentication, to help protect files and data.

SharePoint Online

SharePoint Online is a cloud-based collaboration platform designed to help organizations create, manage, and share content, as well as collaborate with colleagues. One of the key features of SharePoint Online is its ability to create intranet sites (such as Team site, Communication site etc.) and websites. With SharePoint Online, users can create custom sites that can be used to store and share content, such as documents, images, and videos, as well as collaborate on projects, manage tasks, and communicate with colleagues.

- It allows users to customize their sites to meet their specific needs, with features such as custom branding, site templates, and web parts (pre-built components). It also provides a range of collaboration features, such as shared calendars, task lists, and discussion boards, that allow users to work together on projects and share information.

- It provides a centralized location for users to store and manage their content, with features like customize the branding of a site, version control, check-in/check-out, and content approval workflows.

- It has security features such as permissions and access control to ensure that only authorized users can access sensitive information.

OneNote and Planner lie in between the collaboration and productivity section.

OneNote

OneNote is a versatile and powerful digital note-taking application that is part of Microsoft 365. One cross-functional notebook for all your note taking needs. It allows you to create and organize notes in a digital notebook format, making it easy to keep track of your thoughts, ideas, and information in one place and streamline your workflow, as follows:

- Get organized in notebook, you can create different notebooks for different topics, sections for different subjects, and pages for specific ideas or tasks. With easy navigation and search, it is easy to find information and stay organized. It allows user to create their own tags (only available in desktop application).

- OneNote allows to share your notebooks with others, enabling you to collaborate on notes and work together in real-time. OneNote can be accessed from multiple devices, including desktops, laptops, tablets, and smartphones, making it easy to access your notes from anywhere.

- It has multimedia support where you can insert images, audio, and video into your notes, making it an excellent tool for taking lecture or meeting notes. It has a powerful search feature that allows you to find specific information in your notes quickly.

- With the help of OneNote, it is easy to create minutes of meeting and sync the meeting details with calendar. Fifteen spoken languages are provided in dictate functionality and 26 languages are available in preview.

Planner

Planner is a task management and project collaboration tool included in Microsoft 365. It is designed to help teams organize and prioritize tasks, track progress, and collaborate with each other, as follows:

- Planner makes it easy to manage tasks and keep track of deadlines. Users can create tasks, assign it to team members, set due dates, add comments, and attachments to keep everyone on the same page.

- With Planner, users can collaborate with other team members in real-time. They can add comments, attachments, and checklists to tasks, and everyone can see the updates instantly. Planner provides a visual representation of the project's progress, allowing employees to track the status of tasks and identify any potential roadblocks.

- Planner integrates with other Microsoft 365 tools like Outlook, Teams, and SharePoint, making it easy to access all their work in one place. Once you create a Planner, group will be automatically created respective to the planner. As it is a cloud-based application, users can access it from anywhere, on any device with an internet connection.

Productivity applications

The following productivity applications can be used to automate daily tasks:

Power Automate

Microsoft Power Automate, (formerly known as Microsoft Flow) is a tool that allow users to create automated workflows between applications and services. Users can automate mundane tasks, manual process in just one click by automation and boost productivity, as follows:

- Using Power Automate, users can create workflows by using a simple drag-and-drop interface without requiring knowledge of codes. There are a number of pre-built templates available for users to select from or they can customize workflows based on their specific requirements. The workflow can include a variety of actions, such as the sending of emails, the creation of tasks, the updating of records, etc.

- In addition to providing real-time insights and analytics, Power Automate provide users with the ability to track the performance of their workflows and identify areas for improvement. Moreover, it can integrate with various Microsoft services and third-party tools, providing users with the ability to build robust, complex workflows that can automate almost any business process.

- Using Power Automate, you can automate approval workflows, ensuring that requests are routed to the right people and approved in a timely manner. Events can be automatically triggered, based on certain criteria, such as a new email arriving in a specific folder or a new item being added to a SharePoint list.

- It can connect with external services such as Twitter, Dropbox, and Google Drive, enabling users to automate tasks across multiple platforms.

- It helps businesses to become more efficient and productive by automating tasks, streamlining processes, and reducing errors. It can save employees time and effort, allowing them to focus on higher-value tasks and strategic initiatives.

For instance, a finance team receives invoices via email and wants them automatically saved to OneDrive for record-keeping.

Here is a step-by-step process:

1. Open Power Automate and create an automated cloud flow
2. **Choose a Trigger**: Select *When a new email arrives (Outlook).*
3. **Set conditions**: Filter emails with subject line *Invoice.*
4. **Extra attachments**: Add action *Save email attachment.*
5. **Select OneDrive Folder**: Define the folder where attachments should be saved.
6. **Save and test**: Send a test email with an attachment.

In this way, whenever an email comes with an attachment, it is automatically saved in OneDrive's designated folder, reducing manual downloads and file sorting.

Office applications

Office productivity tools such as Word, Excel, and PowerPoint are widely used in a variety of industries and office environments but can also be used for personal purposes. They are designed to be user-friendly and provide a wide range of functionalities to enhance productivity and creativity.

- Microsoft Word is a word-processing software that allows users to create and edit documents, such as letters, reports, and manuscripts. It provides features such as spell-checking, formatting, and the ability to insert tables, images, and hyperlinks.

- Microsoft Excel is a spreadsheet software that allows users to organize and analyze data. It is commonly used for tasks such as creating budgets, tracking expenses, and creating charts and graphs to visualize data. Excel also provides advanced features such as data validation, conditional formatting, and pivot tables.

- Microsoft PowerPoint is a presentation software that allow users to create slideshows for a variety of purposes, such as business presentations, educational lectures, and marketing pitches. It provides features such as slide layouts, themes, animations, and the ability to insert multimedia elements such as images, audio, and video.

Microsoft Stream lies in between the productivity and discovery section

Microsoft Stream

Microsoft Stream is a video hosting and sharing platform that is designed for businesses and organizations to securely share and manage video content within their organization. It is a part of Microsoft 365 suite and allow users to upload, share and collaborate on video content with others in their organizations.

- The platform provides features such as video search, playback controls, closed captioning, and the ability to create playlists and channels. It also integrates with other Microsoft tools, such as Microsoft Teams, SharePoint, and Yammer.

- Microsoft Stream is beneficial for businesses as it allows them to create and share training videos, product demos, and other types of video content with their employees. It also helps organizations to increase engagement and collaboration among employees, as well as improve communication and knowledge-sharing.

As for its expiration date, Microsoft has announced that Microsoft Stream will be replaced by a new service called Microsoft Viva Video, which is currently in preview mode. It has been stated that Microsoft Stream will continue to be available until the new service is generally available and that it will provide ample notice and support to help customers transition to the new service.

Discovery applications

To automate a user's daily tasks, the following applications can be used:

We will discuss each of these as follows:

Power BI

Power BI is also a part of the Power platform component. It is a set of business intelligence and analytics products from Microsoft and is used to analyze and visualize business data sources such as Excel files, databases, and third-party sources like Salesforce and Marketo.

- Power BI provides a user-friendly interface that allows non-technical users to easily create and customize interactive reports and dashboards. Power BI integrates with a variety of data sources, including Excel spreadsheets, cloud-based services such as Azure(Provided by Microsoft, which is like a giant online storage to store data, run apps, and keep their systems running smoothly without needing their own expensive hardware) and Salesforce (It is a tool that helps businesses manage customer relationships to keep track of their sales), and on-premises(company) databases stored on local servers, allowing users to easily access and analyze their data.

- It provides a range of data visualization options, including charts, tables, and maps, that can be customized to suit the needs of individual users. It also provides advanced analytics like **natural language processing** (**NLP**) queries and machine learning algorithms that can help users discover hidden insights in their data.

- A marketing manager can use Power BI to analyze marketing data, such as website traffic and social media engagement. They can create a dashboard that shows the effectiveness of marketing campaigns, identify trends in customer behavior, and make data-driven decisions to improve marketing performance.

Power Apps

Power Apps is a Microsoft Power platform component used to develop custom applications for the organization. It makes the development cycle easy for business applications and equips the business users and developers to build custom native, mobile, and web applications, as follows:

- It is used for creating applications and publishing on mobile apps to assist with business processes. With the help of Power Apps, users can connect to the organization's data fetching from different databases like Oracle, SAP, Salesforce, Office365, etc.

- With the help of Power Apps, users can build and modify business applications quickly, without depending on IT professionals and programmers. They can subscribe to Microsoft Power Apps in Office 365. Power Apps can be divided into three sections, as mentioned:

  o   The Application itself

  o   Connection to the data

  o   Workflows thrown by applications

- Developing mobile applications through Power Apps will take only a few clicks. For customizing and prioritizing the data, we can use the drag-and-drop mechanism. After creating the App, you will have a separate screen for browsing records and displaying the details of documents.

Microsoft Forms

A simple yet efficient way to get opinions is Microsoft Forms, which assists in creating polls, quizzes, and surveys with real-time results, taking up to 5000 respondents into account. Here are some ways that Microsoft Forms can be used:

- **Feedback**: Microsoft Forms can be used to gather feedback from customers, employees, or other stakeholders. This feedback can help improve products, services, or processes.

- **Data collection**: Microsoft Forms can be used to collect data from users, such as contact information or preferences. This data can be useful for various purposes, such as customer segmentation, lead generation, or market research.

- **Training and education**: Microsoft Forms can be used to create quizzes and surveys for training and educational purposes. For example, a teacher can use Microsoft Forms to create a quiz for students to test their knowledge on a particular topic.

- **Event registration**: Microsoft Forms can be used to create registration forms for events, such as conferences or workshops. This can help organizers collect information about attendees and plan the event effectively.

- **Employee engagement**: Microsoft Forms can be used to gather feedback from employees on various topics, such as job satisfaction, work environment, or training needs. This can help to improve employee engagement and productivity.

Microsoft Sway lies in between the discovery and messaging applications.

Microsoft Sway

Sway is an easy-to-use digital storytelling application from Microsoft that makes it easy to create and share interactive reports, presentations, personal stories, and many more. It comes with a built-in design engine to help you create professional designs quickly. Text and multimedia images flow together to enhance the story and are formatted to work on all your devices. It is an excellent tool for newsletters, presentations, stories and many more. Sway is a browser-based application, although there is a mobile app.

Here are a few pointers for Microsoft Sway:

- Create and share interactive reports, presentations, personal stories, and more
- Go from start to finish in minutes
- Tell your story with interactive content
- See suggested search results based on your content
- Instantly transform your Sway with great designs
- Easily share by sending a link or QR Code or embed in a blog/website

Conclusion

By the end of this chapter, we explored Microsoft 365, and it is clear that this suite stands as a cornerstone in modern computing, both for personal and professional use. The Microsoft 365 homepage serves as a gateway to a world of productivity, collaboration, and creativity, offering an intuitive and seamless experience that connects users to an impressive array of tools and features.

Microsoft 365's suite of tools, including flagship applications like Word, Excel, PowerPoint, and Outlook, along with newer additions like Teams, OneDrive, and SharePoint, are ingeniously designed to cater to a diverse range of needs and scenarios. Each tool is a powerhouse, yet when combined, they form an ecosystem that dramatically enhances productivity and efficiency.

The benefits of Microsoft 365 are manifold. From the ease of creating and editing documents in Word, crunching data in Excel, to crafting compelling presentations in PowerPoint, each application is robust and versatile. Outlook's seamless email and calendar integration keep communication streamlined, while Teams facilitate real-time collaboration and communication, essential in today's increasingly remote and dynamic work environments.

OneDrive and SharePoint offer secure and accessible cloud storage solutions, making file sharing and collaboration more efficient than ever. This integration of storage solutions with productivity tools epitomizes the synergy at the heart of Microsoft 365. Moreover, Microsoft 365's adaptability across various scenarios is unparalleled. For students, it is a platform for learning and project development. For professionals, it offers the tools for data analysis, report creation, and effective communication. In each of these scenarios, Microsoft 365 brings its unique blend of functionality, reliability, and user-friendliness.

In the next chapter, you will learn about Microsoft Word which is a word processing application that allows users to create, edit and format documents. You will also learn how to use templates, image, tables, charts to documents and collaborate with team members. You will also learn about different views, layout and many more.

CHAPTER 4

Creating Masterpiece Documents with MS Word

Introduction

Gone are the days when an author, writer, or researcher needed to put back-aching efforts for creating, organizing, and managing their scholarly content in one place, but now in the age of technology and with the wave of enormous ICT-based applications, it has minimized the efforts of every learner. Considering several software applications, prominent **educational technology (EdTech)** giants are introducing promising and reliable software applications with seamless interoperability features.

In this chapter, we will discuss in detail one of the prominent software applications of Microsoft Office 365 suite of applications, i.e., Microsoft Word 365. MS Word 365 is a subscription-based model of MS Office 365, while the traditional Office 2016 (or other versions), built and integrated with Windows, is a one-time purchase. Further, it will elaborate on its seamless features, which are essential for students, learners, educators, researchers, and professionals to write, share, and collaborate with peers.

We will also discuss systematically different sections with the utility of MS Word. A detailed view of each section and tab will be discussed, and the reader will get to know and understand basic to advanced features and functionalities of Microsoft Word.

Structure

This chapter will cover the following topics:

- Unveiling the interface of Microsoft Word
- Functions under the Home tab
- Functions under the Insert tab
- Utilities of Draw tab
- Creating a survey form in MS Word
- Utilities of Design and Layout tab in MS Word
- Functions of Reference tab in MS Word
- Functions and utilities of the Mailing tab
- Functions of Review tab in MS Word
- Functions of View tab in MS Word
- Importance of Help tab in MS Word

Objectives

This chapter would equip learners with comprehensive skills in Microsoft Word by unveiling its user-friendly interface and exploring its various tabs. Specifically, learners will master the functions under the Home tab, Insert tab, Draw tab, and Design and Layout tab to enhance document creation and editing. Additionally, learners will discover how to create a survey form in MS Word and utilize the Reference tab for citation and bibliography management.

This chapter will also cover the functions and utilities of the Mailing tab, Review tab, and View tab, ensuring learners can efficiently manage and finalize documents. Finally, learners will understand the importance of the Help tab in MS Word, ensuring the users can troubleshoot and access resources for continuous learning and improvement.

Unveiling the interface of Microsoft Word

In this section, we will discuss the essential functions and tools for an educationist, researcher, and content writer. Accessibility features are also a highlight of MS Word. The application offers built-in accessibility options that assist users with visual or mobility impairments. These features include screen readers, voice dictation, and keyboard shortcuts, ensuring that individuals with diverse needs can create, edit, and consume documents (Use a screen reader to dictate a document in Word, Microsoft Support, n.d.). The primary use of MS Word is to create a document using the first tab, i.e., file. To create a new document, click on the **File** tab and click **New**. On the other hand, the user can find several online templates, where they need to enter the type of document in the search box and then press *Enter*.

Figure 4.1 shows the steps to create a new document:

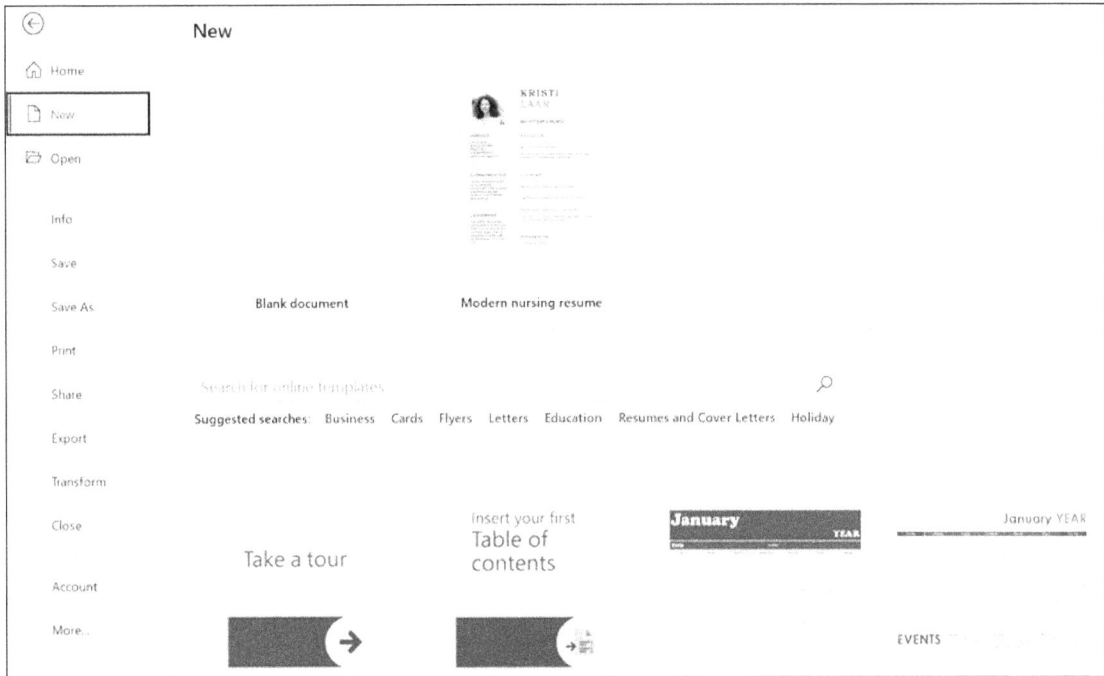

Figure 4.1: *Creating a new document in MS Word*

Functions under the Home tab

The user can access different groups in the first tab of **Home**. Within each group, the user may find several options like **Clipboard**, **Font**, **Paragraph**, **Styles**, and then **Editor**, which allow intelligent spelling and grammar checks that have been improved with sophisticated rules and offer more accurate suggestions and corrections. Editor function use AI and machine learning to suggest improvements based on context and writing style. Further, MS Word has eleven broad tabs, visible in *Figure 4.2*, and has different sub-sections important for efficient document creation, collaboration, and revision as follows:

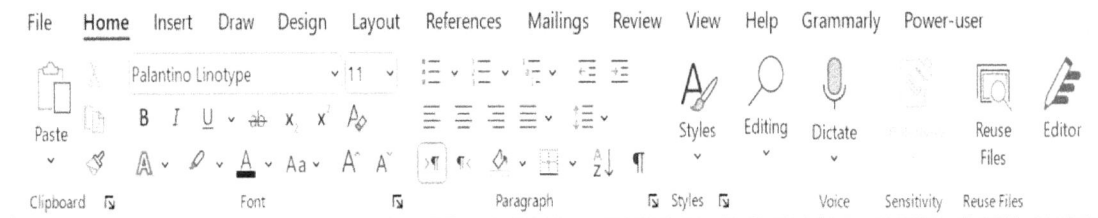

Figure 4.2: *Interface of MS Word tabs*

MS Word provides certain additional features, these are:

- The application offers a thesaurus and a translation feature, enabling users to find synonyms or translate text without leaving the document.

- The clipboard will allow you to see all the items you have copied to it.

- Users can customize their text using advanced font and character options to give it the desired look.

- Moreover, you can finetune the layout of the present paragraph by customizing it with the required spacing, indentation, and more.

- With the editing option in MS Word, you can easily hover and search throughout the entire document.

- The dictate function further gives you two options, i.e., dictate and transcribe. Through the dictate function, the user can use voice typing to author content and voice commanding for a more hands-off experience. On the other hand, while using the transcribe feature, MS Word can only allow you to transcribe your audio or video file, which must be less than 300 MB, and if you upload your file beyond 300 MB file size, then it will show you an error. For reference, see *Figure 4.3*:

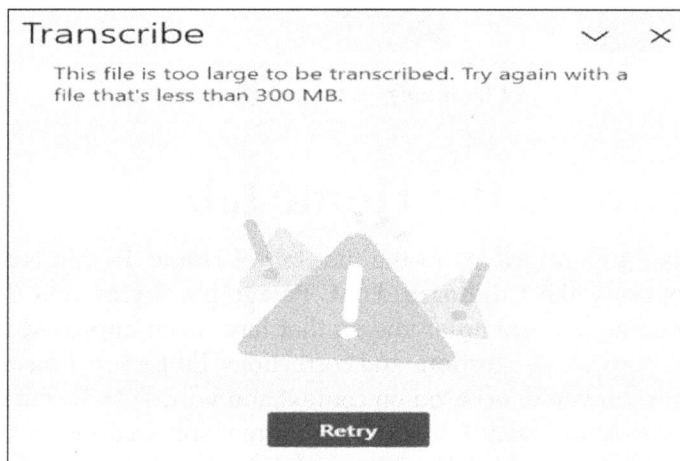

Figure 4.3: Type of error showing in MS Word

- Another essential feature in the Home tab is reflected by the reuse files, allowing an author to find and reuse parts of other documents within your organization.

- Furthermore, users can customize the ribbon and the toolbar to suit their preferences, ensuring quick access to frequently used tools and commands. (*What is new in Word 2019 for Windows*, 2019?)

Moreover, the user can integrate various add-ins into the MS Word application, which is added to the **Home** tab.

Functions under the Insert tab

In this section, MS Word and its various updates showcase traditional word processing by integrating multiple media types, text boxes, shapes, icons, tables, charts, header or footer, equations, and mathematical symbols. For reference, see *Figure 4.4*, which shows a detailed view on the **Insert** tab *(Teaching Learning Center, 2023)*:

Figure 4.4: *Interface of insert tab*

Users can easily insert images from the device, stock images, and a range of online pictures. Under this tab, the user can also insert videos and audio files directly into their documents.

Additionally, the application supports the insertion of online videos and links, allowing users to create interactive and multimedia-rich documents *(Microsoft Support, 2023)*. The link enables the user to click to go to a particular page in the file, an email address, or both. Any website that is referenced in a document must be hyperlinked. If a link within a document is blue, underlined, and looks to be successfully hyperlinked.

On the same tab, users can create cover pages for their documents, which can be books, manuals, reports, and more. To create a cover page for a document, follow the given steps:

1. Clicking on the cover page opens a drop-down menu that allows the user to choose from different cover page templates to set as the front page or cover text.

2. After selecting the templates, the user must enter text in the appropriate fields.

3. The blank page command inserts two-page breaks, one above and one below the current cursor position. Users choose to insert blank page breaks when they want to ensure the entire page has paragraph spacing. The shortcut for page breaks is *Ctrl + Enter*. The page break command expects the next text after the insertion point to be on a new page *(Heisserer, 2023c)*.

In addition, the Table group has a single icon with many built-in features. When executing the `Insert Table` command, the user is prompted to customize the number of rows and columns, as seen in *Figure 4.5*. Besides the `Insert Table` option, users can draw tables, convert text to tables, excel spreadsheets, and quick tables. Selecting an Excel workbook will allow users to place a small Excel workbook in their document at the point of insertion. Excel documents not only appear as tables, but they can also be used to perform many calculations. The latest quick tables feature launches multiple table templates from within Microsoft Word, allowing users to choose from created and formatted tables and choose the template that best suits their project, as shown:

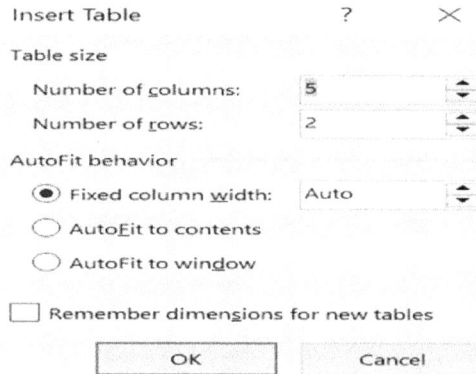

Figure 4.5: Dialogue box of insert table

After the table has been created, adding extra rows and columns, resizing the table, etc. is easy. The table feature automatically adds two modules to the word ribbon, i.e., **Table Design** and **Layout**. The **Table Design** tab allows for manipulation of the appearance of table and includes three sub-options, i.e., table style options, table styles, and borders, which is indicated in *Figure 4.6*:

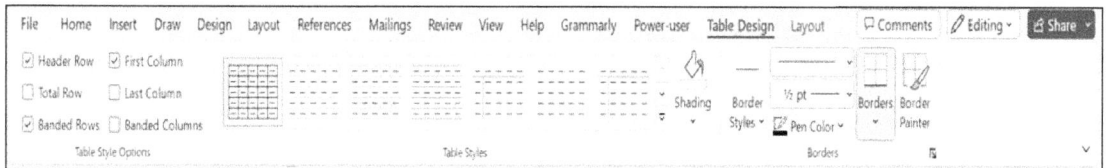

Figure 4.6: Table design within the Insert tab

The most unique feature is the data group, which allows the user to use some features of Excel in a Microsoft Word table. Information can be sorted. The following points discuss the features of the data group section:

- If a table occupies more than one page, select **Repeat Header Rows**, which will display the table header on the next page so the viewer can see the headings.

- Convert to Text removes all table formatting and automatically places each row into paragraphs. After selecting this command, users may need to adjust the table to ensure the data displays how they want it to.

- Finally, the formula allows some features of Excel to be used in the table to perform calculations.

Further, the **Layout** tab consists of sub-options like table, draw, rows and columns, merge, cell size, alignment, and data, as shown in *Figure 4.7*:

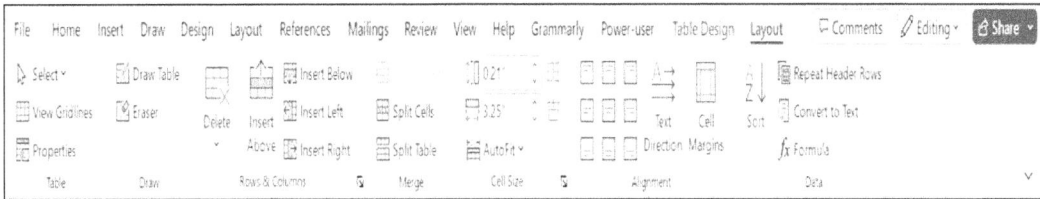

Figure 4.7: *Layout option within the Insert tab*

Users can also approve the positioning of bookmarks in the document. After establishing it, it is necessary to hyperlink and link another text to a bookmark. The user must highlight the text to be bookmarked before selecting the **Insert** tab to bookmark option. The user must construct a hyperlink to link to the bookmark from another location.

Finally, Cross Reference functions similarly to a bookmark except that it shows the exact title of the bookmarked content of the Microsoft document (*Heisserer, 2023*).

Utilities of Draw tab

This section will discuss the utility of the **Draw** tab, giving the reader an idea of its essential functions. The user can be creative and artistic by clicking the **Draw** tab using different options like **Drawing Canvas**, **Stencils**, **Edit**, **Convert**, **Insert**, and **Replay**, as shown in *Figure 4.8*. All in all, the **Draw** tab is a Microsoft Office feature which can help you add notes, create shapes, edit text, and more. Although, the **Draw** tab is available in Microsoft Word, Excel, and PowerPoint (*Anderson, 2021*). See *Figure 4.8* to understand the utilities in the **Draw** tab in MS word:

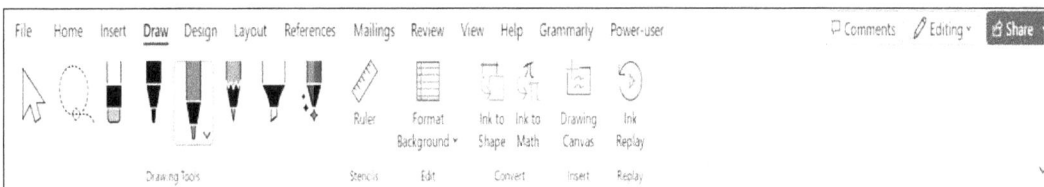

Figure 4.8: *Utilities in the Draw tab of MS Word*

The essential functions of these sections in MS Word are as follows:

- The **Drawing Tools** section contains tools such as **Select, Lasso Select**, **Eraser, Pen, Pencil,** and **Highlighter**, which are used to erase, edit, decorate your images, and highlight text using Ink. The last option is the Action Pen, which is used to edit natural gestures.

- Under the **Stencils**, a **Ruler** is given to draw lines and align objects against a straightedge.

- The **Edit** section will allow the user to format the background of the MS Word document by providing two unique features, i.e., Rule Lines and Grid Lines. Further, it will allow us to apply the changes to the whole page, and the user can provide any desirable color to the entire document.

- The **Convert** section consists of **Ink to Shape** and **Ink to Math**. These two tools convert handwritten shapes and mathematical equations to text form.

- The **Insert** section contains the Drawing Canvas, which will give you a creative space (in the form of a square box to perform some magical creations) to draw in, and it is only featured on the **Draw** tab in MS Word.

- The **Replay** section includes **Ink Replay**. If you have drawn an image using this feature, it will automatically recreate the recent image you created. It improves productivity. For instance: If a teacher marks grammar mistakes on an essay with handwritten corrections. The student replays the ink annotations to see which areas were highlighted first, making it easier to follow feedback and improve their writing.

- The **Ink to Math** tool will give you four options, i.e., write, erase, select, correct, and clear, as shown in *Figure 4.9*:

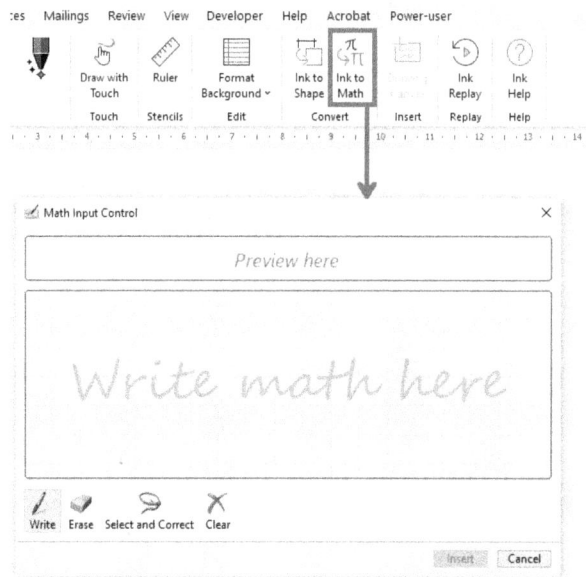

Figure 4.9: *How to use the Ink to Math tool*

Adding the **Draw** tool tab to ribbon in Microsoft Office is described as follows:

Sometimes, if the user does not find the **Draw** tool tab attached to the ribbon and wants to draw something on the MS Word document, they may add it with a few clicks.

The steps for the same are as follows:

1. Open the Microsoft Office application software, i.e., Word, Excel, or PowerPoint. Here, our primary focus is to add the **Draw** tool tab in MS Word.

2. After opening the MS Word document, the user needs to right-click on the blank side of the ribbon and, from there, select **Customize the Ribbon** (see *Figure 4.10*)**,** which will open a new window, as shown in *Figure 4.11*.

3. After opening **Customize Ribbon**, please click on the drop-down menu under Choose commands from, select the menu that says **Tools** tab, check the **Draw** button, and click **OK**.

4. Finally, the **Draw** icon will be visible on the ribbon and ready to use (refer to the *Draw Tool tab in the Ribbon of Microsoft Office if it is missing*, 2021).

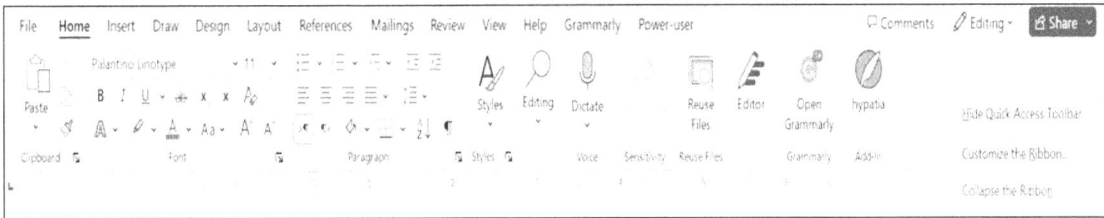

Figure 4.10: Customization of the Ribbon on MS Word

Alternatively, you can open the **Options** section by clicking **File | Options | Customize Ribbon**, or the user needs to press the right click, and the option for customization can appear as follows:

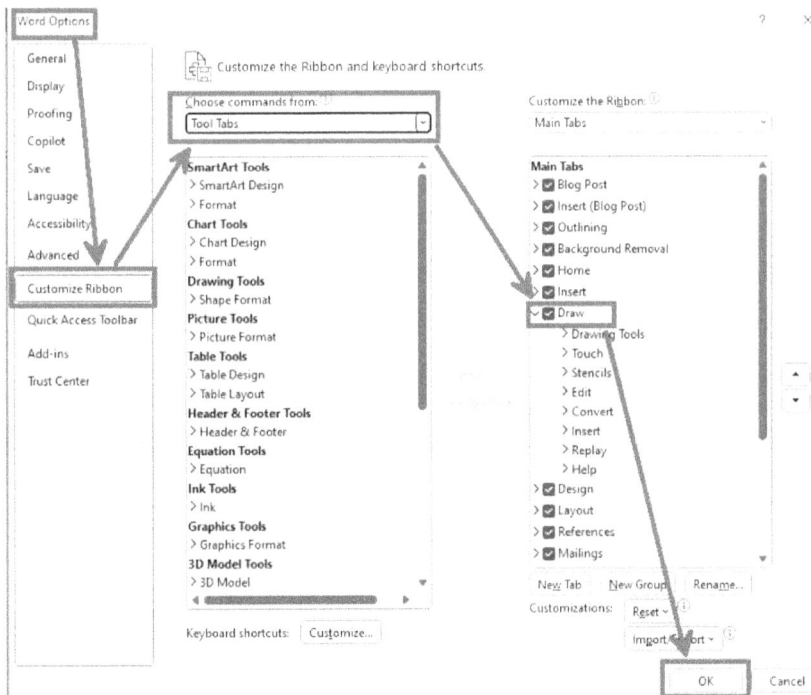

Figure 4.11: Adding the Draw tab to the main ribbon

In this way, the reader can easily be able to customize different tabs over the ribbon as per their nature of work.

Creating a survey form in MS Word

If you are a researcher or any other professional who used to undergo a process to design a survey or a feedback form, then you can do it on MS Word. You may be wondering what is needed for a professional to create it on MS Word when we have a range of online survey creator websites, software, and platforms. Then, the answer is that initially, being a professional, there is a need to design a template of a survey form professionally so that it would look convincing and clear. Further, when a user tries to fill out and start entering data in one of the forms prepared on your MS Word application, you would find the text changes its original place, making these forms challenging to read. Thus, the developer tab is like the icing on the cake to overcome these issues. MS Word application can create forms that allow users to enter data without scattering the text that already exists on the form. These forms can be a course registration, student report, researcher survey questionnaire, or even quizzes for online courses (*Thede, 2009a*).

In the preceding section, you have been introduced to the default ribbon of MS Word, as shown in *Figure 4.2*. However, more tabs are built into the MS Word application, known as the **Developer** tab, to create a form or feedback form. To get this **Developer** tab, the user first needs to follow the following steps:

The user needs to click **File**; different options will appear as follows:

1. Click **More**, and three options will appear. Out of them, click **Options**. Subsequently, a new dialogue box entitled **Word Options** will open.

2. Select **Customize Ribbon, then click Custom Tabs and Groups** (the last option) from the dropdown menu of **Choose commands from**.

3. Check the **Developer** box under the dropdown of **Main Tabs**.

4. Then, Click **OK**.

All these steps have been visualized for the user in *Figure 4.12* as follows:

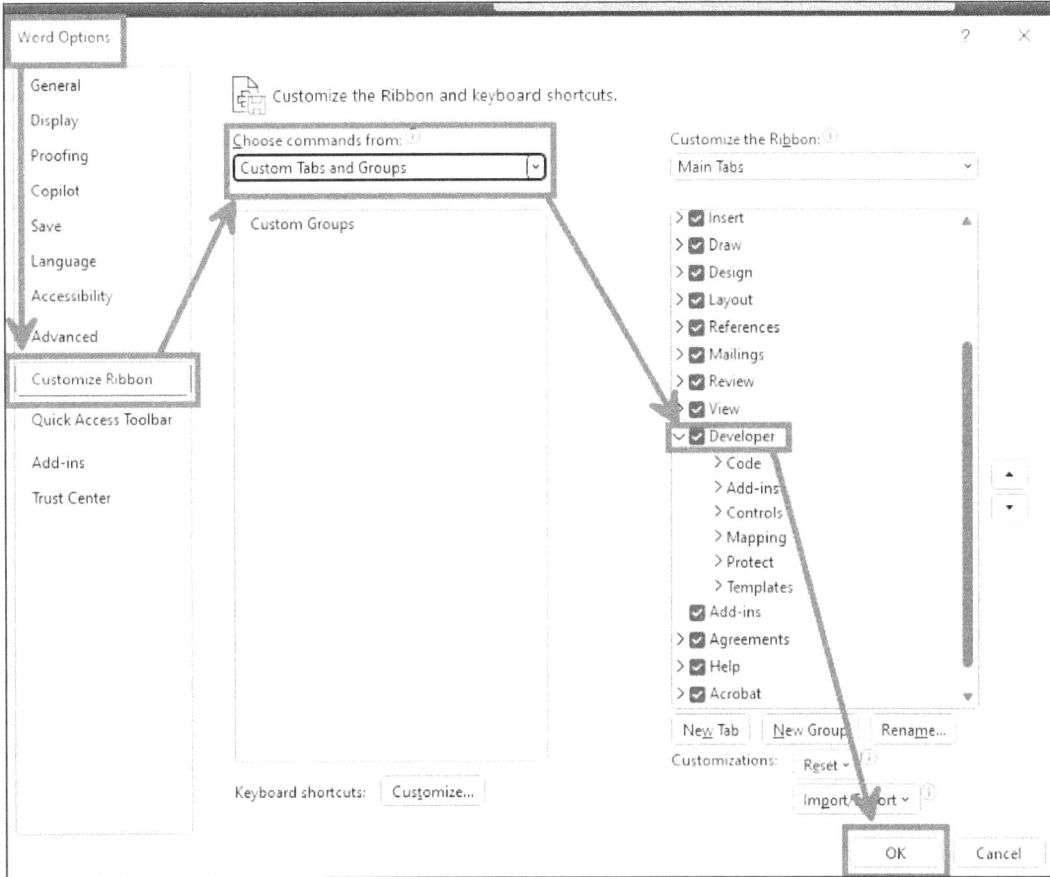

Figure 4.12: *Steps to add Developer tab into MS Word*

After adding the **Developer** tab to the main ribbon, the by-default MS Word ribbon would get changed, as shown in *Figure 4.13*:

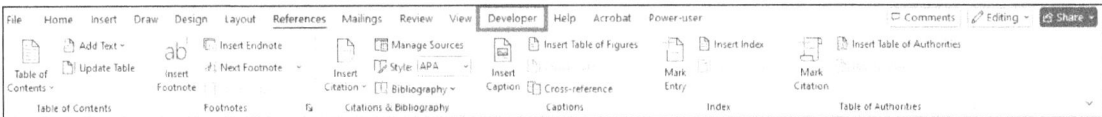

Figure 4.13: *Activating Developer tab in MS Word*

Alternatively, the user can customize the ribbon by right-clicking on the blank side of the ribbon in MS Word, as elaborated in *Figure 4.10*, and it will directly take the user to the window shown in *Figure 4.12*. Once the user has successfully added the **Developer** tab to the MS Word ribbon, they can quickly create or frame the survey form in MS Word. When you click on the Developer tab, there are plenty of ground-breaking options that could change the file format of the Microsoft Word document (**.docx**) to Microsoft Word Macro Enabled Document (**.docm**). This was initially introduced in MS Office 2007 Version, and **.docm** files work exactly like

.docx files; they can also store formatted text, images, shapes, charts, etc., but they are unique as they can execute macros to automate tasks in MS Word (*Fisher, 2023*). In addition, the icons of the saved **.docm** and **.docx** files can be viewed in *Figure 4.14* as follows:

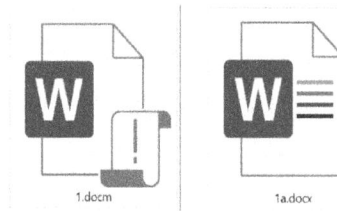

Figure 4.14: Icon of the file formats of .docm and .docx

An overview of the **Developer** tab can be seen in *Figure 4.15*:

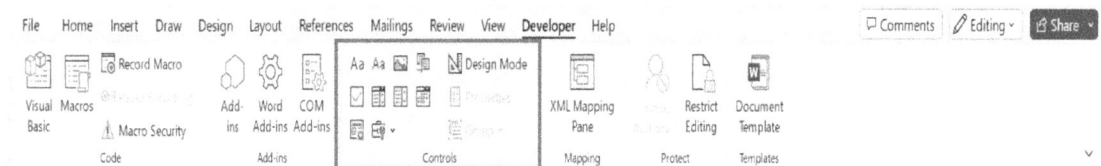

Figure 4.15: Interface of MS Word ribbon after addition of a Developer tab

Now, in this section, the objective is to create a form which is convenient, accessible, and attractive to the readers. For this, the user needs to investigate the **Controls** option (as highlighted in *Figure 4.15*), where the form can be prepared. The overview of the panel used for creating a form is shown in *Figure 4.16* as follows:

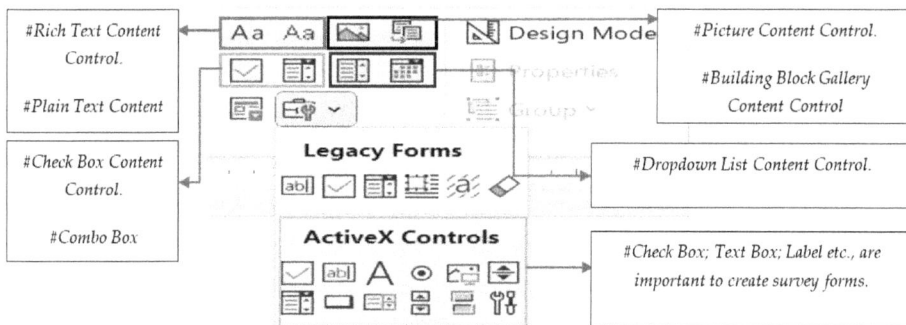

Figure 4.16: Detailed overview of a panel to create a form

The user needs to concentrate on *Figure 4.16* to successfully create a form using its few sub-buttons. The requirement of every user varies depending upon their professional objectives, so in this case, the user needs to reflect and identify the types of data required. Some data types are essential, maybe plain text entry, checkboxes, options buttons, and dropdown boxes. The highlighted description in *Figure 4.16* connotes creating a survey form or a text area needed to get the demographic information.

These features are discussed in detail as follows:

- **Rich Text Content Control**: Rich text content control in MS Word's **Developer** tab offers a powerful way to create dynamic and interactive documents. It allows you to embed various types of content, such as text, images, tables, and even other documents, within a single control. This flexibility makes them invaluable for creating templates, forms, and other structured documents.

- **Plain Text Content**: Under the **Plain Text Content**, the user can display or hide formatting marks (e.g., paragraph marks, spaces, tabs) to visualize the underlying structure of the text and also can remove all formatting from selected text, leaving only plain text.

- The Check Box Content Control is required when we have multiple options, and the options button is necessary when there are various options, but we need to select one out of the total options.

- Picture Content Control is essential for filling out the registration form or any job application form, where an attachment of a passport-size picture is required.

- Most forms need the criteria to fill out the date option, so the Date Picker Content Control is helpful.

These are just some of the many features available in the developer tab of Microsoft, and by using these features, users can efficiently edit, format, and manipulate the text to meet their specific needs.

For reference purposes, *Figure 4.17* indicates the complete form type, which utilizes all the option types (by highlighting them in different colors) required to create an offline survey. Now, these options can be editable once you right-click the chosen button; it will automatically activate the design mode and properties sub-options. Once done with the editing, deactivate the design mode by clicking it again. This way, the user can make any changes in a few clicks.

Furthermore, if the user wants to protect your macro-document, follow the given steps:

1. Click the **Restrict Editing** under the **Protect** option.
2. After clicking the **Restrict Editing** option, a side panel window will pop up asking for three further options, such as formatting restrictions, editing restrictions, and start enforcement.
3. Depending upon the user's requirements, it will further ask you to type the password to protect the file.
4. Enter a password and confirm it by clicking **OK**.

Document protection helps the user prevent unauthorized access to others from changing the form and preserves the design of the form while allowing users to enter data (*Thede, 2009a*). Hence, the **Developer** tab is helpful in many ways, to create applications to use with Microsoft 365 programs, write macros, run macros that you previously recorded, use XML commands, use ActiveX Controls, use form controls in Microsoft Excel, Work and create new shapes and stencils in Microsoft Visio (*Show the Developer Tab, 2023*) as follows:

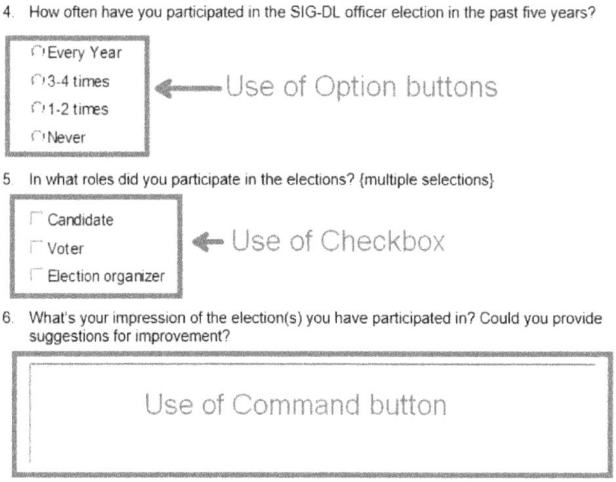

Figure 4.17: Example of a survey form that utilizes the Controls toolbar

This way, a multifunctional, creative, and appealing form can be prepared by activating and using the **Developer** tab in MS Word.

Utilities of Design and Layout tab in MS Word

After executing a range of operations in MS Word documents, there are some unique features of the **Design** tab that allow the user to adjust the arrangement and graphics of the document, as shown in the following figure:

Figure 4.18: Functions of a Design tab

Under the **Design** tab, there are two sections, i.e., **Document Formatting** and **Page Background**, as shown in *Figure 4.18*. The options under the **Document Formatting** are:

- On the left corner, the first option is Themes, which will give the user a range of themes, as we have in MS PowerPoint. A document theme is a uniform set of organizational and stylistic structures that differentiate headings and subheadings and provide easy navigation and comprehension for the reader (*Heisserer, 2023b*).

- Moreover, MS Word has many document style formats and provides a unique range of font arrangements for the whole document.

- Next, the **Fonts** and **Colors** buttons allow you to apply different colors to different document style options, and the font menu applies a single font to the entire document.
- The **Paragraph Spacing**, **Effects**, and **Set as Default** options allow the user to set default paragraph spacing and text effects which are applied to the entire document and Microsoft Word when the document is launched.

Next, we will be discussing the **Page Background** option.

The **Page Background** contains three sub-options, i.e., **Watermark**, **Page Color**, and **Page Border**.

The watermarked document is light colored, which gives different options under three categories, i.e., Confidential, Disclaimers, and Urgent. It also offers an option to customize the watermark under the dropdown menu of the watermark option. Then, the page color dropdown option will change the background color of the entire document.

Finally, the **Page Borders** is used to decorate the MS Word document, and it is applicable whenever the user wants to create a report, proposal, or invitation. This **Page Borders** option further gives different menu options for launching a border and applying shading.

In a nutshell, the Borders and Shading group defines the shading effect of the page border, as well as the thickness and style of the border. Border settings can be applied to a paragraph or the entire document.

Now, we will be discussing the **Layout** tab, which plays an essential role in MS Word. The Layout tab contains three different options, i.e., **Page Setup**, **Paragraph**, and **Arrange**. This tab allows the user to adjust the page setup, line, and paragraph spacing. It also allows the user to assign the margin to the document; the user can also change the orientation of the MS Word document and its sizing and adjust the number of columns. The primary interface of the Layout tab is shown in *Figure 4.19*:

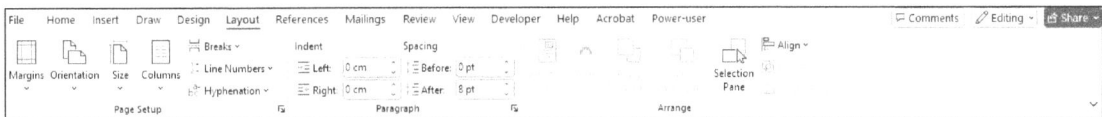

Figure 4.19: *Functions of the Layout tab in MS Word*

The following are the options provided under the Page Setup option:

- In Page Setup, the **Layout** tab allows users to customize the upper, lower, left, and right spacing through its margins' dropdown menu.
- An **Orientation** menu allows the user to change the page layout in portrait or landscape form. The portrait form is vertical, which means the document looks taller than it is broader, whereas the landscape form is horizontal, which means the document looks wider than taller.
- The **Size** dropdown button allows the user to prepare the document in varying sizes like letter size, legal, tabloid, Statement, etc.

- The dropdown option of **Columns** allows changing the text pattern by inserting multiple columns on a Word document. This option is helpful for users who are creating a flyer, newsletter, or any newspaper article. Inserting the columns will let the user fill their text so that once the first column is filled, the following line will automatically go to the next column, and this process continues until the text is filled in all the columns, as suggested by the user.

Furthermore, after these four dropdown options, the next panel within the Page Setup contains three dropdowns altogether, as follows:

- The **Breaks** button allows the user to put various breaks such as page breaks, column breaks, section breaks, and so on. Hence, the section breaks not only allow a break in the text but also allow for different layout options and page orientation settings, whereas page breaks, being in the same section, keep all the same formatting (*Heisserer, 2023d*).

- Under the **Line Numbers** dropdown option will allow the user various options. It will assign a line number before each started line, depending upon the user's requirement, i.e., whether it would be according to the page, a section, or an entire document. This option is helpful for a PhD student or any other professional who wants to help another locate a specific sentence or paragraph. For example, a researcher may be asked to go to line 3527 instead of the fourth sentence in the fifth paragraph on page number 07.

- Finally, the hyphenation option maintains the look of the text on the page, ensuring that text is presented neatly and regularly (*Control Hyphenation, 2023*).

- The last two options within the **Layout** tab will help the user adjust the document indentation and line spacing per their requirements. All these functions can quickly be done in the **Paragraph** sub-panel.

- Another option is to arrange the MS Word document by giving an alignment option in which the grids and guides can be set per the requirement.

To access the Selection Pane, go to the **Home** tab, click on **Select** in the **Editing** group, and then choose **Selection Pane**. The Selection Pane in Microsoft Word is a handy tool for managing objects within your document. The following are some of its key uses:

- **Viewing and selecting objects**: The Selection Pane lists all the objects on the current page, making it easy to select any object, even if it's hidden behind others.

- **Reordering objects**: You can change the order of overlapping objects by moving them forward or backward in the list. This is useful for arranging layers of images, shapes, or text boxes.

- **Hiding and showing objects**: You can temporarily hide objects to work on other elements without distraction. This is particularly helpful when dealing with complex layouts.

- **Grouping and ungrouping objects**: The Selection Pane allows you to group multiple objects so you can move or format them as a single entity. You can also ungroup them if needed.

- **Renaming objects**: For better organization, you can rename objects in the Selection Pane. This is useful when you have multiple objects and need to identify them quickly.

Functions of Reference tab in MS Word

The **Reference** tab is one of the crucial and beneficial tabs across the MS Word ribbon, especially for an author, writer, or researcher for writing a research paper, a book, or an extended technical paper. This tab provides an umbrella for giving and managing the **Table of Contents** (**ToC**), inserting footnotes and in-text citations, creating a bibliography at the end of the chapter, maintaining a content page for figures and tables, and marking the table of authorities, which can be viewed from *Figure 4.20:*

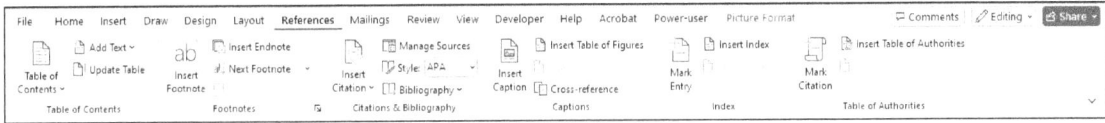

Figure 4.20: Interface of the Reference tab in MS Word

Different groups of the **Reference** tab are discussed as follows:

- **Table of Contents group:** This group helps the user to create a ToCs page at the start of any document, but all the headings and subheadings must be standardized, as discussed in previous sections. Assigning the right format of the heading and subheadings will automatically help the user to create a synchronized ToCs with its appropriate assigned page numbers. When clicking on the ToC icon, MS Word provides the user with various styles of ToC. Every time the document changes, the user should click the **Update Table** button to bring or include the new headings and sub-headings with their exact page numbers.

  Moreover, if the user finds any missing heading or subheading in the ToC, then there may be the case that those headings are not formatted correctly. This would be done by revisiting the **Home** tab, clicking **Styles**, and choosing your preferred style. For each heading you want to be reflected in the ToC, select the heading text and do the desirable formatting in the **Style** menu of the **Home** tab.

  Following is the guide to insert a ToCs in your MS Word document (*Insert a Table of Contents, 2023*):

  1. Put your cursor where you want to add the ToCs, generally on the first page.

  2. Go to **References** | **Table of Contents** and choose any automatic style you prefer.

  3. Finally, if you make any changes, like adding headings or subheadings to your document, those changes will be reflected in the ToC by clicking the **Update Table** icon.

- **Footnotes group:** This group is generally visible on the same page but at the bottom, where the author quotes some information. While choosing the endnotes and footnotes, the user must know the basic difference between the two, which is discussed in brief:

  The endnotes are placed at the end of a document or a section, whereas the footnotes are placed at the bottom of the page where the reference or comment is made. Regarding its usage, endnotes are often used in academic writing to keep the main text clean and uncluttered, while footnotes are commonly used in books and articles to provide immediate references or additional information. Moreover, the endnotes require the reader to flip to the end of the document, which can be less convenient, while the footnotes allow the reader to see the reference or comment immediately without leaving the page. There are three options in the footnotes group, which are discussed as follows:

  o   Footnotes are additional information except for the references, which the author wants to provide to the readers by indicating them by numbers as a superscript. The difference between the footnotes and endnotes is that the footnotes are visible precisely on the same page on which that word is indicated.

  o   An endnote is a reference, explanation, or comment placed at the end of a document or a section of a document. It is used to provide additional information, cite sources, or add context without cluttering the main text. Endnotes are typically numbered and correspond to numbers in the main text. In other words, endnotes are visible or given at the end of the document.

  o   The show notes help the user to locate the footnotes and endnotes provided in the document.

  Thus, inserting a footnote or endnote is not a hard nut to crack; the user needs to click the **Insert Footnote** button where they want to add. Once you click on a footnote, it will automatically get reflected at the end of the same page where it has been indicated (*Heisserer, 2023f*).

- **Insert citation, references, and bibliography:** Writing any subject assignment or research article for school, work, or for publication, giving in-text citations, maintaining references, and finally, preparing the bibliography is found to be a travailing or menial task to perform. In this regard, several reference management software is available in the publishing industry to transform such drudgery tasks into relaxing ones. A few examples of this software are Mendeley (acquired by Elsevier), EndNote (a product of Clarivate), Zotero (developed by Corporation for Digital Scholarship), RefWorks (produced by Ex-Libris, a ProQuest Company), JabRef, and many more. Some of the reference management software is open source and free to use, whereas some are commercial software and need to be purchased. Suppose any user has installed and downloaded the open-source reference management software, for example, Mendeley Reference Manager.

In such a case, it will be attached to the **Reference** tab of the MS Word application and shown in *Figure 4.21*. Then, it can be compared with *Figure 4.20*, which is without the installed Add-in of the Mendeley Reference Management Software:

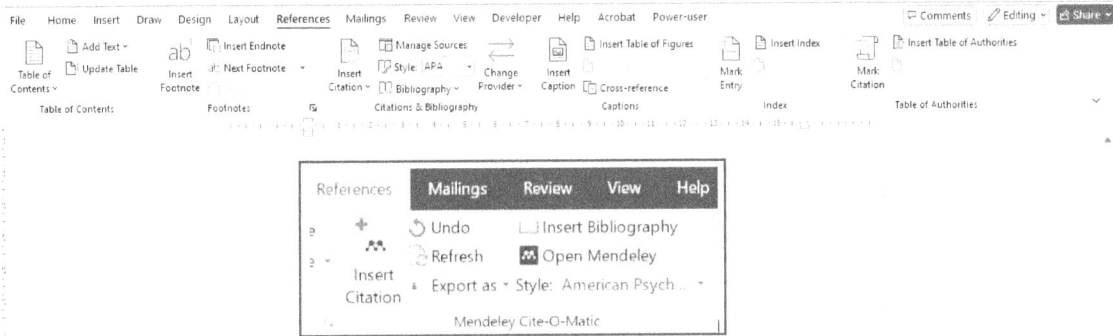

Figure 4.21: *Interface of the Reference tab after adding reference management software*

After comparison, the user will find that both options, i.e., **Mendeley Cite-O-Matic** and **Citations & Bibliography**, will perform all the functions whenever the user wants to cite and reference any document. In addition to this, there are several add-ins available in the Microsoft Store to get it installed on your application, and easy to perform referencing tasks.

For this, the user needs to perform the following steps:

1. **Insert** tab | **Get Add-ins** | In the Search Box, type **Bibcitation** | **Add** | **Continue**.

2. Once the user has successfully installed the Add-in of Bibcitation, it will be visible on the right side of the Home tab. The advantage of this add-in is that the user can effortlessly search, cite, and give the references of any document (be it a journal article, report, website, or video link) in any referencing format, i.e., **American Psychological Association (APA)**, **Modern Language Association (MLA)**, or any other standards of referencing styles. Further, this add-in is helpful for those who do not know the functions of reference management software (i.e., Mendeley, EndNote, or Zotero) efficiently and effectively (*Malik, 2023*).

Alternatively, suppose the user does not want to install software or add-in. In such a case, MS Word provides its basic referencing system via the **References** tab on the ribbon.

The steps for the aforementioned case are shown as follows:

1. Click on **Insert Citation** and select **Add new source**; another dialogue box will appear, as shown in *Figure 4.22*.

2. Next, select the source type and fill in all the bibliographic details of the document you need to cite. The MS Word bibliography manager uses rules to create citations and bibliographies, which need to be entered with care. It will not warn the user about errors or omissions on import.

3. Once the reference is entered into the database; it will not need to be re-imported. It can be used in any document written with this computer system (*LibGuides, 2023*). This function will let you add references to a document and create a bibliography at the end by clicking the **Bibliography** option. Refer to *Figure 4.22* to understand how to enter references using MS Word bibliographic manager:

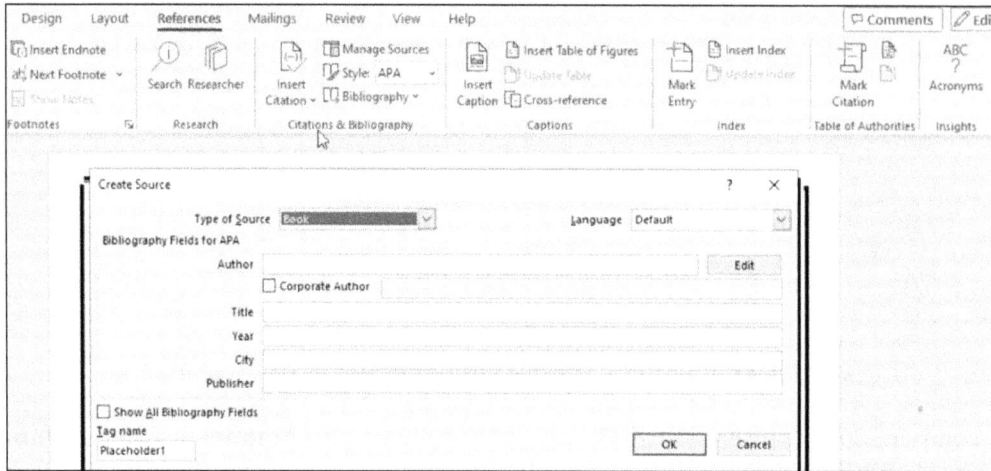

Figure 4.22: Way to enter Reference using MS Word bibliographic manager

4. Finally, the references can be stored in a **Master List**, which can be used to add references to other documents. However, it is less efficient and effective than any other reference management software. It can be accessed when the user clicks the **Manage Sources** option; then again, a pop-up window (see *Figure 4.23*) will open and prompt the user to search for the existing reference and ask you to browse a master list (*Microsoft Support, 2023a*). Refer to *Figure 4.23* to have a detailed view of the dialog box of the **Source Manager** option:

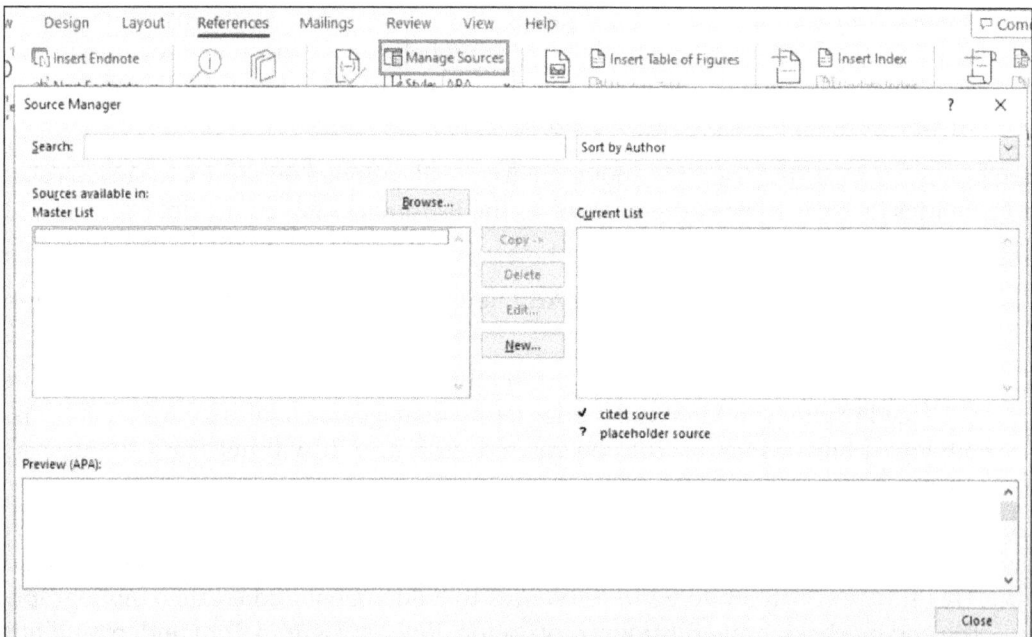

Figure 4.23: Dialog box of Source Manager

In the age of the AI era, when the task can be done quickly and efficiently, the MS Word bibliographic manager is undoubtedly not a panacea. The phrase, *work smarter, not harder* is suitable for free or commercial reference manager software. You will find using it with several limitations because it requires you to key all the bibliographic information, and only then can the user create a database. There is no way to automatically import reference data from a website, journal, or digital library database. Another limitation is that the references you enter cannot be moved and remain on the computer used to create your research paper or other work (*Sewell, 2010*).

Figure 4.24 illustrates how **the Researcher** group is beneficial for doing research work. Explanations are given as follows:

- **Research group:** In MS Word, the research option has two sub-options, i.e., **Search** and **Researcher**, which is highly important for an academician or a researcher. It further allows the user to quickly search any document or file within your system and open or insert a link into your existing document. Next, the researcher option allows the user to locate swiftly accurate information sources from the web, insert them into your document, and include them in the bibliography (*Heisserer, 2023*). This icon is suitable for those engaged in scholarly writing and can be easily added to the document. The researcher option and its subsequent side window can be viewed in *Figure 4.24*:

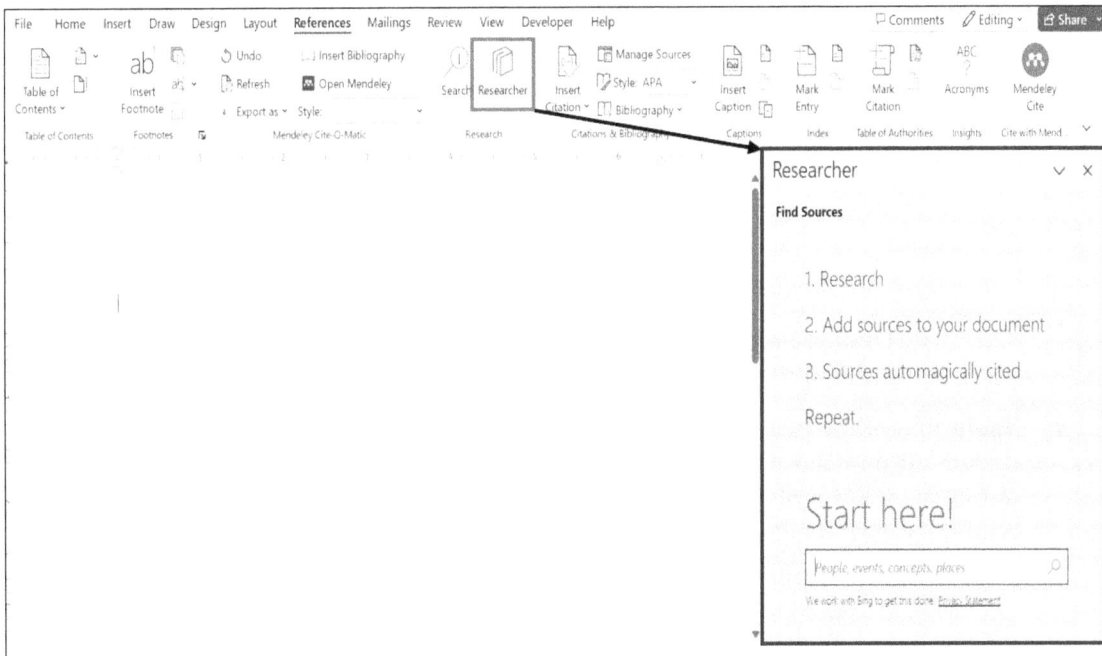

Figure 4.24: *Researcher windowpane on the Reference tab*

- **Captions group:** After writing a complete document by inserting various relevant tables and figures, with proper headings or sub-headings, and by citing the necessary references to create a bibliography, it is then essential to develop a table of figures and a list of tables, unlike the ToCs. Creating a ToCs is related to showcasing all the headings or subheadings used within the document. At the same time, the Captions group allows the user to create a table of Figures and a list of tables altogether in one place, mentioning the exact page numbers on which these are prepared or given. Thus, preparing a list of tables and a list of figures is not burdensome until and unless all their captions are correctly inserted.

Next, cross-references allow the user to quickly place links to a word in a document with some related heading or information. This activity will create a hyperlink to both the set of information, and a reader who is reading that document can easily switch between those hyperlinked information. Moreover, this feature requires using headings or other citations to navigate the document (*Heisserer, 2023a*).

- **Index group:** Index plays a pivotal role in helping the user locate pin-pointed information of any word or phrase found at the end of the book or a lengthy report. Creating an index is a cumbersome process and requires intensive concentration and intellect to execute this task. Still, MS Word is again coming up with the solution to prepare it simultaneously while writing your report or a book.

To highlight a phrase or a word, follow the given steps:

1. The user needs to highlight a word or phrase and select **Mark Entry**.

2. It will open a dialogue box, asking you to fill in the information like main entry, sub-entry, cross-reference, current page, page range, bold, italics, and then **Mark** and **Mark All**.

3. Next, the user must specify how they want that word or phrase to appear in the Index.

4. Further, the **Insert Index** option does the indexing of every selected item.

5. The **Update Index** will automatically get activated, and just clicking it again will update all the new entries to the existing created Index.

- **Table of authorities:** This option lists all the references used primarily in a legal document and the number of pages containing that reference. To create a table of authority, you highlight the citations and Microsoft Word inserts a specific Table of Authority entry field in your document. You can then search for the next long or short citation in the document to highlight, or you can automatically retain each subsequent occurrence of the citation. You can edit or add citation categories if you do not want to use existing citation categories, such as law or business (as shown in *Figure 4.25*). When a user creates an authority table, MS Word searches for tagged citations, sorts them by category, references their page numbers, and displays the authority table (*Microsoft Support, 2023b*). *Figure 4.25* shows how to mark and create the Table of Authorities:

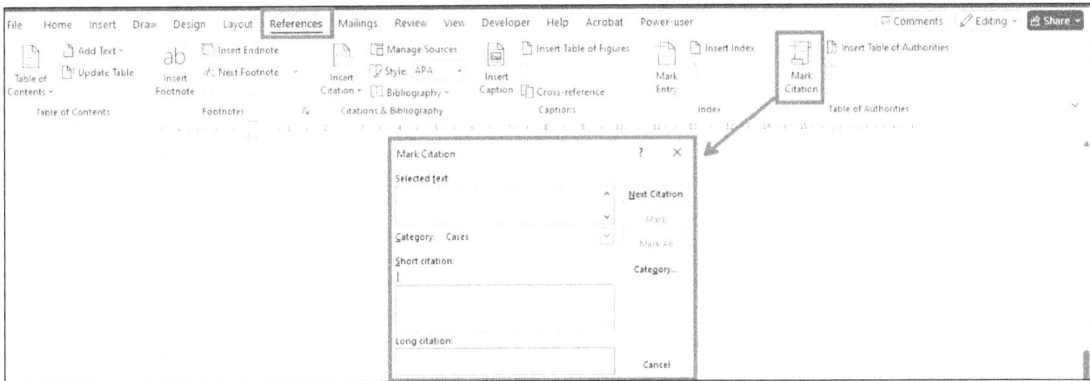

Figure 4.25: Marking and creating the table of authorities

Functions and utilities of the Mailing tab

In this section, you will learn the utility of the **Mailings** tab, whose usage is relatively less for writers, students, authors, or early-career scholars. Still, it is significant for business professionals and IT professionals. This tab is used to send personalized emails, indicating your first name and last name with your initials in an official format, with the proper designation and address of the mail recipient. Such types of emails need to be automated by feeding the required data in separate columns of MS Excel. Attach that Excel Sheet to the MS Word document to automate sending bulk emails. The entire procedure will be elaborated on in the later part of this section. Before that, it is essential to make us aware of its tab in MS Word, as shown in *Figure 4.26*:

Figure 4.26: Interface of the Mailing tab in MS Word document

So, the **Mailings** tab consists of five different options, i.e., **Create**, **Start Mail Merge**, **Write & Insert Fields**, **Preview Results**, and **Finish**. We will discuss them individually, as the last four interrelated options cannot proceed without the other. Here, you may also observe that only two dropdown options are activated, and the rest are deactivated, which will get activated as we move forward and complete the process of mail merge in MS Word.

Different options of the Mailing tab are discussed as follows:

- **Create group:** It allows the user to create customized envelopes or sheets of address & name labels with one address. Once you select the envelope option, the envelopes and labels dialog box will ask you to fill in the delivery address and return address and then with a few options for its settings. Finally, it is ready to get a printed copy, the same as it comes on the envelope.

- **Start Mail Merge:** When you click on the **Start Mail Merge**, a dropdown menu will open, asking you to select the type of document you want to send to several recipients while using the mail merge option. The dropdown menu consists of **Letters**, **Email-messages**, **Envelopes**, **Labels**, a **Directory**, a **Normal Word Document**, and **Step-by-Step Mail Merge Wizard**. Once the user selects the type of document, they are ready to execute the entire process of the Mail Merge (*Microsoft Support, 2023d*).

- Another systematic way is to select the last option, i.e., Step-by-Step Mail Merge Wizard, and then a new window will open in the side vertical panel, as shown in *Figure 4.27*. Then, it will ask you to select the document type and show you Steps 1 to 6, which you need to follow as shown:

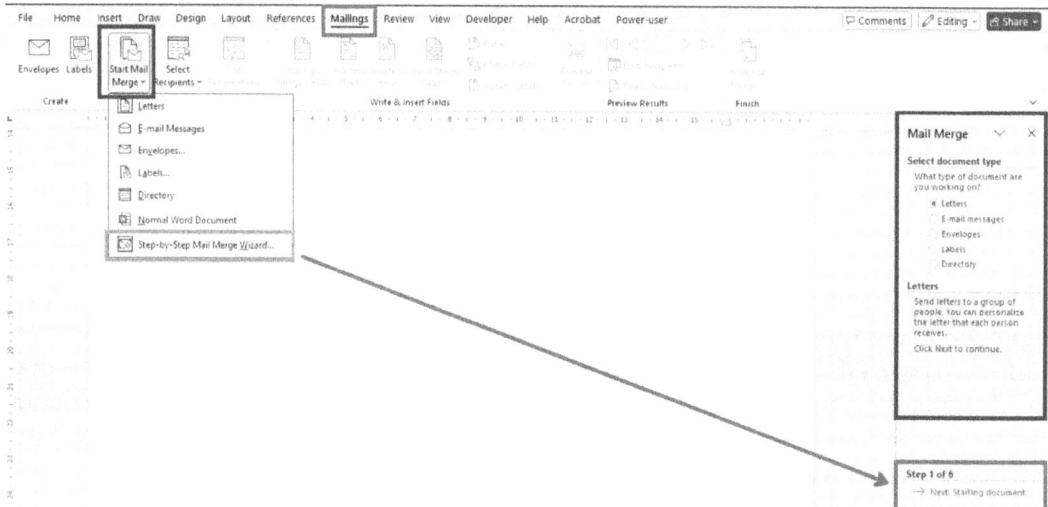

Figure 4.27: *Mail Merge window in the Mailings tab in MS Word*

Once you start following the six steps, you can complete the Mail Merge. As shown in *Figure 4.27*, the first step denotes a forward arrow, indicating the steps from clicking on **Step-by-Step Mail Merge Wizard** to **Step 1 of 6** as follows:

1. Select starting document
   a. Use the current document
   b. Start from a template
   c. Start from the existing document

2. Select recipients
   a. Use an existing list | Browse (you need to choose the already filled-in data from MS Excel)
   b. Select from **Outlook contacts** | Choose **Contacts Folder**
   c. Type a new list | **Create**.

3. Write your document (which you have chosen in the first step) | You need to brown the data fields as suggested above in the 2a. After browsing an MS Excel sheet, it will launch all the remaining options (as shown in *Figure 4.28*) with the loaded list of contacts to whom you intend to send your document through Mail Merge. *Figure 4.28* shows the different options which are used in the Mail Merge process:

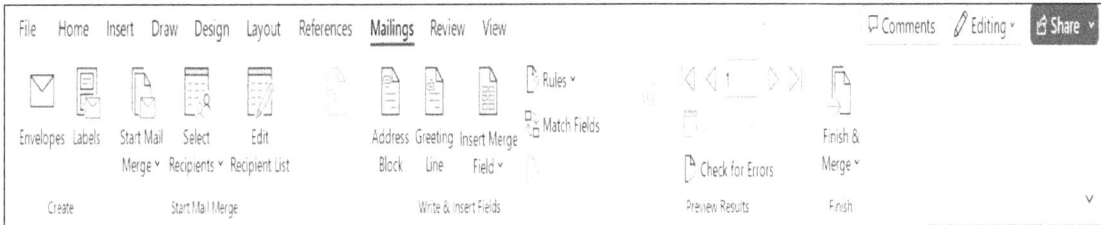

Figure 4.28: Activated options to execute the Mail Merge process

While browsing the data from the Excel sheet, it will ask you two different steps, as shown in *Figure 4.29*. After completing this step, you will have two options, **select a different list** and **edit the recipient list**. You can choose any suggested options if unsure about the selected list. *Figure 4.29* shows the following in-process steps involved in completing the Mail Merge process:

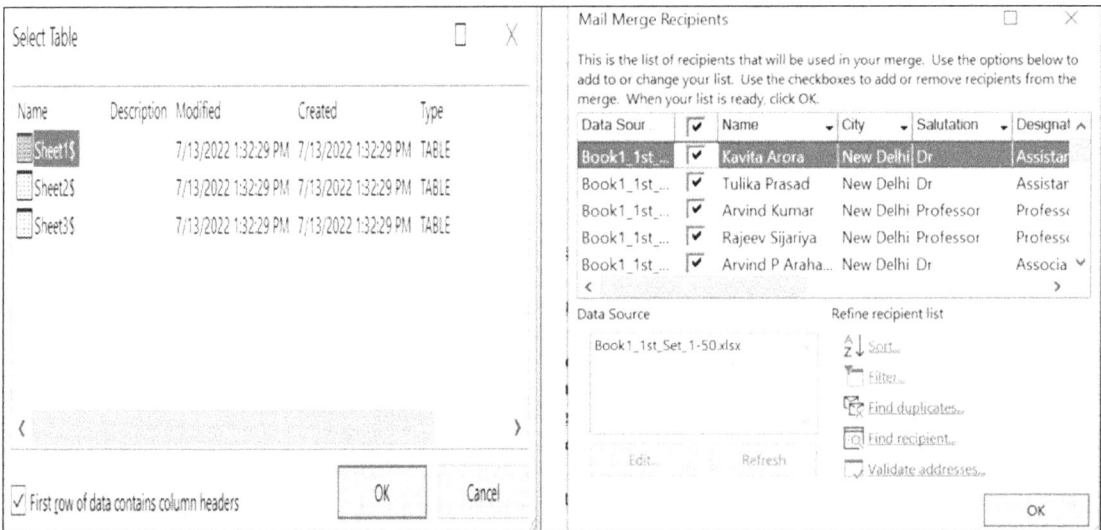

Figure 4.29: In-process steps to complete the Mail Merge process

4. Further, you have to write your intended document (which you wanted to send via mail), which will ask you to modify your list in four different ways. The first is the suggested Address book, Greeting line, Electronic Postage, and a few more items.

5. Then, select the next step, i.e., preview your document. Here, you can see all the recipient lists from the **Preview Results** option.

6. The last step is to complete the merge, which can also be done using the last option in the MS Word ribbon, i.e., **Finish & Merge**. As shown in *Figure 4.30*, you will be asked to select three different options: **Edit Individual Documents**, **Print Documents**, and **Send Email Messages**.

Figure 4.30: Different options under the Finish & Merge section

Here, you may select any of the options, but if you are sending bulk emails, you must choose the third option, i.e., **Send Email Messages**. In this way, the user can easily leverage the Mailings functionality of MS Word.

Functions of Review tab in MS Word

As its name suggests, the **Review** tab means reviewing the already prepared content or proofreading what and how it has been written. This tab also allows the writer, author, researcher, or any content professional to help their colleagues correct the existing document using its various features like spelling and grammar, accessibility, language checker translator, tracking with indicating associated comments, and more. Before going into detail, it is essential to investigate its interface, shown in *Figure 4.31*:

Figure 4.31: Interface of Review tab in MS Word

Figure 4.32 shows there are seven main options, i.e., **Proofing**, **Speech**, **Accessibility**, **Comments**, **Changes**, **Compare**, **Ink**, and **OneNote**, which we will discuss one by one in the coming section.

Different options of the **Review** tab are as follows:

*   **Proofing group:** Proofing allows the user to check for spelling and grammar; once you check Spelling and Grammar, it will open a navigation pane of the editor window on the right side of the document. This editor navigation pane will highlight all the spelling errors and the grammar check across all the words and phrases requiring

correction, as MS Word suggested. Moreover, in the search menu, Thesaurus gives you synonyms, antonyms, and various forms of speech for your chosen word. *Figure 4.32* shows a screenshot of the **Thesaurus** navigation pane, and another arrow shows you the function of the **Word Count** option, given on the Proofing group:

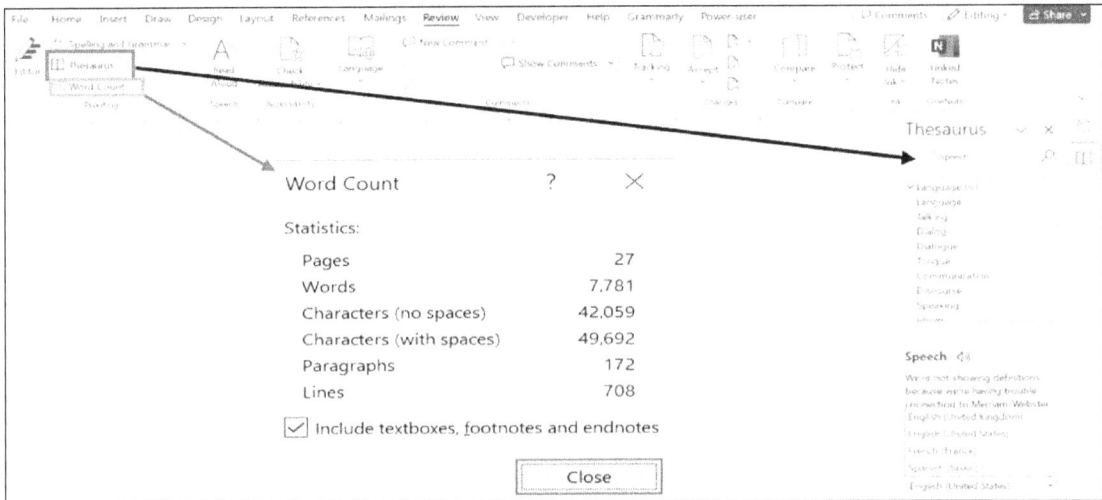

Figure 4.32: Features of Proofing group

- **Speech and accessibility:** Under the **Speech** option of MS Word, the **Read Aloud** feature is shown. When the **Read Aloud** button is selected, MS Word will start reading at the point where the text was inserted.

When you click **Accessibility**, the drop-down menu will present you with five sub-options, i.e., check accessibility, alt-text, navigation pane, focus, and options: accessibility. The Accessibility checker helps you find and edit content in your documents that may be more difficult for people with disabilities to read. Further, you can make your content accessible for people with disabilities by making it convenient for reading by going into the **Alt text** option. The Focus will change the color of your document from white to black or from black to white, meaning the document can be viewed in a darker mode and in a lighter way.

The language dropdown option will allow the user with two sub-options, i.e., **Translate**, which will ask you to translate selection or translate a document. This translation feature helps the user to detect the given language and translate it as per your chosen language. So, this feature is best for those who do not know many languages, but after pasting it into your MS Word document, it will auto-detect its language and convert it as per your desired language. The next option is **Language**, which will ask you to proofread the document in your chosen language, and the user can set language preferences by going into its settings. Thus, both options allow the user to select and set their preferences.

- **Comments:** When the user wants to put a note in the form of a suggestion or question to the author or document writer while reviewing the whole document, then the reviewer can set a new comment by using this Comment group. It is the easiest way to keep track of information about the document without changing its original formatting and meaning. All the set comments can be viewed by using sub-options like **Previous**, **Next**, and **Delete** the existing comment. The author can also give answers to the placed comments by the reviewer, and when we click **Show Comments**, a side navigation pane of **Comments** will open all the placed comments to the document. All these comments will be visible to the user with highlighted lines associated with the comment (*Heisserer, 2023g*).

- **Track Changes in MS Word:** The **Track Changes** mode is helpful for the authors, researchers, reviewers, and editors to make changes as they want in your document. It depends on whether the author accepts or rejects those suggested changes marked by your reviewer or editor. The main functions of this tab are elaborated with the help of *Figure 4.33*, in which a sample of the marked-up document is given. The strikethrough sentences are highlighted in two different colors, meaning that two authors review this sampled document, and all the suggestions can be accepted or rejected. *Figure 4.33* shows a document with enabled **Track Changes** option:

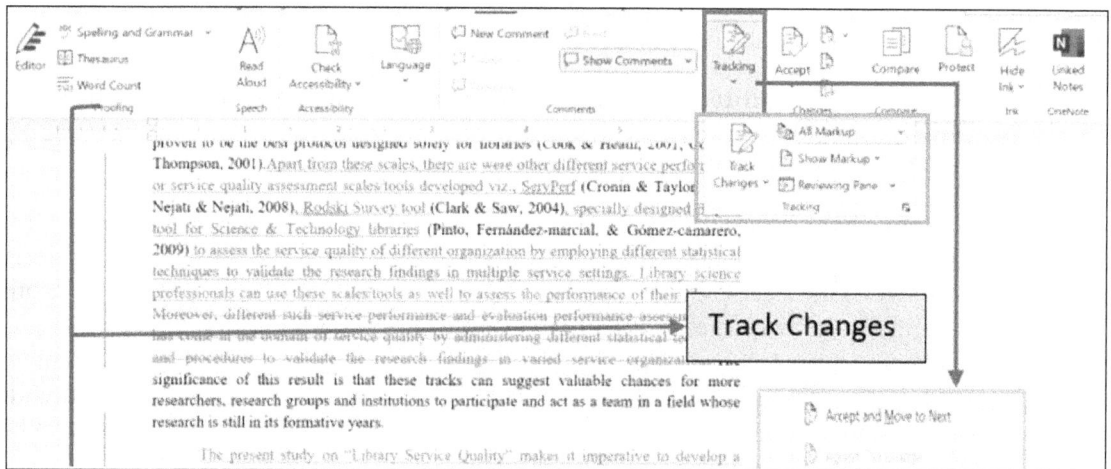

Figure 4.33: MS Word document marked up with Track Changes

The **Accept** dropdown menu is also shown in *Figure 4.33*, which allows the user to perform different actions per the suitability of the sentences in the document. It means the user can accept and move to the next, accept the change, or accept all changes, and finally, accept all changes and stop tracking (*Thede, 2009b*).

- **Compare, Protect, and Ink groups:** The user can finalize the document using Compare and Protect groups. The Compare dropdown gives two further sub-features in which the user can compare two document versions and combine revisions from multiple authors into one document. Since MS Word saves each document version when the author saves it, the user can review each version with the current version. This allows us to preserve the changes to a previous version if significant changes have been incorporated.

The Protect group enables the author to restrict other authors to include the changes to a document and make it a read-only or Restrict Permission document. Clicking **Restrict Editing** will open another window on the right side of the document, which gives three options:

- o **Formatting Restrictions | Limit formatting to a selection of styles**.

- o **Editing Restrictions | Allow only this type of editing in the document | Exceptions**.

- o **Start Enforcement | Enter Password**.

Next, Hide Ink will hide or delete all Ink done in the document.

- **Linked Notes**: In the **Review** tab, the last functionality is **Linked Notes**. Once you click **Linked Notes**, it will open a dialog box, after which the user needs to undertake the following steps:

  1. **Choose a location in OneNote**: In the dialog box, select a location in OneNote where you want to create a new notes page or add to an existing page. Click **OK**.

  2. **Start taking notes**: A OneNote window will open next to your Word document. You can start taking notes in OneNote, and these notes will be linked to the corresponding sections in your Word document.

  3. **Switch between notes and document**: You can click on the OneNote icon in the taskbar or the links in OneNote to switch between your notes and the original content in Word.

This feature is great for keeping your research, thoughts, and references organized while working on a document.

Functions of View tab in MS Word

After going a long way in understanding all the ground-breaking features of MS Word, the last tab is **View**, which is used to help the authors look at the final version of the document. The View tab contains eight different options, i.e., **Views, Immersive, Page Movement, Show, Zoom, Window, Macros, and SharePoint**, as shown in *Figure 4.34*:

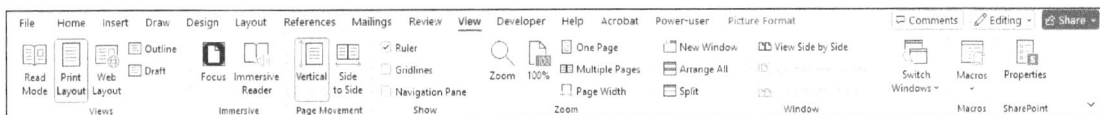

Figure 4.34: Interface of the View tab in MS Word

The following options are provided under the **View** tab:

- The first option of the **View** tab is used to change the layouts of the document by giving different viewing options, whichever is convenient for the readers.

- The **Immersive Reader** option will help the reader read the document by focusing on words, and its reading layout will change once opted.

- Page Movement allows a reader to view the document by scrolling up and down and sliding each page from right to left or left to right (*Microsoft Support, 2010*).

- The **Show** option enables a reader to set a ruler, which can help the reader to measure and see the stuff.

- Further, gridlines help you to place your object perfectly or align the figures and tables with other stuff.

- The navigation pane is like a tour guide for your document because once you click on navigation, the navigation pane will open on the left side of the document, where you can see all the formatted headings and sub-headings. Clicking on any headings or sub-headings will take you right there without scrolling up and down in a normal print layout.

- The **Zoom** feature will adjust your document to the level that is right for you and allows you to adjust your document to zoom 100% at just a single click. So, you can zoom your document so that you can view one page at a time, view multiple pages in one go, and change the width of the page to that of your window.

- The Windows option helps you manage several publisher windows at once.

    o A new window will open the duplicate window so you can view it simultaneously in different places.

    o Clicking the **Arrange All** option will resize your window and move your currently open publisher windows so that they are side by side. Split will allow you to split your document into two sections, making it easier to look at one section while editing another.

    o Switch Windows will allow you to view all open windows and enable you to select and jump to any of those windows.

- The **Macros** option is used to record macros, display a list of recorded macros, run recorded macros, and create or delete macros. A macro is an MS Word program that records work, including mouse actions and keystrokes. For example, a saved job can be any template with a format. The macro function is very useful for repetitive jobs; if we repeat a job occasionally, we can save it with the macro and run it as needed.

- Finally, the SharePoint properties in Microsoft Word can help a user in managing and organizing their documents more effectively. To avail of this feature, the user may follow the following steps under the **View** tab:

1. Opening the Word document that is stored in a SharePoint library.

2. Click on the **View** tab at the top of the Word window.

3. In the **View** tab, look for the **Document Panel** option. This panel allows you to view and edit the SharePoint properties directly within Word.

4. When you click on **Document Panel**, a pane will appear at the top of your document. Here, you can see and edit the metadata properties that are stored in SharePoint, such as title, author, status, and custom properties. Any changes you make to the properties in the **Document Panel** will be saved back to SharePoint when you save the document.

5. Users may also insert SharePoint properties into the document itself by using the **Quick Parts** feature. Go to the **Insert** tab, click on **Quick Parts**, and then select **Document Property** to choose from the available SharePoint properties.

This integration helps ensure that your document metadata is consistent and up-to-date across MS Word and SharePoint.

Importance of Help tab in MS Word

This tab is generally not consulted by the writers, but it will directly lead you to get primary or first-hand product information from its official website. Starting with the help option, it will take you to the newly launched windowpane on the right side of the document, and you will get all the required information directly from trusted web sources.

Further, the contact support, feedback, show training, and **What's New** option will inform the users of all the online training and learning content and let you know the latest updated feature installed on your MS Office application.

Conclusion

Microsoft Word is a highly adaptable and widely utilized word-processing software created by Microsoft Suite. One of its remarkable features is the seamless interoperability between traditional MS Word and cloud-based MS Word applications, enhancing the overall processing experience. With cloud storage services like OneDrive, any user can save and preserve their documents over the cloud, making them accessible from any device and anywhere with a stable internet connection. MS Word is an excellent choice for individuals, students, professionals, and organizations seeking a modern and versatile word-processing solution. It comes out with many efficient writing and editing tools like writing and formatting reports, creating resumes and cover letters, collaborating on documents with team members, and creating newsletters and brochures, which have been discussed in the chapter. Further, providing references is an excellent and ethical practice in the publishing and academic industry while acknowledging an individual's work is always ethical (*Vaidya, 2023*).

In the subsequent chapter, we will explore the management of Excel workbooks and worksheets, as well as delve into the concepts of functions and formulas. The chapter will also include an in-depth study of pivot tables, which enables the quick summarization of extensive datasets.

References

1. Anderson, S. (2021). *How to draw in Microsoft Word using the Draw Tab tools*. The Windows Club. **https://www.thewindowsclub.com/draw-tab-tools-in-microsoft-office**

2. *Control hyphenation*. (2023). Microsoft Support. **https://support.microsoft.com/en-gb/office/control-hyphenation-7d4d2a38-b0e2-4f04-873a-0a8d48ac3923**

3. *Draw Tool Tab in Ribbon of Microsoft Office if it is missing*. (2021). The Windows Club. **https://www.thewindowsclub.com/add-the-draw-tool-in-microsoft-office#google_vignette**

4. Fisher, T. (2023, April 10). *What Is a DOCM File?* Life Wire: Tech for Humans. **https://www.lifewire.com/docm-file-2620747**

5. Heisserer, N. (2023a). *Captions*. LibreTexts Workforce. **https://workforce.libretexts.org/Bookshelves/Information_Technology/Computer_Applications/Computer_Fundamentals_for_Technical_Students_(Heisserer)/13%3A__Design_Layout_References_Mailings_and_Review_Tabs_in_Microsoft_Word/13.04%3A_Captions**

6. Heisserer, N. (2023b). *Design Tab*. LibreTexts Workforce. **https://workforce.libretexts.org/Bookshelves/Information_Technology/Computer_Applications/Computer_Fundamentals_for_Technical_Students_(Heisserer)/13%3A__Design_Layout_References_Mailings_and_Review_Tabs_in_Microsoft_Word/13.01%3A_Design_Tab**

7. Heisserer, N. (2023c). *Introduction to the Insert Tab*. LibreTexts Workforce. **https://workforce.libretexts.org/Bookshelves/Information_Technology/Computer_Applications/Computer_Fundamentals_for_Technical_Students_(Heisserer)/12%3A_Using_the_Insert_Tab_in_Microsoft_Word/12.02%3A_Pages_Group**

8. Heisserer, N. (2023d). *Layout Tab*. LibreTexts Workforce. **https://workforce.libretexts.org/Bookshelves/Information_Technology/Computer_Applications/Computer_Fundamentals_for_Technical_Students_(Heisserer)/13%3A__Design_Layout_References_Mailings_and_Review_Tabs_in_Microsoft_Word/13.02%3A_Layout_Tab**

9. Heisserer, N. (2023e). *Links Group*. LibreTexts Workforce. **https://workforce.libretexts.org/Bookshelves/Information_Technology/Computer_Applications/Computer_Fundamentals_for_Technical_Students_(Heisserer)/12%3A_Using_the_Insert_Tab_in_Microsoft_Word/12.09%3A_Links_Group**

10. Heisserer, N. (2023f). *References Tab*. LibreTexts Workforce. **https://workforce.libretexts.org/Bookshelves/Information_Technology/Computer_Applications/**

Computer_Fundamentals_for_Technical_Students_(Heisserer)/13%3A__Design_Layout_References_Mailings_and_Review_Tabs_in_Microsoft_Word/13.03%3A_References_Tab

11. Heisserer, N. (2023g). *Review Tab*. LibreTexts Workforce. **https://workforce.libretexts.org/Bookshelves/Information_Technology/Computer_Applications/Computer_Fundamentals_for_Technical_Students_(Heisserer)/13%3A__Design_Layout_References_Mailings_and_Review_Tabs_in_Microsoft_Word/13.07%3A_Review_Tab**

12. *Insert a table of contents*. (2023). Microsoft Support. **https://support.microsoft.com/en-us/office/insert-a-table-of-contents-882e8564-0edb-435e-84b5-1d8552ccf0c0**

13. LibGuides. (2023, August 15). *Managing references: Word's References tool*. University of Reading. **https://libguides.reading.ac.uk/managing-references/word**

14. Malik, B. A. (2023, June 24). *Insert in-text citations and references in a Word document without using Mendeley, Zotero, EndNote*. YouTube. **https://www.youtube.com/watch?v=7MetK66V-Hg**

15. Microsoft Support. (2010). *View Tab*. Microsoft. **https://support.microsoft.com/en-au/office/view-tab-08da4abb-5359-4579-97e9-6014f86dd7b7**

16. Microsoft Support. (2023a). *Add citations in a Word document*. **https://support.microsoft.com/en-gb/office/add-citations-in-a-word-document-ab9322bb-a8d3-47f4-80c8-63c06779f127**

17. Microsoft Support. (2023b). *Create a table of authorities*. Microsoft. **https://support.microsoft.com/en-us/office/create-a-table-of-authorities-ddd126ae-52bc-4299-9558-06dd0e4fe8c0#__toc281384145**

18. Microsoft Support. (2023c). *Insert an online video in Word*. Microsoft. **https://support.microsoft.com/en-gb/office/insert-an-online-video-in-word-bf11b812-0243-4f53-a1f9-432fbf7ace2c**

19. Microsoft Support. (2023d). *Use Mail Merge for bulk email, letters, labels, and envelopes*. Microsoft. **https://support.microsoft.com/en-gb/office/use-mail-merge-for-bulk-email-letters-labels-and-envelopes-f488ed5b-b849-4c11-9cff-932c49474705**

20. Sewell, J. P. (2010). Creating a Bibliography with Microsoft Word 2007 and 2008. *CIN: Computers, Informatics, Nursing, 28*(3), 134–137. **https://doi.org/10.1097/NCN.0b013e3181d7bb23**

21. *Show the Developer tab*. (2023). Microsoft. **https://support.microsoft.com/en-us/office/show-the-developer-tab-e1192344-5e56-4d45-931b-e5fd9bea2d45**

22. Teaching Learning Center. (2023). Insert Tab. Dutchess Community College. 19/08/2023 **https://www8.sunydutchess.edu/tlc_web/pdf/Insert_Tab.pdf**

23. Thede, L. Q. (2009a). Creating a Form in Microsoft Word. CIN: Computers, Informatics, Nursing, 27(5), 275–280. **https://doi.org/10.1097/01.NCN.0000360464.08917.7a**

24. Thede, L. Q. (2009b). Track Changes: Using Microsoft Word's Editing Tool. CIN: Computers, Informatics, Nursing, 27(1), 16–17. **https://doi.org/10.1097/01.NCN.0000336471.48305.86**

25. Use a screen reader to dictate a document in Word - Microsoft Support. (n.d.). Retrieved August 14, 2023, from **https://support.microsoft.com/en-gb/office/use-a-screen-reader-to-dictate-a-document-in-word-574a0382-5407-46b8-9d15-37a172726a02**

26. Vaidya, P. (2023, July 8). Day 5 Preventing and Detecting Plagiarism with Digital Tools by Dr Priya Vaidya. In Bharat Digital Academy, YouTube Channel. **https://www.youtube.com/v=FYKBHTtizLE&list=PLEak7vuavrSGEsmwZOPGQUbZmXo44TGXb&index=8**

27. What's new in Word 2019 for Windows. (2019). Microsoft Support. **https://support.microsoft.com/en-us/office/what-s-new-in-word-2019-for-windows-d3d31e5e-2bb8-4433-80bb-08279beef4b3**

28. Anderson, S. (2021). How to draw in Microsoft Word using the Draw Tab tools. The Windows Club. **https://www.thewindowsclub.com/draw-tab-tools-in-microsoft-office**

29. Control hyphenation. (2023). Microsoft Support. **https://support.microsoft.com/en-gb/office/control-hyphenation-7d4d2a38-b0e2-4f04-873a-0a8d48ac3923**

30. Draw Tool Tab in ribbon of Microsoft Office if it is missing. (2021). The Windows Club. **https://www.thewindowsclub.com/add-the-draw-tool-in-microsoft-office#google_vignette**

31. Fisher, T. (2023, April 10). What Is a DOCM File? Life Wire: Tech for Humans. **https://www.lifewire.com/docm-file-2620747**

32. Heisserer, N. (2023a). Captions. LibreTexts Workforce. **https://workforce.libretexts.org/Bookshelves/Information_Technology/Computer_Applications/Computer_Fundamentals_for_Technical_Students_(Heisserer)/13%3A__Design_Layout_References_Mailings_and_Review_Tabs_in_Microsoft_Word/13.04%3A_Captions**

33. Heisserer, N. (2023b). Design Tab. LibreTexts Workforce. **https://workforce.libretexts.org/Bookshelves/Information_Technology/Computer_Applications/Computer_Fundamentals_for_Technical_Students_(Heisserer)/13%3A__Design_Layout_References_Mailings_and_Review_Tabs_in_Microsoft_Word/13.01%3A_Design_Ta**

34. Heisserer, N. (2023c). Introduction to the Insert Tab. LibreTexts Workforce. **https://workforce.libretexts.org/Bookshelves/Information_Technology/Computer_Applications/Computer_Fundamentals_for_Technical_Students_(Heisserer)/12%3A_Using_the_Insert_Tab_in_Microsoft_Word/12.02%3A_Pages_Group**

35. Heisserer, N. (2023d). Layout Tab. LibreTexts Workforce. **https://workforce.libretexts. org/Bookshelves/Information_Technology/Computer_Applications/Computer_ Fundamentals_for_Technical_Students_(Heisserer)/13%3A__Design_Layout_ References_Mailings_and_Review_Tabs_in_Microsoft_Word/13.02%3A_Layout_ Tab**

36. Heisserer, N. (2023e). Links Group. LibreTexts Workforce. **https://workforce.libretexts. org/Bookshelves/Information_Technology/Computer_Applications/Computer_ Fundamentals_for_Technical_Students_(Heisserer)/12%3A_Using_the_Insert_Tab_ in_Microsoft_Word/12.09%3A_Links_Group**

37. Heisserer, N. (2023f). References Tab. LibreTexts Workforce. **https://workforce. libretexts.org/Bookshelves/Information_Technology/Computer_Applications/ Computer_Fundamentals_for_Technical_Students_(Heisserer)/13%3A__Design_ Layout_References_Mailings_and_Review_Tabs_in_Microsoft_Word/13.03%3A_ References_Tab**

38. Heisserer, N. (2023g). Review Tab. LibreTexts Workforce. **https://workforce.libretexts. org/Bookshelves/Information_Technology/Computer_Applications/Computer_ Fundamentals_for_Technical_Students_(Heisserer)/13%3A__Design_Layout_ References_Mailings_and_Review_Tabs_in_Microsoft_Word/13.07%3A_Review_ Tab**

39. Insert a table of contents. (2023). Microsoft Support. **https://support.microsoft.com/ en-us/office/insert-a-table-of-contents-882e8564-0edb-435e-84b5-1d8552ccf0c0**

40. LibGuides. (2023, August 15). Managing references: Word's References tool. University of Reading. **https://libguides.reading.ac.uk/managing-references/word**

41. Malik, B. A. (2023, June 24). Insert in-text citations and references in a Word document without using Mendeley, Zotero, EndNote. YouTube. **https://www.youtube.com/ watch?v=7MetK66V-Hg**

42. Microsoft Support. (2010). View Tab. Microsoft. **https://support.microsoft.com/en-au/ office/view-tab-08da4abb-5359-4579-97e9-6014f86dd7b7**

43. Microsoft Support. (2023a). Add citations in a Word document. **https://support. microsoft.com/en-gb/office/add-citations-in-a-word-document-ab9322bb-a8d3- 47f4-80c8-63c06779f127**

44. Microsoft Support. (2023b). Create a table of authorities. Microsoft. **https://support. microsoft.com/en-us/office/create-a-table-of-authorities-ddd126ae-52bc-4299-9558- 06dd0e4fe8c0#__toc281384145**

45. Microsoft Support. (2023c). Insert an online video in Word. Microsoft. **https://support. microsoft.com/en-gb/office/insert-an-online-video-in-word-bf11b812-0243-4f53- a1f9-432fbf7ace2c**

46. Microsoft Support. (2023d). Use Mail Merge for bulk email, letters, labels, and envelopes. Microsoft. **https://support.microsoft.com/en-gb/office/use-mail-merge-for-bulk-email-letters-labels-and-envelopes-f488ed5b-b849-4c11-9cff-932c49474705**

47. Sewell, J. P. (2010). Creating a Bibliography with Microsoft Word 2007 and 2008. CIN: Computers, Informatics, Nursing, 28(3), 134–137. **https://doi.org/10.1097/NCN.0b013e3181d7bb23**

48. Show the Developer tab. (2023). Microsoft. **https://support.microsoft.com/en-us/office/show-the-developer-tab-e1192344-5e56-4d45-931b-e5fd9bea2d45**

49. Teaching Learning Center. (2023). Insert Tab. Dutchess Community College. 19/08/2023 **https://www8.sunydutchess.edu/tlc_web/pdf/Insert_Tab.pdf**

50. Thede, L. Q. (2009a). Creating a Form in Microsoft Word. CIN: Computers, Informatics, Nursing, 27(5), 275–280. **https://doi.org/10.1097/01.NCN.0000360464.08917.7a**

51. Thede, L. Q. (2009b). Track Changes: Using Microsoft Word's Editing Tool. CIN: Computers, Informatics, Nursing, 27(1), 16–17. **https://doi.org/10.1097/01.NCN.0000336471.48305.86**

52. Use a screen reader to dictate a document in Word - Microsoft Support. (n.d.). Retrieved August 14, 2023, from **https://support.microsoft.com/en-gb/office/use-a-screen-reader-to-dictate-a-document-in-word-574a0382-5407-46b8-9d15-37a172726a02**

53. Vaidya, P. (2023, July 8). Day 5 Preventing and Detecting Plagiarism with Digital Tools by Dr Priya Vaidya. In Bharat Digital Academy, YouTube Channel. **https://www.youtube.com/h?v=FYKBHTtizLE&list=PLEak7vuavrSGEsmwZOPGQUbZmXo44TGXb&index=8**

54. What's new in Word 2019 for Windows. (2019). Microsoft Support. **https://support.microsoft.com/en-us/office/what-s-new-in-word-2019-for-windows-d3d31e5e-2bb8-4433-80bb-08279beef4b3**

Join our Discord space

Join our Discord workspace for latest updates, offers, tech happenings around the world, new releases, and sessions with the authors:

https://discord.bpbonline.com

CHAPTER 5

Sorting and Organizing Data in Microsoft Excel

Introduction

Microsoft Excel is a common spreadsheet application developed by Microsoft. It is part of the Microsoft Office suite, which includes the fundamentals of creating and managing worksheets and workbooks, creating name ranges for cells, applying formulas and functions, and creating charts and objects. Microsoft Excel provides users with a range of features to create, edit, format, share, and manage spreadsheets efficiently.

With Microsoft Excel, users can work on rows and columns. It offers a user-friendly interface with a familiar ribbon toolbar, making it easy to access and utilize its numerous functions.

Users can customize the Quick Access Toolbar and modify worksheets in different views. They can also prepare workbooks for collaboration and distribution.

In this chapter, we will discuss how to manage workbooks, worksheets, and many more. Microsoft Excel is widely used for data organization, analysis, and visualization. Excel includes functions for various operations and graphical data representation, making it a versatile tool in the fields of education, science, finance, and many others.

Structure

In this chapter, we will cover the following topics:

- Overview of Microsoft Excel
- Performing operations using formulas and functions
- Managing tables and charts in Excel

Objectives

By the end of this chapter, we will build a solid understanding of the basics of MS Excel. We will understand how to manage workbooks, worksheets, data cells, and name ranges, manage tables and their properties, and sort, filter, and perform operations using various formulas and functions. We will discuss how to work with charts. Additionally, we will also analyze features and understand how they work.

Overview of Microsoft Excel

To launch Excel, go to the **Start** button | type **Excel** | a menu will pop up, and it will open a new workbook. With MS Excel, data can be streamlined in worksheets (in the form of rows and columns). By default, each workbook has three worksheets: sheet1, sheet2, and sheet3. Every spreadsheet is made up of rows and columns. There are 16,384 columns and 10,48,576 rows. To keep your data distinct, you can add as many worksheets as you wish or start a new workbook; refer to the following figure:

1. Click **File**, and then click **New**.

2. Under **New**, clcik the **Blank workbook**.

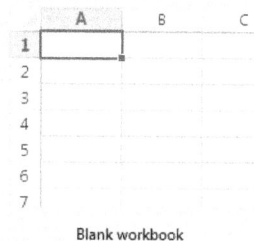

Blank workbook

Figure 5.1: New blank workbook

In Excel, different tabs like **Home** tab, **Insert** tab, draw, design, layout, references, etc., are available. The **Home** tab is divided into subgroups, such as clipboard, font, alignment, number, styles, etc. The **Quick Access bar** is available at the top left corner, as shown in the following figure:

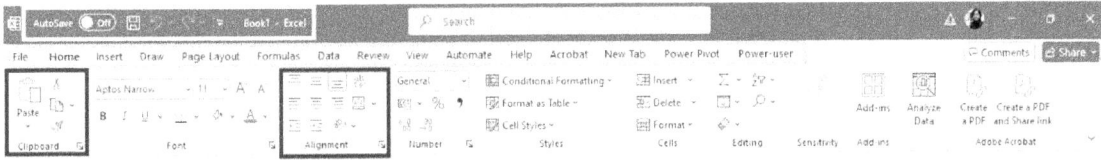

Figure 5.2: *Different tabs in MS Excel*

The Quick Access Toolbar contains a set of commands that are the most common. Quick Access Toolbar can be moved from either location, and buttons you wish to use most often in the worksheet can be added. The size of the command buttons cannot be increased. To add more commands to the Quick Access Toolbar, go to the **File** tab | choose options | select **Quick Access Toolbar** and then select **Add** or **Remove** button to move items between the **Customize Quick Access Toolbar** list and select command from the list as follows:

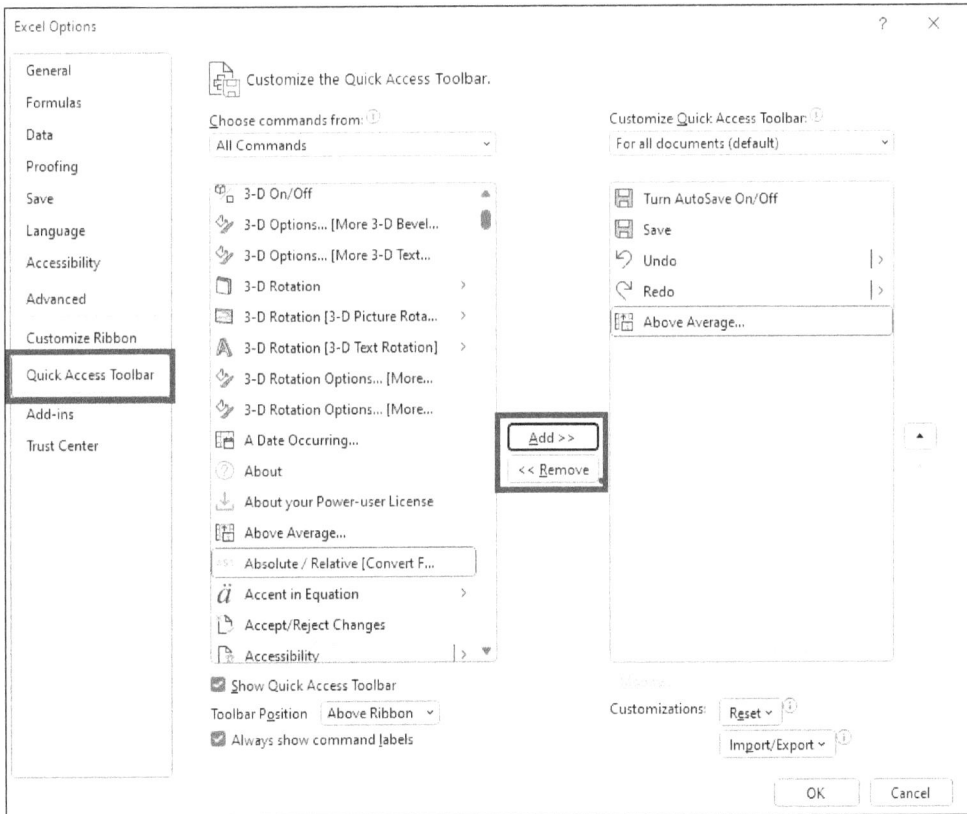

Figure 5.3: *Quick Access Toolbar*

The details are as follows:

- **Backstage menu**: We will discuss one of the most essential tabs, a backstage menu, which can enhance your Excel experience. It provides access to various file-related operations and settings. To access the backstage menu, select the **File** tab, which can be used for behind-the-scenes stuff you do with a file, like creating, opening, saving, sharing, exporting, printing, and managing the file. It is a place where you can manage your files efficiently. It displays the most recent files you have worked on. Choose the **Open** button in the sidebar to see the file locations on the device if the file is not in the list of recent files. You can pin a file to the list to ensure it always stays on the recent list. A pin icon will display to the right of the filename when you hover your pointer over it. To make the file always appear on the list, click it to pin it. Click the pin once again to remove a pinned file from the list. Right-click the file and choose remove from the list to remove an item from the current list. We have various options available over here, like **Share**, which will allow you to collaborate on your file, as shown:

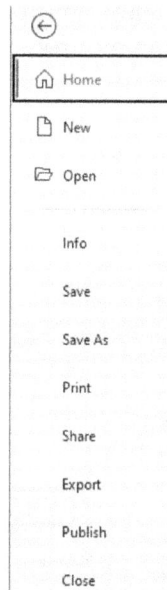

Figure 5.4: Backstage menu

- **Save As:** It enables you to quickly duplicate the active file and save it as a second copy with another name in a different location on the device. Modifications can be made without impacting the initial file. With the help of the **Print** option, you can print and preview files. We have different settings options for the sheet you want to print, like the orientation of the page, page settings, orientation, margins, etc.

- **Share option**: Once you click on the share option, it will help you with the dialog box to enter the recipients' email addresses to share the file with them and make various settings like permission (read or write) for the file. Next, the **Export** option will allow you to export your file into a PDF (change the file type).

- **At the bottom Feedback**: left corner, three options are available to assist you in controlling how Excel functions. Click **Account** to view account details and related services and conveniently save files to or open files from associated services like OneDrive or SharePoint. With the help of **Feedback**, you can provide feedback on how your office app works for you.

- **Options**: It allows you to configure everything related to general settings, formula settings, default file locations, editing choices, spell check, and coloring scheme, customize the access toolbar, and adjust other preferences to make Excel more accessible. To return to the Excel worksheet, select the arrow in the upper left corner of the navigation window. *Figure 5.5* shows the backstage menu options. The account shows the version of Excel where **Options** can help you to do different settings:

Account

Feedback

Options

Figure 5.5: Backstage menu options

Under the **Home** tab, different groups are available, and these are as follows:

- **Clipboard group**: In this group, we have cut, copy, and paste options, along with the format painter, and the paste special is also available as shown in *Figure 5.6* as follows:

  Shortcuts for the cut, copy, and paste commands are *Ctrl+X, Ctrl+C,* and *Ctrl+V,* respectively.

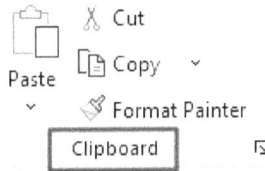

Figure 5.6: Clipboard group options

- **Format painter**: It allows you to quickly apply a format or set of formats to multiple cells. This is useful if you want specific cells to have, for example, both italicized and color-coded information. To do the same, as shown in the following steps:

  1. Select the formatted cell that you wish to replicate.
  2. Go to the **Home** tab.
  3. Choose the **Format Painter** option.
  4. Select an area where you want the formatting to be copied and pasted.

For multiple cells, again go to the **Home** tab, double-click on the format painter icon, and it will remain active until you deselect it.

- **Paste Special**: It provides a variety of choices for pasting only specified elements of copied cells. To execute copy and paste, select and copy the content and open the paste special dialog box. Start hovering the mouse over the **Paste Special** options in the context menu. A drop-down menu will appear with 14 more paste options. Hover over each option to see what it does, and a tooltip will appear. The shortcut for **Paste Special** is *Alt+E*, followed by *S*. The paste special command works in the workbook and worksheet.

- **Paste menu options**: Select the cells with data or any other attributes you wish to duplicate and paste it in another location.

  Use *Ctrl+C* to copy the content from the cell and choose the cell or area where you want to paste. Go to the **Home** tab and click on the arrow next to the **Paste** option, and you will see a paste menu option will pop up.

  The following is a list of options available in the paste menu:

  o **Paste option**: It will replicate all formatting, associated data, and cell contents.

  o **Formulas option**: It will only paste the formulas.

  o **Formulas and number formatting**: This paste only the formula and number formatting applied.

  o **Keep source formatting**: It will paste the cell contents along with the format.

  o **No orders**: All formatting and contents of the cells, excluding the borders.

  o **Keep source column widths**: Paste only column widths.

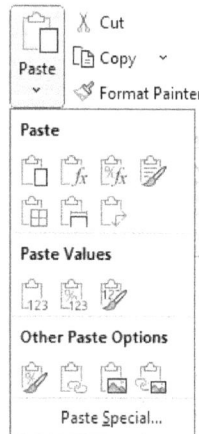

Figure 5.7: Various paste options

  o **Transpose**: When pasting, reorder the contents of the copied cells. Columns are pasted with row data, and vice versa.

  o **Paste values**: These are just the numbers that are visible in the cells.

o **Values and number formatting**: Paste only the values and formatting applied to numbers.

o **Values and Source formatting**: Paste only the values and formatting applied to the source.

o **Formatting**: Copy and paste all the formatting from the source and numbers into the cell.

o **Paste link:** When you paste a link to the data that you copied, Excel inserts an absolute reference to the copied cell or group of cells in the new worksheet location.

o **Paste as picture**: Copy and paste the chosen cells as an image.

o **Linked picture**: Copy the image and paste it with a link to the original cells so that any changes you make to the original cells will also appear in the copied image.

o **Column widths**: This option will duplicate the column width range at a different location.

o **Merge conditional formatting**: The paste area's conditional formatting is merged with the copied cells' conditional formatting.

A few more **Paste Special** options are available through the menu (*Microsoft Support, 2023*), as shown in the following figure:

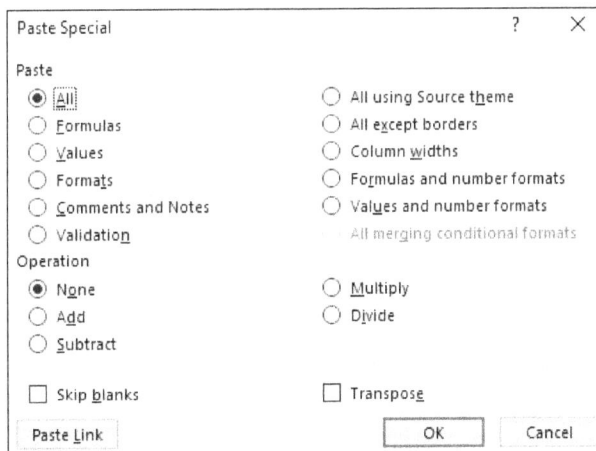

Figure 5.8: Paste Special dialog box

o **All**: By selecting this option, all cell content formatting and related data included will be pasted.

o **Formulas**: It will only paste the formulas.

o **Values**: Place the values only into the cells.

- **Formats**: Formatting and contents of the cells.
- **Comments and notes**: Paste just the cell-related comments.
- **Validation**: Paste only data validation rules.
- **All using source theme**: Every cell's formatting and content follow the same theme as the source data.
- **All except borders**: Paste all formatting and cell contents, excluding cell borders.
- **Column widths**: Paste only the width of a column or range of columns to another column or range of columns.
- **Formulas and number formats**: This setting will only allow you to paste numerical formatting and formulas.
- **Values and number formats**: Only the values and number formatting choices from the chosen cells will be pasted.
- **All merge conditional formats**: The conditional formatting in the paste area will be added to the conditional formatting from the copied cells.

Few basic operation options are available, and these are as follows:

- **None:** Without using any calculation, it will paste the contents of the copied area.
- **Add:** By selecting this option, the values in the paste and copy areas will be added.
- **Subtract**: This option will subtract the values in the copy area from the values in the paste area.
- **Divide:** This option will multiply the values in the paste area by the values in the copy area.
- **Multiply**: By selecting this option, the values in the copy-and-paste areas will be multiplied.
- **Skip blanks**: When blank cells appear in the copy area, it will prevent values or attributes from being replaced in your paste area.
- **Transpose**: When pasting, reorder the contents of copied cells. Columns are pasted with row data, and vice versa.
- **Paste link:** The pasted link (in the form of an image) will also change whenever the original picture is altered.
- **Font_group**: In this group, users can choose the **Font style, Size, Color, Bold, Italic, and Underline**, as shown in *Figure 5.9*. The **Format Cells** dialog box pops up the moment you click on them .

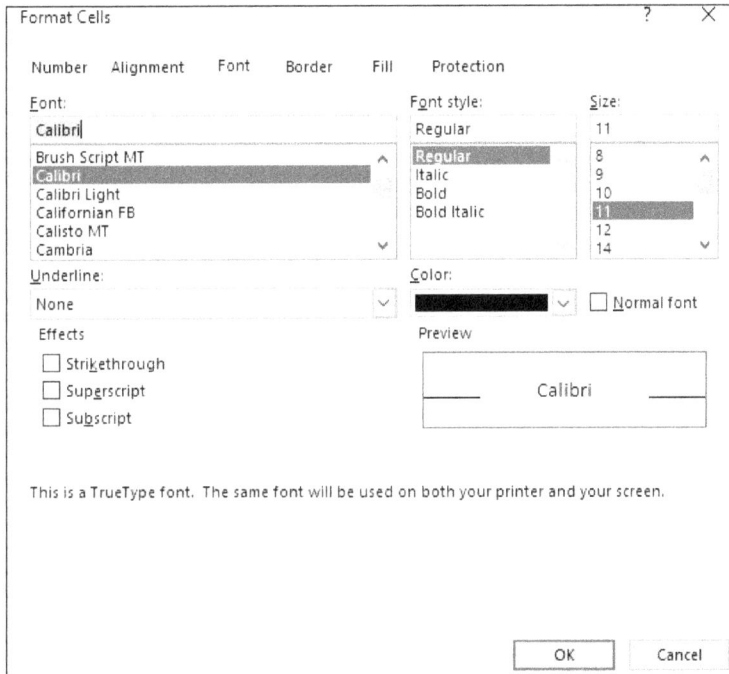

Figure 5.9: Format Cells dialog box

- **Alignment Group**: This allows users to customize how text appears in cells. The first group in the upper left corner is in charge of the vertical alignment of text or numbers in a cell and has horizontal lines. Top alignment, the first icon on the left, aligns the text with the top of the cell. The text is vertically aligned between the top and bottom of the cell when you select the middle alignment icon. Bottom alignment is the final vertical alignment that positions the text close to the cell's bottom. The default vertical alignment is the bottom alignment. (*Heisserer*, 2023) as shown in *Figure 5.10*, as follows:

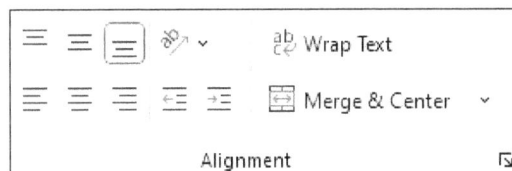

Figure 5.10: Alignment group

Using the next alignment orientation, the user can rotate the text vertically or diagonally ✎ ▾ . A drop-down box with more options allows the user to customize the arrangement of the text in the cell.

Next is **Wrap Text**, which allows users ᵃᵇ Wrap Text to adjust the vertical height of the cell automatically.

The bottom row of the alignment group begins with horizontal alignment settings. The right-hand icons provide the ability to increase or decrease indent, allowing the user to move the cell closer or further away from the cell border based on its horizontal alignment.

The Merge and Center options allow users to treat multiple or highlighted cells as one cell. Four other options are available in Excel for *merging and centering* the text, as follows:

- o **Number Group**: Click the **dialog** box next to number on the **Home** tab to see all available number formats.

- o **Styles Group**: To see all available styles, go to the **Styles** group. You can also create your own style and choose **Style** for the table. In addition, **Conditional Formatting** is available in this group.

- **Conditional formatting:** It is a handy feature for applying various formats to data that satisfy specific requirements. It might help draw attention to trends and patterns in your data, as shown in *Figure 5.11*. It is used by creating rules that determine a cell's format based on its values, text, copy, identical, comparable to, and many more (*Microsoft Support*, 2023).

Figure 5.11: Conditional Formatting Options

A **Data Bar** displays a cell's value in comparison to other cells. The data bar's length indicates the value in the cell. A greater value is indicated by a longer bar, and a lower value is indicated by a shorter bar. When dealing with vast volumes of data, Data Bars help distinguish higher and lower values, such as top and bottom-selling products, in a sales report.

Color Scales are illustrative tools that aid in understanding data variance and distribution. A two-color scale facilitates the comparison of a variety of cells by employing a two-color gradient. Higher or lower values are represented by the color's shade. A three-color scale facilitates the comparison of a variety of cells by employing a three-color gradation. Higher, moderate, or lower values are represented by the color's shade.

Utilize **Icon Sets** to mark up and group data into three to five groups, each divided by a threshold value. Every icon stands for an array of values.

If none of the pre-made ones work for you, you can make a new **rule** from scratch. You can choose to format cells according to their values, format only the cells that include values, or format only the values that rank highest or lowest (e.g., top 3 highest salary), etc. You can find six types of **Rule Types**. Choose the **color** and check the **preview** once you create the rule based on the condition, as shown in the following figure:

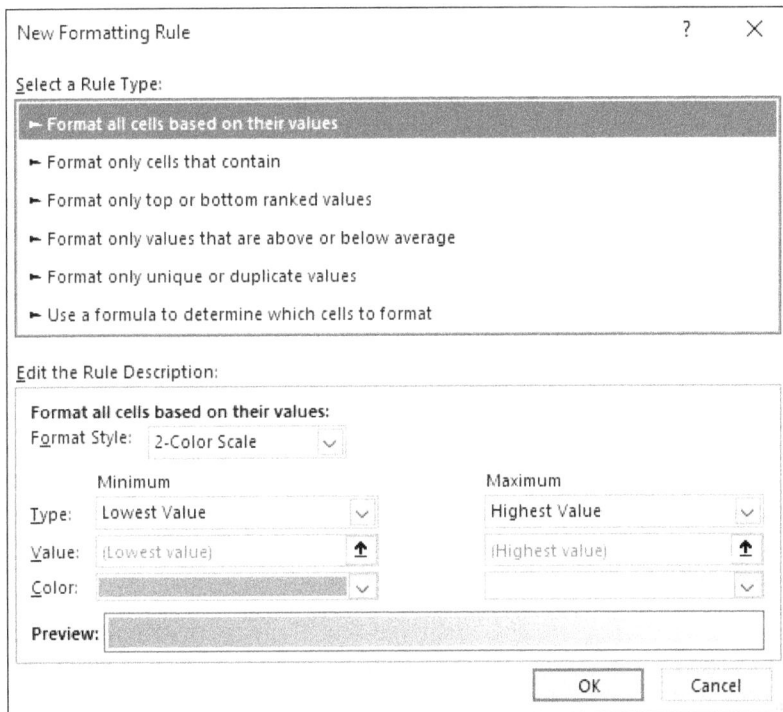

Figure 5.12: Formatting rule dialog box

The cells group is used to insert or delete cells, change the column and **Row Height**, **AutoFit Row Height** and **Column Width**, and many more. Sheets can be organized by renaming, moving, or copying sheets, changing the **Tab Color**, **Protect Sheet**, or **Lock Cell** options. These options are available in the **Home** tab | **Cells group**; go to the **Format** option, as shown in the following figure:

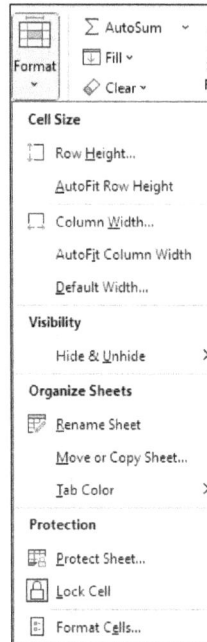

Figure 5.13: Cell group options

- **Sorting and filtering group**: Sorting data is an integral part of data analysis. Sorting helps you instantly analyze and visualize your data and make more effective decisions. Data can be sorted by text, by numbers, by date and time, or by any given condition.

Using a filter, you can quickly show only the relevant data at that moment and hide all other data. Excel worksheets allow you to filter rows based on criteria, format, and value. To display only the data, you want and conceal the rest, use Excel's **AutoFilter** feature or one of the many built-in comparison operators, including **greater than, top 10**, and many more. You can either reapply the filter to view the most current results or clear it to view all of the data once you have filtered it in a range of cells or a table (*Ahmed*, 2023).

In addition to other filtering options, Excel AutoFilter provides relevant sorting options for a given column as follows:

- o   Text values can be sorted by color, alphabetically from A to Z or Z to A.
- o   Sorting by color, largest to smallest, and small to largest are the three options for numbers.
- o   There are three ways to sort dates: from oldest to newest, from newest to oldest, and by color (*Microsoft Support*, 2023k).

  Note: **Data can be sorted by Custom List created by the user. (by cell color, font color, or icon set).**

o **Sort Text**: Select the data that you want to sort. Go to **Home** tab | under editing group | select **Sort & Filter** | **Sort A to Z** for ascending order ⊞ and click **Sort Z to A** for descending order ⊞ as shown in the following figure:

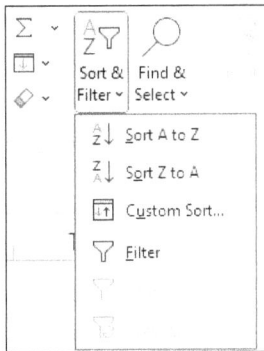

Figure 5.14: Sort and Filter options

o **Sort Numbers:** Select the data that you want to sort. Go to **Home** tab | under editing group | select **Sort & Filter** | **Sort A to Z** for low(smallest) to high (highest) ⊞ and click **Sort Z to A** for high (largest) to low (smallest) ⊞

o **Sort Date or Time**: Select the data that you want to sort. Go to **Home** tab | under editing group | select **Sort & Filter** | **Sort A to Z** for Oldest to Newest ⊞ and click **Sort Z to A** for newest to oldest. ⊞

o **Sort by cell values, cell color, font color, or conditional formatting icon:** If you conditionally prepared a range of cells, you could sort by either cell color or font color. Alternatively, you can sort by an icon set that you can create with conditional formatting.

For advanced sorting, you need to select **Custom Sort**, choose **Sort by box**, and select the column that you want to sort. If your data has a header, then select **My data has headers**, as shown in the following figure:

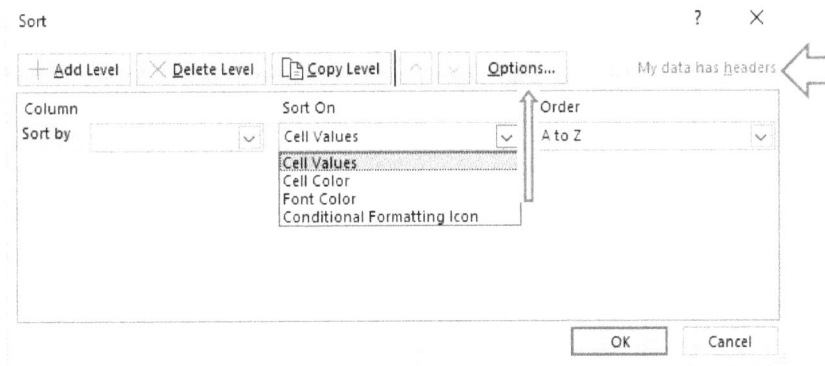

Figure 5.15: Advanced Sorting dialog box

o **Case Sensitive Sort:** When sorting is done through cell values or color, there is one more scenario where you sort data based on case sensitivity. Click on **Options** to get the dialog box, as shown in the following figure, and select **Case Sensitive**:

Figure 5.16: Case-sensitive Sort dialog box

Here is how sorting and filtering in Excel differ from one another:

- In Excel, the whole table is sorted alphabetically from the lowest value to the highest value, or vice versa, when you sort data. But sorting merely rearranges the data; it doesn't obscure any of the input data.

- Excel's filtering feature allows you to see only the data you want to see, and all other data is temporarily hidden from view.

- **Advance_Filtering**: As discussed in the above section, filtering is the most effective method for speedily analyzing data, and the shortcut for filtering is *Ctrl+Shift+L*. So, when we want to apply a filter to a large dataset or create a dashboard, we always use a *Slicer*. Slicers improve your data filtering experience significantly.

It is simple to use, quick, and effective. A group of buttons called an Excel Slicer can filter data from a column. It displays everything that is available for filtering as buttons, unlike a regular filter. It can be customized to your liking in terms of color, font, buttons, and other elements by connecting it to a table or pivot table. Slicers work particularly well with dashboards and summary reports because of their visual characteristics, but you can use them wherever to speed up and simplify the process of filtering data.

o **Insert Slicer in an Excel Table**: To insert Slicer, first of all, you can use the **Insert tab** to transform your data into an Excel table | select tables. It will select the entire range of cells and provide the dialog box (range is visible). If you have headers in your data, then choose **My data has headers** and then select **OK,** as shown in the following figure:

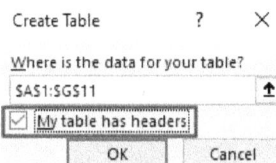

Figure 5.17: Create Table dialog box

Next, click anywhere in the table, select the **Insert** tab │ in the **Filters** group, and click on the **Slicer** button. Once you click on the button, you have the insert Slicer dialogue box, tick off the checkboxes for one or more columns that you want to filter. Press **OK**. After creating a slicer, you can now visually filter the data in your table as follows:

Figure 5.18: *Filter types*

o   **Insert Slicer in a Pivot Table:** Click anywhere in the pivot table, go to **Insert** tab │ select Slicer. Choose the desired column to utilize in the slicer. Here, we have selected zone, then click **OK**. As soon as you put in a slicer, you can filter your data by clicking on any button.

Here, a zone slicer has been inserted. All four highlighted buttons, East, North, South, and West, are selected. Consequently, the pivot displays the data for each of the four regions.

We must now limit our data to the South Zone alone. Select the **South** button. There will be an automatic filter applied to the data in the pivot table, as shown in the following figure:

Zone	Total
East	42540
North	67720
South	143040
West	43060
Grand Total	**296360**

Figure 5.19: *Slicer in a pivot table*

Slicers can be used for a variety of purposes, and these are as follows:

▪   **Select multiple adjacent items:** What happens then if we have to choose the data for more than one region? All you have to do is click on the buttons that need to be filtered by pressing *Ctrl*. We are going to hit *Ctrl* and select **East** and **West** here.

▪   **Clear selected items**: The most important step is to remove the filters. This can be accomplished with a single click on the slicer's top right button.

- **Formatting a Slicer:** A slicer must be formatted. With formatting, it appears cleaner and more organized.

- **Remove headers**: When building a dashboard, we tend to need more space in our reports. Here, in this example, if we do not require the Header Zone

- **Select the Slicer**: Right-click **Slicer Settings** and untick the box against the **Display header**. We could save space because the header has been removed, as shown in the following figure:

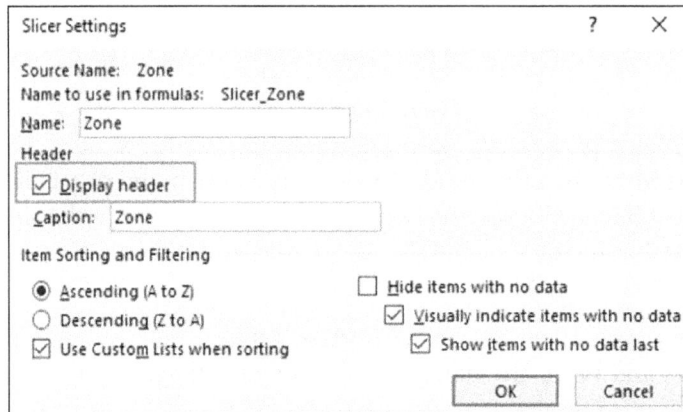

Figure 5.20: Slicer Settings dialog box

o **Change the Font**: To alter a slicer's font, choose the ribbon style that best fits your needs by selecting any style. By right-clicking, choose the replica. This will lead to the **Slicer Elements** dialogue box popping up.

If you overlooked it, right-click on the duplicate slicer style and select modify. Click on the entire slicer now and choose **Format**. Customize the font and borders and fill them to your needs. Choose the duplicate slicer style | **Modify** | **Format** | Border to disable Borders.

o **Eliminate items with no data**: Sometimes, you may come across certain items that are not highlighted because there is no data on them, here, when we do not have sales for the North zone in the year 2019. It is usually advisable to keep these buttons hidden. To accomplish this, right-click on **Slicer**, select **Slicer settings** | Tick the box against **Hide items with no data**.

o **Customize Columns and Buttons**: The slicer sometimes might not fit into your dashboard or report because of its column-style structure. The buttons can be organized in a Slicer. Choose the Slicer Ribbon | Under the buttons group, choose columns. Increase the number of columns, and it is horizontally spread. You can even adjust the dimensions of the slicer using the **Size** option. We can rename a Slicer | Slicer caption, as shown in the following figure:

Figure 5.21: *Customize Columns and Buttons for Slicer*

- **Analysis Group**: **Analyze Data** is available in Excel 2019 or 365. To better represent our ideas into charts, pivots, or some trends, Analyze Data is the best. The analyze feature is used to make data analysis simpler, faster, and intuitive. Analyze Data assists you in comprehending your data by offering high-level graphic summaries, patterns, and trends. (*Microsoft Support*, 2023b).

Choose a cell in your worksheet | Go to the **Home** tab | Select **Analyze Data**. It will investigate your data and return valuable visuals about your data in a task pane. Choose a pivot table, chart, or any other analytics to insert in the worksheet. If you want to ask for specific information about your data, input a question and click Enter within the query box at the top of the pane. Analyze Data will return results in the form of visuals such as tables, charts, or PivotTables that can then be added to the worksheet. Analyze Data also provides personalized suggested questions, which you can access by selecting the query box.

If you do not have any questions in mind, in addition to Natural Language, it provides you with the best results without writing complex formulas. You can save time and get a more targeted analysis by selecting only the fields you want to view. When you choose variables and how to summarize them, Analyze Data removes other accessible data, which expedites the process and presents fewer, more focused options, as shown in the following figure:

Figure 5.22: *Analyze Data to find the insights*

For example, you might only want to view the sum of sales or you could ask **Analyze Data** to display average sales, or you just click on the gear icon represented in *Figure. 5.23*. Select **Which fields interest you the most.** Select the fields and choose from the drop-down to summarize the data, as shown in the following figure:

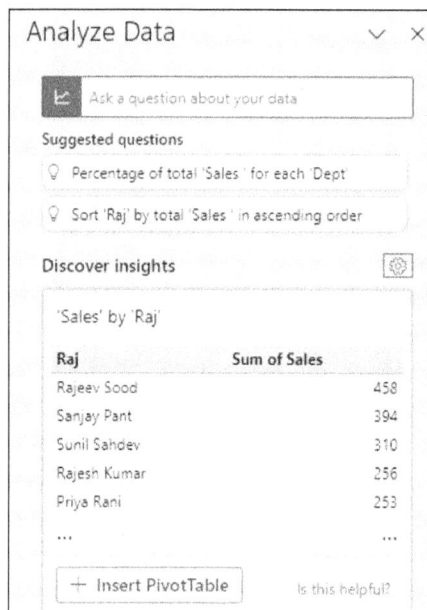

Figure 5.23: Analyze Data dialog box to ask questions

The analyzed data window will display various visualizations and analyses, such as rank, trend, outlier, and majority (*Microsoft Support*, 2023). They are as follows:

o   **Rank**: The largest item is highlighted and ranked higher than the other items.

o   **Trend:** Highlights instances in a time series of data when a consistent trend pattern exists.

o   **Outlier**: Highlights outliers in time series.

o   **Majority:** Finds scenarios where a single element accounts for the majority of a total value.

Note: **When Excel is in compatibility mode (i.e., when the file is in the .xls format), the analyze data function would not function. In the meantime, save your file as a .xlsx,.xlsm, or .xlsb file.**

Performing operations using formulas and functions

You have undoubtedly heard the terms **functions** and **formulas** used in Excel. What differentiates them from one another?

A **Formula** is an expression that calculates the value of a cell, and a **Function** is a predefined formula that is made available for you to use in Excel; it is illustrated in the following figure:

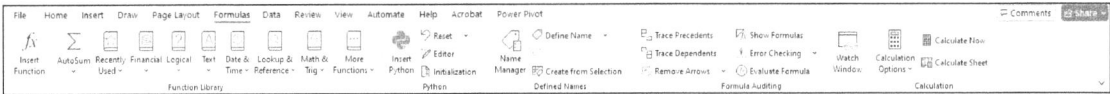

Figure 5.24: Formula functions ribbon

Before we discuss functions and formulas in detail, let us understand **Name Manager** and **Cell Referencing**. These two will play an essential role in creating formulas and using functions in Excel as follows:

- **Cell Referencing**: When we select a cell, it refers to its address, which is known as the cell reference. This reference is used in Excel formulas and functions. There are three kinds of cell referencing that can be used in Excel, i.e., **Relative**, **Absolute**, *and* **Mixed**.

  o **Relative cell referencing:** A relative reference is a cell address that changes or adjusts when copied to another cell. It is used when you want to use the same formula for different cells. Relative cell references contain no dollar ($) sign. E.g., A5

  For example, we must multiply the Price and Quantity values to determine the total. Here, the formula in cell E2 would be =C2*D2. Instead of entering the formula for the rest of the cells, you can copy cell E2 and paste it into the rest of the range. (E3:E8). When you perform this, the reference will automatically adapt to refer to the corresponding row, as shown in the following figure:

A	B	C	D	E
S. No	Product	Price	Qty	Total
1	Charger	150	12	=C2*D2
2	Hard Disk	450	20	
3	Accessories	250	10	
4	LCD Screen	5500	5	
5	LED Screen	9800	10	
6	Lamps	590	25	
7	Bluetooth	800	50	

Figure 5.25: Example of relative referencing

  o **Absolute cell referencing**: An **absolute reference** is a cell address that does not change when copied or moved to another cell. It is used when you want to keep the same cell reference in all formulas. Dollar signs are linked to each letter or number in an absolute reference (i.e., A1).

  When a dollar symbol is placed in front of a row or column number, it makes it absolute (that is, it prevents the row or column number from altering when copied to other cells).

  For instance, if you want to fix the value of cell G2, then you need to put the $ sign before the column and row name, as shown in *Figure 5.27*:

A	B	C	D	E	F	G
S. No	Product	Price	Qty	Total	Total VAT	Tax Value
1	Charger	150	12	1800	=E2*G2	12%
2	Hard Disk	450	20	9000		
3	Accessories	250	10	2500		
4	LCD Screen	5500	5	27500		
5	LED Screen	9800	10	98000		
6	Lamps	590	25	14750		
7	Bluetooth	800	50	40000		

Figure 5.26: Example of Absolute referencing

o **Mixed cell reference:** A mixed reference combines relative and absolute references. It keeps the row or column constant while allowing the other to change. **Mixed cell references** have dollar signs attached to either the letter or the number in a reference but not both (i.e., $A1 or A$1).

- **Name Manager**: To interact with all of the defined names and table names in a workbook, use the **Name Manager** dialogue box. You can examine or update descriptive comments, determine the scope, validate the value and reference of a name, and identify names that contain mistakes. Additionally, you can quickly add, edit, and remove names from a single location, as well as sort and filter the list of names (Microsoft Support, 2023i).

To open the **Name Manager** | Go to the **Formula** tab | **Defined Names** group | **Name Manager** as shown in *Figure 5.28*:

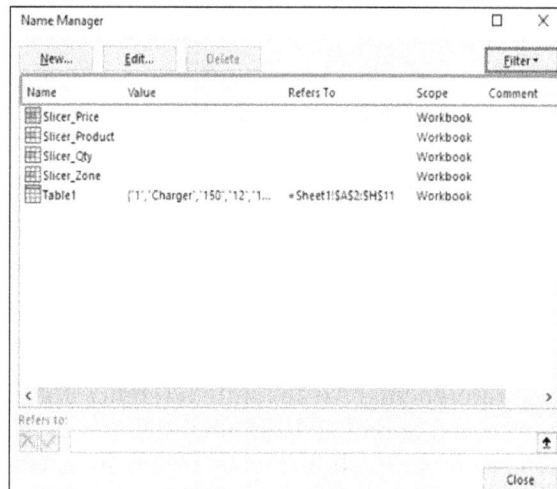

Figure 5.27: Name Manager dialog box

The **Name Manager** dialog box displays the following information about each name in a list box in the form of a column:

o **Name tab** represents a defined name and a table name ▦ ▦ , respectively. Define a name that represents a cell or range of cells, a formula, or a constant value. A table name is a collection of data about a particular subject stored in rows and columns. Excel creates default table names like **Table1** and **Table2**. You can always change the table name by giving a meaningful name.

o **Value** represents the current value of the name, like the formula, and a string constant, etc.

o **Refers To** column represents the current reference for the name.

o **Scope** column represents a worksheet or workbook name (if the scope is the local worksheet level).

o **Comment** represents any other information about the name. It can be up to 255 characters.

o **Refers** denote the reference.

Creating a named range in Excel

To create a name range, the following are some of the steps:

1. On the **Formulas** tab, in the **Defined Names** group, click **Define Name**. In the **New Name** dialog box, in the **Name** box, type the name you want to use for your reference.

   Note: **Names can be up to 255 characters in length**

2. To specify the scope of the named range | in the **Scope** drop-down list box, select **Workbook** or the name of a worksheet in the workbook. A named range set to a Workbook scope can be used across the workbook, whereas a range set to a specific sheet's scope can only be used within that sheet.

3. Enter a descriptive comment of up to 255 characters in the **Comment** field if desired.

4. In the **Refers to:** box, click **Collapse Dialog** (which quickly shrinks the dialog box), select the cells on the worksheet, and then click **Expand Dialog** .

5. To enter a constant, type=(equal sign) and then type the constant value. To enter a formula, type=and then type the formula. Then Click **OK** as shown in the following figure:

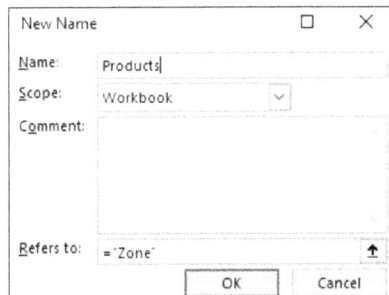

Figure 5.28: Name Range dialog box

Inserting a named range into a formula in Excel

You may swiftly add a named range into a formula in your spreadsheet. Using a named range in a formula improves the formula's appearance and makes it look more user-friendly. The following is an example of calculating with a formula and with a defined name range:

fx =sum(E2:E7)

S. No	Product	Price	Qty	Amount
1	Charger	150	12	1800
2	Hard Disk	450	20	9000
3	Accessories	250	10	2500
4	LCD Screen	5500	5	27500
5	LED Screen	9800	10	98000
6	Lamps	590	25	14750
7	Bluetooth	800	50	40000
				=sum(E2:E7)

fx =sum(TotalAmt)

S. No	Product	Price	Qty	Amount
1	Charger	150	12	1800
2	Hard Disk	450	20	9000
3	Accessories	250	10	2500
4	LCD Screen	5500	5	27500
5	LED Screen	9800	10	98000
6	Lamps	590	25	14750
7	Bluetooth	800	50	40000
				sum(TotalAmt)

Figure 5.29: *Using name range in the formula bar*

- **Formula and functions in Excel**: To start with the formula in Excel, you need to select a cell and start with the = (Equals to) sign. When you enter a formula in a cell, it automatically appears in the formula bar. To calculate the sum of two numbers, pick a cell, then type =, then the function name, and finally, the range within the parentheses. For example = `sum(E2:E7)`.

- **Parts of formula**: A formula can include any function name, references, operators, and constants. A value that never changes is called a constant. A worksheet's chosen cell or range is referred to as a reference. References may come from separate workbooks or from pages in the same workbook. External references, often known as links, are references to cells in other workbooks.

Note: **In Excel 2019, there are 16,384 columns and 1,048,576 rows are available.**

Functions are predefined formulas that perform computations using certain values referred to as arguments. Functions can be used to perform different types of calculations. To **Insert** function, use *Shift + F3*, which will open an **Insert Function** dialog box as shown in the following figure:

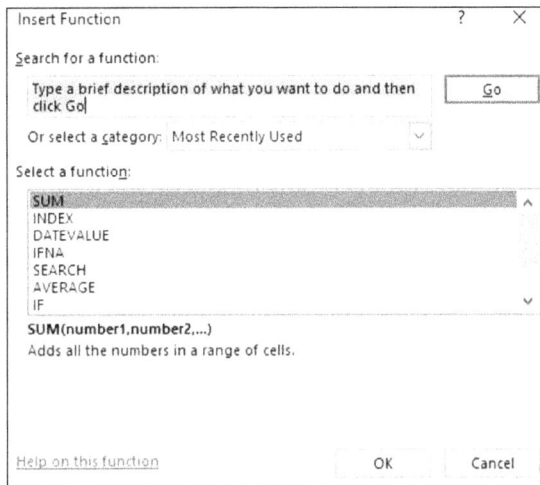

Figure 5.30: *Insert Function dialog box*

Search for a function and click on the **Go** button, as shown in *Figure 5.31* It will launch another **Function Arguments** dialog box, which will display the name of the function, each of its arguments, a description of the function, and each argument, the current result of the function, and the current result of the entire formula. To complete your formula, enter the arguments in the boxes, and you can see the result also as shown in the following figure:

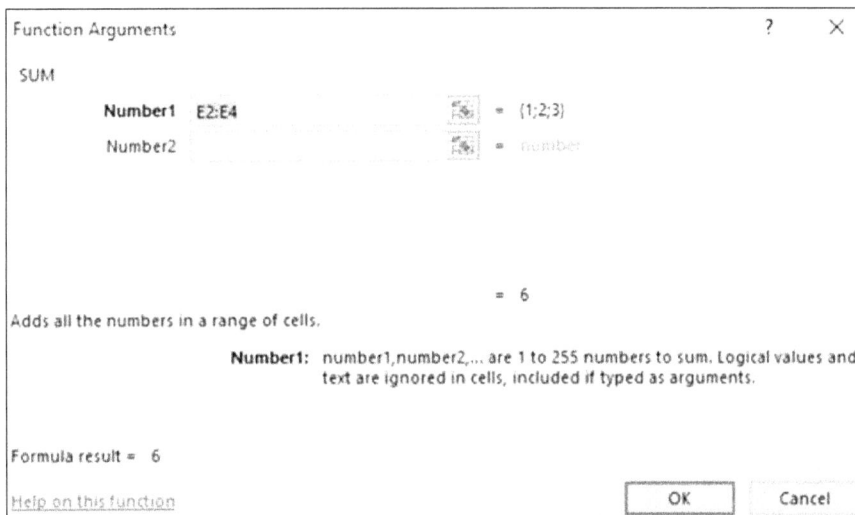

Figure 5.31: *Function Argument dialog box*

There are different types of functions available in Excel, like Financial functions, Logical functions, Text functions, Date & Time functions, Lookup & References functions, and so on.

- **Logical functions**: To work with logical values, Microsoft Excel has four logical functions. They are AND, OR, XOR, and NOT. These functions can be used when there is some comparison or test of multiple conditions. Logical functions return either TRUE or FALSE as output when their arguments are evaluated.

  Following is the explanation of logical functions:

Function	Description of the function
AND	Returns TRUE if all of the arguments evaluate to TRUE.
OR	Excel OR function is a basic logical function that is used to compare two values or statements. Returns TRUE if any argument evaluates to TRUE. and returns FALSE if all arguments are FALSE
XOR	Returns a logical Exclusive Or of all arguments. The XOR function has the same syntax as an OR. Additional logical values are optional, but the first logical assertion (Logical 1) must be stated. Up to 254 conditions can be tested in a single formula; these conditions can be references, arrays, or logical values that return TRUE or FALSE. There are only two logical statements and returns in an XOR formula: TRUE if either argument evaluates to TRUE. FALSE if both arguments are TRUE or neither is TRUE.
NOT	Gives back the argument's logical value in reverse. For example, TRUE is returned if the argument is FALSE, and vice versa.

Table 5.1: Logical functions

- **Using IF with logical functions:** IF function allows you to perform a logical comparison between a value and returning a result if that condition is True or False.

  To create If statement for number, you need to use logical operators like equal to (=), Not equal to (<>), Greater than (>), Greater than or equal to (>=), Less than (<), Less than or equal to (<=).

  If you need to implement IF function with AND, OR and NOT functions, the following is the syntax:

  o   =IF AND (condition1 = True, condition2 = True), output if True, output if False)

  o   =IF OR (condition1 = True, condition2 = True), output if True, output if False)

  o   =IF NOT (condition = True), output if True, output if False)

  Based on your data, you can use the above-given syntax.

- **Using AND, OR, and NOT with conditional formatting:** You can use logical functions mainly to execute conditional formatting with the formula option. You can eliminate the IF function and only use AND, OR, and NOT.

- **Text Functions:** Excel has 33 text functions available. There are three unique functions in Microsoft Excel that allow you to alter the case of text.

They are given as follows:

o You can change every lowercase letter in a text string to an uppercase letter by using the **upper()** function.

Syntax: =upper("hello")

o Text can be made devoid of capital letters with the use of the **lower()** function.

Syntax: =lower("HELLO")

o Each word's initial letter is capitalized, while the other letters are left in lowercase (proper case) using the **proper()** function.

Syntax: =Proper("hEllo")

We have more functions like **Left()**, **Right()**, and **Mid()**, **Exact()**, **Replace()**, **Substitute()**, **Find()**, **Search()**, **Len()**, **Rept()** and **Trim()**.

o The **Left()** function takes two arguments and returns the specified number of characters (substring) from the start of a string. (Note: **It does not work with dates**).

Syntax: =Left("Microsoft",5)

o The **Right()** function takes two arguments and returns the specified number of characters from the end of a text string.

Syntax: =Right("Microsoft",4)

o The **Mid()** function takes three arguments and returns the characters from the middle of a text string given a starting position and length.

Syntax: =Mid("Microsoft",3,5)

o The **Exact()** function checks if the two strings are exactly the same and returns True or False. Exact is case-sensitive.

Syntax: =Exact("AZC","AZC") returns TRUE

o The **Replace()** function is used to replace part of a text string with a different text string.

Syntax: =Replace("AZC Portal",1,3,"News")

o The **Substitute()** function replaces existing text with new text in a text string. (It is case sensitive)

Syntax: =Substitute("AZC Portal","AZC","News")

o **Find()** function finds one text value within another. It returns the starting position of one text string within another text string. It is a case sensitive.

Syntax: =Find(("Portal","NewsPortal",4)

o **Search()** function finds the text value within another text string, reading from left to right. (It is not case sensitive).

Syntax: **=Search("Portal","NewsPortal",4)**

o The **Len()** function provides the text string's character count.

Syntax: **=Len(:NewsPortal")**

o **Rept()** function repeats text a given number of times. It takes 2 arguments.

Syntax: **=Rept("Micro",5)**

o The **Trim()** function trims (removes) all/extra spaces except single spaces from text.

Syntax: **=Trim("Micro   soft")**

We have three functions that will do similar work, **Concatenate()**, **TextJoin()**, and *&* character as follows:

o The **concatenate ()** function joins two or more strings into one string. When you return the current date using the **TODAY()** or **NOW()** function with some text combination, you use the following syntax:

=CONCATENATE(Today is , TODAY()), but in this case, Excel will return **Today is 42198**.

Dates are kept in Excel as numbers that appear as concatenated text string. You can utilize the **Text** function to fix this. For example, combining the **TODAY** function in the **Text** function with the format **dddd d mmm, yyyy** will return the output: **Today is Monday 12 Dec, 2016**

Syntax: **=Concatenate (Today is, Text(Today(),dddd d mmm,yyyy)**

o **TextJoin()** function concatenates a range of cells using a delimiter. It takes three arguments, and the syntax is **=TEXTJOIN (delimiter,ignore_empty,text1, [text2],..)** where:

- **Delimiter**: The character that each text needs to have between it.

- **Ignore_empty**: If you wish to include empty cells, the value should be FALSE, and if you want to exclude them, it should be TRUE. By default, the value will be TRUE.

o *&* character is also used to connect two strings.

- **Lookup and reference function**: In Excel, VLOOKUP is the most commonly used lookup function. Other important lookup functions are HLOOKUP and XLOOKUP.

The **Vlookup()** function searches a vertical list for a specific value. Once it finds it, it uses that row and returns the value from the specified column number.

The new XLOOKUP function is a more sophisticated and user-friendly variant of VLOOKUP that operates in any direction and, by default, returns precise matches. XLOOKUP function finds things in a table or range by row. With XLOOKUP, it will search a range or an array for a match and returns the corresponding item from a second range or array. By default, an exact match is used.

Syntax: `=XLOOKUP(lookup_value,lookup_array,return_array,[if_not_found], [match_mode], search_mode])`

For example, once a country's name is found inside a range using XLOOKUP, the capital of that country is returned. It includes the lookup_value (cell F2), lookup_array (range B2:B10), and return_array (range D2:D1) arguments.Since XLOOKUP generates an exact match by default, the match_mode argument is not included.

The syntax is as follows:

```
=XLOOKUP(F2,B2:B10,D2:D10)
```

Note: **XLOOKUP uses a lookup array and a return array, while a single table array and a column index number are used by VLOOKUP. In such a case, the corresponding VLOOKUP formula would be:**

```
=VLOOKUP(F2,B2:D10,3,FALSE)
```

Country	Abr	Capital			Find the capital?
India	IN	New Delhi		Russia	=XLOOKUP(F2,B2:B10,D2:D10)
China	CN	Beijing			
Russia	RU	Moscow			
Poland	PL	Warsaw			
Portugal	PT	Lisbon			
Nigeria	NG	Abuja			
Banglades	BN	Dhaka			
Mexico	MX	Mexico city			
Indonesia	ID	Jakarta			

***Figure 5.32:** Example of XLOOKUP function*

We can convert the same data in rows using the Transpose function and then apply the **`Hlookup()`** function as follows:

```
=TRANSPOSE(B1:D10)
```

Country	India	China	Russia	Poland	Portugal	Nigeria	Bangladesh	Mexico	Indonesia
Abr	IN	CN	RU	PL	PT	NG	BN	MX	ID
Capital	New Delhi	Beijing	Moscow	Warsaw	Lisbon	Abuja	Dhaka	Mexico city	Jakarta

```
=HLOOKUP(F2,G10:O12,3,FALSE)
```

***Figure 5.32:** Example of HLOOKUP function*

- **Index formula in Excel**: It is used to get the value of a cell in a given table by specifying the number of rows, columns, or both. E.g., to get abbreviation at the 5th observation in the given data, we'll write the formula `=Index (range, 5,2)` and the output will be NG.

Syntax: `=Index(Array, row_num, column_num)`

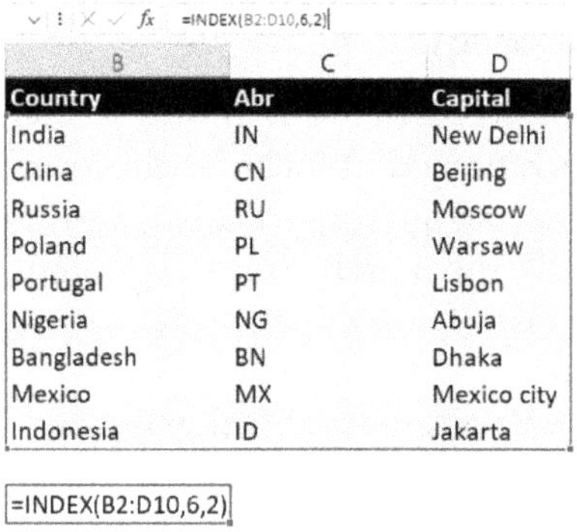

Figure 5.34: Example of INDEX function

- **Match formula in Excel**: It returns the row or column number when a specific string or number is in the given range. We will match the **Country** name, and it will return the position of a value in a given range.

Syntax: `=Match (Lookup_value, Lookup_array, Match_type)`

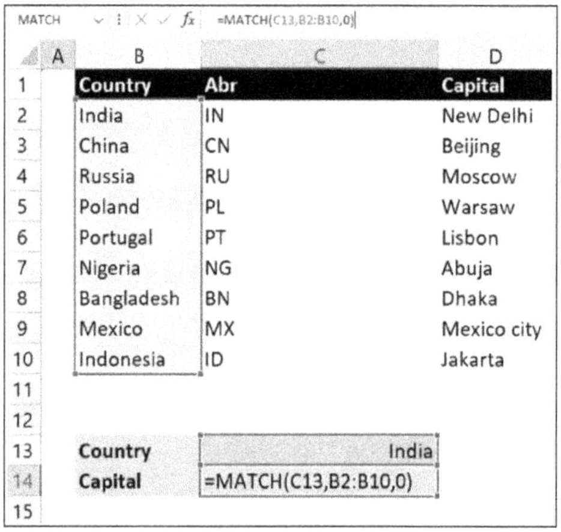

Figure 5.35: Example of MATCH function

- **Wrapcols formula in Excel**: If you want to break down a long list of column data into multiple columns, then use wrapcols formula.

Syntax: `=Wrapcols(vector, wrap_count, pad_with)` whereas Vector refers to reference to wrap

Wrap_count is the maximum number of values per column

Pad_with refers to the value with which to pad. The default is #N/A.

An example is given as follows:

	fx	=WRAPCOLS(B2:B10,3,"-")	
B		**C**	**D**
Country	**Abr**		**Capital**
India	IN		New Delhi
China	CN		Beijing
Russia	RU		Moscow
Poland	PL		Warsaw
Portugal	PT		Lisbon
Nigeria	NG		Abuja
Bangladesh	BN		Dhaka
Mexico	MX		Mexico city
Indonesia	ID		Jakarta

India	Poland	Bangladesh
China	Portugal	Mexico
Russia	Nigeria	Indonesia

Figure5.36: Example of WRAPCOLS function

In the same way you can use Wraprows formula in excel. Wraps a row or column vector after a specified number of values.

Syntax: =Wraprows(vector, wrap_count, pad_with) where vector refers to the reference to wrap(fold).

Wrap_count refers to the maximum number of values per row.

Pad_with refers to the value with which to pad.

$\times \checkmark$ *fx*   =WRAPROWS(B2:B10,2,"-")|

- **Aggregate functions**: In Excel, there are a few aggregate functions like Sum, Average, Min, Max, and Count to calculate the values (in numbers).

- **Date and time function**: In Excel, there are date and Time functions with which you can calculate the difference between two dates, the difference between years, months, days, and weeks (Microsoft Support, 2023h).

Insert the current date and time in Excel worksheet. A static value does not change when the worksheet is reopened. Shortcut to add current date in a cell is Ctrl + ;(Control Key and semi-colon) and current time is *Ctrl+Shift+;* (Control+Shift+semi-colon)

To insert the current date and time, press *Ctrl+;* (semi-colon), then press Space, and then press *Ctrl+Shift+;* (semi-colon).

Insert the date and time whose value is updated. A date or time changes when the worksheet is recalculated, or the workbook is opened, is referred to as **dynamic** rather than **static** (Microsoft Support, 2023d)

Syntax: `=Today()` insert current date (system date)

`=Now()` insert current date and time (system's date and time)

Note: **In order to make dates usable in calculations, Excel maintains dates as consecutive serial numbers. Since January 1, 2008 falls 39,447 days after January 1, 1900, it is assigned serial number 39448 by default, while January 1, 1900 is assigned serial number 1. The majority of routines generate serial numbers from date values automatically.**

Following are a few examples:

Figure 5.37: Example of various date functions

Managing tables and charts in Excel

Excel allows you to create and format tables. To do that, select a cell from your worksheet. Go to the **Home** tab | Format as the table. Choose any predefined style for the selected table in the worksheet. In the **Format as Table** dialog box, set your cell range. Also, choose the option if *your table has headers*, and Click **OK** if you want the range's header row to be the first row (Don, 2023).

Charts enable you to present your data in a way that will significantly impact your audience (Microsoft Support, 2023).

To Insert Chart in Excel, select your data, then go to **Insert** tab | under **Charts** group | Choose a chart on the **Recommended Charts** tab or **All Charts** tab to preview or to select a category for your data, as shown in *Figure 5.39*:

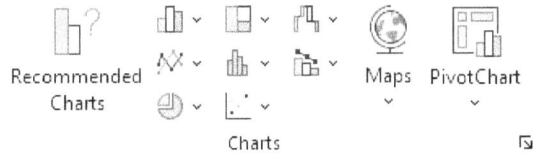

Figure 5.38: Different types of charts

After adding a chart, choose **Chart Design** tab | **Add Chart Element** | Select **Trendline** | then select the type of trendline you want, such as **Linear**, **Exponential**, **Linear Forecast**, *or* **Moving Average**. You can alter the data displayed in the chart or add chart elements such as axis titles and data labels by using the **Chart Elements**, **Chart Styles**, and **Chart Filters** buttons next to the chart's upper-right corner (Microsoft Support, 2023c). To understand the chart easily, you can add the chart title and axis title to any chart. Axis titles cannot be added to charts without axes (like pie or doughnut charts). Choose the **Chart Title** box in the chart and type a new title. If you want to format the chart title, use **Fill** or **Outline,** as shown in the following figure:

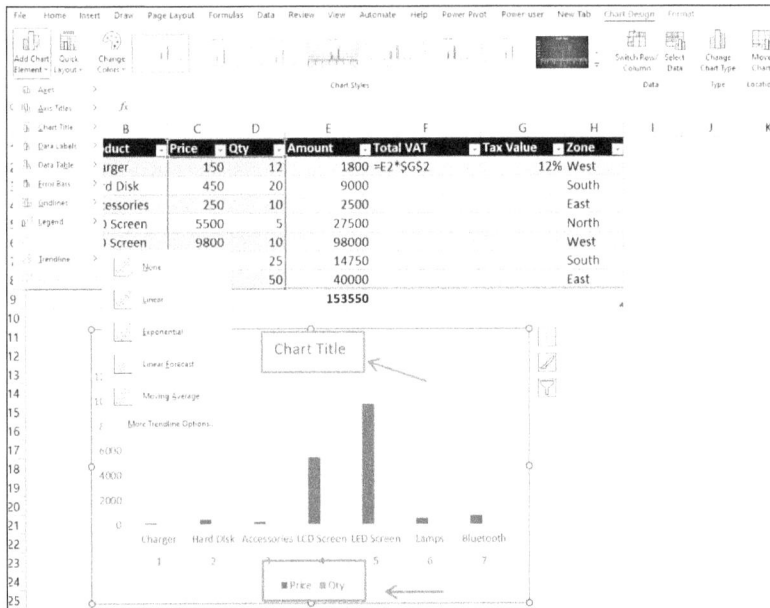

Figure 5.39: Working with Chart elements

The legend of a chart can be revealed or hidden. A legend can help readers understand the chart better if it is shown, but it can also make the chart look cleaner if it is hidden. (Microsoft Support, 2023).

You can place Legends at different positions in the chart, like right-hand side or left-hand side. You can place Legends at Top or Bottom according to your choice, as shown in *Figure 5.41*. Legends show what kind of data is represented in the chart. It is connected to the data source and updates automatically when the data changes. Legends will appear automatically.

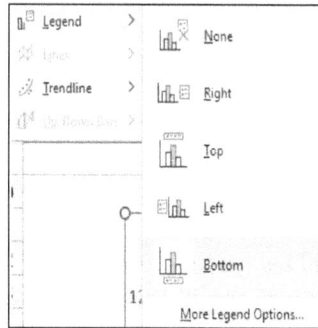

Figure 5.40: Legends placement

- **Change a Chart Type**: If you have chart and you want to change its type then select the chart | Go to the **Chart Design** tab | click **Change Chart Type**. Select a new chart type in the **Change Chart Type** box (Microsoft Support, 2023a).

- **Move Chart**: If you want to move the chart to some other location, you can simply drag and drop the chart. To move the chart to a new worksheet, click the **Move Chart** button on the **Chart Design** Tab, that will help you to move your chart to a new worksheet as shown in the following figure:

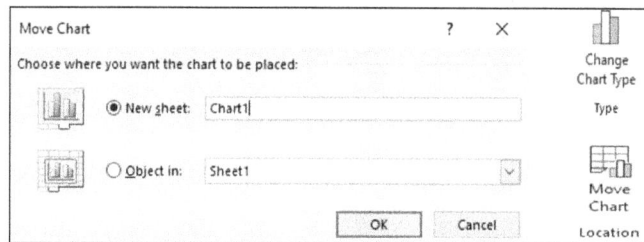

Figure 5.41: Move Chart dialog box

The **Design** tab includes a **Data** section where you may change your chart's data. To open the following window, click the **Select Data** button. You can switch rows and columns.

Figure5.42 shows your data and how it is labeled:

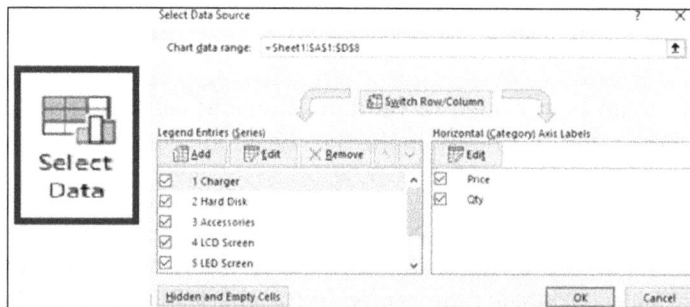

Figure 5.42: Data Source dialog box for various table fields

Conclusion

In conclusion, Microsoft Excel 2019 is a robust and helpful spreadsheet application that continues to be a crucial tool for individuals and organizations across various sectors, such as education or the corporate sector. With its powerful features, Excel empowers users to analyze data, create complex calculations, and visualize information clearly and compellingly. Its user-friendly interface and wide range of functions and formulas make it accessible for beginners and advanced users.

The ability to handle large datasets, create dynamic charts and graphs, and facilitate seamless collaboration through Microsoft 365 integration further solidifies Excel's position as a cornerstone in data management and analysis. Its applications extend beyond mere number-crunching, as Excel is a budgeting, project management, and sophisticated financial modeling platform.

As technology evolves, Excel adapts regularly, ensuring users can access the latest tools and functionalities. Whether used for personal finance, academic research, or business analytics, Microsoft Excel 2019 remains invaluable, empowering users to make informed decisions and derive meaningful insights from their data.

Excel continues to be a key player in enhancing productivity, efficiency, and decision-making processes in the dynamic landscape of data-driven tasks.

In the next chapter, we will discuss Microsoft PowerPoint, a cutting-edge software that empowers users to create stunning, interactive, and professional presentations.

References

1. Ahmed, S. (2023, February 12). *Difference Between Sort and Filter in Excel*. Exceldemy. **https://www.exceldemy.com/difference-between-sort-and-filter-in-excel/**

2. Don. (2023). *How to Create and Manage a Chart in Excel*. Teach Excel. **https://www.teachexcel.com/excel-tutorial/how-to-create-and-manage-a-chart-in-excel_1290.html?nav=sim_bttm_pg**

3. Heisserer, N. (2023). *Alignment Group*. LibreTexts Workforce. **https://workforce.libretexts.org/Bookshelves/Information_Technology/Computer_Applications/Computer_Fundamentals_for_Technical_Students_(Heisserer)/15:_Home_Tab_and_Working_with_Formulas_and_Functions_in_Excel/15.03:_Alignment_Group**

4. Microsoft Support. (2023a). *Add or remove titles in a chart*. Microsoft. **https://support.microsoft.com/en-us/office/add-or-remove-titles-in-a-chart-4cf3c009-1482-4908-922a-997c32ea8250**

5. Microsoft Support. (2023b). *Analyze Data in Excel*. Microsoft. **https://support.microsoft.com/en-us/office/analyze-data-in-excel-3223aab8-f543-4fda-85ed-76bb0295ffc4**

6. Microsoft Support. (2023c). *Available chart types in Office*. Microsoft. **https://support.microsoft.com/en-us/office/available-chart-types-in-office-a6187218-807e-4103-9e0a-27cdb19afb90**

7. Microsoft Support. (2023d). *Calculate the difference between two dates*. Microsoft. **https://support.microsoft.com/en-us/office/calculate-the-difference-between-two-dates-8235e7c9-b430-44ca-9425-46100a162f38**

8. Microsoft Support. (2023e). *Copy and paste specific cell contents*. Microsoft. **https://support.microsoft.com/en-us/office/copy-and-paste-specific-cell-contents-a956b1c3-cd5a-4245-852c-42e8f83ffe71**

9. Microsoft Support. (2023f). *Create a chart with recommended charts*. Microsoft. **https://support.microsoft.com/en-us/office/create-a-chart-with-recommended-charts-cd131b77-79c7-4537-a438-8db20cea84c0**

10. Microsoft Support. (2023g). *Get insights with Analyze Data*. Microsoft. **https://support.microsoft.com/en-us/office/get-insights-with-analyze-data-aa105149-1e48-446d-b3df-872dff70a866**

11. Microsoft Support. (2023h). *Insert the current date and time in a cell*. Microsoft. **https://support.microsoft.com/en-us/office/insert-the-current-date-and-time-in-a-cell-b5663451-10b0-40ab-9e71-6b0ce5768138**

12. Microsoft Support. (2023i). *Names in formulas*. Microsoft. **https://support.microsoft.com/en-us/office/names-in-formulas-fc2935f9-115d-4bef-a370-3aa8bb4c91f1**

13. Microsoft Support. (2023j). *Show or hide a chart legend or data table*. Microsoft. **https://support.microsoft.com/en-us/office/show-or-hide-a-chart-legend-or-data-table-5d663010-fee5-4953-a2ab-18f529543fd5**

14. Microsoft Support. (2023k). *Sort data in a range or table*. Microsoft. **https://support.microsoft.com/en-us/office/sort-data-in-a-range-or-table-62d0b95d-2a90-4610-a6ae-2e545c4a4654**

15. Microsoft Support. (2023l). *Use conditional formatting to highlight information*. Microsoft. **https://support.microsoft.com/en-us/office/use-conditional-formatting-to-highlight-information-fed60dfa-1d3f-4e13-9ecb-f1951ff89d7f**

CHAPTER 6

Designing Professional Presentations with Microsoft PowerPoint

Introduction

Microsoft PowerPoint is a popular presentation application that was developed by *Microsoft*. It is part of the *Microsoft Office suite*, which includes various productivity applications. *PowerPoint* is a versatile and widely used application that is part of the *Microsoft 365* suite of applications and is primarily designed for creating engaging and impactful presentations. Microsoft PowerPoint helps you to learn and create professional presentations that grab attention and make your data more presentable. Anyone can create a presentation using slides and add images and videos according to the topic. Think of blank slides as a canvas; they allow you to showcase your creativity with the help of pictures and words.

Gradually, with each version, the application became more creative and interactive. It offers a user-friendly interface with a familiar ribbon toolbar, making it easy to access and utilize its numerous functions. This application is widely used for creating and editing educational, professional, and personal documents. This lesson is perfect for those looking for new features and how to beautify a presentation. We will understand how to use Office 365's cross-functionality through *OneDrive* and *PowerPoint Online* so you can save, edit, and share presentations.

Structure

In this chapter, we will discuss the following topics:

- Overview of PowerPoint
- Managing slides and presentations
- Different presentation views
- Configure and present slide show
- Configure print settings for presentations
- Insert various objects in the slide
- Apply transitions and animations
- Tips and tricks to save time

Objectives

By the end of this chapter, we will understand the basics of PowerPoint, different presentation views, visual features like photo albums, how to insert slides using various methods, setting basic file attributes and printing preferences for presentations, and exploring how videos and audio can be used and edited within the presentation itself. This chapter also explains more advanced features so we can create captivating presentations for your business and other office work.

Overview of PowerPoint

In this section, we will discuss the basic features, explore ribbons, learn how to start the PowerPoint program, and start with a presentation. It is time to create a presentation from scratch.

When you open PowerPoint, you will see some built-in themes and templates. It seamlessly integrates with other Microsoft Office applications, such as Word and Excel, enhancing your ability to create cohesive documents [OBJ]. When creating a new presentation, it usually asks whether you want to start with a blank template or a pre-defined one.

To create a new presentation, click on **File** | Select **New** | Select a predefined template or a blank presentation as follows:

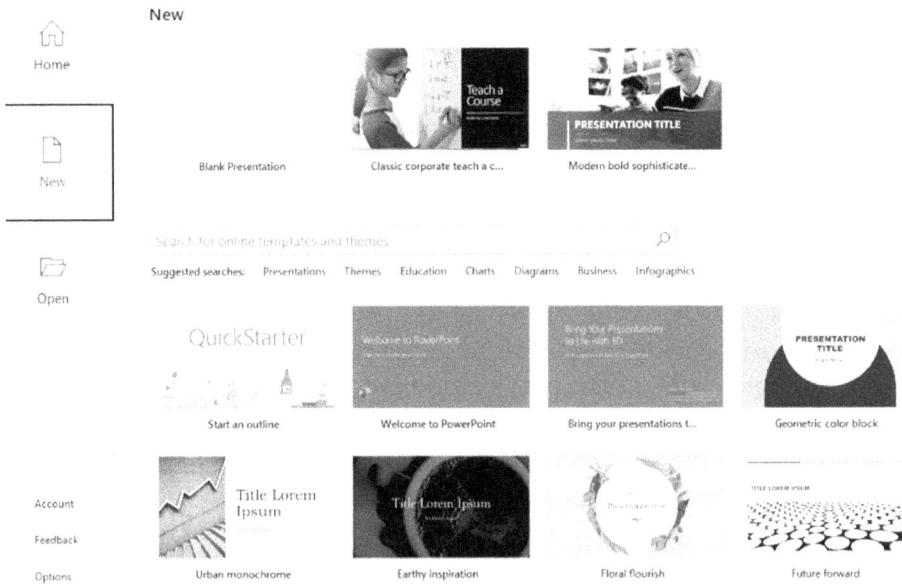

Figure 6.1: *Available pre-defined templates in PowerPoint*

Start with a blank presentation. You will have a normal view where you can edit the slide according to your requirements. When you click on **File** menu, it will take you backstage, where you can open an existing presentation, save, print, send, or close it. The most common tab is the **Home** tab, where you can have cut, copy, and paste options, which are available in all office applications. You can change the font style, size, and other formatting options like bold, italic, underline, etc.

In the paragraph group, you can change the alignment, bulleted list, numbered list, increase or decrease indent, and the paragraph into 2 or 3 columns. Line spacing can be adjusted, and under the text direction, you can change the orientation of the text to stacked or horizontal or rotate the text to 90 and 270 degrees (or any desired direction).

Bulleted text can be changed into Smart Art graphics easily, as shown in the following figure:

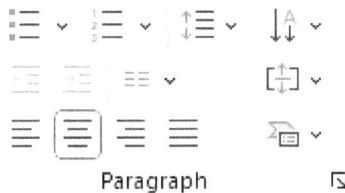

Figure 6.2: *Paragraph group options*

To enable the dictate functionality, go to | **Home** tab | **Dictate** to add content to presentation placeholders and SLI. Once you click on the **Dictate** option, a microphone icon will appear on the screen (for the first time). Wait for the button and start speaking to see text appear.

Your content will automatically be transcribed and added to the slide. It offers various languages; you can add punctuation by saying them explicitly (*Go Hands-Free and Dictate Text in PowerPoint*, 2022).

The benefits of using Dictate are that it will speed up your work, increase productivity while authoring presentations, reduce the time spent creating presentations, and, of course, require no typing skills.

Managing slides and presentations

When more slides are added to a presentation, ensuring that all elements remain well-organized often becomes challenging. PowerPoint provides individual slides with placeholders to keep all elements properly. To insert a new slide, use the **Home** tab or the **Insert** tab. This tab allows you to add new slides for your presentation, create duplicate slides, and reuse slides from Outline.

Inserting slides using various methods

There are various ways through which we can insert the slides in our presentation; these are as follows:

- **Slides from Outline:** PowerPoint allows you to use a Word outline to create new slides in a presentation. When the Word document is formatted correctly with the correct heading styles, you can insert the Word document into PowerPoint, and it will convert the information into slides with the appropriate headings and bullets. Make sure your Word document is formatted correctly. Microsoft Word has nine levels of heading styles, starting from Heading 1 to Heading 9. If your text is in Heading 1, then PowerPoint will translate it into Slide Titles. Heading 2 will be converted as first-level bullet points, and so on. To do this, go to the **Home** tab | **Slides** group | **New Slide** menu | Select Slides from Outline | Navigate to the file in your local device | Select and click the **Insert** button as follows: (PowerPoint converts word outline document into presentation.)

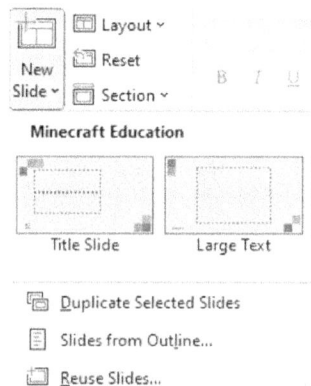

Figure 6.3: Different ways of adding slides to a presentation

- **Import slides from another presentation:** Refer to *Figure 6.3*. If you click on **Reuse Slides**, it will open presentations on the right-hand side and ask you to open the content from the presentation you have selected, and then you can choose one or more slides to add to your presentation without having to open the other file. (By default, a copied slide inherits the slide design you are inserting it once its in the destination presentation. However, you can keep the formatting of the slide you copied instead). Whenever you import a slide from one presentation to another, it is simply a copy of the original slide. Changes you make to the copy do not affect the original slide in the other presentation (*Dawn*, 2015).

- **Duplicate selected slides:** Refer to *Figure 6.3*. If you want to make a duplicate copy of the existing slide in the presentation, select the **Duplicate selected slides** option. The shortcut to create a duplicate slide is *Ctrl+D,* or right-click the slide thumbnail that you want to duplicate and select the duplicate slide option. The duplicate slide is inserted immediately after the original slide.

- **Insert slides and select slide layouts:** Every theme in PowerPoint includes a set of slide layouts that are predefined arrangements for the slide content. Placeholder boxes provide you with a place where you can insert content without manually formatting or arranging it. You can choose layouts from the menu and add content according to your requirements. Some predefined layouts can be accessible under the slides group from the **Home** tab. The predefined layouts include a title slide to begin with. We have layouts containing placeholders for text, videos, pictures, charts, shapes, clip art, images, tables, and many more. The layout also contains the formatting for those objects, like theme, colors, fonts, and effects.

- **Insert sections into your slide:** Once you create a presentation and want to divide it into different categories, you can easily insert sections between the slides to create a more cohesive presentation. You can create sections to organize your slides into meaningful groups like you use folders to organize your files.

  Right-click between slides and select the **Add section**. Type a name in the section name field and select **Rename**. You can collapse the section and see the number of slides in each section. To move or delete a section, select **View | Slide Sorter**. From here, you can select **Move Section Up** or **Move Section Down**, or to delete a section, select the **Remove section** option.

- **Rearrange the order of slides:** In the presentation, select the thumbnail of the slides from the left pane that you want to move to another location, then drag it to the new location. To select multiple slides, hold the control key and then select the slide you want to move. Upon releasing the control key, drag the selected slides as a group to the new location in your presentation.

- **Insert summary Zoom Slides:** To make presentations more dynamic and exciting, we have another option, namely Zoom Slides. To summarize the entire presentation on one slide, add summary zoom. Go to the **Insert** tab, under the links group -> Select **Summary Zoom**; it will ask you to quickly select any section or slide to move to the summary slide. Once you add slides to the summary slide, you can click on any thumbnail icon to take you to that slide. Again, you will automatically return to the Summary Zoom slide. Summary zooms are like landing pages, where you can see all the pieces of your presentation at once.

- **Insert Section Zoom:** Choose the section or sections you want to insert. When you are presenting, select it to zoom to the corresponding section. At the end of the section, we will automatically return to the slide you zoomed in from.

- **Insert Slide Zoom:** Adding a slide zoom to your presentation can help make it more dynamic, allowing you to navigate freely between slides. If you want to focus on specific content, make a slide zoom, a small thumbnail is added to your slide. You can easily click on the thumbnail.

To show selected slides only, choose **Slide Zoom** as follows:

Figure 6.4: Different zoom options

Different presentation views

PowerPoint files can be viewed in various ways, depending on your work. Some views are helpful when creating the presentation, and some are most helpful when delivering the presentation.

There are different views in PowerPoint. Go to **View** tab | under the presentation group to check that. We have different views, as follows:

Figure 6.5: Different presentation views

- **Normal view**: This is the editing mode where you will work most frequently to create the slides. The normal view displays slight thumbnails on the left, a large window showing the current slide, and a section below where you can type your speaker notes for that slide.

- **Outline view**: The outline view can be used to create an outline or storyboard for the presentation. It displays only the text on your slide, not pictures or other graphical items. You must get the outline view from the **View** tab.

- **Slide sorter view**: It displays all the slides in your presentation in horizontally sequenced thumbnails. It is helpful if you need to reorganize your slides. You can just click and drag them to a new location or add sections to organize them into meaningful groups.

- **Notes page view**: This is helpful when checking the speaker notes. It is located beneath the slide window. An empty notes pane prompts you with text that says, **Click to add notes**. You can show or hide your speaker notes with the notes button at the bottom of the slide window. The notes can be printed and included in the presentation to be used during the presentation (*Katewa*, 2023).

  During the presentation, the speaker notes are visible on your monitor but not visible to the audience, so the notes pane is the place to store talking points that you want to mention when you give your presentation. If notes exceed the allotted length of the notes pane, a vertical scroll bar appears on the side of the pane. You can also enlarge the notes pane by pointing your mouse at the top line and then dragging upward after the pointer turns into a double-headed arrow.

- **Reading view**: The reading view lets you read your entire presentation without slide show mode. You can access this mode from the taskbar at the bottom of the slide window. It is beneficial when you want to review the PowerPoint presentation without a presenter. The reading view displays the presentation in full-screen mode (like a Slide show) and gives you basic controls to make it easy to flip through the slides.

The **View** tab allows you more options; the master view tab is one of them. We will discuss it in detail as follows:

- **Master views:** The master view group includes Slide Master, Handout Master, and Notes Master. Master view provides the advantage of making universal style changes to every slide, common notes page, or handout associated with the presentation with a single button click. PowerPoint's Master View provides users with the ability to oversee the comprehensive appearance and style of their presentations. Through the customization of slide masters, it is possible to achieve consistent formatting, font choices, color palettes, and layouts across every slide, which aids in producing sophisticated and professional presentations. This exploration will highlight how Master View can optimize the design process and amplify the impact of the presentation as follows:

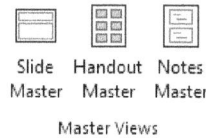

Figure 6.6: Master views group

o   **Slide master:** In the slide master, you want all your slides to contain the same font, style, header, footer, and images like logos or the company name. You can make those changes in one place, which is known as the master slide, and all the formatting will be applied to all the slides. In the Master Slide, you will get Slide Master and Layout Master.

Any changes you make to the slide master will be reflected in all slides based on it. However, most of the changes you will make will likely be available in the layout master, which is related to the master only. The advantage of making any changes to the slide master or layout master is that people working on your presentation in Normal Mode cannot change or delete anything from the slide. Your slide formatting will remain intact. The moment you click on **Slide Master**, it will provide a new menu where you can insert different layouts insert different placeholders for content, Text, Pictures, Charts, Table, Smart Art graphics, Media, or any online image. You can also insert Titles and Footers for all the slides.

Companies can customize branding **colors**, **fonts,** and different **effects** for the master slides, as shown in the following figure:

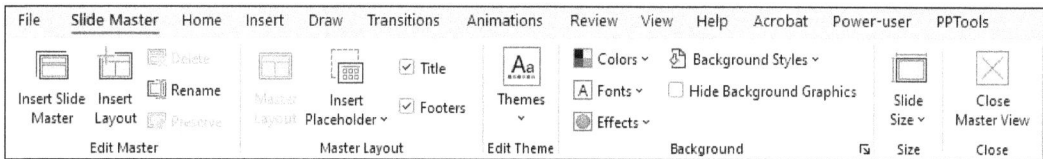

Figure 6.7: Slide Master tab options

You can also change the slide size to **Standard** or **widescreen** for printing newsletters or any campaign printouts as follows:

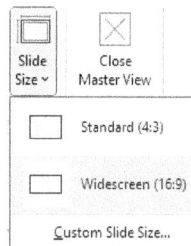

Figure 6.8: Way to change the slide size

Handout Master and Motes Master will work in the same manner as Slide Master.

Configure and present slide show

The **Slide Show** tab is about managing and presenting your slides to the audience. This tab gives you many options to show up your presentation. Use slide show mode once your presentation is ready and you want to present it to the audience.

The **Slide Show** menu allows you to present the slides either from the beginning or from the current (selected) slide under the **Start Slide Show** group from your device as follows:

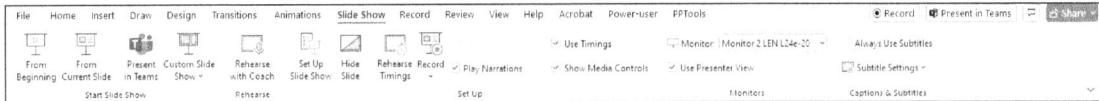

Figure 6.9: Slide Show ribbon

This is the best way to view or preview your presentation to ensure it is focused and has an impact on the audience. Once you start the slide show, you can select commands that are available during the slide show, such as *go next* and *previous*. A semitransparent toolbar will appear in the lower-left corner of the screen.

Press *W* if you need a Whiteboard to share your ideas during the slide show. This will give you a Whiteboard on which you can share your thoughts.

There are many options available during the slide show, as follows:

- **Create custom slide show**: As the name suggests, a custom show allows you to customize your presentation according to the audience's needs. Assume we are creating our playlist to listen to songs, and in the same way, we can present or create a subset of the slides from a **custom slide show**. A basic custom show consists of a separate presentation or one incorporating portions of the original presentation.

- **Rehearse with Coach:** The Speaker Coach assists you in preparing in private to deliver more effective presentations. A Speaker Coach analyzes how you speak, how you pace yourself, how you make your pitch, whether you use filler words, informal language, synonyms, and culturally sensitive terms, and can detect when you are overly wordy or simply reading text from the slides, as shown in the following figure:

Rehearse
with Coach

Rehearse

Figure 6.10: Rehearse with Coach option

After each rehearsal, you will be provided with a report that includes statistics and suggestions for improvements. Speaker Coach is compatible with Edge, Chrome, and Firefox browsers. To start with Speaker Coach, you must be ready with the presentation, then select the **Rehearse with Coach** option from the **Slide Show** Tab. The presentation will open in a full-screen view like a Slide Show, then the screen will appear at the lower right hand on your screen with a **Welcome** message, and then select the **Start Rehearsing** button as follows:

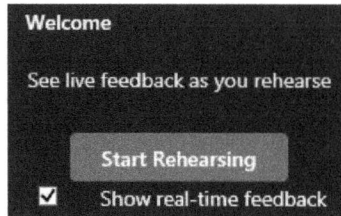

Figure 6.11: Rehearse Coach dialog box

Once you start speaking, your pace, speed, pitch, language, informal language, and fillers will be considered. When you are through your presentation or slide deck, you must exit the full-screen view and stop the presentation.

It will then be prompted with a report that gives you a summary and offers recommendations.

Please read the report. If you want to review it again, select **Start Rehearsing** or consider all the points highlighted in the report.

When using Speaker Coach, sit in a quiet place with a microphone. A good internet connection is required for this. After you close the rehearsal report, it disappears. If you want to take or save a copy, you need to take a screenshot and save it on your device, as shown in the following figure:

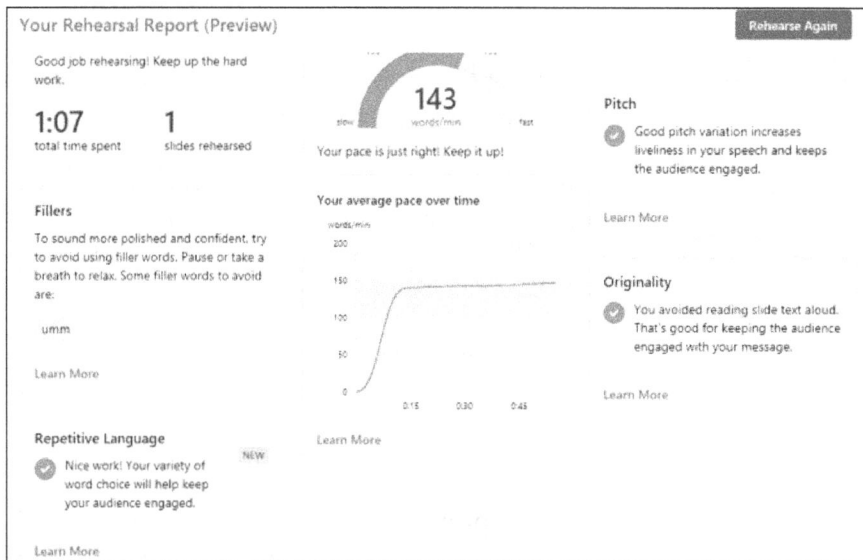

Figure 6.12: Rehearsal Report

- **Set up slide show:** This option allows you to set up your slide show. To start a custom show from within PowerPoint, go to the **Set Up Slide Show** | dialog box, which will open with various options. You can use various options according to your preference. There are different ways to make your slides run automatically. As soon as the **Set-up Slide Show** window opens, select the **Presented by a Speaker** option, which refers to manually advancing your slides by clicking (Lia, 2023), as shown in the following figure:

Figure 6.13: Set-Up Slide Show option

- **Browsed by an individual:** It allows you to create a self-running presentation. It will enable you to deliver the presentation within a window. Ensure that the present option's use timings are enabled, so that this feature functions correctly.

- **Browsed at a Kiosk:** It automatically allows you to run a full-screen continuous slideshow. Make sure your slide show will continue until you press the escape key as shown in the following figure:

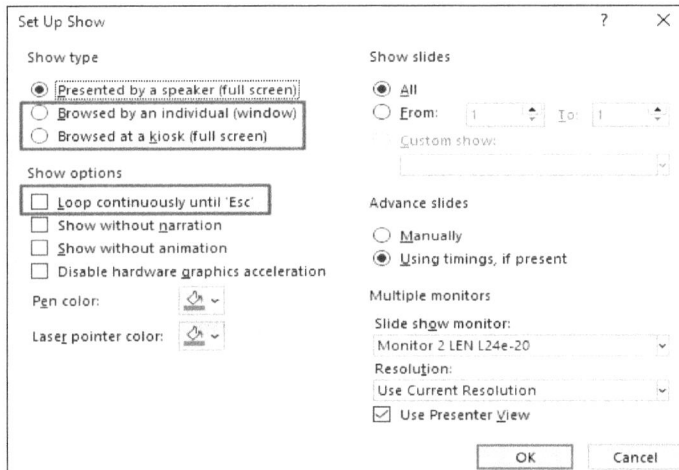

Figure 6.14: Set Up Show dialog box

The next is the **Rehearse Timings** option. This will help you spend your time on the presentation and do a dry run(rehearsal) before the actual presentation as follows:

Figure 6.15: Rehearse Timings option for dry run

The following figure shows the dialog box:

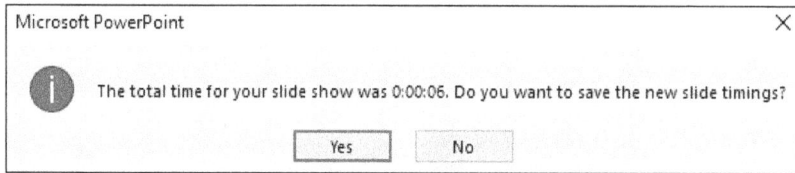

Figure 6.16: Set Up Show dialog box

Setting your timings will define how much time you want your slideshow to spend on each slide before going live. Rehearse Timings allows you to review your presentation slide by slide and record how much time you spend on each slide. It will help you prepare well in advance before any big day. Once you are done, a message will save you time. Click the **Yes** button to save time on each slide.

- **Record**: This option will help you record your presentation; editing can be done later. It is available under the Slide Show menu.

- **Always use Subtitles**: You can add subtitles to your PowerPoint presentation, and it is a helpful way to enhance accessibility and understanding, especially during a live presentation. In the slide show tab, look for the **Always Use Subtitles** option. You will likely be prompted to choose the language for your subtitles. Select the appropriate language for your presentation. PowerPoint will start generating subtitles. There are customization options available. You can adjust the subtitles' size, font, and color and access these settings through the **Subtitle Settings** option.

We have Subtitle settings under **Captions and Subtitles** in PowerPoint, where you can choose Spoken language and Subtitle language. You can also manage where your subtitles will be displayed, i.e., at the **top, bottom, above,** or **below** the slide.

To stop the subtitles during the presentation, return to the slide show tab, click the **Subtitle/CC** option again, and choose **End Subtitles** as follows:

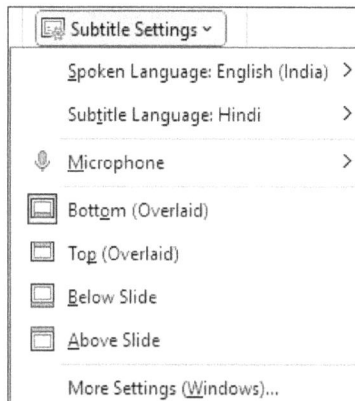

Figure 6.17: Subtitle settings

Several factors affect the accuracy of automatic subtitles, such as the quality of your microphone, your speaking speed, and the presence of background noise.

If necessary, reviewing and editing subtitles for accuracy is always a good idea.

Configure print settings for presentations

Microsoft PowerPoint has various printing preferences using the **Print** option. It allows users to print physical or digital copies in various formats. Whether you require handouts for an audience, speaker notes, or high-resolution PDF, it provides adaptable printing options to meet the user's requirement. Users can print complete slides, notes pages, or several slides on a single page, making it an invaluable resource for meetings, training sessions, and documentation purposes as follows:

- **Print your presentation**: Select **File** | **Print** | from **Settings**. Select the options according to your preference, as shown in the following figure:

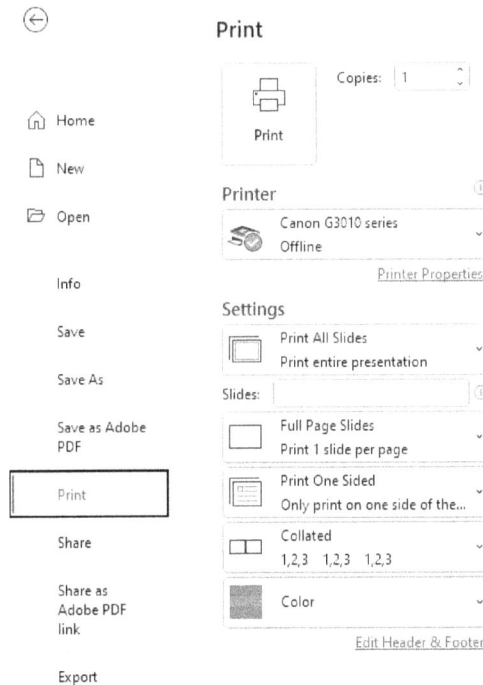

Figure 6.18: Print settings for Presentation

- **Print all slides**: To print each slide once you choose this option.
- **Print selection**: Only print the selected slides, separated by a comma.
- **Print current slide**: It only prints the current slide.
- **Custom Range**: Specify which slides to print.

- **Slides:** Once you print all slides, select slides or the current slide. In the Slides box, type which numbers you want to print separated by a comma, as shown in the following figure:

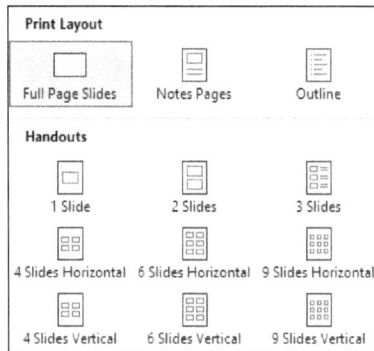

Figure 6.19: Print Layout of the slides

- **Print Layout**: Choose to print just the full-page slides, just the Notes pages (speaker notes), an outline, or handouts. You have the option to choose the slides per page to be printed. This is an effective way to save paper and provide handouts to the audience. Once you select the **Outline** option, it will only print the text available in the slides without the images (*Print Your PowerPoint Slides, Handouts, or Notes*, 2023).

- **Collated**: Once you select collated, it will print all the slides in the presentation.

- **Non-collated**: This option will print all copies of the first slide, followed by other slides.

- **Color**: This option allows you to choose whether to color grayscale or pure black and white for printing the slide.

- **Edit header and footer**: It will allow you to edit the header and footer before printing.

Insert various objects in the slide

Various objects, such as links, tables, charts, text, shapes, images, and audio/video, can be inserted into the slide for presentation. Align shapes and insert hyperlinks. Convert text into SmartArt graphics and replace fonts throughout the presentation, as shown in the following figure:

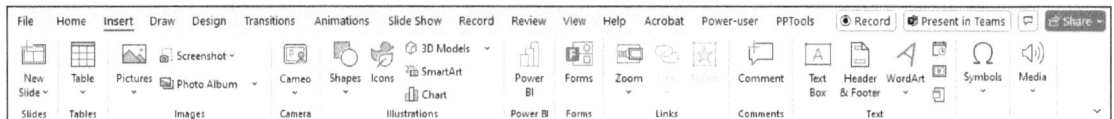

Figure 6.20: Manage text, formatting, shapes, images and work with SmartArt graphics, 3D objects, and media

If you want to add a table to the slide, click the **Insert** tab, Select **Table**, **Insert Table**, enter the number of rows and columns, and click **OK**. The table will be added to your slide.

Under the **Images** tab | You can add pictures from your device, online images, or stock images. Here, you can screenshot any window on your desktop and attach it to your document.

Here, you can create a beautiful presentation for your favorite photo collection. A photo album is an option in PowerPoint presentations that you can use to display business photographs. To make one, click **Insert** tab | Under **Images** subgroup | Select **Photo Album** | **New Photo Album**. It will open a dialog box.

Select **File/Disk** under **Insert picture from** option | select the folder containing the image you want to insert, then click the **Insert** button. In the **Photo Album** dialog box, click **Create**. There are options, like adding captions for each picture. If you want to add captions for all pictures, select **Captions** below all pictures.

You can do various settings here based on your preference, as follows:

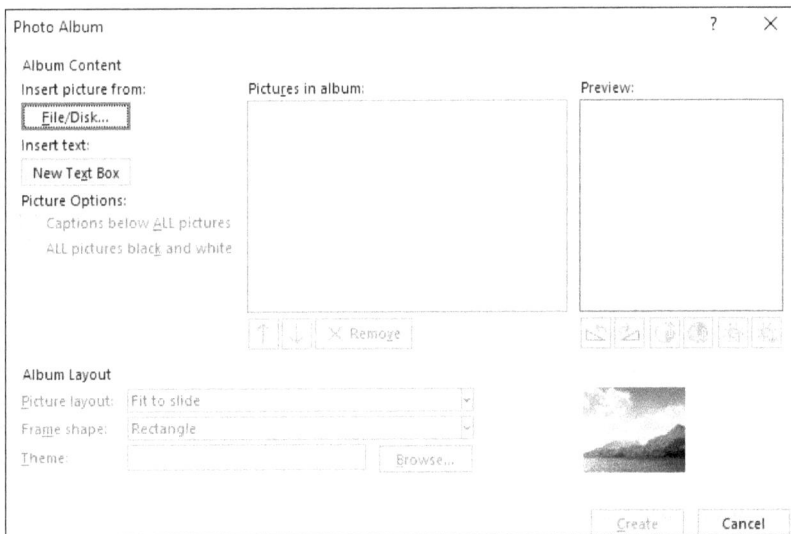

Figure 6.21: *Photo Album settings*

Cameo is a feature available to Microsoft 365 subscribers in the desktop app for Windows and macOS. With Cameo, you can insert your live camera feed directly on a PowerPoint Slide, as follows: (*Presenting with Cameo*, 2023)

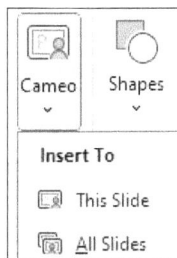

Figure 6.22: *Cameo settings for the slides*

To add, go to **Insert** | Select **Cameo**. A placeholder for the camera feed will appear on the slide. Select the **Preview** icon in the placeholder to turn on the camera feed. In the **Camera** tab | Select the arrow below the **Preview** button to select other cameras. Remember that only one video feed can be used on a slide.

Once you add a video feed to the slide, the Camera format tab allows you to apply effects like **Camera Style, Camera Shape, Camera Border, and Camera Effects**. Use Slide Show to present using the cameo feature as follows:

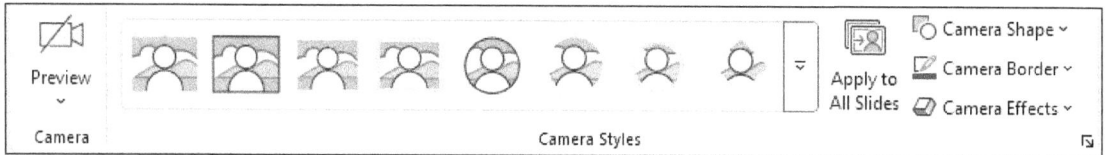

Figure 6.23: Different camera styles

The **Insert** tab allows you to use different shapes, icons, 3D Models, SmartArt, and charts in your presentation.

It will also allow you to add Microsoft Forms to the slide so that it is easy to provide to the audience during the presentation, as follows:

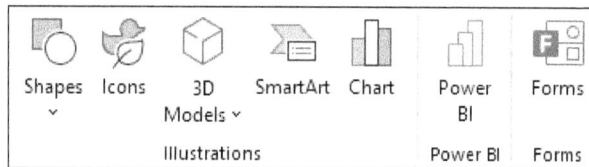

Figure 6.24: Work with shapes, 3D Models, and SmartArt in slides

PowerPoint allows you to add a text box, WordArt, Header and footer, Date and time, and the Slide number. Also, if you want to add a Word document, Excel file, or PDF document to the slides, add it as an object.

It will be added as a support document, and an application icon will be placed on the slide so you can open and view it during your presentation as follows:

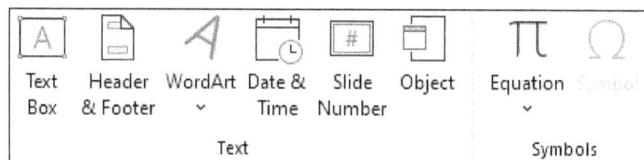

Figure 6.25: Work with Text group and Symbols in presentation

PowerPoint allows you to insert a PDF file as an object, making it easy to include reference materials, reports, or any supplement document within the presentation. This feature ensures that important information is accessible directly from your slides, as follows:

- **Insert PDF file as an object**: Go to **Insert** | Select Object from the Text subgroup to add a PDF file. In the **Insert Object** dialog box, select the **Create from file** option, select the PDF file location from your device, and then select the **OK** button as shown: (Insert PDF file content into a PowerPoint Presentation, 2023).

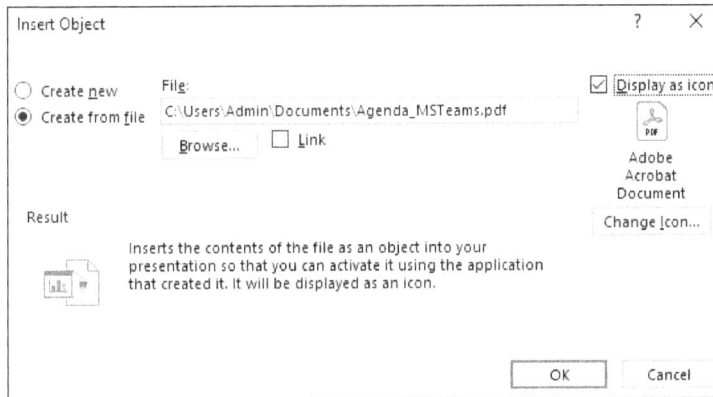

Figure 6.26: Insert PDF in slides

- **Open the PDF from a Slide Show**: To open the inserted PDF file during a Slide Show, attach an action to it. In the Slide, select the PDF file icon, then go to **Insert** | **Links** | **Action**, as shown in the following figure:

Figure 6.27: Work with Links group

In the **Action Settings** dialog box, select the **Mouse Click** tab to open the PDF with a click or the **Mouse Over** tab to open the PDF file when you move the pointer over it.

Select **Object action**, then select Open in the list, as shown in the following figure:

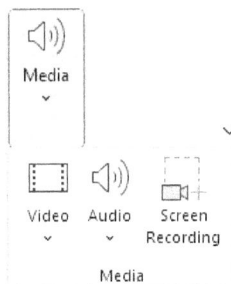

Figure 6.28: Work with Media controls

- **Insert a video from YouTube:** You can add/insert an online video in your presentation. Go to the **Insert** tab of the ribbon | Select **Media** | Select **Video** | Choose **This Device**, **Stock Videos**, or **Online Videos**.

In the **Online Video** dialog box, paste the **Uniform Resource Locator** (**URL**) of the video you want to add to the presentation. Select **Insert**. Once a video is successfully inserted, you can play it. A play button will appear on the video in Normal View. In Slide Show Mode, you can interact with the video as you do in an Edge browser.

Moreover, you can play the video without clicking on the Play button. Tapping the Spacebar to advance to the next step in your click sequence would be best, as shown in the following figure:

Figure 6.29: Insert different videos in Slides

In the same way, you can insert audio like music, narration, or sound bites into your slide by just clicking on the **Audio** button. It would be best to use a microphone; your computer must have a sound card and speakers.

During the slide show, you can play the audio you have recorded. PowerPoint provides playback options that can be changed and configured according to user requirements.

When a slide appears, you can add background music to it. The background music starts automatically with the Slideshow and plays during other slides until you stop or move to the next slide.

- **Record your screen in PowerPoint:** You can record your computer screen and related audio, then embed it in your PowerPoint slide or save it as a separate file. For this, go to the **Insert** tab | select **Screen Recording**. The moment you choose screen recording, it will take you to the last opened window and ask you to choose an area to record with the cross-haired cursor + then select and drag the area of the screen you want to record. Select Record and use Pause or Stop when you are done. Your video is added to the slide. Once you select the video, a **Playback** tab will be available, allowing you to trim or change the video. If you want, you can save your screen recording as a separate file.

Apply transitions and animations

First, before you apply transitions or animations in your presentation, you must understand the difference between the two. A transition is a unique effect when you exit one slide and move on to the next during a presentation (*The Difference between Animations and Transitions*, 2023).

The following are the basics of transition:

- A transition is applied to an entire slide.

- Only one transition effect can be applied to a slide.

- Select the slide where you want to add a transition, then select and apply an effect. The effect will appear when the previous slide gives way to the slide that has the transition effect.

- Morph is a transition effect that looks like the animation on the slide. It creates smooth movement of objects from one position to another. Morph is a versatile and efficient option used for generating fluid animations between slides. It operates by identifying elements that are identical or closely related on two successive slides and facilitating a smooth transition of their transformation.

The following are the steps to incorporate Morph into your presentations:

- **To add, change, or remove transitions between the slides**: Once your presentation is ready, and if the user wants to add, change, or remove the transitions, the user can add sound, control the speed, and customize the look of the transition effects also. The steps are given as follows:(*Add, Change, or Remove Transitions between Slides*, 2023)

Figure 6.30: Transitions between slides using the Morph feature

The following are some steps to add transitions to the slide:

- o Select the slide where you want to insert the transition.

- o Go to the **Transitions** tab and select the type of transition you want to apply for.

- o Click on **Preview** to view what the transition looks like.

- o Select **Apply to All** to add the transition to the entire presentation. If you want to add different types of effects to the transition, such as where and how it should appear on the screen, select **Effect Options** and choose the desired ones.

- o In the **Timing** group, you can change the duration of the effect, enter the desired time for the transition, and specify whether the effect occurs after a mouse click or after a certain amount of time passes. There are options to add a sound to the transition effect. Sounds are best used in moderation.

To remove a transition, select the slide, and go to the **Transitions** tab | Select **None**.

Select the **Apply to All** option under the **Timings** subgroup if you want to remove the transitions from the presentation.

To change the transition to a different one, go to the **Transitions** tab and select the effect you want to apply. In PowerPoint, there are three categories of unique transitions: Subtle, Exciting, and Dynamic Content.

- **Subtle:** The most basic type of transition is Subtle. There are 13 types of transitions, including Morph, Fade, Push, Wipe, Spill, Reveal, Cut, Random Bars, Shape, Uncover, Cover, and Flash. They use simple animations to move between slides (*Elena*, 2022; *PowerPoint: Applying Transitions*, 2023).

  - **Fade**: Slide gradually becomes visible.
  - **Push**: Slide appears from the left or right sides, bottom or top.
  - **Wipe**: It is used to wipe content to a slide area from a specified direction.
  - **Split**: Units' halves of a slide from a specified direction.
  - **Uncover**: The previous slide uncovers the following one from a specified direction.
  - **Cover**: It is the opposite of uncover.
  - **Zoom**: The current slide zooms in/out or zooms and rotates to show the following.
  - **Morph**: This transition is a feature that allows smooth, animated continuity between presentation elements, as shown in the following figure:

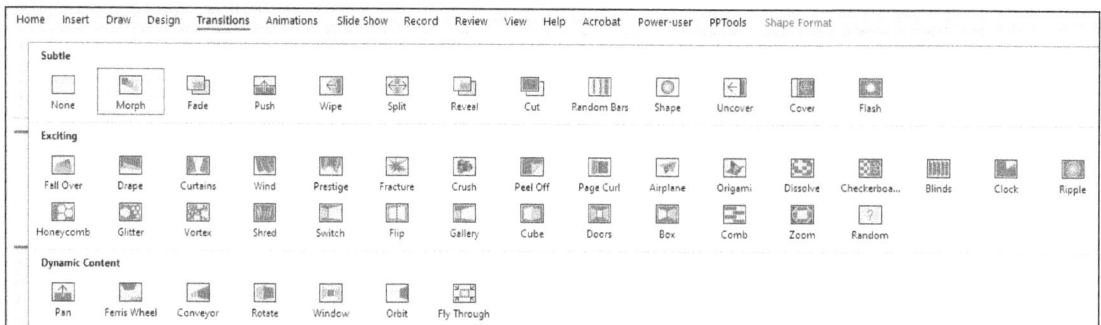

Figure 6.31: Various categories of transitions

- **Exciting**: PowerPoint has 29 types of transitions, and Dynamic Content has seven types of transitions available. The more complex transitions can be used between slides to make your presentation look professional.

- **Dynamic Content:** In this transition, dynamic transitions will solely affect the placeholders rather than the slides of similar layouts used in two similar slide layouts. The use of dynamic transitions can enhance the cohesion of the slides and elevate the overall quality of your presentation.

Understanding how to apply animations

An animation is a special effect that applies to a single element on a slide, such as text, shape, image, tables, SmartArt graphics, etc. Effects can make an object appear, disappear, or move. They can also respond to mouse clicks, giving your presentation an interactive feel.

The following are the basics of animation:

- There is no restriction on the number of animation effects that can be applied to a slide. So, one slide can have several animation effects applied to it.

- Entrance effects make an object appear.

- Exit effects make an object disappear.

- Emphasis effects draw attention to an already visible object.

Motion paths move an object from one position to another, as shown in the following figure:

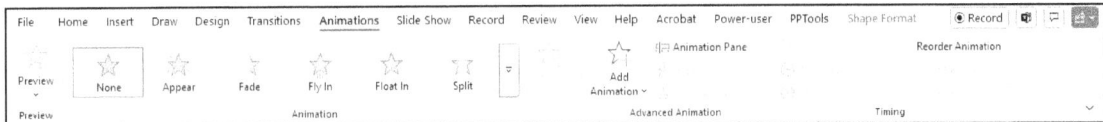

Figure 6.32: *Animation styles*

We have different types of animations and previews to see their effect on the slide.

To add animations to text, pictures, and shapes, select the object or text you want to animate. Then, select the **Animations** tab, choose an animation, and select **Effect Options**. Finally, select **Add Animation** and select an animation. There are four types, **Entrance, Emphasis**, **Exit**, and **Motion Paths**, as shown in the following figure:

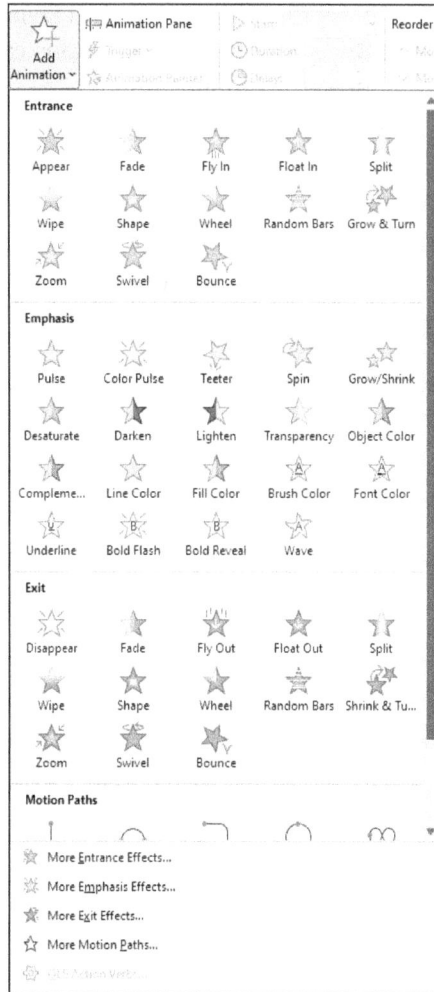

Figure 6.3: Different categories of animations

The following are some of the ways to manage animations and effects in your presentation:

- **On Click**: Start an animation after clicking on a slide, as follows:

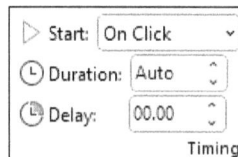

Figure 6.34: On Click animation after clicking

- **With Previous**: Play animation simultaneously with the previous animation in the sequence.

- **After Previous**: Start an animation immediately after the previous one, as shown in the following figure:

Figure 6.35: Animation after previous settings

- **Duration**: Specify the length of an animation.

- **Delay**: Play the animation after a certain number of seconds.

- You can change the order of animations; for example, there are two options, such as **Move Earlier** and **Move Later**. Also, add an animation to grouped objects, text, and more. Press *Ctrl* and select the objects you want. Select **Format | Group | Group to group objects together**. Select **Animations** and choose an animation.

- **Work faster with Animation Tool:** When animating various objects that use the same actions, it is helpful to use the **Animation Painter Tool**. This tool copies the animation from the original object to the new one and saves you time, so you do not have to animate each one individually.

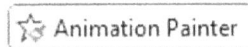

  o   Select the object with the animation you wish to copy.

  o   On the **Animations** tab of the toolbar, click **Animation Painter**.

  o   Finally, click on any object you want to apply the animation to.

Tips and tricks to save time

The following tips and tricks can be handy while making a presentation: (Mihaila, 2022):

- **Dictate functionality:** Planning everything before creating a presentation is always good practice. It will help you to put your thoughts into the slides quickly. You can plan your presentation using the **Dictate** functionality to type anything in the slide.

- **Turn a Word document into a presentation:** If you are working in a Word document, use different styles like H1, H2, and H3 for your text to convert it into a PowerPoint presentation quickly.

- **Use PowerPoint templates:** If you do not have time to apply animations, transitions, or any theme, the best way to create a presentation is to use templates. This way, your presentation will have a cohesive design, as templates contain fonts, effects, backgrounds, layouts, and content. PowerPoint offers a variety of templates. Once you use them, you can personalize them.

- **Use Master Slides:** Master slides are a great way to ensure that all slides are uniform in design. You can quickly change the design or apply the theme by editing the master slide. Slide Master is always a great way to create impressive and uniform presentations. If you want to keep the company logo, company name, date, or page number, the best way to do it in Master Slides is not to do it every time on every slide.

- **Always prefer the personalized Quick Access toolbar:** If you often use a few commands in the presentation, keep those commands in the Quick Access Toolbar, which appears at the top left corner of the presentation.

- **Use keyboard shortcuts:** If you want to speed up your work, always use keyboard shortcuts. They will save you time, and you will not have to go through PowerPoint's tabs every time (*Can I Use Portrait and Landscape Slide Orientation in the Same Presentation?*, 2023).

- **Use the Reuse Sides feature:** If you want to copy a few slides in your current presentation, always use the **Reuse Slides** option. It will allow you to open the presentation on the right-hand side in the thumbnail view, and then you can open the presentation, and it will open/show all slides. Use **source formatting** to use already applied formatting, or check the checkbox. Then select it, and it will automatically add to your current presentation.

- **Use PowerPoint add-ins**: Add-ins can enhance your Office applications by adding new features or commands. Several free add-ons are available online that can assist you in inserting pictures, creating QR codes, or making the presentation more engaging overall.

- **Format Painter:** Use Format Painter to apply formatting to objects or text. To apply it to different slides, double-click the Format Painter icon. It will keep the formatting until you de-select it (*5 Ways to Save Time in PowerPoint from Presented*, 2022).

The following are some keyboard shortcuts:

If you are keyboard savvy, shortcuts are beneficial and work more effectively. For users with mobility or vision disabilities, keyboard shortcuts can be easier than using the touchscreen and are always a must-have alternative to using a mouse.

Frequently used shortcuts	
Starting from A to Z	
Create new presentation	*Ctrl + N*
Open a presentation	*Ctrl + O*
Add a new slide	*Ctrl + M*
Cut selected text, object or slide	*Ctrl + X*

Frequently used shortcuts	
Starting from A to Z	
Copy selected text, object or slide	*Ctrl + C*
Paste selected text, object or slide	*Ctrl + V*
Apply bold on selected text	*Ctrl + B*
Insert a hyperlink	*Ctrl + K*
Open the font dialog box	*Ctrl + T*
Insert a new comment	*Ctrl + Alt + M*
Undo the last action	*Ctrl + Z*
Redo the last action	*Ctrl + Y*
Start the Slide Show	*F5*
End the Slide Show	*Esc*
Save the Presentation	*Ctrl + S*
Close the entire Presentation	*Ctrl + Q*
Duplicate selected slide	*Ctrl + D*
Print a presentation	*Ctrl + P*
Copy the formatting of the selected text	*Ctrl + Shift + C*
Paste the formatting of the selected text	*Ctrl + Shift + V*
Select all objects on the slide	*Ctrl + A*
Group the selected objects	*Ctrl + G*
Insert equation	*Ctrl + = (Equal Sign)*
Open the Find dialog box	*Ctrl + F*
Open the Replace dialog box	*Ctrl + H*
Repeat the last Find action	*Shift + F4*
Center your selected content	*Ctrl + E*
Italics your selected text	*Ctrl + I*
Justify the selected text	*Ctrl + J*
Align your content to the left	*Ctrl + L*
Align your content to the right	*Ctrl + R*
Underline your selected text	*Ctrl + U*
Close the current presentation	*Ctrl + W*

Table 6.1: *Frequently used shortcuts*

Some keyboard shortcuts work with views and panes. The following table helps you understand how to use them while presenting a Slide Show: (*Use Keyboard Shortcuts to Create PowerPoint Presentations*, 2023).

Frequently used shortcuts	
Use while presenting	
Start/Switch to Presenter view	*Alt + F5*
Switch to Slide Show view	*F5*
Go to the next slide during the Slide Show	Press *N* or right arrow key (->)
Go to the previous slide during the Slide Show	Press *P* or left arrow key (<-)
White screen (during presentation)	*W*
Black screen (during presentation)	*B*
Use Pen while using Slide Show for annotations	*Ctrl + P*
Start the laser pointer (for pointing during the Slide Show)	*Ctrl + L*
Change the pointer to an arrow	*Ctrl + A*
Change the pen pointer to an eraser	*Ctrl + E*
Hide the arrow pointer	*Ctrl + H*
Show or hide ink markup	*Ctrl + M*
Erase on-screen annotations	*E*
Toggle between Outline and Thumbnail view	*Ctrl + Shift + Tab*
Switch to full screen	*Ctrl + F1*
Show or hide guides	*Alt + F9*
Show or hide the grid	*Shift + F9*
Select all slides in the Slide Sorter view	*Ctrl + A*
Show the help menu	*F1*
Display the context menu	*Shift + F10*
Increase the font of selected text	*Ctrl + }*
Decrease the font of selected text	*Ctrl + {*
Rename a focused text	*F2*
Move up, down, left or right	Use arrow keys

Table 6.2: Shortcuts while presenting the presentation

Conclusion

By the end of this chapter, we discussed how the PowerPoint application allows us to present our ideas through a presentation by adding animations, transitions, videos, graphics, images, text, and more. PowerPoint is a versatile canvas for ideas and stories.

Microsoft 365 makes it easy to access the online PowerPoint version and make real-time document changes while collaborating with others. PowerPoint has a versatile range of uses.

It can be used for business presentations, pitch decks, marketing plans, induction for new employees, seminars, educational purposes, and more.

This chapter covered various topics, including how the PowerPoint application can be used for multiple purposes. Users can modify the slides according to their preferences. We also discussed different views of presentations and how they can be used. The comprehensive array of formatting options, transition effects, and animation tools empowers users to transform concepts into captivating visual narratives. PowerPoint provides features like real-time co-authoring and cloud-based sharing, fostering collective creativity in the digital age.

In the next chapter, you will learn about Microsoft Access, which is a powerful database management system. This database has a user-friendly interface with robust tools for creating, managing, and analysing data. This database enables users to store data in a structured format, link related information, and generate insightful reports.

References

1. *5 Ways to Save Time in PowerPoint from Presented.* (2022). Presented. **https://presented.co.uk/5-ways-to-save-time-in-powerpoint/**

2. *Add, change, or remove transitions between slides.* (2023). Microsoft Support. **https://support.microsoft.com/en-us/office/add-change-or-remove-transitions-between-slides-3f8244bf-f893-4efd-a7eb-3a4845c9c971**

3. *Can I use portrait and landscape slide orientation in the same presentation?* (2023). Microsoft Support. **https://support.microsoft.com/en-us/office/can-i-use-portrait-and-landscape-slide-orientation-in-the-same-presentation-d8c21781-1fb6-4406-bcd6-25cfac37b5d6**

4. *Create and share a photo album.* (2023). Microsoft Support. **https://support.microsoft.com/en-us/office/create-and-share-a-photo-album-6febdf8b-5179-4e63-90a6-0fb68df97ec6**

5. Dawn. (2015). *How to Import Slides from a Word Outline into PowerPoint.* Office Skills Training. **https://officeskills.org/how-to-import-slides-from-a-word-outline-into-powerpoint/**

6. Elena. (2022). *Transitions in PowerPoint presentations: a big guide.* **https://www.onlyoffice.com/blog/2022/04/powerpoint-transitions**

7. Escobar, V. (2023). *PowerPoint 101: The Ultimate Guide for Beginners.* 24Slides. **https://24slides.com/presentbetter/powerpoint-101-the-ultimate-tutorial-for-beginners**

8. *Go Hands Free and Dictate Text in PowerPoint.* (2022). Free PowerPoint Templates. **https://www.free-power-point-templates.com/articles/dictate-in-powerpoint/**

9. *Insert PDF file content into a PowerPoint presentation.* (2023). Microsoft Support. **https://support.microsoft.com/en-us/office/insert-pdf-file-content-into-a-powerpoint-presentation-5e7719d5-508c-4c07-a3d4-68123c373a62**

10. Katewa, S. (2023). *What are the Main Features of Microsoft PowerPoint? – Art of Presentations.* Art of Presentations. **https://artofpresentations.com/what-are-the-main-features-of-microsoft-powerpoint/**

11. Lia. (2023). *How to Play PowerPoint Slides Automatically.* 24Slides. **https://24slides.com/presentbetter/how-to-make-powerpoint-slides-advance-automatically**

12. Mihaila, R. (2022). *13 Time-Saving Tips for Microsoft PowerPoint.* Make Use Of. **https://www.makeuseof.com/time-saving-tips-powerpoint/**

13. *PowerPoint: Applying Transitions.* (2023). GCF Global: Creatig Opportunities for a Better Life. **https://edu.gcfglobal.org/en/powerpoint/applying-transitions/1/**

14. *Presenting with cameo.* (2023). Microsoft Support. **https://support.microsoft.com/en-us/office/presenting-with-cameo-83abdb2e-948a-47d0-932d-86815ae1317a**

15. *Print your PowerPoint slides, handouts, or notes.* (2023). Microsoft Support. **https://support.microsoft.com/en-us/office/print-your-powerpoint-slides-handouts-or-notes-194d4320-aa03-478b-9300-df25f0d15dc4**

16. *The difference between animations and transitions.* (2023). Microsoft Support. **https://support.microsoft.com/en-us/office/the-difference-between-animations-and-transitions-bae174a4-dad3-4268-bf9c-c201a70995f1**

17. *Use keyboard shortcuts to create PowerPoint presentations.* (2023). Microsoft Support. **https://support.microsoft.com/en-us/office/use-keyboard-shortcuts-to-create-powerpoint-presentations-ebb3d20e-dcd4-444f-a38e-bb5c5ed180f4#bkmk_frequentlyusedwin**

Join our Discord space

Join our Discord workspace for latest updates, offers, tech happenings around the world, new releases, and sessions with the authors:

https://discord.bpbonline.com

CHAPTER 7

Developing and Administering Database using Microsoft Access

Introduction

Microsoft introduced the database management system known as Microsoft Access. This application serves as a database solution, offering a user-friendly interface for the creation, management, and analysis of the data. It is a part of the Microsoft Office 365 suite and uses the Access Jet Database Engine to store data in a unique format. Data is crucial for any organization, encompassing raw facts and figures, and it represents the details of entities like people, departments, products, projects, transactions, and various others. Databases serve as organized collections of data arranged in rows and columns, facilitating efficient storage, retrieval, and manipulation of information. MS Access facilitates integration with SharePoint and OneDrive, enabling users to store and share databases in the cloud. However, it is primarily intended as a desktop application rather than a comprehensive cloud-based solution. Microsoft Excel is also a database management system used for creating and managing databases.

Unlike SQL Server and other **relational database management systems (RDBMS)** such as MySQL or PostgreSQL, MS Access is a file-based system that does not require a dedicated server to operate. While SQL Server is designed for high-performance, large-scale data handling with advanced security and concurrent user support, MS Access is more user-friendly and suited for individual users or small teams needing a simpler database solution.

In this chapter, we will discuss the components of the RDBMS, which allows users to organize data into related tables, which can be linked through relationships, reducing redundancy and improving data integrity. We will also cover different types of data types and how to store values while creating tables in Microsoft Access.

Upon mastering the fundamentals, the emphasis will shift towards incorporating data and developing queries that enable users to efficiently search, filter, and conduct calculations on the data.

Structure

We will discuss the following topics in this chapter:

- Introduction to MS Access
- Components of RDBMS
- Datatypes in MS Access
- Creating databases and tables
- Adding data and creating query
- Normalization
- Types of relationships
- Wildcards in MS Access
- Creating reports in MS Access

Objectives

By the end of this chapter, we will understand the concept of a database management system. Various components of a relational database system facilitate the collection and organization of data. Microsoft Access accommodates a range of data types that specify the nature of data contained within the fields of a table. The selection of each data type is determined by the characteristics of the data, thereby facilitating precise storage and processing. In this chapter, you will gain insights into the process of inserting data into tables and generating queries. Additionally, this chapter will enhance our understanding of normalization and the various types of relationships that can exist within tables.

Introduction of MS Access

As we know, Microsoft Access is a well-known database that can store data in huge amounts in the form of a table. It has multiple tables in Microsoft Access, when it comes to fetching the data from various tables, you need to create a relationship between the tables. This is important for maintaining data integrity and ensuring that related information is linked correctly, and that is why this application is known as RDBMS. Access has much more to offer and enables enterprise users to manage data in a structured manner.

Users can easily retrieve data from the database using queries. These queries allow you to filter, sort, and extract data based on specific criteria. Access also provides tools to create data entry forms, making it easier for users to input data into a database. It also allows you to generate reports based on the stored data.

Access supports basic data analysis through sorting, filtering, and grouping.

When creating a new database, you need to open the application. It will ask you to create a blank database. Then, you can go to more templates and select the **Database** category. It will help you with various templates. *Figure 7.1* shows various templates available while creating a new database:

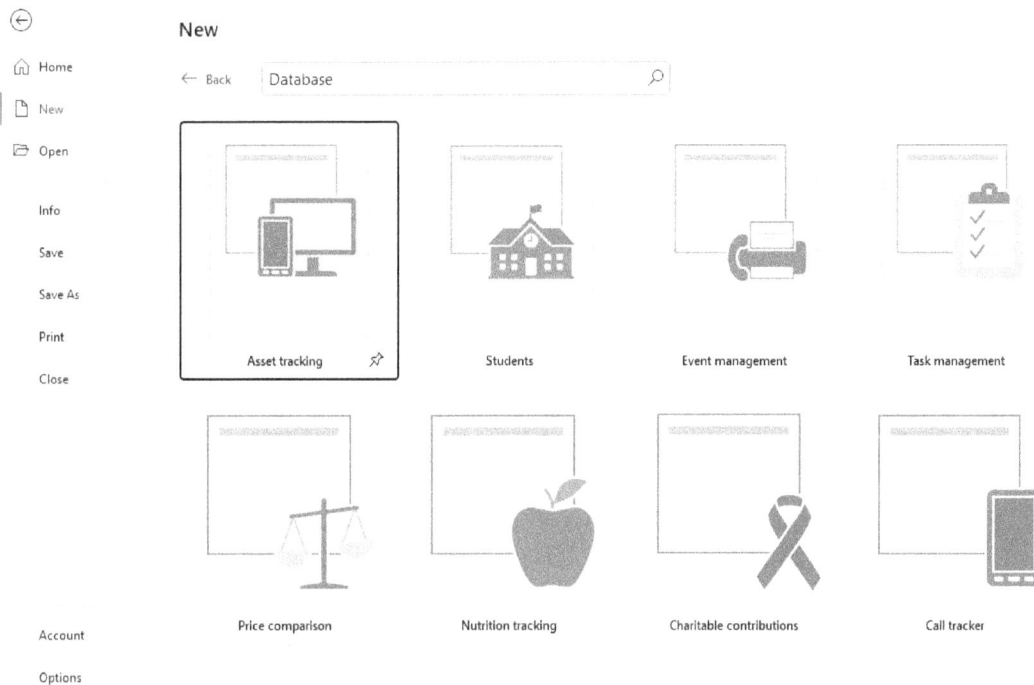

Figure 7.1: *Various templates in Microsoft Access*

If you choose the **Students** database option, the program will use the template to build and manage an extensive database of students and their guardians. You will also be able to construct queries and get various helpful results. Additionally, access may import data from other programs and databases or create direct links to them. Direct data export and import from word processing, spreadsheet, and database files are supported. Microsoft Access is a tool that developers can use to create applications.

When it comes to appearance and navigation, Microsoft Access looks and feels just like other Office apps. However, it is a database, more precisely, a RDBMS.

Before Microsoft Access 2007, the file extension was ***.mdb;** however, it was changed to ***.accdb** starting with MS Access 2007. MS Access 2007 and later versions can read and modify earlier versions of Access, but earlier versions cannot read **.accdb** extensions. A complete RDBMS is an Access desktop database (**.accdb** or **.mdb**).

It offers all the functions for data definition, modification, and control, including data query, that you require to handle massive amounts of data. Access is the RDBMS when developing an application that uses an Access desktop database.

Components of RDBMS

RDBMS is a tool for collecting and organizing data. The significant components of MS Access are as follows (*Database Basics*, 2023):

- **Tables:** The fundamental components of any database are tables. Data from Microsoft Access is kept in tables with rows and columns. A database is referred to as **Flat** when the data is kept in it or in the form of a plain text file. A **Relational** database is one that contains data that is kept in a format where the data items are connected to one another and support numerous tables (arranged in rows and columns) (*Introduction to Tables*, 2023).

  Data regarding products will be kept separate from data about branch offices in a separate table. **Normalization** is the term for this procedure. A table's rows are referred to as records in this context. Every record has one or more fields in it. Columns in the table are referred to as fields. Whether a field contains text, dates, times, numbers, or another sort of data, it needs to be marked as that data type.

- **Queries:** As its name suggests, a query is a specific request for information from a database. Queries can be simple, involving basic data retrieval, or complex, combining and analyzing data from multiple tables. The main function of a query is to retrieve data from the tables and allow you to view it in a single datasheet. Queries can be of two varieties, **select** queries and **action** queries.

  The data is retrieved and made usable with a select query. The query's output can be used as the record source for a form or report, or it can be viewed on the screen, printed, copied, or pasted to the clipboard.

  An action query uses the data to carry out an operation. Action queries can be used to edit, remove, or add data to already-existing tables.

- **Relationships:** In MS Access, relationships exist between two or more tables. Each table can be connected or interrelated with each other.

- **Forms:** It is a desktop database object whose main function is data input. Forms are used to customize how data that your application pulls from tables or queries is presented. With the use of forms, users can construct an interface that is easy for anyone to fill out, and after the form is submitted, the data is saved in the database. Forms are widely used because they provide a simple means of assisting users in accurately inputting data. You can use drag-and-drop items (tools and controls) to customize forms.

- **Reports:** Users can create reports using Access by using the data that has been stored. Before printing a report, you can view it on the screen. Decision-making is aided by reports' ability to display and analyze data in an understandable manner. Sorting, labeling, summarizing, and grouping data for easy sharing or printing is made simpler with reports. A report's appearance can also be altered to improve its visual attractiveness.

- **Macros:** A Macro is a set of actions that can be automated and executed as a single unit. It allows users to automate common tasks and processes within a database without having to write code in a programming language like VBA. Instead of writing code, users can use the Macro Designer in Access to visually create a sequence of actions that Access will perform automatically when the macro is run. Macro contains actions that perform tasks, like opening a report, running a query, or closing the database. For instance, create a macro to a command button on a form so that the macro runs whenever the button is clicked. With the help of macro, operations can be automated.

- **Modules:** A Module is a container for storing and organizing **Visual Basic for Applications** (**VBA**) code. VBA is a programming language that is integrated into Microsoft Access. Modules in Microsoft Access allow users to automate tasks and write and store custom procedures, functions, and code that can be executed to perform specific tasks within the database, among many more.

  A module is categorized as a **Standard Module** and a **Class Module**. Class modules are associated with reports or forms, handling events like button clicks or form loads. General operations included in standard modules are unrelated to any other object. It contains reusable VBA functions and procedures that can be used across the database.

  o **Example of Class Module:** Showcasing a greeting message when a form opens.

  o **VBA Code:**
  ```
  Private Sub Form_Open(Cancel As Integer)
  MsgBox "Welcome to the ABC Database!", vbInformation, "Greetings"
  End Sub
  ```

  o **Example of Standard Module:** Automating data entry with a function.

  o **VBA Code:**
  ```
   Function GenerateCustID(LastName As String, ID As Integer) As String
  GenerateCustID = UCase(Left(LastName, 3)) & "-" & Format(ID, "000000")
  End Function
  ```

  After a function has been created, it can be invoked within a query. This query will return a unique customer ID like COT-000117 for a customer named Solomon Cotmore with ID 117

  ```
  Select FirstName, LastName, GenerateCustID([LastName],[CustID]) As
  UniqueCustomerID from Customers;
  ```

- **Data definition language:** In data definition, you must define the data according to your application. The type of data you have and how it should be stored can be specified with an RDBMS. The integrity of your data can be guaranteed by the RDBMS using the rules you create. Validation rules are used to prevent users from inadvertently storing alphabetic letters in a field intended for a number.

- **Data manipulation language:** DML statements can be used to manipulate data while utilizing the instructions. You can work with your data in a variety of ways with an RDBMS. For example, you can use a single command to edit multiple records or just one field. Additionally, you may create programs that employ RDBMS commands to retrieve the data you wish to show and enable user data updates (*Microsoft Learn*, 2023).

- **Data control language:** DCL statements in RDBMS allow you to share your data with multiple users to update with more flexibility, and additionally, it has safeguards in place to make sure that no two users can alter the same data simultaneously. You can also set some restrictions on your data.

- **Data query language:** A DQL statement in RDBMS allows you to create a query based on the data. For creating a query, we will always use a **select** statement. Using the **select** statement, we can create a query and fetch the data from the database.

We have already covered database components that assist the user in organizing data and provide tables, queries, forms, reports, macros, and modules. These items or parts enable you to input, store, process, and gather data (*Peterson*, 2023).

Figure 7.2 shows different SQL commands used to create a query when fetching data from the database:

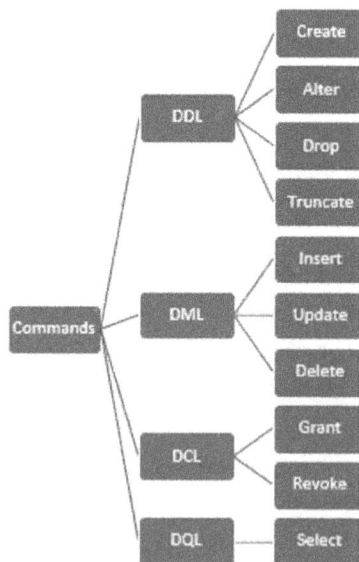

Figure 7.2: Categories of SQL commands

Datatypes in MS Access

Microsoft Access can efficiently store substantial amounts of data in a tabular format. Each field in a table includes properties that determine its attributes and behaviors. The data type of a field is considered the most essential feature. When you save data into the table, you need to select the data type of that column to store the data. Microsoft Access has multiple data types, including newly introduced data types that facilitate integration with modern tools like Power BI and support for JSON. Once the data type is defined, it provides the accuracy to enter the correct data (*Data Types for Access Desktop Databases*, 2023).

The following are the data types used in Microsoft Access. Access 2013 and the subsequent versions allow only one kind of data to be stored in each field:

- **Attachment:** Stores files like digital images, documents, spreadsheets, or charts.
- **Auto Number:** Access, or the user can provide an auto number when a new record is created.
- **Calculated:** Generates an expression using information from one or more fields.
- **Currency:** Stores currency values and numeric data stored with four decimal places of precision.
- **Date or Time:** Stores date and time information for a year range between 100 and 9999.
- **Hyperlink:** Stores a combination of numbers and text, used as a hyperlink address.
- **Long Text:** Typically used for lengthy alphanumeric or text data, up to 63,999 characters (like sentences and paragraphs).
- **Numbers:** Numeric data used for storing mathematical calculations.
- **OLE Objects:** This data encompasses audio, video, and other Binary Large Objects.
- **Short text:** Stores text and numbers not used in calculations like alphanumeric data. (up to 255 characters).
- **Yes or No:** Only stores the logical values of Yes and No.
- **Lookup wizard:** When you choose this data type, a wizard starts to help you define either a simple or complex lookup field.
- **JSON data support:** Microsoft Access does not natively support a *JSON* data type, it can parse and manipulate JSON data using VBA functions. This improves data exchange with APIs and modern applications.
- **BigInt (Large Number):** This 64-bit integer data type allows better compatibility with SQL Server and other databases.
- **Deeper Power BI Integration:** Access databases can now be more effectively linked to Power BI, which enhances the capability for real-time data analysis and visualization.

- **Date/Time Extended:** A new data type allowing more precise time values with higher accuracy, useful for scientific and financial applications.

MS Access vs. other RDBMS

MS Access, along with other RDBMS such as SQL Server, MySQL, and PostgreSQL, employs various data types to effectively store and manage data. However, MS Access is designed to be user-friendly and is adequate for smaller applications, while other RDBMS applications provide more scalable and secure data management solutions suitable for enterprise-level needs.

The following table is a comparative analysis of various data types:

Data Type	MS Access	SQL Server	MySQL	PostgreSQL
Text/ String	Short Text (255), Long Text (Memo)	VARCHAR, NVARCHAR, TEXT	VARCHAR, TEXT	VARCHAR, TEXT
Numeric	Integer, BigInt, Single, Double	INT, BIGINT, FLOAT, DECIMAL	INT, BIGINT, FLOAT	INT, BIGINT, FLOAT
Boolean	Yes/No	BIT	TINYINT	Boolean
Date/Time	Date/Time, Date/Time Extended	DATE/TIME	DATE/TIME, TIMESTAMP	TIMESTAMP, DATE, TIME
Auto Number	Auto Number (Long)	IDENTITY, UNIQUEIDENTIFIER	AUTO_INCREMENT	SERIAL, BIGSERIAL
JSON Support	Handle via VBA/ linked tables	JSON, JSONB	JSON, JSONB	JSON, JSONB
Binary Data	Attachment, OLE	VARBINARY, IMAGE	BLOB, VARBINARY	BYTEA

Table 7.1: Comparative analysis of various data types

Creating database and tables

When creating a new database, you can choose between a blank database or a template. It depends on the project requirement, complexity, and the level of customization required. Carefully crafted templates facilitate efficient database creation (Create a Database in Access, 2023).

To create a database, we have the following options:

- From external data (*Figure 7.3* shows how to add data to the database).
- From predefines templates.
- From blank database.

Situations for using a blank database compared to a template: A blank database is useful when you have the blueprint ready for the data you are creating, like an inventory system or client tracking system that does not fit a predefined database.

Templates are pre-built databases that include tables, forms, reports, and relationships tailored for specific tasks. They are best when you need quick setup without extensive customization of pre-built components like **customer relationship management** (**CRM**), student database, etc. Templates are good for beginners where minimal design is required.

The following are the steps to be followed:

1. Open Microsoft Access, choose **File** | **New** | Select **Blank** database | Type in the database's name, choose a location, and click **Create** to start creating one.

2. Once the Excel worksheet is open, choose the range of data and ensure that each column has a title and a consistent data type.

3. Choose **External Data** | **New Data Source** | **From file** | **Excel,** as shown:

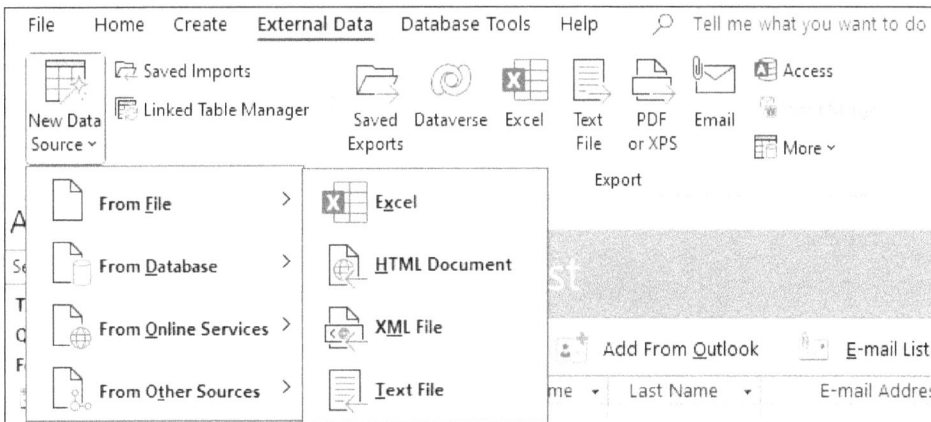

Figure 7.3: Steps to create a blank database

4. Click **Browse** | Locate the Excel file, accept the default settings, and click **OK**.

5. Click **Next** after selecting, *does the first row of your data contain column headings?*

6. After completing the remaining wizard panels, click **Finish**.

   Here, we have used the template **Student Database**. Once you have it, you can view all the additional objects included with this database by clicking the **Navigation** pane on the left side, as shown in the following figure:

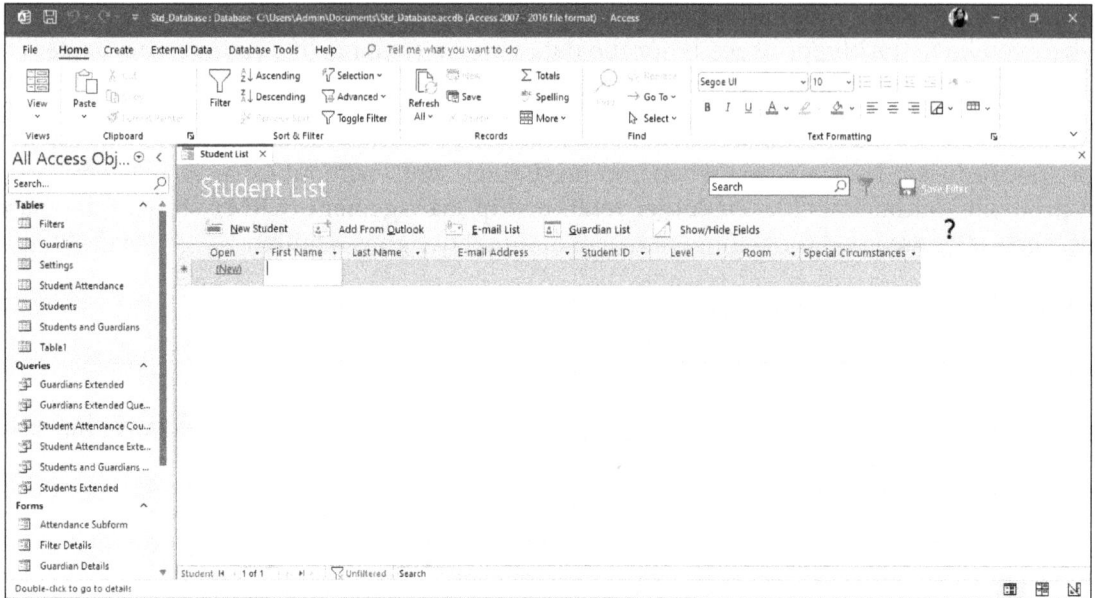

Figure 7.4: Student Database Sample

7. Click the **All Access Objects** arrow key to view different options in the menu. Selecting **Object Type** will show all the object types, **tables, queries, forms, reports, macros,** and **modules**.

Figure 7.5 shows the different types of objects that are used in the database:

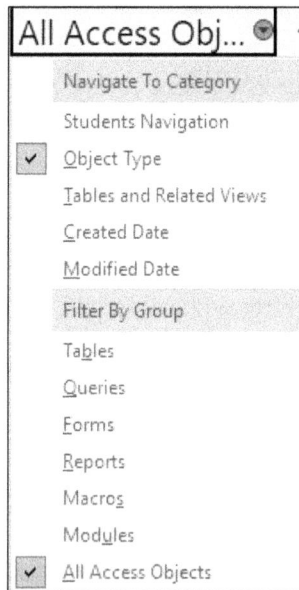

Figure 7.5 Different types of objects

8. Once you create a table, you need to define the datatype of the table fields.

Figure 7.6 will show the **Table Fields** ribbon:

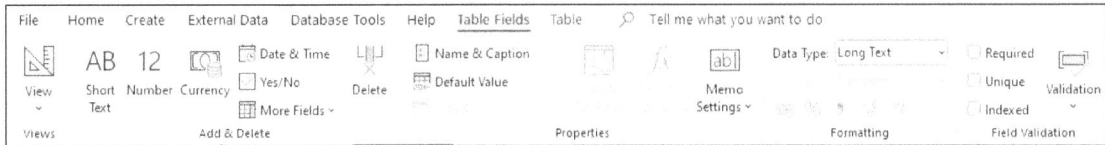

Figure 7.6: *Table Fields menu*

A table field menu option in Microsoft Access refers to the various settings and properties that can be applied to fields (columns) within the table. These options are crucial for defining the data type, characteristics, and constraints of the data that can be entered into each field. Properly configuring these options ensures that your database is efficient, accurate, and user-friendly.

The following is a list of some of the key menu options you may find when working with table fields in MS Access:

- **Data type:** This is the most important option under the **Formatting** subgroup. It establishes the types of data that can be stored in a field, including text, numbers, date/time, currencies, yes/no, and more. The right data type must be selected for effective data storage and retrieval.

- **Field size:** This option allows you to specify the maximum data size that can be stored in a field. For instance, setting a field size for a text field determines the maximum number of characters it can hold.

- **Format:** This option lets you define how the data in the field will be displayed. For example, you can format a date field to show dates in a specific format (like *MM/DD/YYYY*) or a number field to display currency.

- **Input mask:** The input mask controls how data is entered into a field. It is particularly useful for ensuring consistency in data entry, such as phone numbers or social security numbers.

- **Default value:** This setting allows you to define a default value that will automatically appear in the field for each new record. It is useful for fields that have a common value across many records.

- **Required:** When this option is set to *Yes*, the field must contain data; a record cannot be saved without a value in this field.

- **Validation rule and validation text:** These options are part of the Filed Validation subgroup and are used to define rules for data entry in a field (like a range of acceptable values) and to notify users when they enter invalid data.

- **Indexed:** This option can be used to create an index on the field, which can improve search and query performance. However, it is important to use it judiciously, as too many indexes can negatively affect database performance.

- **Lookup wizard:** The lookup wizard is a helpful tool in MS Access that allows you to create a field that lets users select a value from another table or a list of options, facilitating data entry and ensuring data integrity.

- **Name and caption:** This is a label for the field that you can use to display a more readable or understandable name for the field in forms and reports.

- **Description:** Here, you can add descriptive text about the field, which can be helpful for documentation purposes and to guide other database users.

- **Different views in MS access:** There are three views that can be used while working with forms such as, Form View, Layout View, and Design View. Each of these views serves a different purpose and is useful in various stages of form creation and modification. *Figure 7.7* shows three types of views available in Microsoft Access:

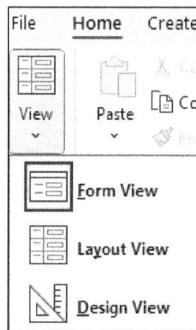

Figure 7.7: Different types of views in Microsoft Access

- o **Form View:** In this view, you can enter, edit, and view records in the form. You can interact with all the controls, and it is ideal for entering new data, modifying existing data, and navigating through records. It also shows data as it appears in the database.

- o **Layout View:** In this mode, you may examine real-time data while designing the form. It is a mix of Form View and Design View that enables layout adjustments to be made while the form is in use. Changes are reflected instantly with real data, making it easier to customize the look and feel of the form.

- o **Design View:** This view is used for the detailed creation and modification of form structures. You can add, remove, or modify fields, controls, and their properties and write VBA code.

  It is ideal for creating a new form from scratch, making structural changes, or performing advanced customization that Layout View cannot achieve.

Apart from this, you have two views usually available when you work with tables and queries, i.e., **Datasheet View** and **Design View**. *Figure 7.8* illustrates both the datasheet view and design view, enabling the user to modify the table design:

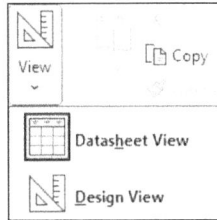

Figure 7.8: Different views to manage the table structure

The **datasheet view** is used for viewing and editing data directly. It is like an Excel sheet where you can see rows and columns. This view is useful for data entry, data, and viewing the data.

Design View is used for creating and modifying the structure of tables and queries. It provides a more detailed interface for defining field properties, relationships, and query criteria. This view does not display actual data but focuses on the architecture and logic behind the data. In the tables group, several options help manage tables.

Figure 7.9 shows various menu options like **Primary Key**, property sheets, etc., as follows:

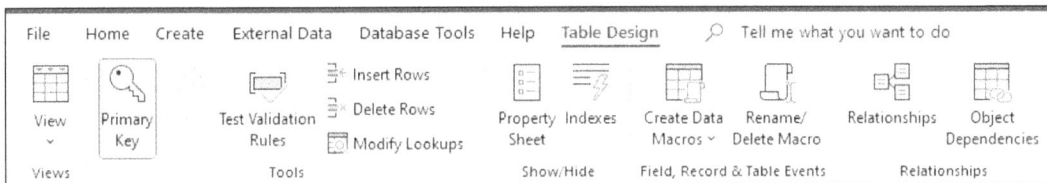

Figure 7.9: Table Design menu options

Some keys that play a significant role in creating tables are as follows:

- **Primary key:** The small key icon next to the field is visible. This indicates that the field is a component of the main key of the table. A **primary key** is also referred to as a unique identifier since it is the only key that can be used to identify every record in a database uniquely. The primary key field value cannot be the same in two records. It must always have a unique value for each record and cannot be null (which means it cannot be blank). For example, the **AutoNumber data type** is used for primary keys to ensure uniqueness.

Figure 7.10 represents the datatype and auto-assigned primary key to column ID:

Figure 7.10: Primary key represents with a key before the field name

The primary key is important because it allows each record in a table to be uniquely distinguished from others, which is important for data accuracy and integrity. It is also essential in defining relationships between the tables and helps maintain data integrity by ensuring that no duplicate records are entered (Primary Keys and Foreign Keys in Access, 2023).

- **Foreign key:** A replica of the primary key is called a foreign key. A field in one table is used to identify a row in another table in a unique way. Although it refers to the main key in a different table (the parent table), the foreign key is defined in a child table.

- **Composite key:** This key is a combination of two or more columns in a table that can uniquely identify each record in that table. It is used when a single column is not sufficient.

- **Unique key:** It guarantees that every value in a column (or set of columns) is distinct for every entry in the table. A unique key, in contrast to a main key, can accept one null value. It is useful for data integrity, ensuring that certain fields do not have duplicate values in the table.

- **Index key:** Not a **key** in the traditional relational database sense, but rather a mechanism to speed up the retrieval of records from the database. An index in a database is like an index in a book. It can be created on one or more columns to speed up searches or queries on those columns. However, excessive use of indexes can slow down data insertion, deletion, and update operations.

The following are some of the best practices:

- **Primary key selection:** Always choose primary keys carefully, ensuring they are stable and not subject to frequent changes.

- **Redundancy and performance:** Overusing foreign keys and indexes can lead to redundancy and affect database performance. Use them carefully.

- **Normalization:** Keeping database normalization rules in mind while defining keys to ensure efficient and logical data organization.

- **Data integrity:** Foreign keys help maintain referential integrity by ensuring consistent relationships between tables.

Create a primary key to relate data between several tables. Add a primary key to a table using the following steps:

1. Right-click on a table in the **Navigation** pane and choose **Design View**.
2. Decide which field or fields to utilize as the main key.
3. Click on **Primary Key** under **Design**.

   Figure 7.11 illustrates the connection of the primary key in establishing relationships among multiple tables:

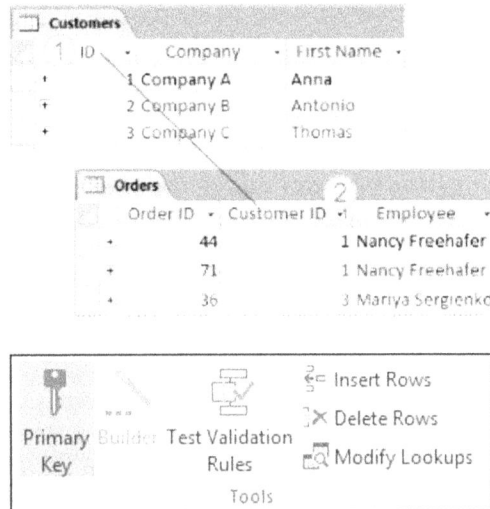

Figure 7.11: Relationship of Primary key to relate data between several tables

Adding data and creating query

An Access database comprises numerous items, including tables, forms, reports, queries, and many more, all of which are necessary for the database to operate correctly. We have understood how to construct tables with fields and attributes. The table's datasheet view, which we covered previously in this chapter, allows us to examine, modify, add, or remove data from a table within Access.

The following are a few steps to check how to add the data to a table:

1. Without further formatting, you can view your data in rows and columns on a datasheet.

2. Access automatically generates two views you can use immediately for data entry whenever you create a new table.

3. When it is open in Datasheet View, you can enter data into one or more fields in a table that appears like an Excel worksheet.

4. It is not necessary to save your data explicitly. When you move the cursor to a new field in the same or different row, Access commits your changes to the table.

5. An Access database's fields are configured by default only to accept particular kinds of data, like text or numbers. The type of data the field configures to allow must be entered. Access shows an error message if you do not.

We are looking for a query in the table or data. We can use a query to answer a simple question, fetch data, or calculate any specific column data. With a query, you can apply a filter so that we get the appropriate data.

The following are a few pointers that we need to keep in mind when working with the query part:

- As tables grow in size, it is difficult to look for the specific record, and here, we need to apply a query.
- After executing the query, you can utilize the filter to retrieve the desired data and obtain the information you need.
- Select queries are those that are used to get data out of tables and do calculations.
- Action queries are those that give you the option to add, edit, or remove data.
- You must know everything about the query before applying it.
- The query can be used to create a form or report.

When you do not know how to create a query, always use the **Query Wizard**, as shown in the following figure. It will guide you with step-by-step instructions, and you can enter the required details accordingly, as follows:

Figure 7.12: Different types of Query Wizard

1. Once you click on **Query Wizard**, it will give you a dialog box, and *Figure 7.13* shows the wizard.

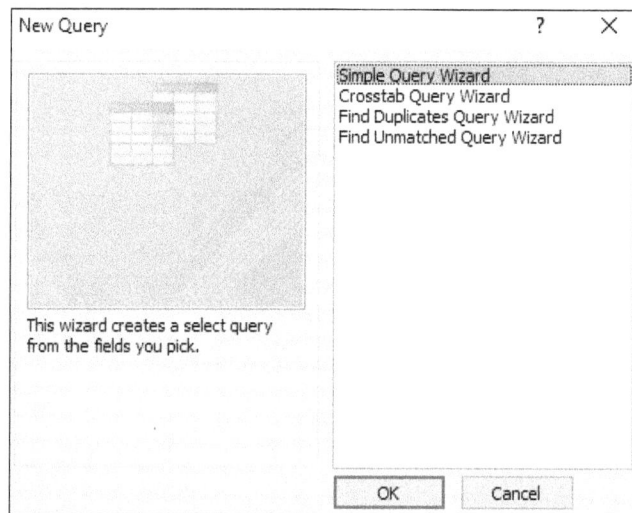

Figure 7.13: Steps in Query Wizard

2. Next, it will ask you to drag the field names required for creating a query as follows:

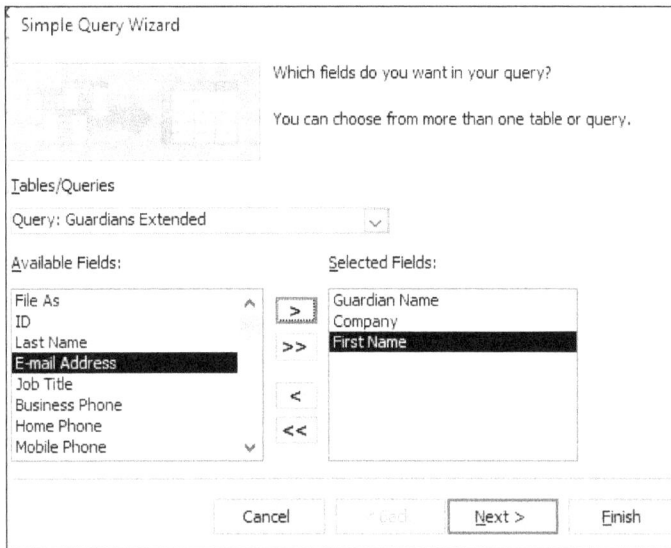

Figure 7.14: *Drag the field names to the right of the wizard*

3. Once you have completed the field's name, save your query as follows:

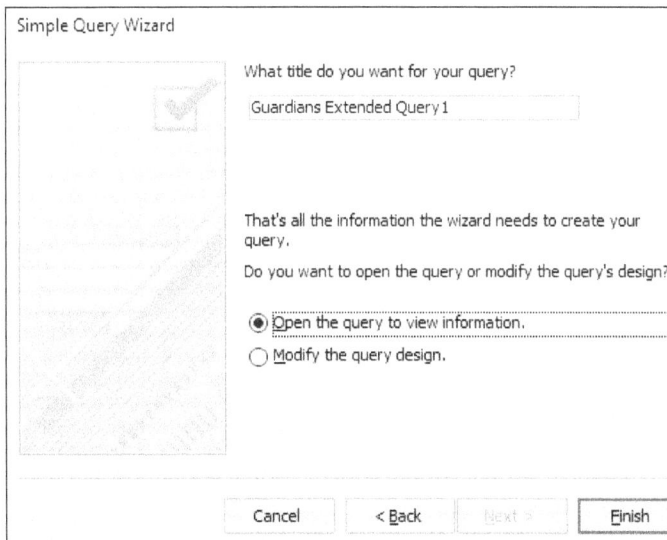

Figure 7.15: *Provide title to query*

4. Another way to create a query is through the **Query Design** tab. Click on it. You can then click on **Add Table** to select the **Tables**. Select the tables to add, and then create queries to the query design as follows:

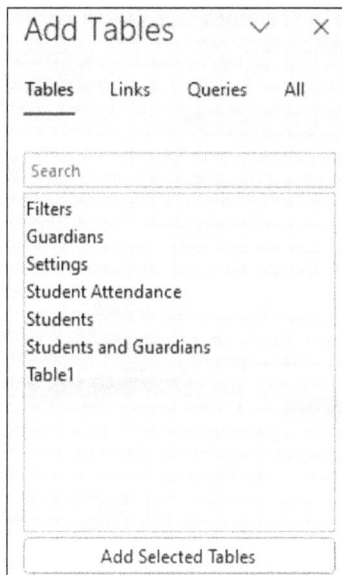

Figure 7.16: Select an appropriate table from the list

5. **Query Design** menu will help you with submenus like **Add Table**, **Query Type** subgroup, and many more.

Figure 7.17 illustrates the query design menu to check various types of components that need to be added to the query:

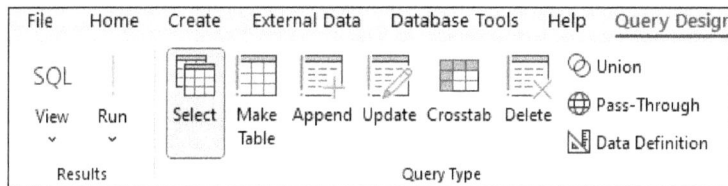

Figure 7.17: Query design menu

You must specify the criteria while creating a query to obtain particular records from the database. A query criterion is an expression that Access compares to query field values to decide whether to include the record containing each value.

A query can perform various actions on the table in the database. Microsoft Access provides four types of action queries. These queries perform an action on the data rather than selecting and displaying data. Action queries are potent tools for batch updating, deleting, and managing data efficiently, as follows:

- **Append query**: This query adds new records to an existing table. Records can be sourced from another table or query. The append query also adds a few records from one table to another table, as shown in the following figure:

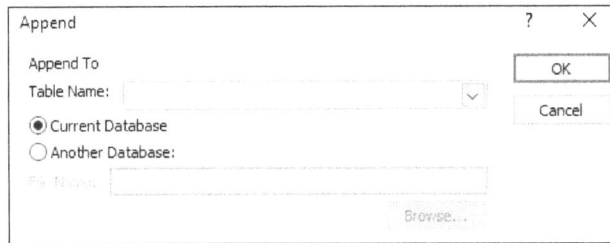

Figure 7.18: Append query dialog box

- **Update query**: This query allows you to modify the data in existing records in a table. It is useful when you need to update multiple records at once, like changing the address of several users who live in a specific city that has been renamed, as shown in the following figure:

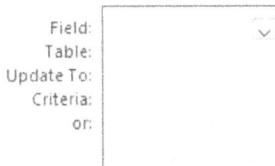

Figure 7.19: Update multiple records at once

- **Delete query**: This query removes records from a table. It is suitable if you need to delete records under certain conditions.

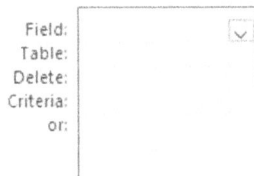

Figure 7.20: Removes record from a table

- **Make table**: This function creates a new table and populates it with data selected from other tables. It is also useful for creating a backup of records or a table with a subset of data for a specific purpose, like a targeted marketing campaign as follows:

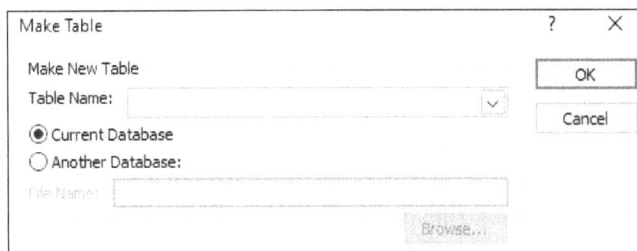

Figure 7.21: Make a new table dialog box

- **Crosstab query**: Crosstab queries are powerful tools for summarizing and analyzing data in a compact and readable format (in a cross-tabular format). They are beneficial when you need to understand relationships and patterns across two dimensions of your data, one running down the left side (row header) and one across the top (column header). It is also used to summarize data in data aggregation functions (like sum, average, count, min, max). For instance, it can sum sales figures by product (row heading) for each month (column heading), as shown in the following figure:

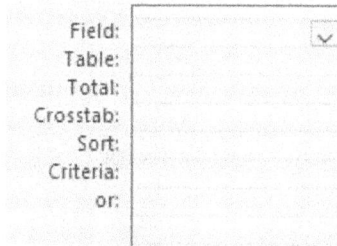

Figure 7.22: Crosstab field used for summarizing and analyzing

The following are some important considerations when using action queries:

- Always back up your database before running an Action Query, as these changes can be hard to undo.

- If possible, test the query on a small subset of data to ensure it behaves as expected.

- Since Action Queries modify data, they should be used carefully. Incorrect use can lead to data loss or corruption.

- Depending on your database settings and environment, you may need special permissions to run Action Queries, especially in a shared or networked database scenario.

- Crosstab queries can significantly aid in interpreting complex data sets, but understanding the underlying data is important to make accurate interpretations.

- One unique aspect of crosstab queries is that the column headings (fields that appear across the top) can change dynamically based on the data. For example, if you summarize monthly sales data, new columns will automatically be created for new months as data is added.

Normalization

After designing a database, it is also vital to ensure that the data in the tables is consistent and relevant. Normalization refers to reducing the redundancy of data in a relational database. In other words, normalization is the process of organizing data (columns, i.e., attributes, and tables, i.e., relations) to minimize the redundancy from a relation or set of relations in a database (*Barick*, 2023).

Redundancy

Repeating data is referred to as redundancy. A crucial component of database normalization and architecture in MS Access is comprehending and controlling redundancy. Unwanted features like Insertion, Update, and Deletion Anomalies are removed via normalization. It creates tiny tables from the main one and connects them with relationships.

Normalization offers several advantages. Fewer NULL values, quicker sorting and index generation, and database compression are all made possible by it. It aids in streamlining the table's structure as well.

The following pointers need to be followed to create a good database design:

- Columns should not have a NULL value.

- Data for a single kind of entity should be kept in each table.

- There ought to be an identity for every table.

- It is best to steer clear of repeating values or columns.

Various types of anomalies and inconsistencies are not introduced in the database, which is ensured by the normal forms (*DBMS Normalization*, 2023). A table structure is always in a definite normal form. The normal form is used to reduce redundancy from the database table. There are several types of normal forms, including 1NF, 2NF, 3NF, BCNF, 4NF, and 5NF (*NF* stands for Normal Form). We will discuss each of these in this section as follows:

Dr. E. F. Codd originally defined the first, second, and third normal forms. Later, *Boyce and Codd* introduced the *Boyce and Codd Normal Form.*

- **First Normal Form (1NF):** A table is said to be in the first normal form when each cell contains only one value. It is shown in the following table:

Student ID	Stream	Subjects	Number of hours (course completion)
A101	Science	Physics	120
		Maths	154
		Chemistry	90
A128	Arts	Geography	100
		English	80
		Hindi	60
A136	Humanities	Civics	101
		History	88

Table 7.2: First Normal Form

The data in the table is not normalized because the cells in the **Subjects** and **Number of hours** columns have more than one value.

By applying the first normal form to the above table, table data can be arranged in each cell so that, according to the definition, each cell contains only one value.

- **Second Normal Form (2NF):** When a table is in the first normal form, and each row's attribute depends functionally on the entire key rather than simply a subset of it, it is said to be in the second normal form. For instance, the entire key, or Employee Code, is functionally dependent upon the employee's data, such as name and birthdate.

- **Third Normal Form (3NF):** When a table is in 2NF and each column name, which is a non-key attribute, depends on the primary key for functionality, the table is said to be in third normal form. For instance, according to 3NF, all non-key characteristics (all columns) must be functionally reliant solely on the primary key, even if one column depends on another, but that column is not the primary key.

- **Boyce and Codd Normal Form (BCNF):** Its goal is to get rid of unwanted features, including insertion, update, and deletion anomalies, and minimize redundancy. Any table is said to be in BCNF if and only if each determinant is a potential key, which extends the concepts of 3NF. Any attribute that is completely functionally dependent on another property is called a **determinant**. It has the names of *Edgar F. Codd* and *Raymond F. Boyce*, two computer scientists.

The following are the key aspects of BCNF:

  o BCNF addresses situations that 3NF does not cover, particularly regarding tables with composite keys (keys made up of more than one column).

  o It aims to eliminate redundancies and anomalies in database tables that could lead to inconsistency. This includes insertion, update, and deletion anomalies.

  o In BCNF, for any non-trivial functional dependency (A → B), A should be a superkey. This means that B is functionally dependent on A, and A is either a candidate key or a superset of a candidate key.

  o Achieving BCNF can sometimes lead to more tables than what one might have in 3NF due to further decomposition. While this enhances data integrity, it might sometimes affect query performance due to the increased number of joins.

Consider a table with attributes (columns), **{StudentID, CourseID, Instructor}**; here, the **StudentID** and **CourseID** can determine the instructor. However, suppose that **CourseID** alone can determine the instructor. In this case, the table is not in BCNF because the instructor depends on the part of the key (**CourseID**) and not the whole key (**StudentID, CourseID**). To convert this table to BCNF, you must split it into two tables to separate these dependencies.

Types of relationships

The term **relationship** is defined between relations (tables). It means that the primary key in one table is a foreign key in another table. In other words, a relationship is defined as **an**

association among the entities. There is a relationship between an employee and a company. It represents that the company has many employees, and an employee serves one department of the company.

There are three types of relationships, **One to One (1:1)**, **One to Many (1:M)**, and **Many to Many (M:M)**.

- **One to one:** In a one to one relationship, one occurrence of an entity belongs to only one occurrence in another entity. For instance, in college, there can be only one principal for one college.

  Figure 7.23 shows one to one relationship:

  Figure 7.23: *One to one relationship*

- **One to many:** In a one to many relationship, one occurrence of an entity belongs to many occurrences in another entity. For instance, one student would have registered for many subjects, as shown in the following figure:

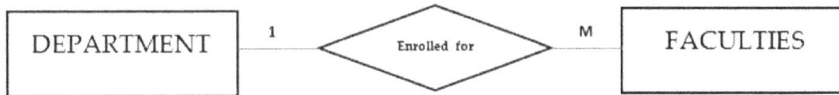

  Figure 7.24: *One to many relationship*

- **Many to many:** In a many to many relationship, many occurrences of an entity belong to many occurrences in another entity. For instance, many students would have registered for many subjects as follows:

  Figure 7.25: *Many to many relationship*

Wildcards in MS Access

In Microsoft Access, wildcards are special characters used in query conditions to represent one or more characters in a string. They are particularly useful in search and filter criteria, allowing for more flexible and powerful search capabilities but with different data. Wildcards can enhance your ability to work with data, especially with text data.

As access supports two different Structured Query Language standards, it can support two sets of wildcard characters, ANSI-92 and ANSI-89. According to regulation, ANSI-89 wildcards ("*" and "?") can be used when performing queries and find-and-replace operations against access databases like ***.mdb** and ***.accdb** files.

When running queries such as access files attached to SQL Server databases, you can use ANSI-92 wildcards ("%", "_").

The following are some common wildcard characters used in the Access database:

- **Asterisk (*):**
  - **Usage:** Represents any number of characters. You can use an asterisk (*) anywhere in a character string.
  - **Example:** LIKE "Comp*" would find "Computer", "Company", "Competition", etc.

- **Question Mark (?)**
  - **Usage:** Represents a single alphabetical character.
  - **Example:** LIKE "Comp?ter" would find "Computer", "CompuTer", etc., but not "Computing".

- **Square Brackets ([ ])**
  - **Usage:** Matches any single character within the brackets.
  - **Example:** LIKE "Comp[uy]ter" would find "Computer" and "Compyter", but not "Compter".

- **Hyphen (-) within Square Brackets**
  - **Usage:** Specifies a range of characters.
  - **Example:** LIKE "C[a-c]t" would find "Cat," "Cbt," and "Cct," but not "Cdt."

- **Exclamation Mark (!) within Square Brackets**
  - **Usage:** Represents any character not in the brackets.
  - **Example:** LIKE "Comp[!a]ter" would find "Compter", "Computer", etc., but not "Computer".

- **Hash (#)**
  - **Usage:** Represents any single numeric character (0-9).
  - **Example:** LIKE "1234#" would match "12345", "12346", etc., but not "1234A".

The following is a wildcard comparison table: ANSI-89 vs ANSI-92:

Wildcard	ANSI-89 (default in MS Access)	ANSI-92 (used in SQL Server)	Usage Example
*	Matches zero or more characters	Not used	Like "Aj" finds Ajay, Ajith
%	Not used	Matches zero or more characters	Like "Aj%" find Ajay, Ajith
?	Matches a single character	Not used	Like "R?te" finds Rate, Rote
_	Not used	Matches a single character	Like "R_te" finds Rate, Rote
!	Matches a single character	Not used	Like "Mi[!a-c]e" finds Mide, Mike but not Miae, Mibe, Mice
#	Matches a single numeric digit (0-9)	Not used	Like "P#2" finds P12, P22, P32

Table 7.3: Comparison of Wildcards used in ANSI-89 and ANSI-92

The following are some essential notes that need to be considered while using Wildcards:

- **Syntax in queries:** Wildcards are typically used within a **LIKE** clause in a query. For example, **SELECT * FROM Table WHERE "FieldName" LIKE "Comp*"**.

- **Note about case sensitivity:** By default, wildcard searches in Access are not case-sensitive.

- **Combining Wildcards:** You can combine wildcards for more complex patterns. For example, **LIKE "A*[!0-9]"** would find any string that starts with "A" and does not end with a number.

- **Different database engines:** If you are using Access with a different database engine (like SQL Server), the wildcards might differ. For instance, SQL Server uses the percent sign (%) instead of the asterisk (*).

Calculated expression

In Microsoft Access, you need to do calculations, which is known as an expression. Operators, constants, functions, and identifiers are examples of expressions. It is possible to compute values with expressions not included in the data. It can define a default value and be used for validating data, like what type of values a user can enter in every column (Introduction to Expressions, 2023).

Let us take an example, if you want to combine the **FirstName** and **LastName** fields in a separate column, then you need to create a calculated field in the table or in a query as follows:

E.g.: **[FirstName] & " " & [LastName].**

Here, ampersand (&) combines the value in the **FirstName** filed, a space character, and the value available in the **LastName** field.

If you want to define a default value for a field, then use the **Date()** function. (It will set the default value for the current date.)

If you want to define a validation for your field, then set the value in the Validation Rule property box: **>=Date()**

You can also use an expression to define the query criteria.

An expression consists of different components that can be used to generate a result (*Examples of Expressions*, 2023).

These components are as given as follows:

- **Identifiers**: An identifier is the field name, control, or property. An identifier can be used to refer to a value in an expression that is associated with a field, property, or control.

- **Functions**: Functions are the built-in procedures that can be used in an expression. There are many functions that can be used to calculate values like sum and average and manipulate text and dates. A few common functions that can be used are as follows:

    o **DATE()** function.
    o **Now()** function.
    o **DateDiff()** function.
    o **DatePart()** function.
    o **Sum()** function.
    o **Average()** function.
    o **Left()** function.
    o **Right()** function.
    o **Min()** & **Max()** function.
    o **Count()** function.
    o **If()** function.
    o **Round()** function.
    o **Concatenate()** function.

    In these functions, you can pass the arguments within the parenthesis.

- **Operators**: There are several operators in Microsoft Access; some of them are listed as follows:

    o Arithmetic operators represent addition, subtraction, multiplication, and division, including +, -, *, and /.

- o When comparing values, comparison operators such as <, >, <=, and >= (less than and more than) are useful.

- o Text operators, such as & and +, are used to join text together.

- o Logic operators for assessing true or false values include AND, OR, and NOT.

- **Values**: Literal values can be used in an expression. When you use text string values, put them within quotation marks to make sure that Access interprets them correctly.

- **Constants**: A constant is a value that can be defined once and cannot be changed. True, False, and Null constants are commonly used in expressions.

Creating form in MS Access

A form can create a user interface for a database application. With the help of forms, users can add, edit, delete, or display the data in a graphical user interface. You can give different designs to your form (Introduction to Forms, 2023).

You can create two basic types of forms:

- **Bound forms**: Bound forms are used to input or amend data in a database and are directly tied to an underlying data source, such as a table, query, or SQL statement.

- **Unbound forms**: These do not have a direct link to an underlying data source or record. To use the application, you may need to interact with dialogue boxes, switchboards, navigation forms, labels, or other controls.

With MS Access, a variety of bound form types can be constructed.

- **Single item form**: The most common form is the single item form, in which each record is shown one at a time.

- **Multiple item form**: This allows for the simultaneous presentation of various records.

- **Split form**: This form is split in half equally, either horizontally or vertically. One-half shows a single item, whereas the other half shows several entries from the underlying data source in a list or datasheet view.

To create a form, go to the **Create** tab and click on **Form**. Access will create and display the form in Layout view, where you can make changes while it shows data. The form can also be created through the **Form Wizard**, which is best for first-time users.

Figure 7.26 shows various elements used in Forms:

Figure 7.26: Form design elements

If you click on **More Forms** under the **Forms** group, you will get multiple options, as follows:

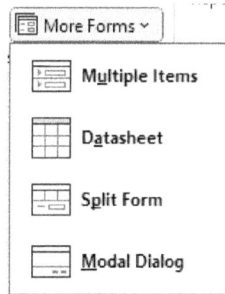

Figure 7.27: Different types of forms

- **Multiple forms**: Creates a form that shows multiple records at once.

- **Datasheet**: Create a form showing multiple records on a datasheet, with one record per row.

- **Split form:** Make a split form with the datasheet displayed in the upper sections and a form view for inputting details about the record that has been selected in the datasheet in the lower portion. When you pick a field in one area of the form, it also gets selected in the other area. When you work with Spilt, you get the advantages of both formats in one.

- **Model dialog**: A model dialog form requires the user to interact with it before they can return to any other part of the application. Model dialog forms capture the user's attention by preventing interactions with other open forms or controls until an action is completed. They are often used to collect critical information from users.

Modifying a form

Upon creating a form, it is essential to use the controls on the form. Controls are used to display data and perform actions or items used for decorations, such as a line.

The following menu will help design the form layout. You have controls listed under the controls group. *Figure 7.28* shows various controls that can be used in creating a form:

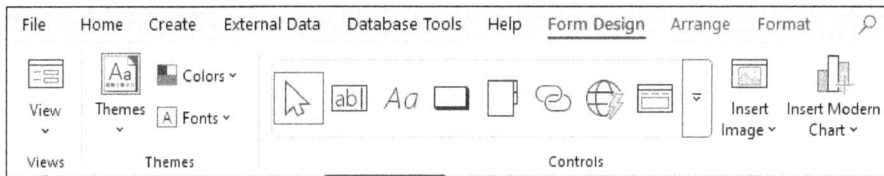

Figure 7.28: Various controls available in MS Access

- **Text box control**: It displays text, numbers, date, time, and alphanumeric data.
- **Label**: It is used for label controls that contain fixed text.

- **Command button**: This control activates a macro and navigates back and forth in the form. You can also link a hyperlink address when a user clicks the button.

- **Link**: Use this option to add a hyperlink to the form.

- **Web browser**: This control is used to display the content of web pages directly inside the form.

- **Image**: This control uploads any image from the browser or local device.

- **Check box**: It is used to hold an on/off value. A true/false or yes/no value is used to check the box.

- **Chart**: Use the chart control to add a chart to the form grid.

- **Combo box**: This control contains a list of potential values for the control and an editable text box.

- **List box**: This control contains a list of potential values for the control.

- **Line**: It adds lines to a form to enhance appearance.

- **Navigation**: This is used to give users a simple method to access the many reports and forms in your database.

Creating reports in MS Access

Reports provide a summary of information from your database. Reports can be customized based on specific business needs through filters, grouping, sorting, and conditional formatting. If reports are created for sales and revenue, it will summarize daily, weekly, or monthly sales using grouped reports. To create a report in Access, go to the **Create** menu and click on any of the tools available in the **Reports** group.

Figure 7.29 illustrates various types of reports:

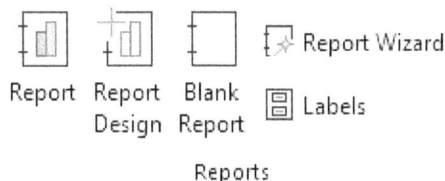

Figure 7.29: *Different types of reports available in MS Access*

The following is a description of what the aforementioned report tool does and the record source types that are created by default:

- **Report**: All the fields from the data source will be included in a straightforward tabular report that is created. Before you click the tool, you must select a table or named query in the **Navigation** pane.

- **Report Design**: It will launch a blank report in the design view, allowing you to add controls and fields according to the specifications. From the property sheet's record source drop-down list, you may choose a table or named query. If you drag fields from the field list task pane, the embedded query is the default record source type.

- **Report Blank**: Access opens a blank report in the Layout view and shows the Task Pane for the filed list, where you can drag fields to the report.

- **Report Wizard**: This is the easiest way to create a report. It displays multiple steps that allow you to specify fields, grouping/sorting levels, and choose layout options. The wizard will provide you with the report according to the selections you make. It will ask you to add data from either one or more than one table. The data source will depend on your table selection.

- **Labels**: It displays a wizard that allows you to select standard or custom label sizes and the fields you want to display in the report. Again, you must select the table or named query before clicking on the tool.

Microsoft Access Reports can be integrated with Excel, PowerPoint, and Word, and you can easily share them via email.

Note: **While creating reports, data can be highlighted by using conditional formatting rules for each control or group of controls. From the Layout View, various themes can be applied, and the preview can be checked. It depends upon the user whether you want to add a logo or any background image to a report.**

Record sources to create reports in MS Access

The **record source** is an essential element that determines where and how the data for the report is retrieved. Reports give you the flexibility to reassemble the data and display it. You need to select three main record sources while creating a report, as follows:

- **Table**: A table is used as an existing table in your database as the record source. It is ideal when your report data comes directly from a single table without the need for complex filtering, calculations, or joining data from multiple tables. For instance, a report listing all items in an inventory table.

- **Named query**: A named query is also called a query that has been saved as a database object. Queries allow more complex data manipulation, including filtering, sorting, and combining data from multiple tables. They are best for reports requiring aggregated data, specific filtering, or data from multiple tables. For instance, a sales report aggregating sales data by region and month requires data from sales and region tables.

- **Embedded query**: An embedded query is automatically generated whenever you utilize the labels, blank report, or Report Design tools. If you choose data for the report from many tables, it can also be created using the report wizard.

The following are the best practices for selecting a record source:

- **Clarity and maintenance**: Use the simplest source that meets your needs. Queries are often preferred over SQL statements for ease of understanding and maintenance.

- **Performance considerations**: Direct table sources can be faster but need to be more flexible. Queries and SQL statements offer more power but can be more resource-intensive, especially with large datasets.

- **Dynamic data needs**: For reports that require runtime data determination (like based on user input), consider using form controls or VBA-generated record sets.

Conclusion

By the end of this chapter, we must reflect on the fundamental components and concepts that make it such a powerful tool in data management and analysis.

We covered the core components of RDBMS and how Microsoft Access implements these to provide a robust and user-friendly environment. Creating databases and tables in MS Access was demystified, highlighting the process's simplicity and intuitiveness yet underscoring the importance of thoughtful design. We understood how to structure data in tables efficiently. Query creation, a cornerstone of data management in Access, was explored in depth. We discussed how normalization in Access streamlines database design and enhances performance and maintainability. Relationships are the heart of a relational database system like Access. They enable the system to draw meaningful connections and insights from disparate data points, transforming raw data into valuable information.

In the next chapter, we will discuss Microsoft Teams, a powerful application that is used to connect with colleagues and share data on the Teams site. This application serves as a collaborative workspace chat platform, unifying individuals, discussions, and documents within a single environment.

References

1. Barick, A. (2023). *Normalization Process in DBMS*. GeeksforGeeks. **https://www. geeksforgeeks.org/normalization-process-in-dbms/**

2. *Create a database in Access*. (2023). Microsoft Support. **https://support.microsoft.com/ en-us/office/create-a-database-in-access-f200d95b-e429-4acc-98c1-b883d4e9fc0a?wt. mc_id=otc_access**

3. *Data types for Access desktop databases*. (2023). Microsoft Support. **https://support. microsoft.com/en-us/office/data-types-for-access-desktop-databases-df2b83ba-cef6-436d-b679-3418f622e482**

4. *Database basics*. (2023). Microsoft Support. **https://support.microsoft.com/en-us/office/ database-basics-a849ac16-07c7-4a31-9948-3c8c94a7c204**

5. *DBMS Normalization.* (2023). Javatpoint. **https://www.javatpoint.com/dbms-normalization#Types%20of%20Normal%20Forms**

6. *Examples of expressions.* (2023). Microsoft Support. **https://support.microsoft.com/en-us/office/examples-of-expressions-d3901e11-c04e-4649-b40b-8b6ec5aed41f#bmcalculatedfields**

7. *Introduction to expressions.* (2023). Microsoft Support. **https://support.microsoft.com/en-us/office/introduction-to-expressions-5cad6e24-65a3-4a95-82cc-92b4b1bd4b8b**

8. *Introduction to forms.* (2023). Microsoft Support. **https://support.microsoft.com/en-us/office/introduction-to-forms-e8d47343-c937-44e8-a80f-b6a83a1fa3ae#bmsimpleformtool**

9. *Introduction to tables.* (2023). Microsoft Support. **https://support.microsoft.com/en-us/office/introduction-to-tables-78ff21ea-2f76-4fb0-8af6-c318d1ee0ea7**

10. Microsoft Learn. (2023). *Data manipulation language (Microsoft Access SQL).* Microsoft. **https://learn.microsoft.com/en-us/office/client-developer/access/desktop-database-reference/data-manipulation-language**

11. Peterson, R. (2023, December 9). *SQL Commands: DML, DDL, DCL, TCL, DQL with Query Example.* GURU99. **https://www.guru99.com/sql-commands-dbms-query.html**

12. *Primary Keys and Foreign Keys in Access.* (2023). CDA Computer Tips. **https://cdacomputer.tips/primary-keys-and-foreign-keys-in-access/?doing_wp_cron=1704200429.2934861183166503906250**

13. Terra, J. (2023, April 24). *What is Microsoft Access? An Introductory Guide.* Simplilearn. **https://www.simplilearn.com/what-is-microsoft-access-article**

Join our Discord space

Join our Discord workspace for latest updates, offers, tech happenings around the world, new releases, and sessions with the authors:

https://discord.bpbonline.com

CHAPTER 8

Transforming Learning with Microsoft Teams

Introduction

Microsoft Teams stands out as the most demanding application within the Microsoft 365 suite. It is a workspace chat application that brings people, conversations, and files into a single location and enables everyone on your team to have instant access to collaborative data files, conversation history, and much more. It seamlessly integrates with other Office 365 including office online tools and SharePoint. Furthermore, it is designed to be mobile-friendly, serving as a central hub for collaboration rather than merely a chat application.

In this chapter, you will explore the various types of channels and meetings available in Microsoft Teams. The discussion will encompass notification management and a range of features, including presenter modes, different icons, and the integration of third-party applications like weather, praise, stock, places, it, and much more.

Structure

In this chapter, we will discuss the following topics:

- Overview of Microsoft Teams
- Microsoft Teams interface
- Comparing standard, private, and shared channel

- Activity in Teams
- Types of meetings in Teams
- Types of presenter modes
- Different views during Microsoft Teams meetings
- Set your status in Teams
- Manage notifications in Microsoft Teams
- M365 Copilot in Microsoft Teams
- Mobile version of MS Teams

Objectives

By the end of this chapter, you will gain a foundational understanding of Microsoft Teams and its role in facilitating collaboration, communication, and productivity within organizations. You will explore the layout and components, including the navigation element, chat features, different types of channels and their use cases, and how to decide which type to use for different collaboration scenarios. You will learn different meeting views, including Gallery, Large Gallery, Together Mode, and Focus Mode, and how to customize your view to suit your needs along with the presenter modes. We have also introduced Copilot, an AI-powered assistant in Teams that can help streamline workflows and enhance productivity.

Overview of Microsoft Teams

Microsoft Teams is the hub for teamwork. It is a cross-functional application that promotes collaboration and communication in Microsoft 365 and integrates the people, content, and tools your team needs to be more engaged and effective. Teams bring everything together in a shared workspace where you can chat, meet, share files, and work with business apps.

Microsoft Teams is the digital hub that brings conversations, content, assignments, and applications together in one place. It performs various functions, including text and video, conference calls, and file storage. With an A3 license, you can promote equity and student voice with collaborative classrooms, connect in professional learning communities, and communicate with staff, all from a single experience in Microsoft 365 Education.

A central location for every type of teamwork, connect to professional learning communities to continue lifelong learning. Streamline staff communication using custom Staff Notebooks and conferences in any meeting with HD video, VoIP, and dial-in audio conferencing options.

It is also the perfect location for working on projects with colleagues, curriculum adoptions, or even whole organization initiatives.

Microsoft Teams is designed to make managing workstreams easier and more intuitive. *Figure 8.1* illustrates the functions of MS Teams.

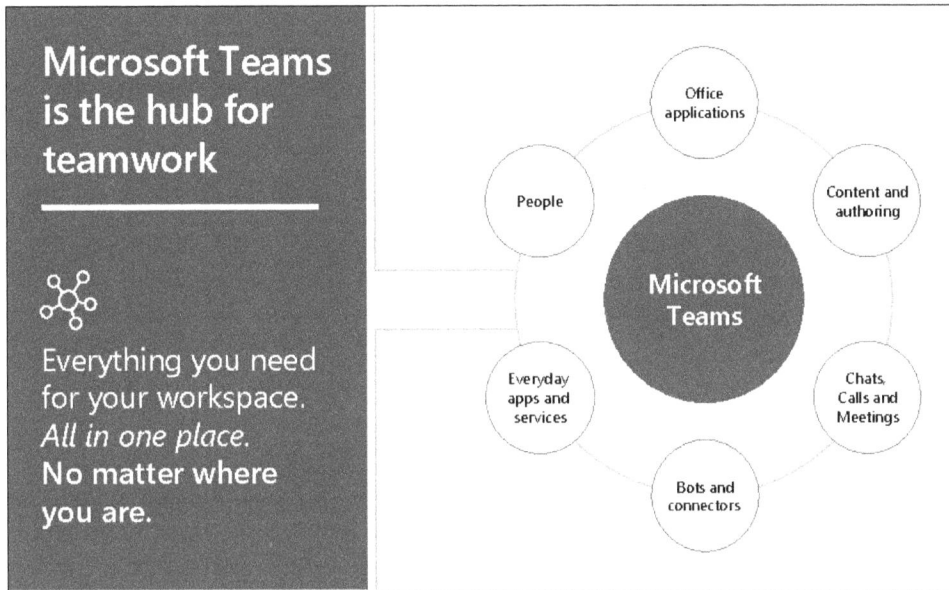

Figure 8.1: *Hub for teamwork in Microsoft Teams*

Note: **After March 31, 2024, users still on classic Teams will be automatically upgraded to the new Teams experience.**

Advantages of Microsoft Teams

Integration is possible with Office applications along with third-party applications. Private chat and group chat are possible. Communicate with everyone (Employees, end users, and everyone in the organization) on a single platform. It offers various features like uploading files, pinning favorite teams or channels, checking for insights, assignments, and grading available for A3 licenses like educational institutions. Communicate with everyone on a single platform. Schedule online meetings/webinars/Live meetings with support up to various numbers of attendees, respectively.

Once the user schedules a Webinar, it can be published on the SharePoint site, on the blog, or in the public domain so that users can register directly for it and receive a calendar invite. High-level security is available, and 1:1 group online audio and video calls can be done.

As a part of Microsoft Office 365 suite, apps such as Microsoft Word, Microsoft Excel, Microsoft PowerPoint, Microsoft Outlook, Microsoft OneNote, Microsoft Publisher (PC only), and Microsoft Access (PC only) can be integrated seamlessly. This integration allows users to access and collaborate on files directly within Teams, streamlining workflows and improving productivity. Inform and engage with communication sites and team sites throughout your(organization) intranet using SharePoint. Enterprise video service for securely creating, managing, and sharing videos across an organization.

Microsoft Teams is suitable for businesses of all sizes, from small teams to large enterprises. It offers scalability and flexibility to accommodate organizations' growing needs, whether they are expanding their workforce, adding new departments, or entering new markets. With the rise of remote work, Teams provides essential tools and features to support remote collaboration, including virtual meetings, screen sharing, and remote desktop access. This enables teams to stay connected and productive regardless of their physical location.

Microsoft Teams prioritizes security and compliance, offering robust data encryption, multi-factor authentication, and compliance with industry standards and regulations such as GDPR and HIPAA. This ensures that sensitive information shared within Teams remains secure and protected.

Microsoft Teams interface

In the given figure, on the left side, you will find some icons available, namely Activity, Chat, Teams, Calendar, Files, and many more. With the help of the Apps icon, you can add Microsoft 365 or third-party applications in Microsoft Teams. A search bar at the top of the screen helps you find colleagues, files, team chat, or channel conversations. Here, you can use the **slash (/)command** for shortcuts. Teams offer a robust collaboration feature called teams and channels. Microsoft creates specific workspaces for the team to collaborate and produce work collectively. It provides a structured way to organize and manage workspaces, content, and groups of people.

Figure 8.2 illustrates the interface of MS Teams:

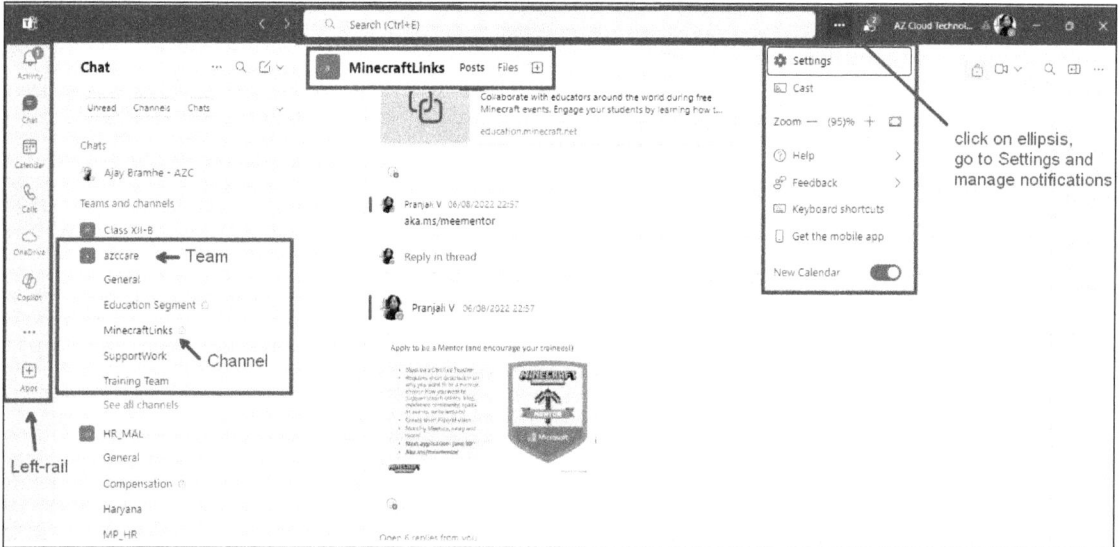

Figure 8.2: Microsoft Teams interface

The options presented in *Figure 8.2* are outlined as follows, along with a comprehensive explanation like Teams and channels are available on the left-rail and associated contents are available on the right-hand side. There is a **Search box** also available at the top of Microsoft Teams to search or use slash commands (For instance, use forward slash /, and a list of all commands will be displayed). On the top right-hand side, click on three dots to manage different types of Settings like notifications, audio and video, etc.

- **Teams:** The aforementioned image shows various teams. A team is a group of people gathered for discussion. Teams are made up of channels, which are the conversations you have with your colleagues. Once you create a team, the **General** channel is available by default. You can create more channels according to project requirements. Teams can have standard, private, or shared channels. Each team has its own dedicated SharePoint, known as Teams Site, and each channel will have a dedicated folder to maintain documents for that workspace, known as document library. By default, all members of a team can create channels. A standard channel is public for all, and anything posted is searchable. You can create up to 1000 channels over the life of a team. It includes channels you create and delete later. You can't convert a standard channel to a private channel and vice versa.

  You can create private channels if you need to discuss sensitive information. Once you create a private channel, it is linked to the parent team and cannot be moved to a different team. It is identified with a lock beside it. Private channels within a Team are accessible only to owners and members specifically added to them. Each Team can have up to 30 private channels throughout its existence. Owners have the authority to manage membership by adding or removing members from private channels. These channels can have multiple owners and accommodate up to 250 members.

  However, there are certain limitations associated with private channels. For instance, scheduling meetings directly within a private channel is not possible. External guests can join a meeting only if a member of the private channel shares a meeting link with them. During the meeting, guests have temporary access to chat, files, and Whiteboard features, but this access is not retained after the meeting concludes.

  Furthermore, files shared within a private channel are exclusively viewable by channel members and are stored separately in SharePoint from the rest of the team's files.

- **Channels:** A channel is a term given to an area within Teams where you and your colleagues can communicate around a specified subject. Think of a channel as being a topic, department, or project. When a team is created, a **General** channel is generated by default. At present, you cannot rename or delete this default channel. Channels are listed in alphabetical order, with the General channel positioned at the top. You cannot hide the General channel. It can also be used to share an overview of what the team wants to achieve or other high-level information through an announcement feature. A team can have up to 200 channels. Clicking on the channel name will display the conversations in the main area of the window (*First Things to Know about Channels in Microsoft Teams*, 2024).

- **Edit, delete, hide, or leave a channel:** When you delete a channel, its entire conversation history is lost. Although channels can be restored within 21 days, it is important to note that during this period, no new channels can be created with the same name as the deleted ones. Additionally, you will still find OneNote sections associated with the deleted channels on your team's SharePoint site. To manage channels, select **More options**… next to the channel name, where you can edit, delete, hide, or leave the channel.

- **Chat vs Channel:** Chats are usually used as one to one or in a group or pull together up to 250 participants in a chat. Chat in Teams is fast, intuitive, and has guilt functionality that is easy to adopt. While communicating via chat, anyone can share a screen, add to a chat, and share all or part of the chat history (*First Things to Know about Chats in Microsoft Teams*, 2024). Chats are intended for instant messaging and sending files, links, emojis, stickers, and GIFs. In contrast, Channel Posts are threaded and intended to maintain context throughout an ongoing conversation, and yes, conversations are still **persistent**. Channels function within teams like how files reside within folders. They serve as open spaces for transparent collaboration, allowing the entire team to participate and access shared resources. **Standard channels** are accessible to all team members, providing centralized interaction. In contrast, **private channels** are reserved for discussions that should only be visible to some. Additionally, **shared channels** facilitate collaboration with individuals both inside and outside your team or organization (*Create a Standard, Private, or Shared Channel in Microsoft Teams*, 2024).

- **Posts and Files:** When you go to any channel, the first visible tabs are **Posts** and **Files**. Whosoever has access to the channel can view the messages on the **Posts** tab. Here, threaded conversations can be made, which means team members can revert to a channel message and stay attached to the original message. Next is the **Files** tab, where all the team members' files are stored or uploaded. You can add more tabs by selecting the + icon.

Comparing standard, private, and shared channel

In Microsoft Teams, varying names of channels bring distinct features and functionalities for users to leverage their utmost potential. As the name suggests, standard channels provide an open platform where all team members can participate and collaborate with each other, promote transparency, and share the resources that are stored in the team's document library. However, private channels are useful for scheduling confidential discussions and thus confined only to a group of team members. Lastly, shared channels do not need to create a guest account for having inter/intra collaboration and are best suitable for cross-organization partnerships.

The following table elaborates clear differences between the types of channels:

Features available in channel	Standard channel	Private channel	Shared channel
Moderation can happen	Yes	No	No
Copy link to channel	Yes	No	No
Schedule Meetings	Yes	No	Yes
Integration of Planner Application	Yes	No	No
Extension of bots, connectors and messaging	Yes	No	No
Analytics is available	Yes	Yes	No
Tags can be done	Yes	No	No
Guest can participate in channel	Yes	Yes	No
People can be added to the channel without adding them to the team	No	No	Yes
Channel membership is limited to a subset of the team	No	Yes	Yes
Channels can be shared directly with other teams	No	No	Yes

Table 8.1: Comparison of channels

- **Restrictions with private channels**: Private channels are accessed only by owners or members of the private channel. It can be used to create focused spaces for team collaboration. You can identify a private channel through a lock icon associated with it. Only members of the private channel can see and participate in all channel communication. When creating a private channel, it remains associated with the parent team and cannot be transferred to a different team. Notably, private channels cannot be converted into standard channels, nor can standard channels be turned into private channels. The individual who initiates a private channel becomes its owner, and only the owner has the authority to directly add or remove members. Additionally, the private channel owner can delete the channel, which can be restored within 30 days after deletion.

  Note: **If a private channel owner leaves your organization or is removed from the Microsoft 365 group associated with the team, a member of the private channel is automatically promoted to become the new private channel owner.**

- **Private channel settings:** Private channel settings are managed separately from the parent team settings. The owner has the authority to add or remove members, integrate tabs, and utilize **@mentions** within the entire channel. While private channels initially inherit settings from the parent team, these settings can be modified independently thereafter.

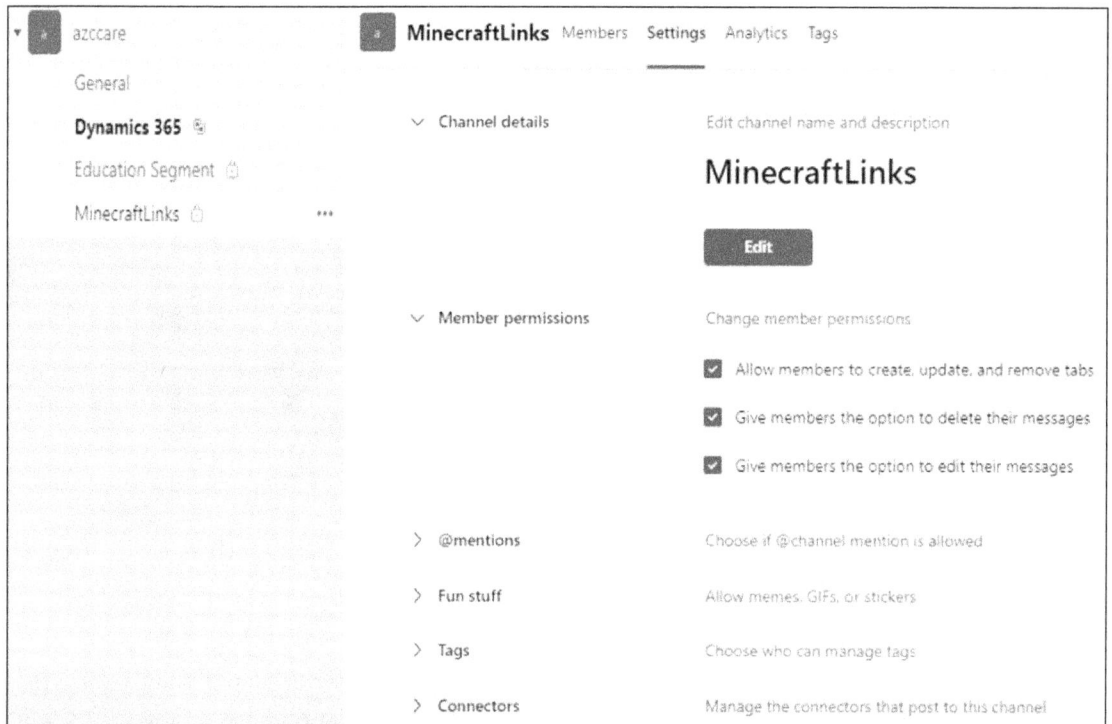

Figure 8.3: Private channel settings

To manage the channel, go to private channel | click on **...** dots | Select **Settings** tab. From here, the owner can add or remove members and edit settings.

- **Private channel SharePoint sites**: Each private channel is associated with a distinct SharePoint site. The purpose of the separate site is to ensure that only private channel users may access the files. By default, these sites include a document library, which can be easily enhanced through the site administration interface to become fully functional websites. Each site is developed within the same geographical area as the parent team's site.

- **Channel notification:** To manage channel notifications, select the channel | select **...** (ellipsis) | **Channel notifications**. This will allow you to manage all new posts and whenever anyone mentions a channel name. Notifications will be sent to your mobile and to Activity, located at the upper left corner of the Teams app when you select **Custom** | **Banner and Feed**. Feed will appear in your activity feed and will not send notifications to your desktop. *Figure 8.4* shows the **Channel notifications** for any of the channels present in Teams.

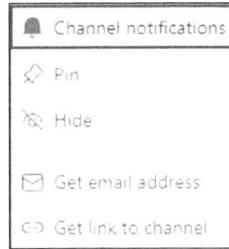

Figure 8.4: Channel notification of specific channel

Activity in Teams

The **Activity** tab is located at the top left corner of the Teams application (in the left rail). *Figure 8.5* shows the icon:

Activity

Figure 8.5: Activity icon present in MS Teams

It enables you to focus on all your important events, notifications, or actions taking place across the teams, channels, chats, and apps you have access to. If someone notifies you, that is also available in the **Activity** tab. It keeps track of everything that is happening in the Teams channels or chats so that we do not miss anything (for example, someone replied to your post in a channel or someone mentioned you in Teams). It is represented by a bell icon with a number in the red circle to inform you about the number of notifications.

Configuring the activity feed in Teams

You can configure the activity feed from the settings of the logged-in user. Go to your profile icon | Click on ellipsis (**...**) | select **Settings**. A dialog box will open. Select the **Notifications and Activity** option from the left-hand side, as shown in *Figure 8.6*:

Settings

Figure 8.6: Associated Settings for activity feed

You can now set notifications for missed activity emails, chat notifications, channel notifications, likes and reactions, replies to my channel post, and replies, as well as meeting notifications. *Figure 8.7* shows the settings for notification and every notification will be displayed in the **Activity** tab, as shown in the following:

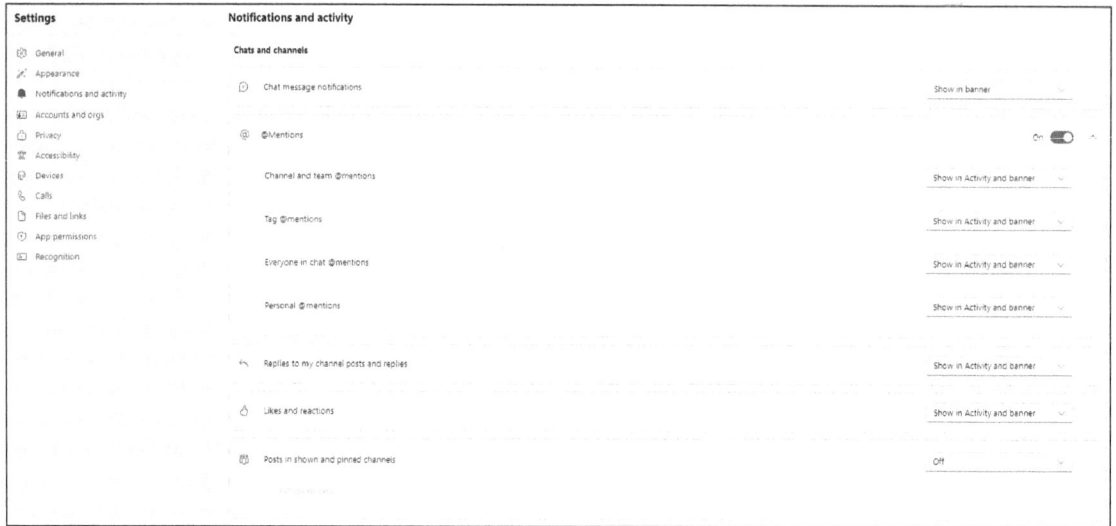

Figure 8.7: Notifications and activity

Filtering the activity feed

You can filter your **Activity** based on the type of notification you want to see, such as mentions, likes, or replies, as shown in *Figure 8.8*:

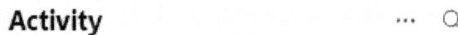

Figure 8.8: Three dots to filter the activity feed

Navigate to the **Activity** button to see the activity feed, and we can select the **Filter** button to show only certain types of messages there, as illustrated in *Figure 8.9*.

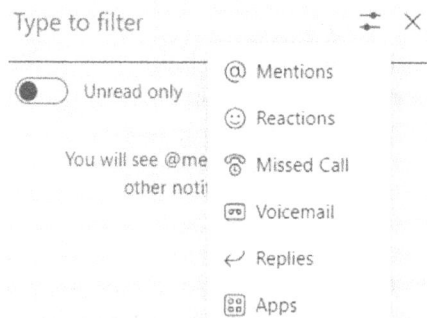

Figure 8.9: Activity filter options

It does not give us the option to perform a deep filter, such as checking the **@Mention** notification for a particular date range or from a specific person.

If anyone mentions you in Teams using the *@ sign*, if someone reacts to your message, if someone calls you and you miss that call, or if you have a voicemail, you will be notified by the **Activity** tab.

We have a search box at the top of Microsoft Teams where we can use slash commands to search for specific items, as shown in the following figure:

For instance, Type **/unread** in the search bar to view your unread channel notifications, or Type **/mentions** to view all your **@mentions**.

Figure 8.10: Search box available at top of MS Teams

We can click on the ellipses of any feed to manage it (for example, mark a notification as read or unread). *Figure 8.11* shows the activity feed icons available in Teams.

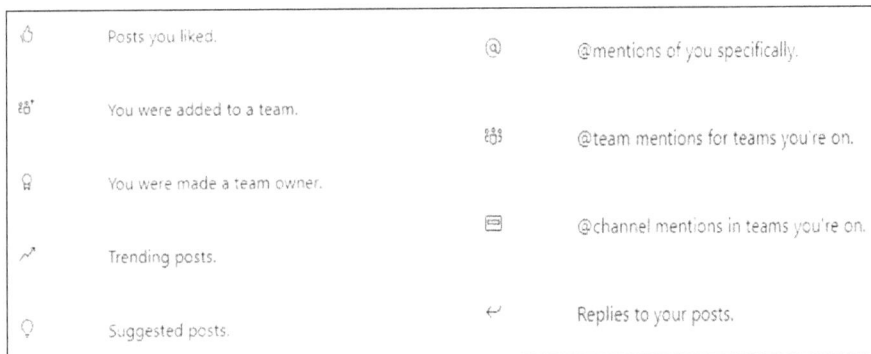

Figure 8.11: Activity feed icons

The advantages and disadvantages of the **Activity** tab are that you will always stay up to date with notifications and better focus on all important activities. Sometimes, irrelevant notifications disturb you, and they cannot be turned off. If you are a part of any Teams, you will automatically receive the notifications.

Types of meetings in Teams

On the left-hand panel of the Teams application, go to the **Calendar** option through which you can schedule different types of meetings. Team Meetings can also be scheduled through Outlook. The Exchange calendar and your calendar in Teams are linked. Put differently, a meeting that you set up in Outlook will appear in Teams and vice versa. Every meeting that is arranged in Teams gets converted to an online meeting by default.

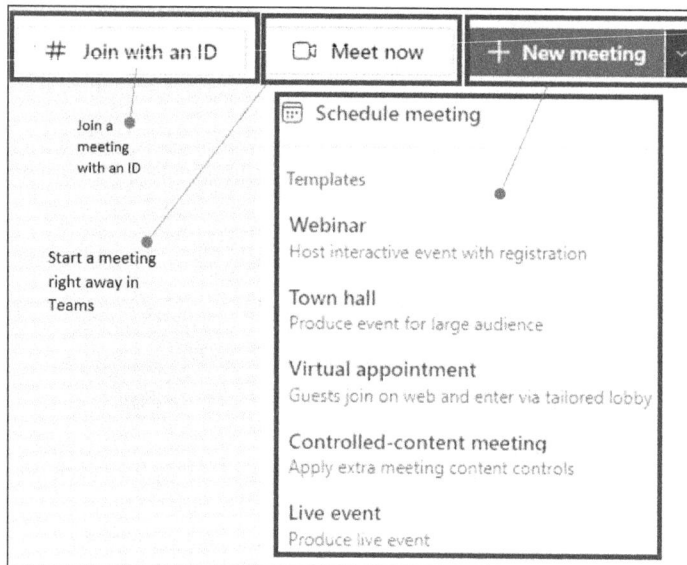

Figure 8.12: Types of Meetings

Here, we will discuss different types of meetings, such as Schedule meetings, Webinars, Town Hall (formerly known as Live Events), Virtual appointments, Controlled-content meetings, and Live events (which will be decommissioned by the end of 2024).

Schedule meetings

The calendar option is available in the navigation bar from the side rail, which helps to schedule a normal meeting, or a meeting can be scheduled within the channel itself. Scheduled meetings are visible in the Outlook calendar; this means all your meetings are stored in a single location, but multiple apps can display how your day looks (apps include Outlook, Teams, and Calendar). When you create a new meeting, you will be given a new screen asking for necessary meeting details like the **title** of the meeting, **required attendees**, **date**, **and time**; select the **recurring type**, and if the meeting is to be placed in the Channel, then select the **Add Channel** option. You can also add additional information about the meeting in the **editor box** at the bottom of the page. When finished, select the **Send** button in the upper-right corner. Your attendees will automatically receive an email about the scheduled meeting. You can use the **Scheduling Assistant** if you find it challenging to find a mutually convenient time. *Figure 8.13* shows the **Schedule Meeting** option available in MS Teams.

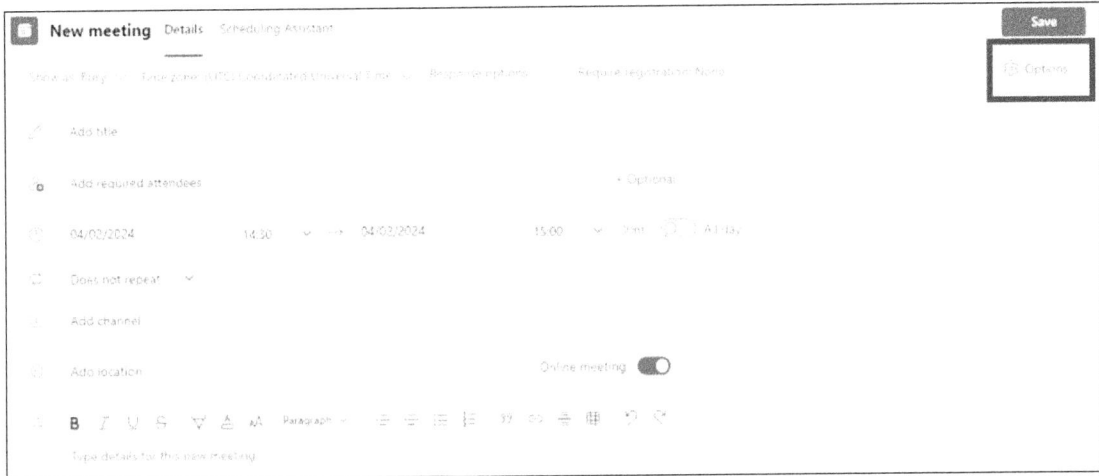

Figure 8.13: Schedule a meeting

After a meeting is scheduled, click on **Meeting options** to change the settings. Meeting options can be set before or during meetings (*Meeting Options in Microsoft Teams*, 2024), illustrated in *Figure 8.14*.

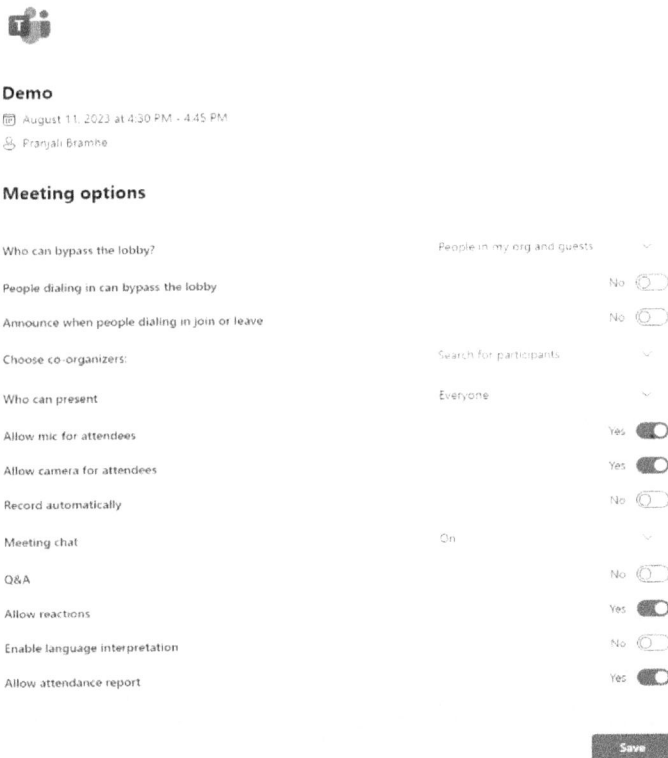

Figure 8.14: Meeting options

Organizers can set these settings according to their preference to enable specific capabilities during a meeting. Various **meeting options** show the engagement and interaction of participants during a meeting. Once you are done, select **Save.**

The subsequent options will be available solely when a meeting has been scheduled and the user wishes to modify the meeting settings. We will find the descriptions for each of the available options as follows:

- **Who can bypass the lobby?:** This option will decide who gets into the meeting directly and who should wait to be let in by using the lobby. After enabling, people from trusted organizations can bypass the lobby. They need not wait in the lobby.

- **People dialing in can bypass the lobby**: By enabling the toggle, anyone can join the meeting by phone to enter immediately without waiting in the lobby. This feature will help reduce the number of people waiting and streamline the flow of the lobby easily.

- **Announce when people dial in to join or leave:** By enabling it, it will receive alerts when people dial in to join or leave the meeting if you want to keep track of who is still in your meeting and who has left.

- **Choose co-organizers**: The Organizer can select a co-organizer to manage the meeting.

- **Who can present**: This option is available to manage who will present during the meeting. If you have a co-organizer's name, add the name to the list.

- **Allow mic for attendees**: If it is enabled, participants can unmute and participate in the meeting.

- **Allow camera for attendees**: If it is enabled, participants can turn off their cameras during the meeting.

- **Record automatically**: Once it is on, recording will start automatically.

- **Meeting chat**: If it is *on*, it will allow participants to chat during the meeting. If it is **Off**, it will not allow me to participate in the meeting. If it is **In-meeting only**, it will allow participants to chat only during the meeting.

- **Q&A**: It will allow attendees to ask questions and post replies during a meeting and make the event/session more interactive.

- **Allow reactions**: Participants can use emojis to express their emotions.

- **Enable language interpretation**: By enabling, it allows you to add a professional interpreter who can translate the speaker's language into another in real-time.

- **Allow attendance report**: After enabling, the attendee report is available. Attendance reports can contain meeting details, duration of the meeting, and more.

A few factors that need to be considered in a meeting are as follows:

- **Before:** Setting the stage and exchanging agendas prior to the meeting are essential for its success. Each team meeting has a unique dialogue. Before the meeting, participants can communicate and share content. You can bring that discussion and its contents right into the meeting.

- **During a meeting:** After the meeting starts, participants can make use of a number of tools that promote inclusivity, increase focus, and increase involvement. These consist of a digital Whiteboard, real-time document collaboration, coauthoring with Office 365 apps, screen sharing, high-fidelity audio and video, and live captioning. Using Whiteboards for idea sharing and brainstorming is facilitated by team gatherings.

- **After the meeting:** All of the meeting materials are kept in the meeting chat after the meeting, allowing attendees to evaluate and advance the work. The chat area also offers features for recording meetings and attendance.

Webinar

Webinar in Microsoft Teams allows you to manage events, manage attendee registration, and go live with an interactive presentation. Webinars are more structured because, as an organizer, you need to fill out the details and customize the registration page and theming. Furthermore, you can personalize your event by adding a presenter bio and the look of your site. Later, publish the link either on a SharePoint page blog or website where users can view the details about the event and register themselves for the same. Once participants register for the event, they will receive an email with a `.ics` file. It means after registering, they will receive a calendar invite *(Get Started with Microsoft Teams Webinars*, 2024).

Note: **By default, audio and video permissions are turned off for attendees.**

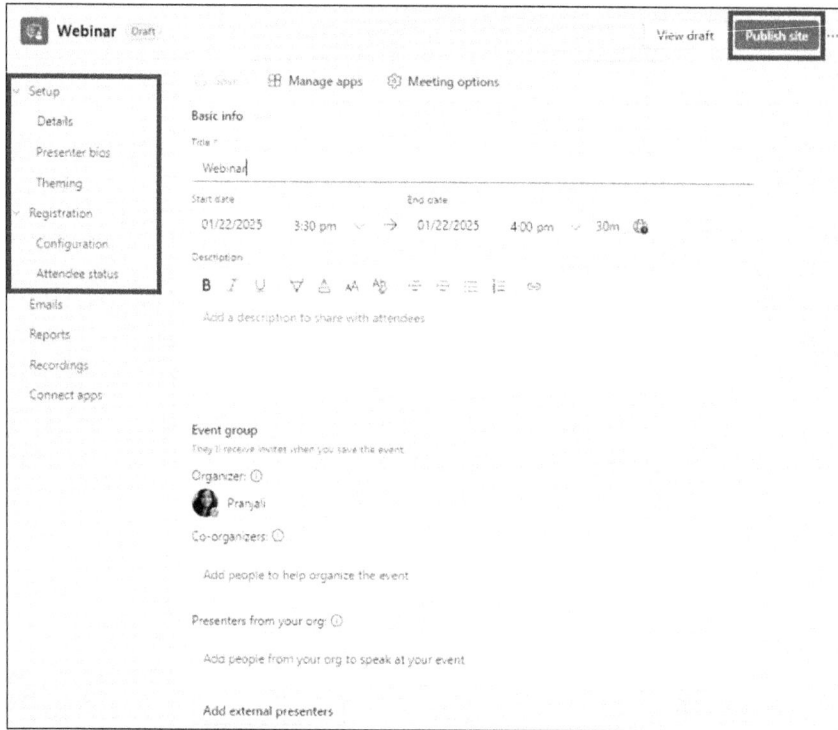

Figure 8.15: *Scheduling a Webinar*

Important features of Webinar

The following are the various significant attributes associated with a Webinar:

- **Registration:** Use registration settings like event capacity (for setting limits) can be checked and managed. Make a customized form with questions for prospective guests to get more information about your audience.

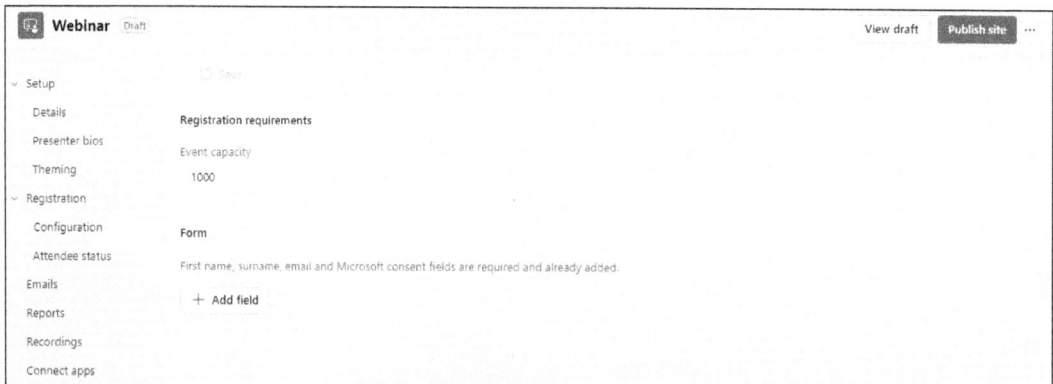

Figure 8.16: *Setup Registration*

- Using the attendee status, you can gain an overview of your event registration. To manage the Webinar, go to **Registration | Attendee status**, as displayed in the following figure. You can check the registered participants by clicking on **Attendee status** as shown in the following figure:

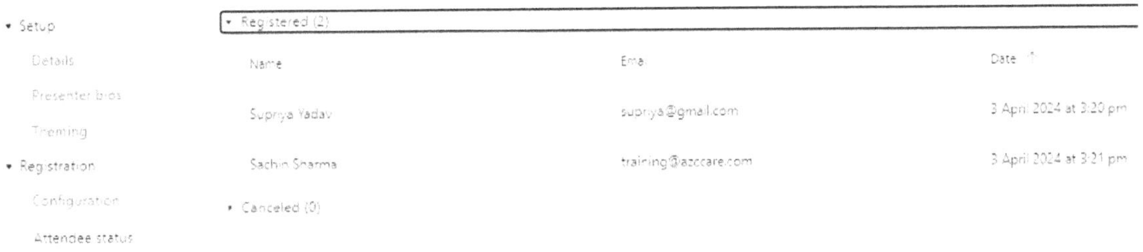

Figure 8.17: Registered Participants

Once the event page has been published on the SharePoint site, users can view it. Organizers can also distribute live registration links via various social media networks. *Figure 8.18* shows the published event page.

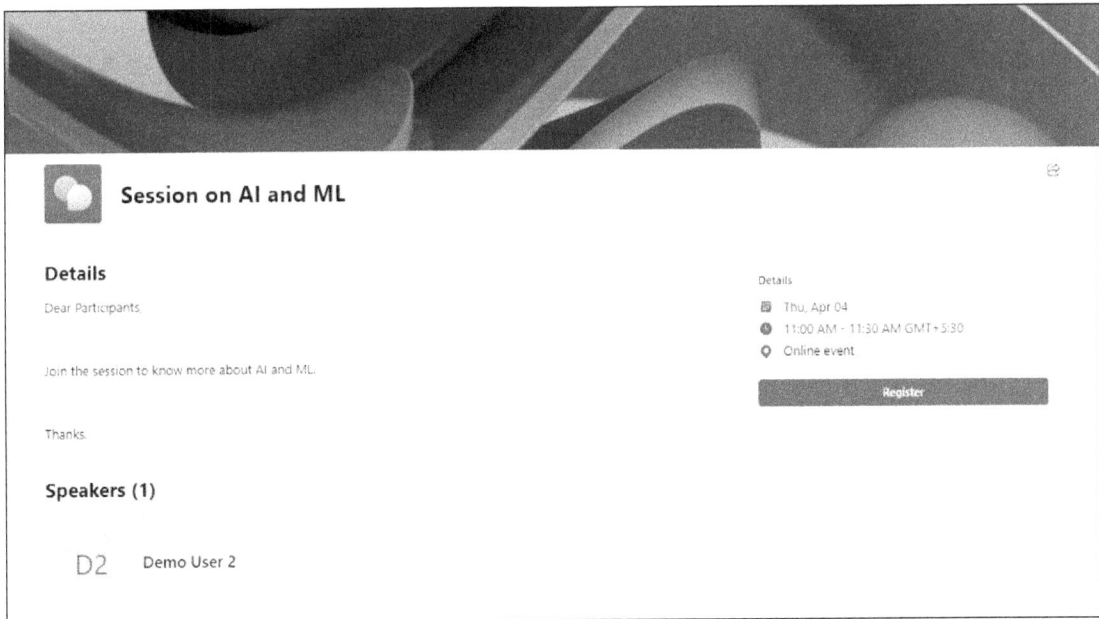

Figure 8.18: Event page

Once users register for the event, they will receive an email and confirmation message, as shown in the following figure:

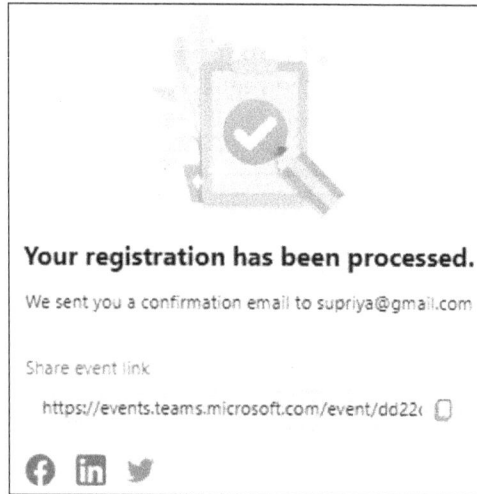

Figure 8.19: Registration confirmation message

- **Lock a meeting**: In Teams, organizers can select to lock their meeting to prevent subsequent join attempts. No one will be allowed to attend the meeting after it is locked, but those invited can still access the chat, recording, and other meeting materials. Once you are in a meeting, select **Participants | … | Lock the meeting.**

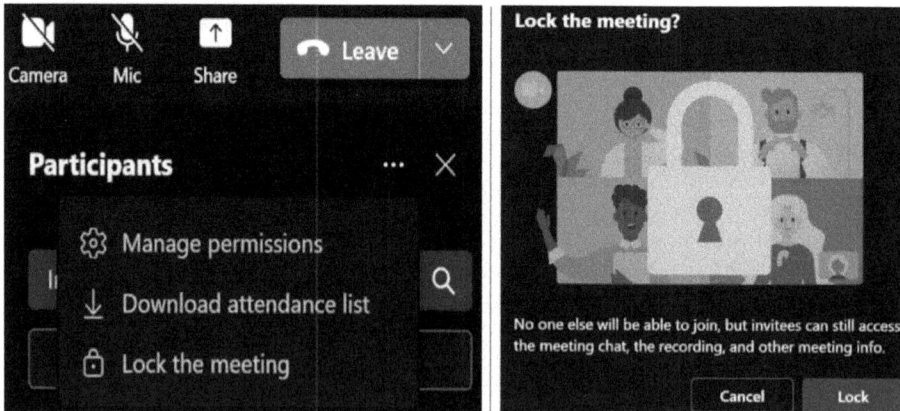

Figure 8.20: Lock a meeting

Town hall

A town hall (**formerly known as Live Events**) is a new type of meeting in Teams that will replace Teams live events by September 30, 2024. Town hall provides a dynamic and inclusive platform to engage the customers or end-users on a large scale. Town hall facilitates company-wide communication, enabling leadership to share important updates, annual town hall meetings, strategic initiatives, etc. Town hall events in Teams would allow leaders to engage their workforce transparently and engagingly through robust features like live video broadcasts, interactive Q&A sessions, and real-time polling, building a sense of community and aligning around shared objectives (*Get Started with Town Hall in Microsoft Teams*, 2024).

Town hall can accommodate 10,000 users and up to 20,000 with Teams Premium. For town hall, the maximum duration is 30 hours. Town halls provide a one to many experience, allowing attendees to watch presenters, share content, and participate in Q&A sessions. However, during town hall events, attendees cannot activate their microphones or cameras or chat with other attendees. Organizers automatically send email invitations to town hall attendees when creating the event, and if the event is recorded, attendees receive emails with links to the recording.

Live-translated captions enhance accessibility by allowing users to view captions in their preferred language. In live events, attendees can choose from six pre-selected languages as the event organizer determines. Similarly, town hall attendees can select live-translated captions from the same language options, with the possibility of ten languages if the organizer has Teams premium.

The following steps are required to schedule a town hall:

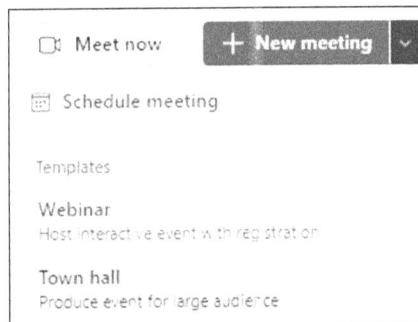

Figure 8.21: Selecting Town hall from New Meeting drop-down

1. Select **Teams Calendar** ❘ Select **New meeting** ❘ **Town hall** from the dropdown menu. In **Details** ❘ enter the basic details like **Title, date and time**, **Description, Co-organizers**, and **Presenters**, and select the option for **Event access**. Whether the event is open to anyone (public) or only for the people within the organization, once done, select **Save**.

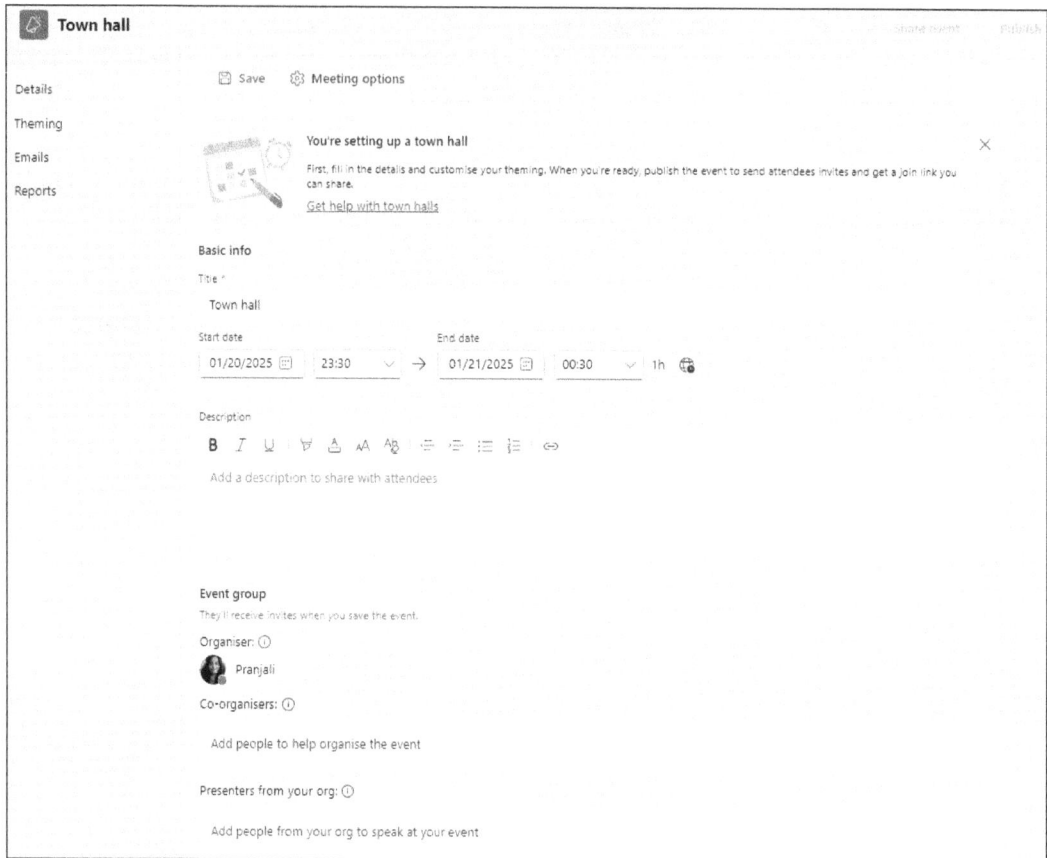

Figure 8.22: Town hall

2. Once you schedule the town hall, it will be displayed on the calendar. Open your calendar invite within Microsoft Teams and select **Manage event** to make any changes to your event (*Schedule a Town Hall in Microsoft Teams*, 2024).

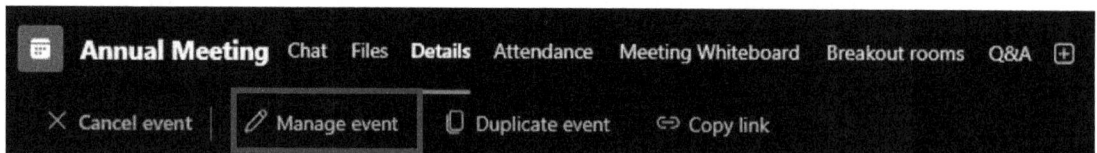

Figure 8.23: Manage event from Teams Calendar

3. Under **Theming** | Add colors, logos and custom images to the emails which participants will receive. Under the **Email** section, you can preview the email invitation which attendees will receive and the email regarding the event recording.

4. Once everything is done, select the **Publish** option available in the upper right corner to schedule the town hall and invite attendees as follows:

All set and ready to share

Your webinar is now published. Share it with your
network to get the word out.

Share link

https://events.teams.microsoft.com/event/f1c0254d-b9f3-4b4b-af67 ⬚

Figure 8.24: Joining link for town hall

5. **Add external presenters:** Up to 20 presenters from outside the organization could simply be added by the organizer for the town hall. Guests who are anonymous, federated, or unfederated are known as external presenters. An exclusive joining link will be issued to the external presenter upon their addition, enabling them to join the event right away and avoid the lobby line. Presenters who do not have Microsoft accounts can still join by clicking the link and inputting their names beforehand.

   Note: Presenters outside the organization must join the Teams desktop town hall. Currently, support for external presenters via web and mobile join is unavailable.

   To include an external presenter, select Add external presenter and input the presenters' email addresses. To send invitations, choose Save, as shown in. the following figure:

Presenters from your org: ⓘ

Add people from your org to speak at your event

Add external presenters

Event access

○ Public	⦿ Your organisation	○ People and groups
The event is open to anyone. Choose this if there will be attendees outside your organisation.	The event is only open to people in your organisation and guests of your organisation.	Only invited people and groups in your organisation can watch the event.

Figure 8.25: Adding external presenters

Note: External presenters will receive unique join links, and they can join up to 3 devices. These links should not be forwarded or shared.

6. **Duplicate a town hall:** The Organizer can duplicate or copy the settings of the scheduled town hall to create another upcoming town hall, which will be reflected in the Team Calendar. When you duplicate an existing town hall setting, the new one will have the same details and settings embedded within it.

7. **Town hall Email invites:** Once you schedule the town hall, attendees will receive an email invite. This invitation will contain all the details, including the name of the event, date and time, and description of the event. If the organizer wants to edit the email, they need to click on the **Email** | Select **Email Invitation** | **Edit** option to make some necessary changes. Users can always click on Preview email to see how the email will appear to invitees.

8. **Publish a town hall**: When you have finalized the details of your town hall and the email invitation template, publish the town hall so that attendees will be automatically invited.

Managing a town hall

The following are a few points to keep in mind while managing a town hall:

- **Host a town hall:** Hosting a town hall in Microsoft Teams provides a powerful platform to engage a large audience. When you host a town hall, an organizer or presenter can manage the event from start to end. Organizers and co-organizers can manage green room settings, spotlight presenters, and many other things beforehand.

  To prepare a green room, you need to be ready with co-organizers and presenters in the green room before starting a town hall. Check audio and video settings and the content you want to share. Attendees will wait in the lobby until you start the event if they join early. Once you join the green room, bring all presenters on screen, set up all content, and then **Start meeting** (to start a town hall).

Figure 8.26: Toolbar appears in town hall to start a meeting

  The event recording will automatically start. Start the presentation and bring other presenters to the screen. You can showcase up to nine presenters at a time or up to seven presenters (*Town Hall Insights in Microsoft Teams*, 2024).

- **Bring presenters on and off screen**: During a town hall, you select which presenters to bring on and off screen. When a presenter is on screen, participants can watch the content and the presenter in addition to the video.

  To bring presenters on the screen, select the People option from the meeting controls, select the participant, and hover over the name of the presenter you want to **Bring on**

screen. Once you bring them on screen, if you are going to take them off-screen, again hover over the name, select **...** (ellipsis), and then choose the option **Take off screen,** as shown in the following figure:

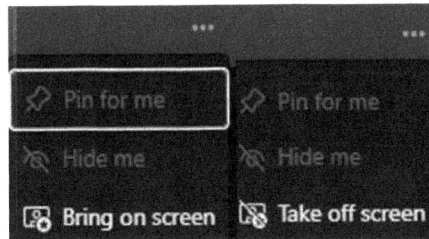

Figure 8.27: To bring presenter on/off screen

- **Manage Q&A:** During the town hall, organizers and other presenters can answer questions, and participants can ask questions. To manage the Q&A settings, select the settings icon as follows:

Figure 8.28: Settings icon

To prevent participants from posting queries, turn off the **Questions** toggle. By default, it is **On**. To prevent participants from replying to posted queries, turn off the **Replies** toggle. By default, it is **On**. Turn on the **Anonymous posts** toggle to allow participants to post queries anonymously. To review questions by an organizer before posting them, turn on the **Moderate questions** toggle.

Once you turn on the feature, you can view three headings in the Q&A thread. They are given as follows:

- o **In review tab:** Every new question submitted by participants will appear on the **In review** tab. Any moderator (organizer or co-organizer) can review the questions and decide whether to publish or reject them so that all participants can see them.

- o **Published tab:** Published questions will be moved to the **Published** tab and visible to all town hall participants.

- o **Dismissed tab**: Dismissed questions will be moved to the **Dismissed** tab. It is not visible to the participants except organizers and co-organizers. Dismissed questions can be published later if required.

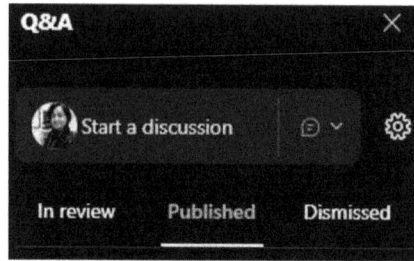

Figure 8.29: Three tabs once moderation is on

Here, we can see **Q&A settings** through which we can change the **Attendee permissions**, as shown in the following figure:

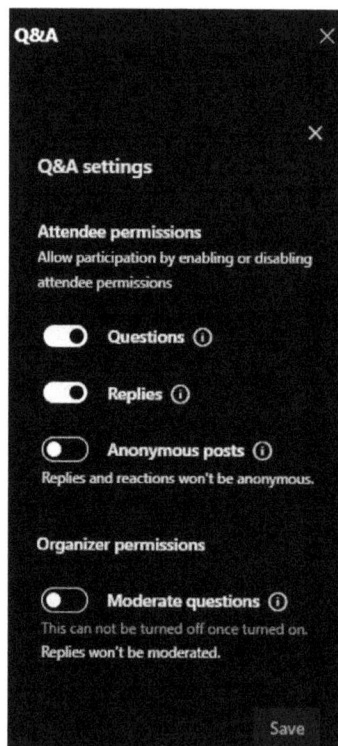

Figure 8.30: Settings for QnA in town hall

In an unmoderated meeting, participants' queries will appear in the Q&A feed immediately.

Once you are done with the change, click the **Save** button.

Note: **Once you turn on the Moderate questions toggle, you cannot turn it off. Replies would not be moderated.**

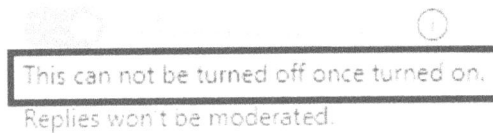

Figure 8.31: Moderate toggle on

- **Participant Q&A experience:** In the Teams meeting on Teams Desktop, Teams Mobile, and Teams Web, participants can participate in Q&A. Q&A is intended for conferences that need additional organization. There will only be one Q&A feed shown to guests regardless of whether the meeting is moderated. The Q&A feed lets them publish, respond, and interact with queries.

  If moderation is enabled, when participants ask questions, they will receive a notification that their question has been received and will be published after the moderator approves it.

- **Reports under town hall**: All reports and analytics are available once the town hall is over. During a town hall, organizers can see real-time event analytics like viewer count and participants' country or region, including charts and graphs. You will also get information about when a participant leaves or joins.

  After a town hall ends, select the **Reports** under town hall and then choose **Download** to view the report on your device.

  After you start at the town hall, share the content or bring speakers on the screen. The content will be visible to participants, as shown in *Figure 8.32*:

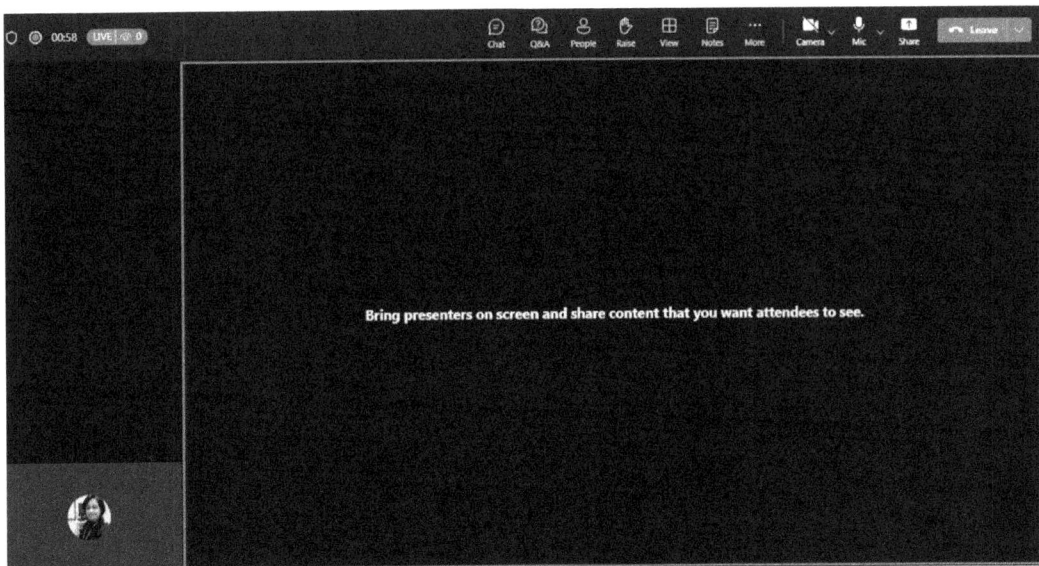

Figure 8.32: Screenshot of town hall live

- **Virtual appointment:** These are meant to schedule lightweight client appointments. A virtual appointment provides external guests with a lean, browser-based meeting experience that makes joining easy. Guests will receive a tailored meeting invitation, can join from any device, and will enter a friendly pre-appointment virtual lobby until they are ready to begin (*Use a Teams Meeting Template to Create a Virtual Appointment*, 2024).

The organizer can invite external guests, and attendees outside your organization can join from any device. Installing Microsoft Teams is unnecessary, and attendees can enter a pre-appointment virtual lobby.

Note: External guests will receive a tailored invitation for this scheduled online meeting. They will join from a mobile or web browser and experience a virtual lobby before the appointment begins.

Organizers can also invite participants within the organization.

You can add appointment details, and this tailored invitation includes the appointment description and relevant information to make joining easy. Once everything is ready, your invitation will go out to all attendees, and the event will be added to your calendar, as shown:

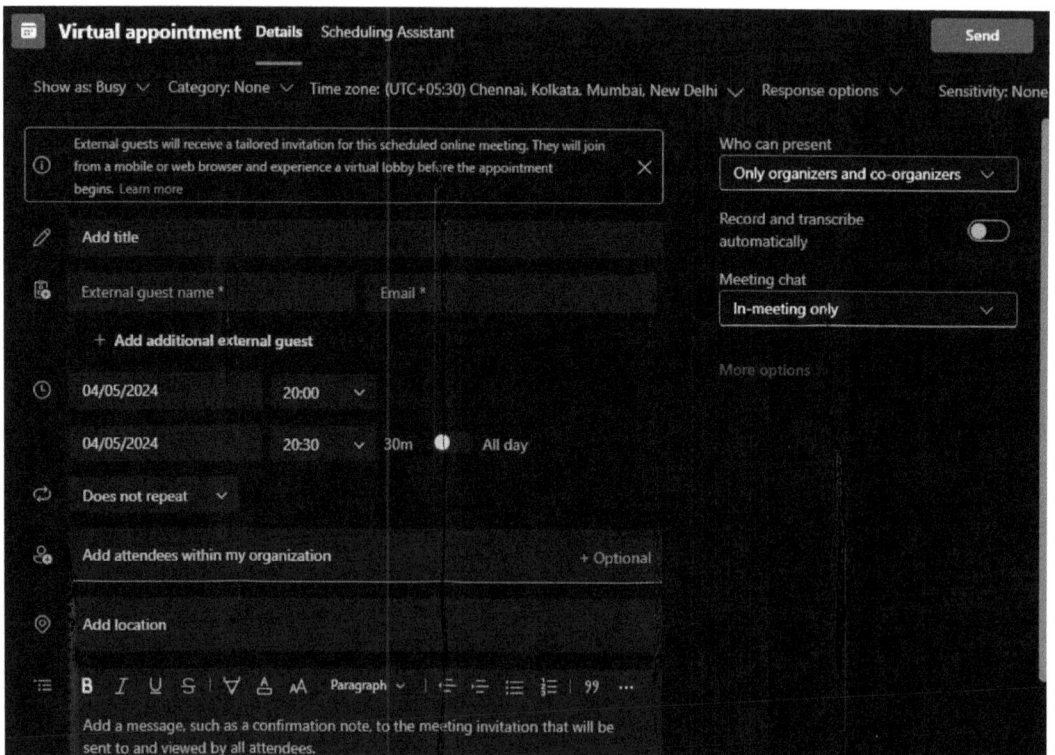

Figure 8.33: Screenshot of Virtual appointment

- **Live Meetings:** Live meetings will be decommissioned by the end of September 2024. They are meant to organize events with larger groups of audiences, with interactive conversations, questions, and answers. Live events are scheduled from the Teams Calendar. To do so, go to the **Teams Calendar| Live event**. This will open another window where the organizer will add all the details, including Presenters' and Producers' email IDs, as shown in the following figure:

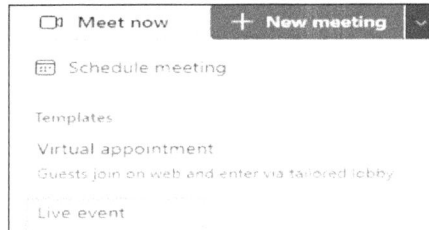

Figure 8.34: Scheduling Live event

The live meeting supports up to 10,000 concurrent participants. The producer can share the presenter's screen along with the video feed. Real-time closed captioning and translation are possible. Moderated Q&A is available. Attendance and engagement reports are available after the event. Events are recorded automatically and transcribed so the organizer can search the recording for specific content.

The following are the responsibilities of an organizer, producer, and presenter:

Roles	Responsibilities
Organizer	Schedules a live event and ensures the event is set up with the right permissions for attendees and the event group, who will manage the event. Creates the live event. Sets attendee permissions. Select production method. Configures event options (for example, the moderated Q&A) Invites attendees. Select event group members. Manages reports generated after the event is over.
Producer	As a host, make sure attendees have a great viewing experience by controlling the live event stream. Starts and stops the live event. Share own video, Share participant video. Shares active desktop or window. Selects layouts.
Presenter	Presents audio, video, or a screen to the live event Can moderate the Q&A

Table 8.2: Responsibilities of Producer, Presenter, and Organizer in Live Event

Meeting Toolbar options

Figure 8.35 illustrates meetings toolbar provides options such as **Chat, People, Raise Hand**, live **React**, different **Views** for meeting participants, taking meeting **notes**, Breakout **Rooms**, adding applications like **Polls**, **muting and unmuting mic**, and many more.

Figure 8.35: *Meeting Toolbar options*

The organizer can turn on the camera and set the background. In a Teams meeting, participants can personalize avatars and express themselves virtually through animated gestures and reactions.

Organizers or presenters can share screens in a meeting using **Share content** control. They can also select whether to present an entire screen, a window, a PowerPoint file, or a Whiteboard.

Types of presenter modes

Engage your audience with different types of presenter modes in Teams. It is an interactive guide that provides visual cues without overwhelming users with information. You actively participate and enhance your presentation by opting for presenter mode rather than simply sharing screen or window content. **Presenter mode** allows presenters to adjust the content orientation on the screen and resize the video to fit well within the presentation. *Figure 8.36* illustrates different presenter modes available while presenting in MS Teams.

- Normal mode (default mode)
- Standout mode
- Side-by-side mode
- Reporter mode

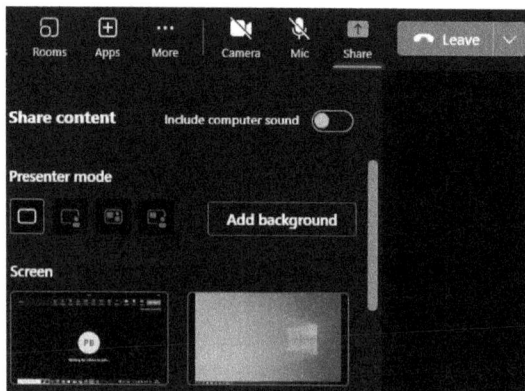

Figure 8.36: *Meeting Toolbar options*

Engage your audience with presenter modes in Microsoft Teams as follows:

- **Initiate your meeting**: Once your meeting is underway, navigate to the upper-right corner of Teams. Click on **Share content** to access the meeting presenter modes and additional options.

- **Select your presenter mode**: Within the **Presenter mode** section, choose the mode that best suits your needs. Ensure that your camera is activated.

- **Customize your presentation**: Before commencing your presentation, click on **Customize** and select a background image. Pick a screen or window on your PC or device to start your presentation.

- **Begin your presentation**: Choose a screen or window on your PC or device to initiate your presentation.

- **Presenter toolbar**: A brief toolbar will appear at the top of your screen when your presentation begins. In this toolbar, you can dynamically switch presenter modes, grant control to another participant, and include computer sound.

- **Reveal the toolbar**: To display the toolbar again, hover your pointer at the top edge of the screen where it initially appeared.

- **Stop sharing**: To cease sharing a screen or window, select **Stop presenting** in the presenter toolbar or choose **Stop sharing** in the meeting controls at the lower-right corner.

The following table describes what to remember while sharing screens during a meeting:

Share your...	If you want to...	Great when...
Desktop	Show your entire screen, including notifications and other desktop activity.	You need to seamlessly share multiple windows.
Window	Show just one window, and no notifications or other desktop activity.	You only need to show one thing and want to keep the rest of your screen to yourself.
PowerPoint	Present a PowerPoint file others can interact with.	Share your presentation slides through PowerPoint and users have the ability to navigate the slides themselves.
Whiteboard	Collaborate with others in real time.	You want to sketch with others and have your notes attached to the meeting.

Table 8.3: Sharing screens while presenting in MS Teams

The following are some of the best practices while sharing content and presentations:

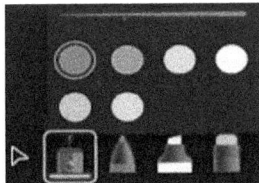

Figure 8.37: Markers available while sharing content

- Share only what you want to display. Include computer sound when sharing audio or video files.

- Give and take control of shared content.

- Focus the viewer's attention on the inking pens, laser light, and eraser during the presentation.

- Turn on Live captions if necessary. Enable Mute when you are not speaking.

- Send your reaction using the emojis icon and raise your hand if you want to say something.

Different views during Microsoft Teams meetings

Microsoft Teams provides different views while you are in a meeting with a video feed. While turn on your video, users can change what appears behind them in the video meeting or call; users can either blur the background, replace it entirely with any image, or use Teams virtual background template.

You can switch your views at any time during the video call. *Figure 8.38* illustrates different views while you are in a meeting, such as Gallery view, Large Gallery view, and Together mode view.

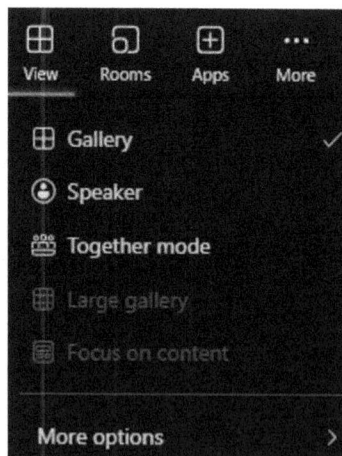

Figure 8.38: Different Views in Teams

You can change the view depending on the number of attendees in the session or meeting. By adding views, you can personalize the way you view other people's videos in a Teams meeting. For instance, in a big conference, you should simultaneously view as many video feeds as possible (*Switch Views during a Video Call in Microsoft Teams (Free)*, 2024).

The details are as follows:

- **Gallery mode:** This is the default view when joining a meeting on a desktop or mobile. When using pop-out, Gallery view will show up to nine video participants on any device.

- **Large gallery mode:** Teams' wide gallery view allows up to 49 participant videos to be displayed at once in a 7x7 format in the meeting window during large meetings. This option would not appear unless ten or more individuals activated their cameras. When more than 49 people join a Teams meeting, all of them can be viewed in a page-filled gallery. When there are more than 49 participants in the large gallery view, navigation controls (< >) will show up at the bottom of the gallery. Navigate using these buttons to see or interact with additional people in videos.

  Note: **If no one shares the video, the large gallery will not be selectable in the menu.**

- **Together mode**: Together mode gives the impression that everyone in the meeting is in a shared area, collaborating virtually on your call. When there are five or more participants in the meeting, the Together mode is accessible. Each person's name, reaction, and other information will be displayed next to their name labels and status icons.

  During your meeting, choose **View** | **Together mode** to activate Together mode. When there are five or more participants in the meeting, the Together mode is accessible.

  To alter the situation, undertake the following steps:

  1. In the lower-left corner of your screen, click the name of the scene.
  2. Under **Choose**, select the desired scenario and click **Apply**. The scene will alter for everyone in Together mode.

  To assign seats in **Together mode**, the following steps need to be undertaken to allocate chairs during a meeting:

  1. In a meeting, activate the **Together** mode.
  2. Choose to assign seats under the **Change scenario**.
  3. Under **Select a participant**, select and hold down the **name of a participant**. Then, drag them to the seat of their choice to make it theirs.
  4. To allocate a seat to a participant, select it, hold down on it, and then drag it to their name under Select a participant.
  5. To implement the changed seating arrangement, choose **Assign**.
  6. In Together mode, everyone will see the updated seating arrangement by default. To allow guests to adjust their perspective, deselect **Make this the opinion of all**.

  Note: **Only the meeting organizer can assign the seats.**

Set your status in Teams meeting

In Microsoft Teams, users can set team status. People will get to know when you are available or if you are away from your desk. Sometimes, Teams will automatically set the status, such as when you are in a meeting or presenting in a meeting/call. *Figure 8.39* shows how to set the status explicitly. (*Change Your Status in Microsoft Teams*, 2024)

- **Available:** This status shows that you do not have anything in the calendar and are available to chat. Please be aware that Teams will automatically switch your status from **Available** to **Away** once your computer is locked or enters idle or sleep mode.

- **Busy:** This status reflects that you want to focus on something. If you are in a meeting, Teams will automatically set your status to **In a meeting** or **In a call**.

- **Do not disturb:** This status indicates that you want to focus on or present your screen and do not want notifications to pop up.

- **Be right back:** This shows when you want to notify others that you have been away for some time. It is never set automatically.

- **Appear away:** This shows when you need to focus or work on some projects but do not respond immediately.

- **Appear offline:** This shows that you are only ready to respond to people once you are online. However, you will receive notifications if someone messages you.

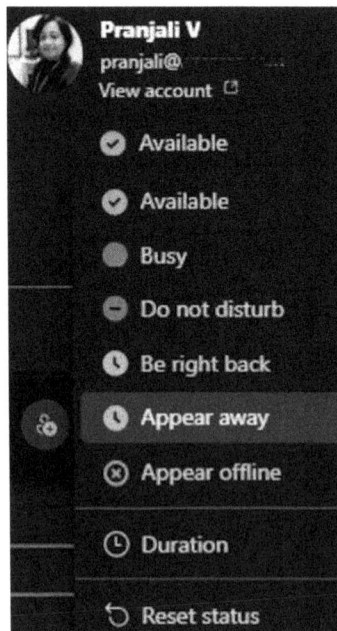

Figure 8.39: Set the Teams status

Set duration and status messages in Microsoft Teams

Suppose you want to change the status for a specific period for some important stuff. In that case, you can do so by going into the **Duration**, selecting the **time** and **status**, and resetting the status after so that Teams can automatically reset the status to default.

It is a great way to change the status message if you want to share a specific message for your contacts to view. To do this, go to the profile picture and select | **Set status message** | type the message or use the @ *sign* to mention someone in your status. Select the check box for **Show when people message me;** also, if you want to **clear the status message after** a certain duration of time, select that from the dropdown, as shown in the following figure:

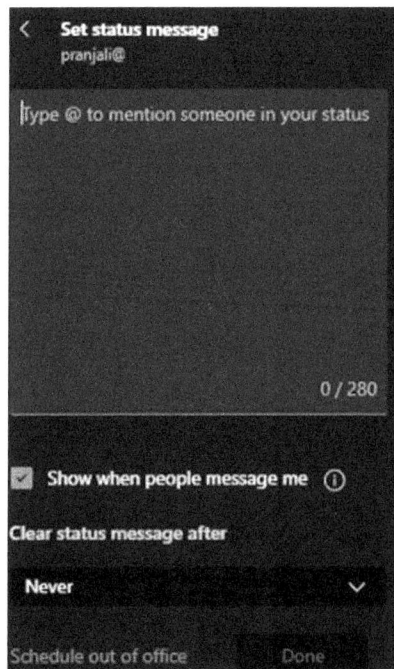

Figure 8.40: Setting Teams status

Schedule an out of office status

Users can set up **out of the office** via Microsoft Teams as well as from Outlook. Your out of office status will sync with automatic replies in your Outlook calendar. When your contacts hover the mouse over your name, they can view your out of office message and know that you are not available for that duration. While setting **up out of office**, you can select **Send replies outside my organization** and tailor your out of office message to this audience. *Figure 8.41* illustrates various options like start **date and time** and specific check boxes.

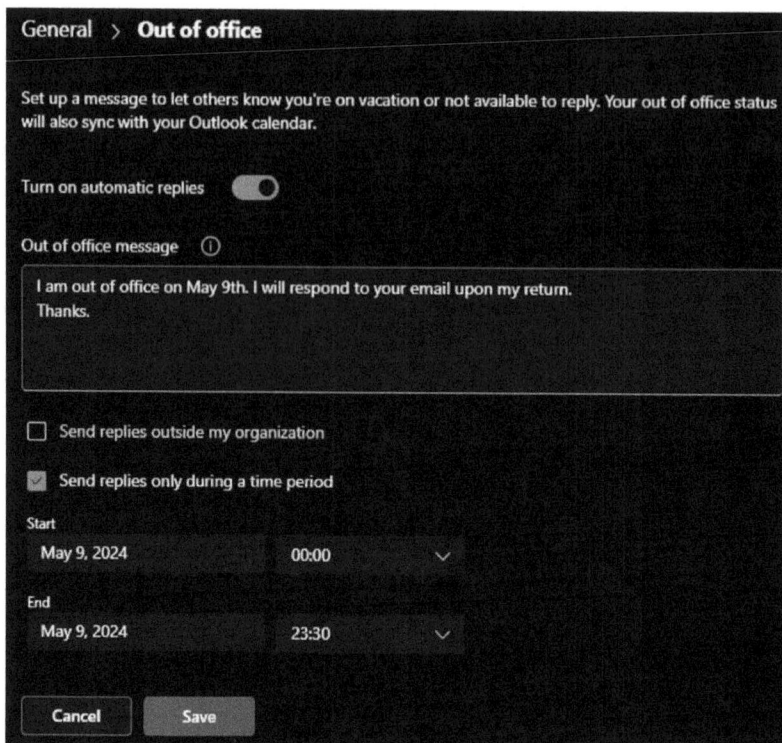

Figure 8.41: *Set out of office in Microsoft Teams*

Manage notifications in Microsoft Teams

Microsoft Teams provides various methods for accessing, receiving, and managing notifications. These settings encompass options for the appearance, timing, and location of your notifications, customized preferences for channels and chats, visual and auditory cues, disabling particular messages, and more (*Manage Notifications in Microsoft Teams*, 2024).

To manage notifications, select **Settings and More...** at the top right of **Teams | Settings | Notifications and activity**. In the **General** section of **notifications and activity**, you can set up notifications that best suit your working style.

Figure 8.42 illustrates the **Missed activity emails** section, which shows the frequency of summary emails that outline your missed activity or disable this feature altogether and **Meeting** section illustrates all notifications related to meetings, like meeting start notification or meeting chat notification, which can be set to mute, unmute, or mute until I join or send a message.

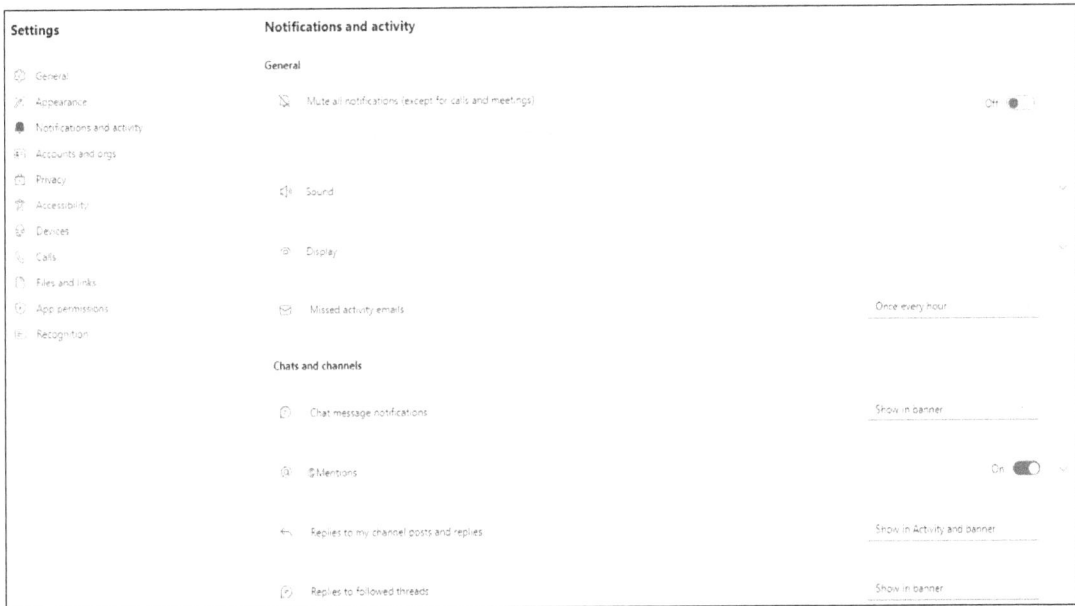

Figure 8.42: Notifications and Activity in Teams

You can customize **Chats and channel** notifications at a granular level to your work style. You can manage **chat message notifications** and **@ mentions** when someone notifies you. In fact, if someone likes or reacts to your message, Teams will notify you according to the settings you have made.

The following are some of the best practices for notifications in Microsoft Teams:

- It is advised that you follow only chats and channels that are relevant to you. Pin important channels so they are available on top of all chats.

- Mute and unpin the chats and channels that are no longer relevant to you. The best option is to **leave** chats that are of no use.

- It is advisable to change your status when you need to focus. Use **Viva Insights** to focus your attention, and it will automatically block your calendar.

- Teams have various ways to manage **notifications and activity** across different features, such as email notifications, banner notifications, or your activity feed. If the company's email culture is strong, educating end users on how to set up (email) notifications in Teams may improve adoption.

- Use the @ sign to mention someone. It is the easiest way to let users know something needs their attention in Teams. It notifies users, and it is highlighted in the Activity area, making it easy to find where the conversation is.

- Try to keep an eye on the **activity feed**, which will help you stay on top of all your notifications.

- Use the **Search text box** at the top of the Teams to look for people, messages, files, Teams and channels, and many more. Searches cover your entire organization. You can use the **slash (/) command** to set your status quickly.

M365 Copilot in Microsoft Teams

Microsoft 365 Copilot is an AI-powered tool that helps with your daily work tasks. Copilot uses the capabilities of Azure OpenAI's **large language models** (**LLMs**) to assist you with various tasks within familiar Microsoft 365 applications. Copilot uses pre-trained LLMs from Azure Open AI, trained on massive datasets. These models perform tasks like text summarization, content creation etc. Copilot taps your data through the Microsoft Graph. It does the grounding process and dive into your emails, chats, meetings, contacts, everything that you have permisson to. Copliot can access information from the web to enrich its response. Copilot is built on Microsoft's security framework, it respects your permission, keeps sensitive data safe, and take care of compliance.

Copilot in Microsoft Teams enhances collaboration and helps you get the most out of your Teams chats and meetings. It can generate insights and actionable items or suggestions alongside your important touch points *(Get Started with Copilot in Microsoft Teams Meetings,* 2024).

M365 Copilot is available across over 10+ applications within Microsoft 365 ecosystem. It helps users to start from scratch and turn blank page into proposal in MS Word, condensing lengthy email threads in Microsoft Outlook, visualizing and analyzing data in MS Excel and generating presentations from existing documents (limited to Word and PDF only) in PowerPoint, comparing and summarizing documents in OneDrive and many more.

Unlock productivity with Copilot in Microsoft Teams. If you have a valid license, you can use Copilot in your meeting with an enabling transcription feature. Copilot in Teams is available on Windows, Mac, Web, Android, and iOS. Copilot will help you summarize key discussion points, including who said what and all the action items, all in real time during a meeting.

If you are joining a meeting with recording and transcription *on,* participants will receive a message that they can use Copilot during and after the meeting. Click on **Open Copilot** from the meeting controls located at the top of your meeting window and wait for the summary to appear on the right side of your meeting window.

The following are the steps to install Copilot in Teams:

1. Select **Apps** from the left side of Teams.
2. In the search box, type Copilot.
3. Locate M365 Chat/Copilot Chat/Bizchat and select **Add**.
4. It will add Copilot as a chat in your Teams chat list.
5. Select Chat from the left-hand side and find the **M365 Chat** that was added, as shown:

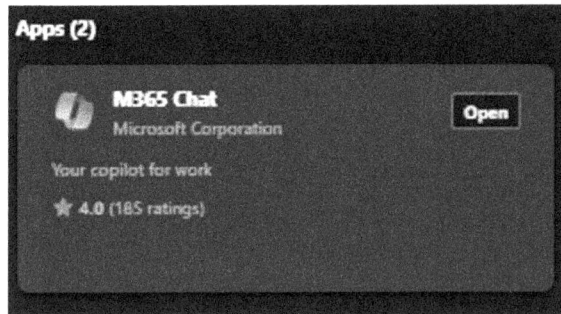

Figure 8.43: Adding M365 Chat from Apps

When you first open in chat, it will show some best practices for using Copilot and suggest **prompts**. *Figure 8.44* shows a few prompts to use in the M365 chat environment:

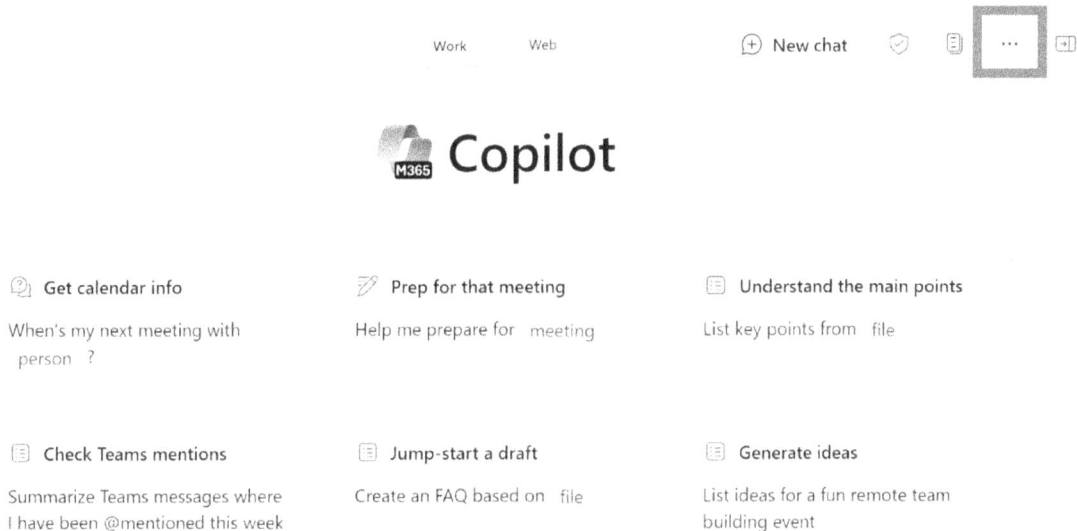

Figure 8.44: M365 Chat experience

You can get sample prompts from the **Copilot Prompt Gallery (https://copilot.cloud.microsoft/ prompts)**. Users enter a prompt in Copilot Chat environment and Copilot responds with AI-generated information. The responses are in real-time and can include internet-based content and work content that users have permission to access. To open Copilot Prompt Gallery, type the url: **https://copilot.cloud.microsoft/prompts**

Microsoft 365 Copilot Chat in Teams

Copilot collaborated with you to integrate information from your documents, presentations, emails, calendar and contacts within Microsoft Teams. It empowers you to accomplish tasks in innovative ways through AI capabilities. Copilot app can be found in MS Teams, and you can pin it and engage with Copilot in Teams chat. Providing Copilot with instructions using natural language and adding more details enhances its effectiveness.

You can enhance outcomes by honing your instructions and iterating. Request a summary of the items you need to catch up on, such as your files, messages, and contacts. Copilot can also assist you in locating and utilizing information buried within documents or lost within conversations. Working together, you can create content incorporating all of these elements.

For example – In the Copilot Chat, type your prompt "`Summarize all unread messages from <person>`." Select **Send**. Copilot generates a response and provide the sources at the end.

Mobile version of MS Teams

Always stay connected with your team through Microsoft Teams. Download the app from the respective Play Store for Android or iPhone and sign in with your work account. Stay connected with a consistent experience across all devices. It is also available in Edge and Chrome browsers; *Figure 8.45* illustrates various mobile platforms where MS Teams can be used.

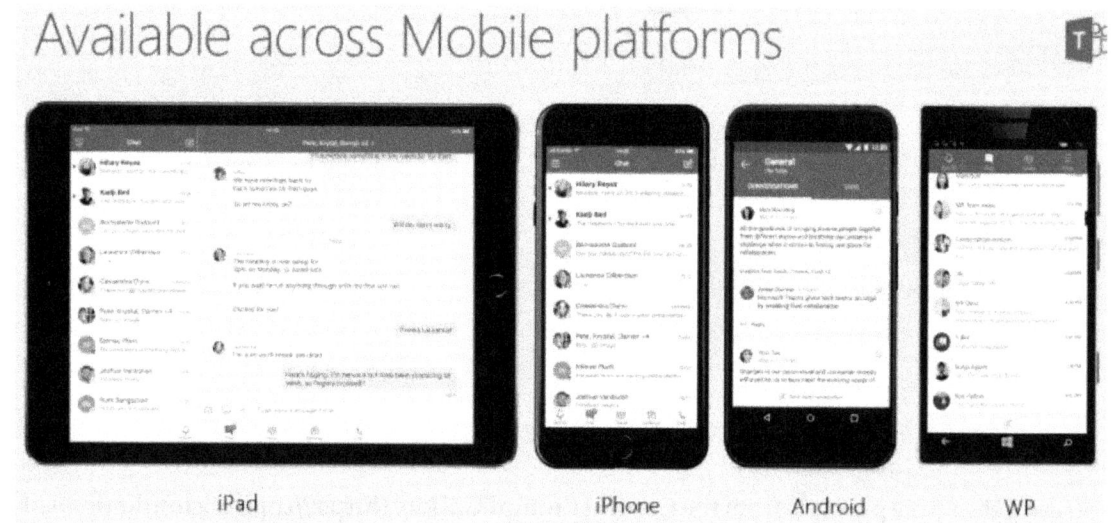

Figure 8.45: Different types of mobile platforms

Conclusion

In this chapter, we covered all the crucial functionalities that Microsoft Teams cater to their users efficiently and effectively. The Microsoft Teams application is undoubtedly the best example of the blend of convergence and collaboration through which the users cannot only collaborate with peers but also integrate various apps into one single application. The **Apps** feature helps a user to leverage top trending apps, manage work desks and meeting rooms efficiently, and simplify tasks with Copilot plugins. This video conferencing tool also promotes healthy habits by suggesting a range of built-in applications to boost your productivity. Thus, Team collaboration in organizations accelerates better work delivery and employee engagement. It has been observed that in the post-COVID era, most organizations have leveraged MS Teams efficiently to engage their workforce and emphasize efficient employee collaboration (*Yang et al.*, 2022).

In the next chapter, we will be introduced to OneDrive, a cloud storage solution, as well as SharePoint. Both applications are integral components of the M365 suite. Participants will gain insights into file sharing and co-authoring within documents, in addition to exploring the various elements of SharePoint.

References

1. *Change your status in Microsoft Teams. (2024). Microsoft Support.* **https://support.microsoft.com/en-us/office/change-your-status-in-microsoft-teams-ce36ed14-6bc9-4775-a33e-6629ba4ff78e**

2. *Create a standard, private, or shared channel in Microsoft Teams. (2024). Microsoft Support.* **https://support.microsoft.com/en-us/office/create-a-standard-private-or-shared-channel-in-microsoft-teams-fda0b75e-5b90-4fb8-8857-7e102b014525**

3. *First things to know about channels in Microsoft Teams. (2024). Microsoft Support.* **https://support.microsoft.com/en-us/office/first-things-to-know-about-channels-in-microsoft-teams-8e7b8f6f-0f0d-41c2-9883-3dc0bd5d4cda**

4. *First things to know about chats in Microsoft Teams. (2024). Microsoft Support.* **https://support.microsoft.com/en-us/office/first-things-to-know-about-chats-in-microsoft-teams-88ed0a06-6b59-43a3-8cf7-40c01f2f92f2**

5. *Get started with Copilot in Microsoft Teams meetings. (2024). Microsoft Support.* **https://support.microsoft.com/en-us/office/get-started-with-copilot-in-microsoft-teams-meetings-0bf9dd3c-96f7-44e2-8bb8-790bedf066b1**

6. *Get started with Microsoft Teams webinars. (2024). Microsoft Support.* **https://support.microsoft.com/en-us/office/get-started-with-microsoft-teams-webinars-42f3f874-22dc-4289-b53f-bbc1a69013e3**

7. *Get started with town hall in Microsoft Teams. (2024). Microsoft Support.* **https://support.microsoft.com/en-us/office/get-started-with-town-hall-in-microsoft-teams-33baf0c6-0283-4c15-9617-3013e8d4804f**

8. *Manage notifications in Microsoft Teams. (2024). Microsoft Support.* **https://support.microsoft.com/en-us/office/manage-notifications-in-microsoft-teams-1cc31834-5fe5-412b-8edb-43fecc78413d**

9. *Meeting options in Microsoft Teams. (2024). Microsoft Support.* **https://support.microsoft. com/en-us/office/meeting-options-in-microsoft-teams-53261366-dbd5-45f9-aae9-a70e6354f88e**

10. *Schedule a town hall in Microsoft Teams. (2024). Microsoft Support.* **https://support. microsoft.com/en-us/office/schedule-a-town-hall-in-microsoft-teams-d493b5cc-9f61-4dac-8027-d837dafb7a4c**

11. *Switch views during a video call in Microsoft Teams (free). (2024). Microsoft Support.* **https:// support.microsoft.com/en-us/office/switch-views-during-a-video-call-in-microsoft-teams-free-3a4247bf-09ca-484a-a9f3-b96d1906a75e**

12. *Town hall insights in Microsoft Teams. (2024). Microsoft Support.* **https://support.microsoft. com/en-us/office/town-hall-insights-in-microsoft-teams-def99575-61bf-4ea2-ad0e-c6e75dce7741**

13. *Use a Teams meeting template to create a Virtual Appointment. (2024). Microsoft Support.* **https://support.microsoft.com/en-us/office/use-a-teams-meeting-template-to-create-a-virtual-appointment-6a9e8cbb-c0ed-4598-851e-3b1750a4a747**

14. *Yang, L., Holtz, D., Jaffe, S., Suri, S., Sinha, S., Weston, J., Joyce, C., Shah, N., Sherman, K., Hecht, B., & Teevan, J. (2022). The effects of remote work on collaboration among information workers. Nature Human Behaviour, 6(1), 43–54.* **https://doi.org/10.1038/s41562-021-01196-4**

Join our Discord space

Join our Discord workspace for latest updates, offers, tech happenings around the world, new releases, and sessions with the authors:

https://discord.bpbonline.com

CHAPTER 9

OneDrive for Business and SharePoint

Introduction

In this chapter, we will discuss OneDrive for Business. It is a cloud storage and collaboration service from Microsoft. It allows you to store, share, and co-author files with internal and external users. When everything is based on data, it is very important to save your data in a safe place and ensure you do not have a space crisis. With Microsoft 365, users will get ample space to keep all their data on a cloud, i.e., a virtual space. OneDrive is part of your organization's subscription to SharePoint in Microsoft 365 or through an on-premises installation of SharePoint Server. We will also discuss SharePoint; to put it simply, it can be described as a type of Intranet that allows for the use of sites created within SharePoint exclusively for organizational purposes. Additionally, we will discuss the various components of SharePoint.

Structure

In this chapter, we will discuss the following topics:

- Understanding OneDrive for Business
- Interface of OneDrive for Business
- Sync and share files using OneDrive
- Overview of SharePoint

- Components of SharePoint
- Working with document content
- Elements of a SharePoint team site
- Saving files to OneDrive or SharePoint
- Difference between OneDrive, SharePoint, and MS Teams

Objectives

By the end of this chapter, we will understand the concept of OneDrive for Business and cloud management. It is a space where organizational employees can securely store, access, and share files from the cloud, offering seamless collaboration and advanced security features to ensure data protection. Users can take advantage of numerous benefits, including centralized management and enhanced protection of sensitive business data through compliance-ready encryption and monitoring tools, which leads to increased productivity and scalability.

Understanding OneDrive for Business

Google Drive, Dropbox, and OneDrive for Business are all cloud storage solutions, but OneDrive for Business stands out due to its seamless integration with Microsoft 365, ensuring robust security and compliance for enterprises. Google Drive is particularly strong in collaborative features, especially with Google Docs, whereas Dropbox is known for its effective file-sharing capabilities. OneDrive is ideal for companies that use Microsoft 365 licenses. It allows users to safely access, store, manage, download, and share files and enables employees to collaborate in real-time and access documents seamlessly from any device, including PCs, laptops, iPads, and smartphones. All that is required is a connection to your organization's Microsoft 365 service (*Sajid, 2023*).

Figure 9.1 shows the logo of OneDrive for Business:

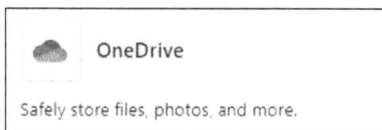

Figure 9.1: *OneDrive application available in Microsoft 365 ecosystem*

Documents can be created, opened, and edited within OneDrive, which allows employees to work together on documents to get simple and quick feedback from their peers and share it across the business. With seamless integration into the Microsoft 365 ecosystem, including applications like Microsoft Teams, Word, and SharePoint, it supports efficient workflows and team collaboration. OneDrive for Business offers cloud storage starting from 1 TB (terabyte) to 5 TB (depending upon the organization's policy and user license). OneDrive for Business offers enterprise-grade security features such as end-to-end encryption, ransomware detection, and file recovery options, ensuring the protection of sensitive information. Administrators can easily manage storage, monitor usage, and enforce compliance policies, making it an essential tool for modern cloud management. Its robust capabilities, such as version history, offline access, and advanced sharing controls, make it a versatile solution for both individual and team needs in a dynamic, cloud-driven work environment.

Interface of OneDrive for Business

OneDrive for Business is available in the Microsoft 365 suite, which allows users to access, download, collaborate, and edit documents from any connected device. Files stored on OneDrive are automatically backed up and saved and can be accessed from any suitable device, including PCs and laptops. To open OneDrive, you must open *microsoft365.com* and log in with M365 credentials (*What Is OneDrive for Work or School? 2023*).

Figure 9.2 shows available options in OneDrive on the left navigation pane:

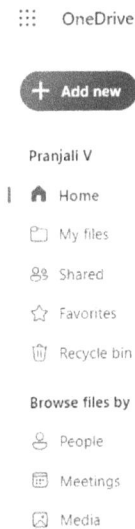

Figure 9.2: *Various options available in OneDrive for Business*

Upon navigating to the left side, a range of options is available to utilize, as follows:

- **Home**: You will be directed to the home page of OneDrive for Business.
- **My files:** It displays all next level files and folders stored in OneDrive for Business.
- **Shared**: It will display the files that have been shared with you by other individuals in addition to the files you have shared.
- **Favorites:** This is the place that shows you all your favorite files.
- **Recycle bin**: It holds all files and folders deleted from your device (which is stored on OneDrive) or directly from the OneDrive location. You can recover the deleted files.

- **Browse files by:** There is a category that shows **Browse files** *by*, where you can search for **People** and **Meetings and Media**.

  o Clicking on the **People** tab will show the files that you have shared.

  o The **Meeting** tab will show the past meetings and the files that have been shared during a meeting.

  o The media option will display all pictures.

Sync and share files using OneDrive

As long as you do not share your OneDrive files, they remain private. When it comes to sharing your files, select a file that you want to share.

Figure 9.3 will show you more options by clicking on three dots:

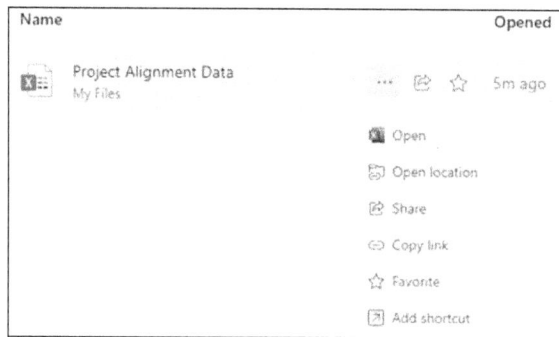

Figure 9.3: List of options available

Upon clicking on the **Share** button, a dialog box will open. When you share a file using OneDrive for Business, you enable others to access a file or folder, all the while ensuring that you retain full control over that file. You can **add a name, group, or email** and **add a message** (*Share OneDrive Files and Folders*, 2023).

Figure 9.4 illustrates the dialog box that allows you to provide access control:

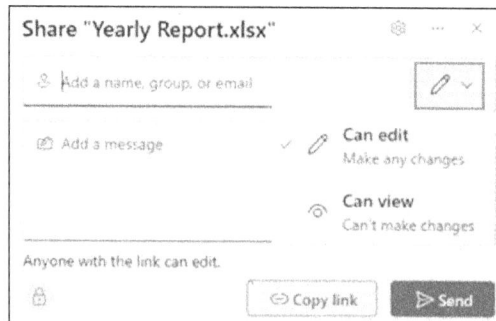

Figure 9.4: Sharing and Enabling Editing/Viewing rights

Before clicking the **Send** button, select the **pencil icon** to change the permission, such as **Can edit** or **Can view**. The recipient will be notified through an email in Outlook.

Note: **When you grant edit permissions for shared folders, individuals with whom you share can incorporate those folders into their OneDrive accounts.**

Any updates they make with the shared folder will sync, so users with access to the folder are up to date.

Figure 9.5 demonstrates that clicking on the gear icon will bring up the **Link settings** dialog box:

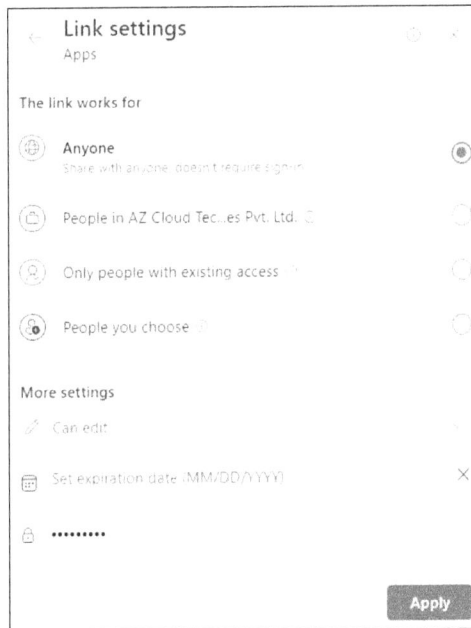

Figure 9.5: Link settings dialog box

The following are the individual components that comprise the share settings:

- **Anyone**: This option gives anyone who receives the link access, whether they receive it directly from you or forwarded it from someone else. At times, this option is disabled for data protection reasons.

- **People within your organization:** You can give the link ABC Pvt Ltd access to people who work within your organization. Recipients can share the link internally.

- **Only people with existing access**: Use this to grant access to existing recipients.

- **People you choose**: The link only works for the people you specify, internally or externally, and requires the recipient to be logged into a Microsoft 365 account. If you or another user forwards the link, it will not work.

Under **More settings**, there are other options, as follows:

- **Editing**: You have the option to block the file from being downloaded. This prevents other users from downloading the file and sharing it independently. You can set a password and date while sharing the file. The same permission level is set for everyone on the invitation, so you must send separate invitations if different permissions are required.

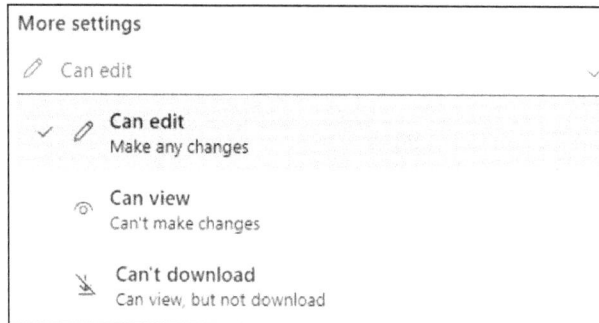

Figure 9.6: Link settings dialog box

- **Cannot download:** This option prevents the download access for files and folders. Turning the slider off means that user can download the files on their devices.

- **Set expiration date:** This allows you to set a date for the link to expire. Once you set the date, the link will not work, and you will need to create a new link for the users requiring access to your file or folder.

- **Set password**: This allows you to apply a password to access the file. Once you set the password for a file, the user will be required to use the password to open and view the document. You will have to provide this password separately to anyone you want to share the file with.

When an item is shared, the status in the Sharing column is updated to display a symbol representing people. To remove or change sharing, click **Manage Access** by clicking on **three dots** (ellipsis).

Figure 9.7 illustrates the dialog box representing different sharing links:

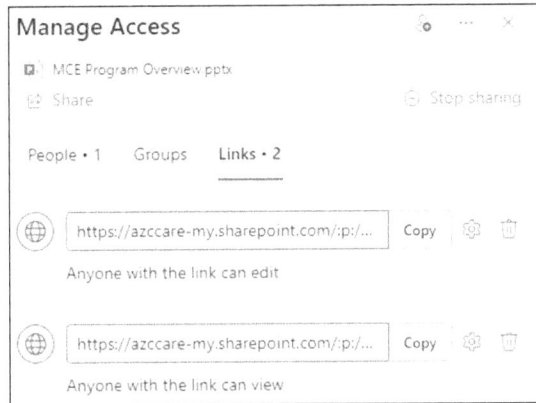

Figure 9.7: *Manage Access*

The dialog box reflects how the file has been shared. To remove access, click **Stop sharing.**

The following are the best practices for secure sharing in OneDrive for Business:

- **Activate multi-factor authentication** (**MFA**): It will allow users to securely access their accounts.

- **Restrict external sharing**: Always share with trusted individuals and disable anonymous links.

- **Set expiry date**: Make sure to set an expiry date on shared links to restrict long-term access.

- **Limit permission**: Ensure that read-only access is provided if collaboration is not required.

- **Utilize sensitivity labels**: Apply labels to classify and protect sensitive information.

Adhering to these practices ensures safe and controlled file sharing while safeguarding sensitive business information.

Co-authoring documents in OneDrive for Business

Co-authoring in OneDrive for Business enables multiple users to work on the same document simultaneously, fostering real-time collaboration and productivity. Users can edit, comment, and update shared files without version conflicts. Documents can also be co-edited in the desktop application. Choose any document to **Open in the desktop app,** and you may require a setting to enable editing to work in the document.

When the document opens, you may need to **enable editing** to work with the file. A reference to **Autosave** will appear in the desktop app, and the **Save** icon will indicate that changes will be synced with the OneDrive copy. Changes are automatically saved and synchronized, allowing team members to see updates in real time, even when working from different devices or locations. Co-authoring supports advanced features such as inline comments, track changes, and notifications for edits, ensuring effective teamwork and communication.

Figure 9.8 depicts the **AutoSave** option available in the office application at the top left corner:

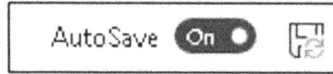

Figure 9.8: *AutoSave option*

To connect Microsoft Office to OneDrive, sign into any desktop app by clicking the **File** tab and choosing **Account**. You will need to enter your username and password. You will now be connected to your OneDrive and SharePoint services, as shown in *Figure 9.9*:

Figure 9.9: *Connected Services dialog box*

When opening or saving existing or new files, choose **OneDrive** to view content in OneDrive.

If you are using the desktop apps to edit a file stored in OneDrive, you can share the file from the **ribbon** at the top right corner. If the file has been saved locally, you will be prompted to **Save to Cloud** before sharing, as shown in the following figure:

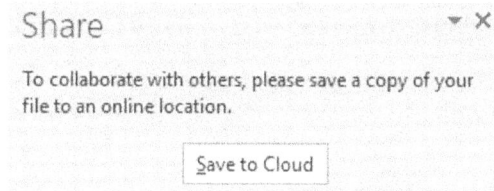

Figure 9.10: *Share option*

You can also share from the **Backstage** view by clicking on the **File** menu.

To sync your device with OneDrive for Business, open or save files in desktop mode, and it will ask where to save. If your OneDrive is set up on your device, you can save files so that you can access documents offline instead of online.

A few symbols that appear before the file or folder are as follows:

- ☁ : This file is only available online; you need the internet to access it.

- ⊘ : This file is available locally. When you open an online-only file, it downloads to your device and is available without the internet. To change the file back to **online only**, right-click on the file and select **Free up space** (refer to Figure 9.11)

- ☁ ⋅ : This file is on the cloud and shared.

Right-click on a file to share or change sync options as follows:

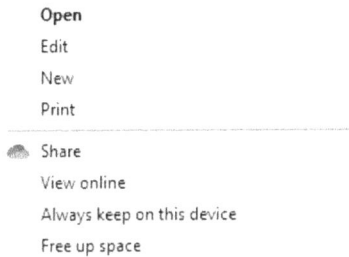

> **Open**
> Edit
> New
> Print
> ──────────────
> ☁ Share
> View online
> Always keep on this device
> Free up space

Figure 9.11: Context menu

The Microsoft Office Online applications consist of Word, Excel, PowerPoint, and OneNote. They are used for document creation, **light touch** editing, and viewing.

Note: **The apps can be used across various devices, although the functionality depends upon the device and browser.**

Reading and editing directly in OneDrive for Business

To view a document's contents, simply click its filename. OneDrive for Business will open the document in a separate tab, where you can view or edit the file.

Both online and desktop applications incorporate tabs and ribbons as key features. This shows the *simplified ribbon*. Search *(Alt+Q)* is an interactive help feature.

Any changes made to the document are automatically saved. You can edit, review or view the file in online mode. If you want to use all the functionality of MS Word, it is always better to use the **Open in Desktop App** option, as follows:

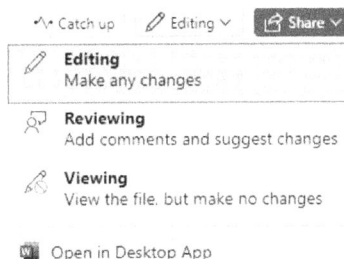

> ⌃⌄ Catch up   ✎ Editing ⌄   📢 Share ⌄
> ──────────────
> ✎ **Editing**
>   Make any changes
> ──────────────
> ⤶ **Reviewing**
>   Add comments and suggest changes
> 🖉 **Viewing**
>   View the file, but make no changes
>
> 📄 Open in Desktop App

Figure 9.12: Sharing options

Every time a document is edited, a new version is saved using the same filename. With a selected file, click or tap the *ellipsis (three dots)* on the command bar to view **Version History**. All versions are visible. You can go to … (ellipsis) and open any version, restore, or delete, as shown in the following figure:

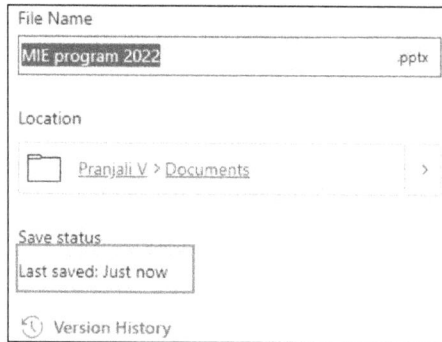

Figure 9.13: Version history

When a file or folder is deleted from OneDrive for Business, it is sent to the **Recycle Bin** once you confirm moving it. The following are the options:

- Select the item or items and then choose **Delete**.
- Right-click the item and select **Delete** from the menu.
- Select the item or items and press **Delete** on the keyboard.

All options then display the following dialog box:

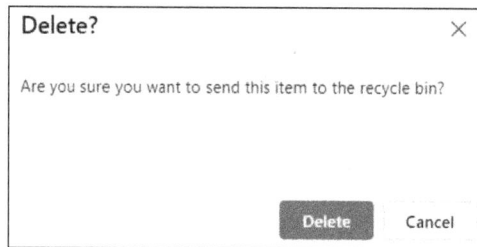

Figure 9.14: Recycle bin Dialog box

Select **Delete** to send the item(s) to the Recycle Bin. The bin's contents can be viewed by selecting the **Recycle bin** button available in the left pane.

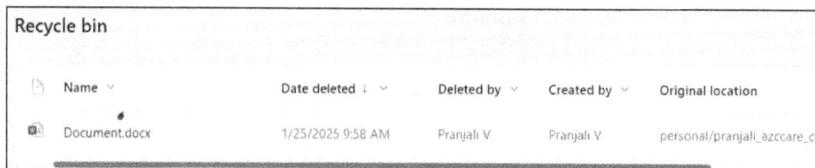

Figure 9.15: Recycle Bin documents

To restore the document, select the document, and you will get the **Restore** button.

Figure 9.16 shows the available options for **Delete** and **Restore**:

🗑 Delete   ↩ Restore

Figure 9.16: Restore button

The default setting for the Recycle Bin is to retain deleted items for 90 days each. Items deleted from the Recycle Bin can be retrieved from the **Second stage recycle bin,** as illustrated in *Figure 9.17*:

Can't find what you're looking for? Check the Second-stage recycle bin

Figure 9.17: Second Stage recycle bin

Overview of SharePoint

Microsoft SharePoint is a user-friendly cloud-based intranet solution that provides a document management and collaboration platform, as shown in the following figure:

Figure 9.18: SharePoint Availability

SharePoint is used to create Intranet sites within the organization. It can used internally to store, organize, share, and access information within the team from any device. It is a secure place to keep all your documents. You need a web browser to access the SharePoint sites. Open microsoft365.com and open SharePoint. It is a collaborative working tool based around sites. Each SharePoint site acts as a central repository for information that is stored by individual teams or departments. Documents and files are stored in the SharePoint app, known as a document library. Each site will contain one or more libraries, depending on how the site is configured. Access to these sites can be restricted by security features called using site permissions (*What Is SharePoint?*, 2023).

With the help of SharePoint, you can build intranet sites (available within the organization) and create pages, document libraries and lists, and web parts to customize your content. It will also show important news, visuals, and updates with a team or communication site.

It allows you to manage your workflows, forms, and lists where anyone can sync and store files in the cloud and your team can work on these files.

You can also catch up on the latest while on the go with the mobile app. Once you open the interface, it will allow you to **Create site or Create news post**, as shown in the following figure:

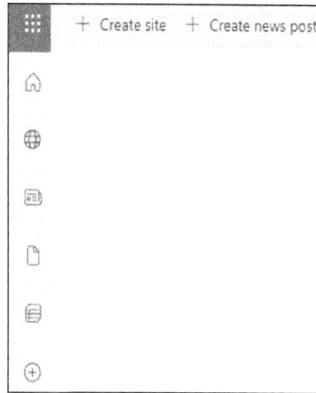

Figure 9.19: Create Site or news post

Components of SharePoint

When you click on the *+ icon from the left rail*, you can create a **News Post**, **Page**, **Site**, **Document**, **Spreadsheet**, **Presentation**, **Notebook**, **List**, etc., as shown in *Figure 9.20*:

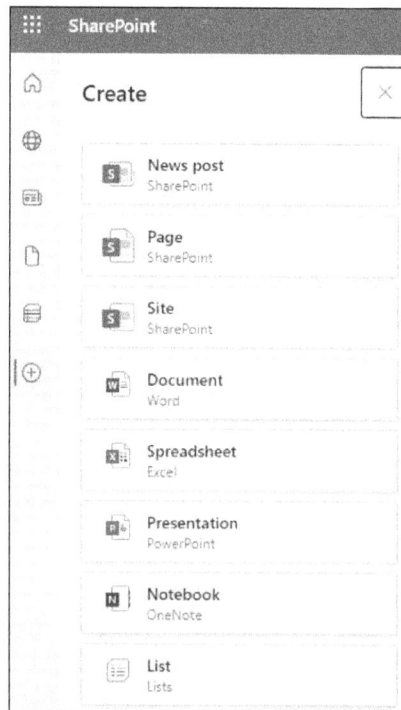

Figure 9.20: SharePoint components

Organizations can create **News Post** via SharePoint. When a site is created, different pages can be associated with that site, which contain the information related to it.

SharePoint sites can differ from each other, but most of them will have a similar structure.

The site name and links to other sites are displayed above the logo. Clicking on the logo of your site takes you to the site's home page (*Get Started with SharePoint*, 2023).

The following sharing and editing links are given on the right-hand side of the site:

Figure 9.21: Follow button appears on the right side

These links will allow you to add the site to your follow list (the Following keyword is shown in the upper right-hand corner) or share it with other users. You can also edit if you have editing permission. It will also help you see whether it is a public or private group.

Once you are on your site, the user will be able to see several options. If you click on **Documents**, it will show you all documents available on your site.

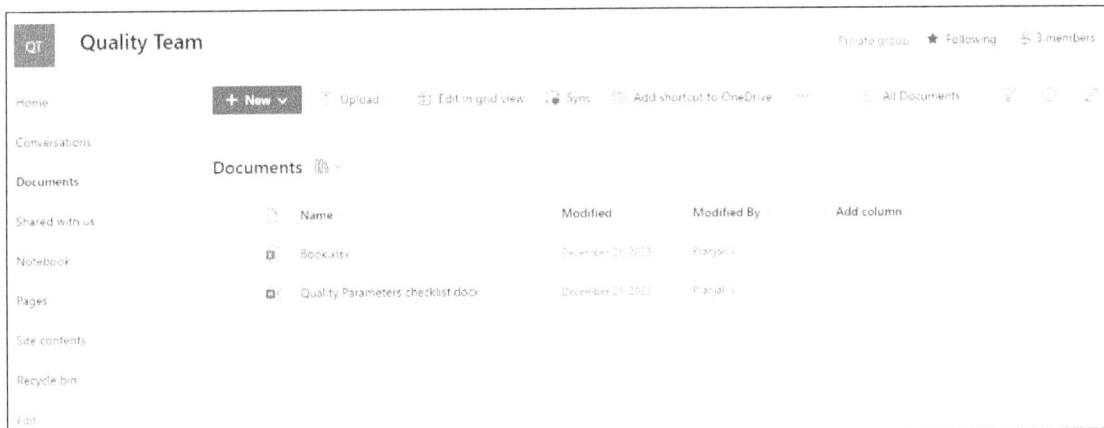

Figure 9.22: Document library

The Toolbar runs across the top of the **Content** pane. On the left are icons that allow you to make changes to your site's content. This bar will vary in appearance based on the type of content being accessed.

Figure 9.23 illustrates various options:

Figure 9.23: *Various options available on the site main page*

The site page will display the content you have accessed on the site. It will vary based on what you are looking at or have searched for. It is shown in the following *Figure 9.24:*

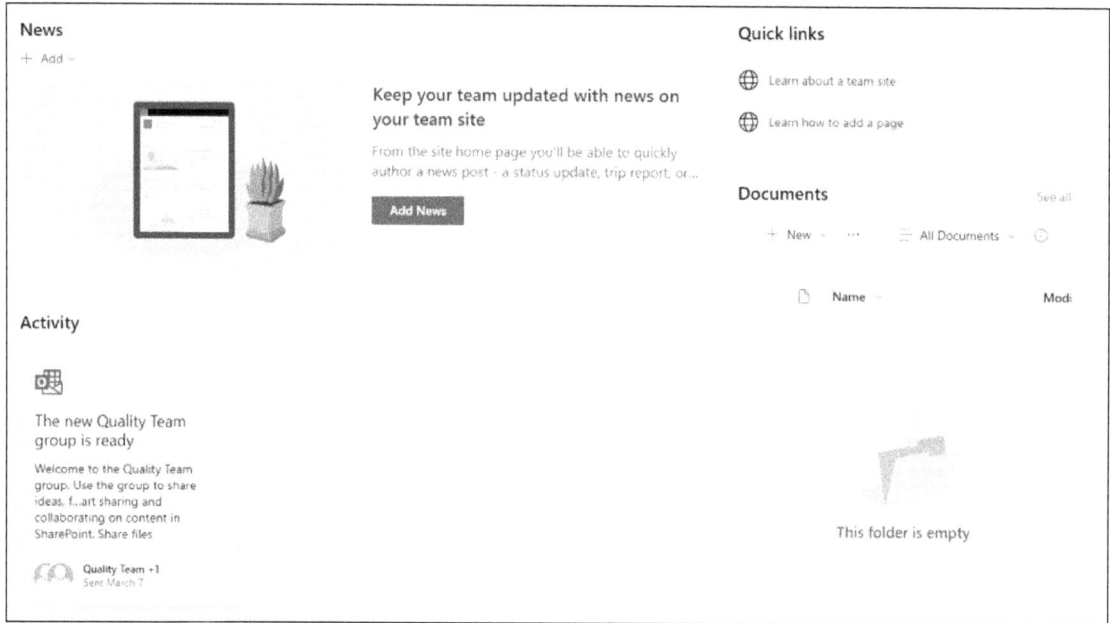

Figure 9.24: *Content Pane in SharePoint*

The following are the mentioned section covers key functionalities of SharePoint Library apps to help users maximize productivity and ensure seamless file management:

- **SharePoint Library apps**: The most common use of SharePoint is as a central repository for documents and files. Documents and files are stored in a SharePoint app known as a document library. Each site will contain one or more libraries depending on how it is configured (*Create a Site in SharePoint*, 2023).

- **Working with SharePoint Library apps**: To reach the SharePoint library, many sites have a single document library named **Documents.** When working in the document library, you must use the toolbar to change a document and its properties. The toolbar changes its appearance depending on how many documents have been selected.

  Additionally, actions can be found by clicking the ellipsis button at the end of the toolbar. Alternatively, you can click on the **Show Actions** button against a document to display a full menu of options available, as provided in *Figure 9.25:*

Figure 9.25: More option will display after clicking on three dots

You can open a document and see a preview of it. By clicking on the *ellipsis*, you can share the file with teammates or copy the link and paste it into Teams chat or email.

You can use the **Manage access** option to stop access. You can also delete the file.

We have download and rename options. If you have many files in the document library, use the **Pin to top** option. Click the **Version history** option to check the file's version history.

- **Manage items**: Once you have added documents to a library, the information they use can be changed to enable you to quickly find specific documents in the future. This is controlled by understanding metadata and creating views.

Understanding metadata

Metadata is essentially **Data about data**. It can be understood as the field used to categorize a document, such as the date created or modified.

Metadata can be split into two types:

- **Intrinsic metadata:** This is information controlled by SharePoint itself, such as the name of the person who uploaded the file, the name of the person who last edited the file, the date the file was edited, and so on.

- **Descriptive metadata**: It helps describe the file. This could be the document's file type, size, or an arbitrary label to help categorize the file.

Metadata can be seen in the columns displayed in the library.

The following example shows the Modified columns, which display the time the document was last edited, and the Modified by column, which shows who edited the document.

You can also view all the properties of the document. Select a single document in the library and click on the command to open the **Details** pane, which is located at the top right-hand corner. The editable properties of the document can be seen around a quarter of the way down the **Details** pane. You can click on each property to edit the information displayed or click on the **Edit All link** option to open a form to change the metadata.

Note: **Only the Name and Title metadata fields are displayed in the aforementioned example. Depending on how your site has been set up, additional fields may need to be edited in other SharePoint sites.**

There are different settings for documents. The following are a few options that are available on a SharePoint site:

- **Managing views**: A view is a page that displays information in SharePoint. Different views will be displayed for different app types on a SharePoint site. For simplicity, we will limit ourselves to views we can create in a document library.

  By default, a document library contains a single view called **All documents**. This view includes metadata information such as the type of icon, the document name, the modified date, and the modified fields.

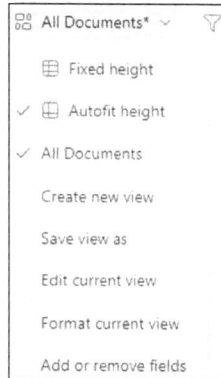

Figure 9.26: Options available for All documents

- **Adding fields**: As a user, you can click | add a column, which will show a dialog box with multiple options or metadata fields that can be added to the list as shown in the following figure:

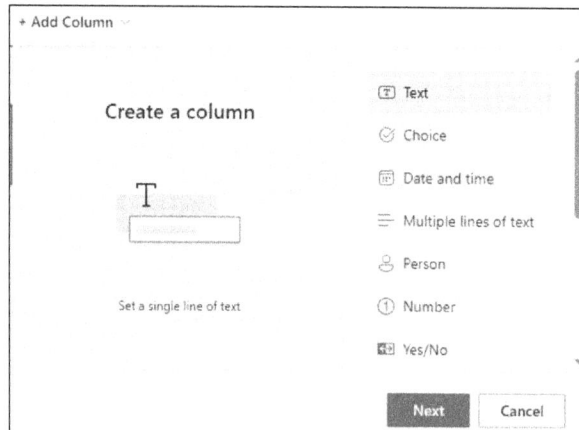

Figure 9.27: Datatypes available for columns

This option displays a list of additional columns or metadata fields that can be added. Select any option you wish to add, then click **Next** to fill in all the options accordingly.

- **Re-ordering fields:** To change the order of the fields, click on the title of the metadata field you want to move and drag and drop it to its new position.

- **Hiding fields:** Fields can be hidden from a view by clicking the existing fields heading, clicking on, and selecting **Hide this Column**.

- **Saving views:** If you add, move or hide metadata columns, you can change the look of the view where the columns are displayed.

    If a view has been edited, its name displays an asterisk. To save your changes, click the Views name and select **Save View As**. A dialog box will appear as shown in the following figure:

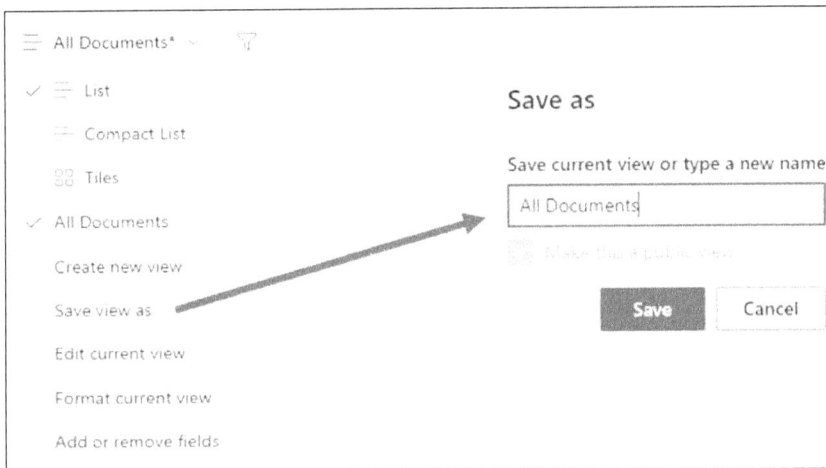

Figure 9.28: Save View options

To save the current view, do not change the name. Click **Save** to save the current view. To create a new view, type a new name, choose whether to make the view public, and click **Save**.

Note: **All members can see a public view of the SharePoint site. A non-public or Private view can only be seen by the creator of the view.**

Sorting, filtering, and grouping data

You can enhance views by sorting columns, creating groups based on repeated information, or filtering the view only to display specific records as follows:

Sorting

To sort a column, click on the column's heading and select the **sort type**. If the column contains text, you can sort it alphabetically as shown in the following figure:

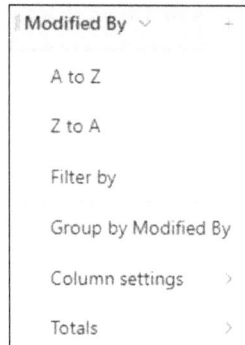

Figure 9.29: Sorting options

If it contains dates, you will be able to sort by date as follows:

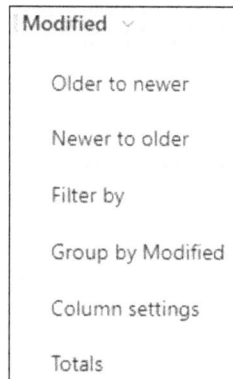

Figure 9.30: Sort by date options

Similarly, if it contains numbers, you will be able to sort by smaller to larger and vice versa.

Grouping

If a column contains repeated information, such as a date, a person, or a category, you can create a view that groups information by that data. Click on the column's heading and select **Group by...** The library will now display documents as a group.

You can expand or collapse the group heading if needed. To ungroup the column, click on the column name again and select **Group** once more to ungroup.

Filtering

To filter data, click on the column you wish to filter by and select **Filter By**. A task pane will appear to the right of the screen. Select the items you wish to Filter By and click **Apply**. To clear a filter, select the name of the filtered column again, choose **Filter by**, and this time click **Clear All**.

You can filter by multiple fields by clicking the **Filter** command on the right of the screen. This will open the **Filters** pane. As you select any of the options, the list of data will filter automatically. Select the **clear filters icon** at the top of the filters pane to remove all filters.

Working with document content

When you work with a document in a library, you can edit it as if it were stored in a Windows folder. You can also edit documents in the online web app and the desktop application.

The document can be edited in the Office 365 web app using the following steps:

1. Select a single document from your library.
2. Click the **Open** command and choose **Open in the browser.**
3. The document opens in the appropriate web app. Make your changes to the file as needed; they will be saved automatically in SharePoint.

The document can be edited in a desktop program using the following steps:

1. Select a single document in your library.
2. Click the **Open command** and choose **Open** in the app.
3. You may be prompted to open the item in the desktop application.
4. The document will open in its native desktop program.

Using alerts

An alert is an automatic reminder that can be set up so that you receive an email if a specific document has been edited.

Create an alert as follows:

- Select a single document in a library.
- Click the ellipsis icon on the command bar and choose **Alert Me**, as shown in the following figure:

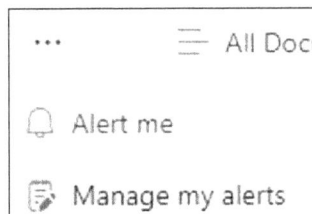

Figure 9.31: Alerts box

- A dialog box appears. Use this to determine what condition will create the alert and when you want to receive the alert email. Click **OK,** as follows:

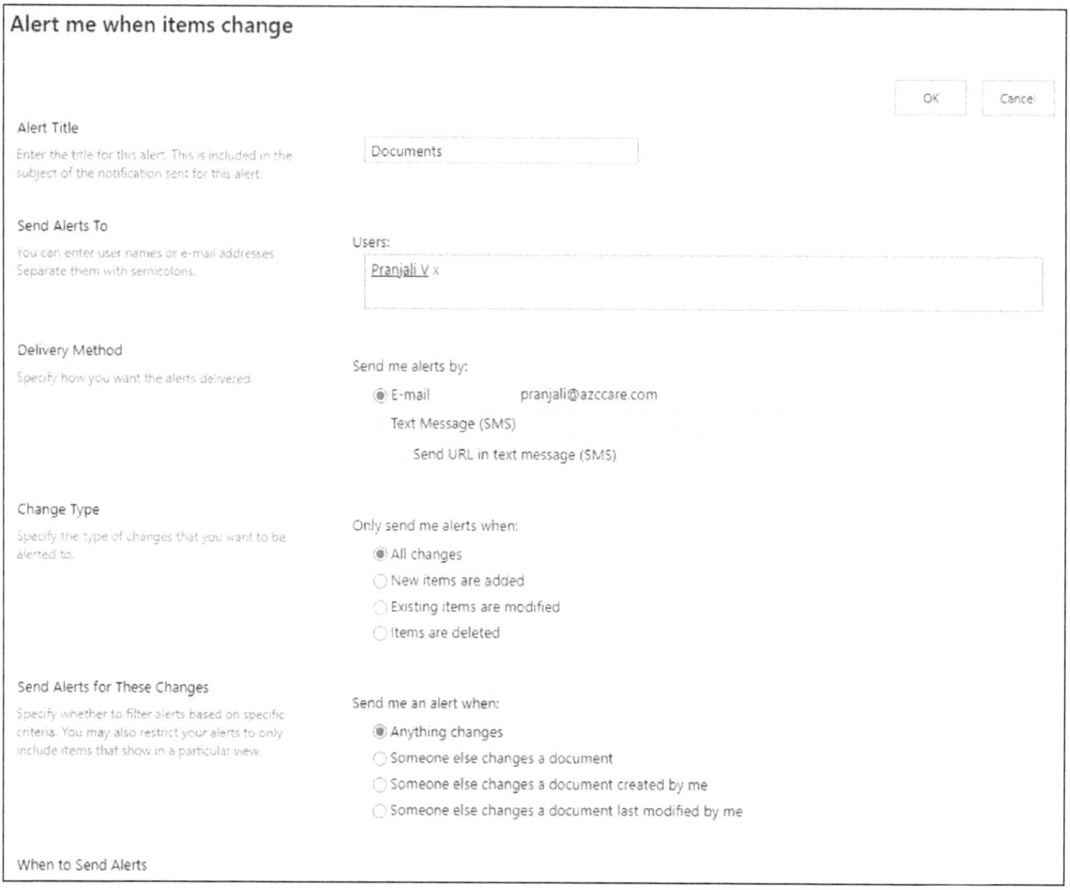

Alert me when items change

OK   Cancel

Alert Title
Enter the title for this alert. This is included in the
subject of the notification sent for this alert.

Documents

Send Alerts To
You can enter user names or e-mail addresses.
Separate them with semicolons.

Users:

Pranjali V x

Delivery Method
Specify how you want the alerts delivered.

Send me alerts by:
◉ E-mail   pranjali@azccare.com
   Text Message (SMS)
     Send URL in text message (SMS)

Change Type
Specify the type of changes that you want to be
alerted to.

Only send me alerts when:
◉ All changes
○ New items are added
○ Existing items are modified
○ Items are deleted

Send Alerts for These Changes
Specify whether to filter alerts based on specific
criteria. You may also restrict your alerts to only
include items that show in a particular view.

Send me an alert when:
◉ Anything changes
○ Someone else changes a document
○ Someone else changes a document created by me
○ Someone else changes a document last modified by me

When to Send Alerts

Figure 9.32: Creating an alert

Document collaboration and co-authoring

Up to 99 users can co-author a document simultaneously. Except for Excel, which can only be co-authored in the browser, OneNote, PowerPoint, and Word can be co-authored in the browser app and desktop program as follows:

- To co-author a document, two or more users need to open the document at the same time.

- You will be able to see which co-author is working on which part of the document at the same time as you are.

- A document will stop being co-authored once all other users have closed the document.

Note: **Co-authoring will not work if a document is checked out.**

Apply and customize SharePoint site templates

SharePoint offers various site templates containing pre-populated pages, page templates, news post templates, and web parts that can be tailored to meet your organization's needs. Once you create a communication or team site, you can change the site's name, description, logo, privacy level, and site classification. You can also set permissions for the site (*Apply and Customize SharePoint Site Templates*, 2023), as follows:

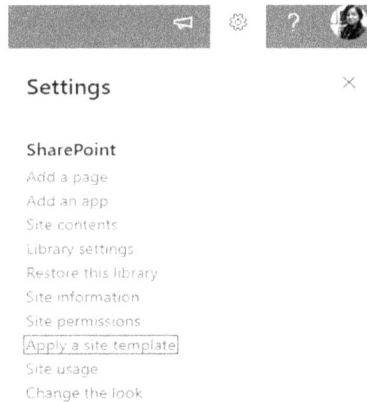

Figure 9.33: *Customize SharePoint site*

Click the **Next Steps** or **Settings** icon (gear icon) to **apply a site template,** as shown in the following figure:

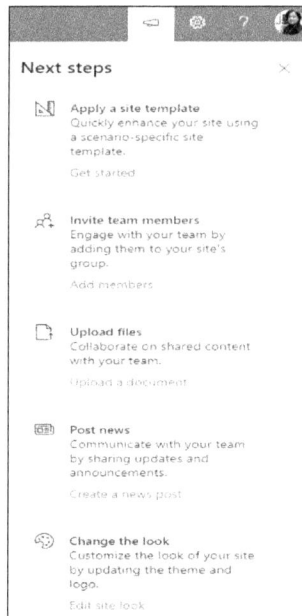

Figure 9.34: *Options to improve your site*

Select a site template to display additional information. If it meets your organizational needs, select **Use Template.** Review everything in the Site content and then Republish your site to make the SharePoint site available to viewers. SharePoint site can be accessed by internal employees (within the organization).

Elements of a SharePoint team site

A SharePoint team site is a collaborative workspace designed to help teams organize, share, and manage information and resources effectively.

The following are the key elements of a SharePoint team site:

- **News and announcements:** It is a place where the team can share the latest developments regarding the project, important news, and achievements with other members of the team.

- **Outlook Calendar**: As you know, the Outlook group calendar is available to every team site you create. So, anyone can check the upcoming team meetings right there on the site page.

- **Quick links**: You can easily share bookmarks or links with the team members.

- **Recent documents**: If you are on a SharePoint site, you can easily navigate to view the latest activity regarding your documents. It will also show you which document was updated when, along with the date and time and the person's name who modified it.

- **Document library**: It is a place where you can store documents for all the team members. Every SharePoint site has a document library, and it is the default one.

- **Quick launch links to Outlook, Teams, Planner, and OneNote notebook**: A team site has quick links available on its left-hand navigation that allow users to link to other resources related to the project. Links can also be added directly to Microsoft 365 applications like Microsoft Planner, Outlook Calendar, and Microsoft Teams.

- **Add a web part**: In any SharePoint site, a web part can be added according to the requirement by clicking on the plus sign. Select the web part and add it where you want to insert the content. Select the web part you want to use, such as **Text, Image, File viewer, Date, Link,** etc. (*Zelfond*, 2019), as follows:

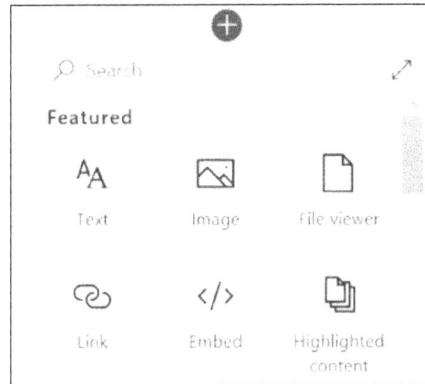

Figure 9.35: Add a web part

- **Hero Web Part**: Hero Web Part is the most frequently used web parts in the tiles layout categories that can be used to display five tiles layout options like images, texts and documents, etc. By default, SharePoint displays the site page with links to relevant info and colorful images/tiles and it can be transformed in terms of look and feel.

Get your news and content from anywhere, at work, home, or on the go. Set up the SharePoint app on your mobile device (*Set up Your Mobile Apps*, 2023), as follows:

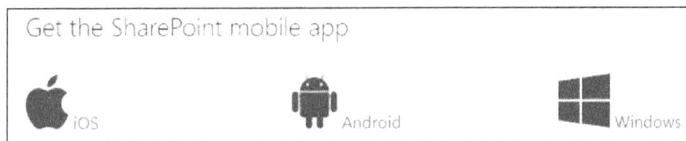

Figure 9.36: SharePoint mobile apps available on different devices

Saving files to OneDrive or SharePoint

When you work on any Office application like Word or Excel, save the file on OneDrive for Business. Unless you share your OneDrive files with others, they remain private. This is particularly useful if you still need to create a team. It is recommended that you save your files where your team works if you are already working in Microsoft Teams, SharePoint, or Outlook because OneDrive for work and connects you to all your shared libraries, too (*Should I Save Files to OneDrive or SharePoint?* 2023).

OneDrive allows teams to collaborate by creating a shared library and adding members. Shared libraries are accessible within Teams, SharePoint, and Outlook, and the team can comfortably use or copy the files whenever necessary.

Difference between OneDrive and SharePoint and Teams

OneDrive for Business is a place where all your work files reside. You can share files with others through MS Teams, and others can also share files with you. As a user of OneDrive, you will enjoy a consistent, intuitive file experience across all your systems, including web, mobile, and the desktop of a Windows or whatever device you use.

SharePoint in Microsoft 365 provides the content services for all files in Microsoft 365, including files you work on. SharePoint is powered by content collaboration across Microsoft 365 and manages your files. Beyond files, SharePoint enables portals, news, pages, lists, and a platform for business apps within the organization.

Conclusion

In this chapter, we focused on OneDrive for Business and SharePoint.

SharePoint and OneDrive are cloud-based platforms designed for online file storage, enabling users to retrieve their files from any device with internet connectivity. It is important to note that access to this online storage is contingent upon an active internet connection. OneDrive for Business offers 1TB of cloud storage, with the potential to expand to 5TB based on the user's role and the license provided by the IT department. By syncing SharePoint and OneDrive with your device, you can access files stored within these applications similarly to how you would access folders on a Windows 10 device, even in the absence of an internet connection.

The next time your device connects to the internet, the changes you made to files on your OneDrive or SharePoint will sync with cloud storage, updating your documentation. Similarly, any changes made by others will sync down to the files on your device. The SharePoint team sites in Microsoft 365 make it easy for project teams, departments, and divisions to collaborate efficiently and effectively.

In the next chapter, we will discuss Microsoft Forms, the capabilities of Outlook, Microsoft Planner, and Viva Engage. These applications form a crucial part of the Microsoft 365 suite. Microsoft Forms allows users to create surveys and polls, while Microsoft Outlook is primarily used for email communication and offers a variety of additional features that will be discussed in the upcoming chapter. We will also discuss the task management tool and the method for assigning tasks to your colleagues. Lastly, the chapter will address Viva Engage, a social media platform specifically for Microsoft 365 users within an organization.

References

1. *Apply and customize SharePoint site templates.* (2023). Microsoft Support. **https://support.microsoft.com/en-us/office/apply-and-customize-sharepoint-site-templates-39382463-0e45-4d1b-be27-0e96aeec8398**

2. *Create a site in SharePoint.* (2023). Microsoft Support. **https://support.microsoft.com/en-us/office/create-a-site-in-sharepoint-4d1e11bf-8ddc-499d-b889-2b48d10b1ce8**

3. *Get started with SharePoint.* (2023). Microsoft Support. **https://support.microsoft.com/en-us/office/get-started-with-sharepoint-909ec2f0-05c8-4e92-8ad3-3f8b0b6cf261**

4. Sajid, H. (2023, June 29). *What Is OneDrive for Business and What Does it Do?* ShareGate. **https://sharegate.com/blog/what-is-onedrive-for-business-and-what-does-it-do**

5. *Set up your mobile apps.* (2023). Microsoft Support. **https://support.microsoft.com/en-us/office/set-up-your-mobile-apps-539608ac-4725-455e-aea0-9ca1f769849f**

6. *Share OneDrive files and folders.* (2023). Microsoft Support. **https://support.microsoft.com/en-us/office/share-onedrive-files-and-folders-9fcc2f7d-de0c-4cec-93b0-a82024800c07**

7. *Should I save files to OneDrive or SharePoint?* (2023). Microsoft Support. **https://support.microsoft.com/en-us/office/should-i-save-files-to-onedrive-or-sharepoint-d18d21a0-1f9f-4f6c-ac45-d52afa0a4a2e?ui=en-us&rs=en-us&ad=us**

8. *What is OneDrive for work or school?* (2023). Microsoft Support. **https://support.microsoft.com/en-us/office/what-is-onedrive-for-work-or-school-187f90af-056f-47c0-9656-cc0ddca7fdc2**

9. *What is SharePoint?* (2023). Microsoft Support. **https://support.microsoft.com/en-us/office/what-is-sharepoint-97b915e6-651b-43b2-827d-fb25777f446f**

10. Zelfond, G. (2019, August 21). *SharePoint site examples built with out of the box features.* SharePoint Maven. **https://sharepointmaven.com/sharepoint-site-examples-built-with-out-of-the-box-features/**

Join our Discord space

Join our Discord workspace for latest updates, offers, tech happenings around the world, new releases, and sessions with the authors:

https://discord.bpbonline.com

CHAPTER 10

Microsoft Forms, Outlook, Planner, and Yammer

Introduction

In this chapter, you will learn various applications available in the Microsoft 365 suite. Here, we are going to learn about Microsoft Forms, Microsoft Outlook, Microsoft Planner, and Yammer, which is now known as **Viva Engage**. Microsoft Forms is an application that allows users to create surveys, quizzes, and polls, create effective forms with easy-to-use tools and clear design suggestions. Users can access Microsoft Forms through a web browser or a dedicated mobile app. We will also learn about Outlook, which is an email client and includes a robust calendar feature that allows users to schedule appointments, meetings, and events. We will also learn about Microsoft Planner, which is a task management tool, and used for team collaboration. We have Yammer, which is known as **Viva Engage**, and is a social media platform for Microsoft 365 users within the organization.

Structure

The following applications will be covered:

- Overview of Microsoft Forms
- Accessing and creating forms
- Microsoft Outlook

- Microsoft Planner
- Microsoft Yammer

Objectives

By the end of the chapter, you will learn how to collect better data and make well-informed decisions using Microsoft Forms and how to create quizzes and get feedback effortlessly with surveys, polls, and quizzes. You will also learn to share overviews and benefits of Microsoft Outlook, and how to assign work with the help of Microsoft Planner and track all the plans.

Overview of Microsoft Forms

Microsoft Forms is a browser-based application that can be used to create surveys, quizzes, or polls within Office 365. Anybody can be invited to complete the survey or take part in the quiz on virtually any device, outside or within the organization. All they need is an invitation. Results are shown immediately/in real-time and can be exported for analysis with built-in analytics. It is easy to add different types of questions, make those questions mandatory or optional, and customize the look as per business requirements.

Microsoft Forms allows you to choose different types of settings while sharing the form with others. It also gives collaboration access to your colleagues, as shown:

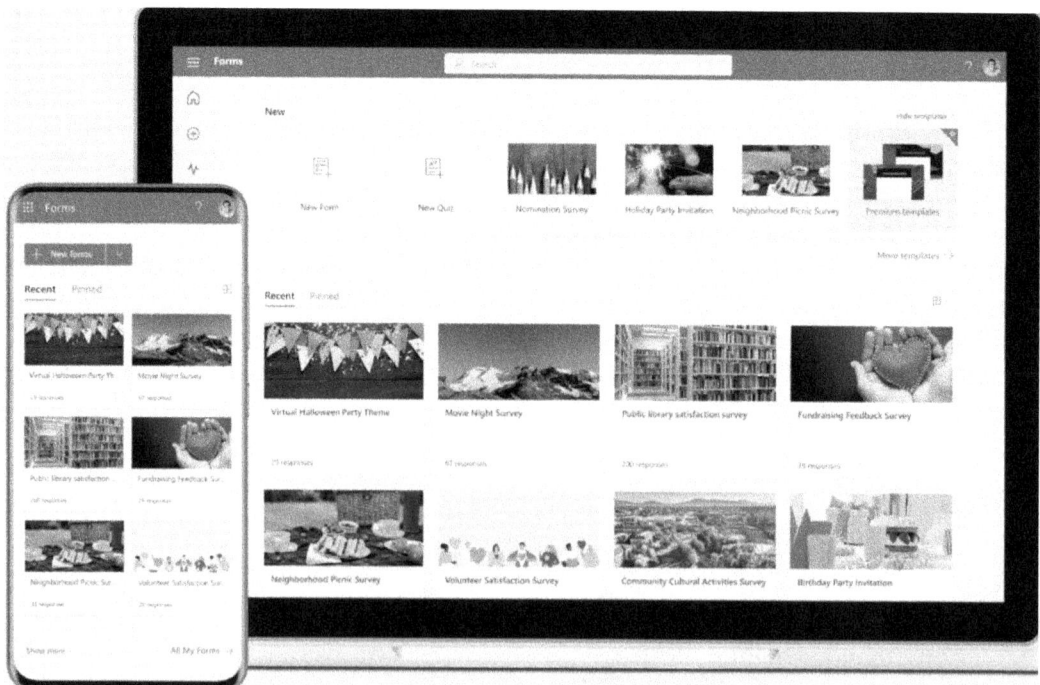

Figure 10.1: Microsoft Forms outline

Accessing and creating forms

Starting Microsoft Forms is straightforward. Once you have logged in to Microsoft 365 (**https://portal.office.com**), use the tile found in the list of M365 apps.

Alternatively, open a web browser and enter:

https://forms.office.com

Figure 10.2: Microsoft Forms icon

You may be prompted to log in using your Microsoft 365 or organizational account.

Navigating forms

After clicking on Forms, a new form titled **Untitled Form** will open. Enter a title for the form. While adding a description is optional, it is recommended to help clarify the form's intended purpose. Users can also include terms and conditions in the description section if needed. (*Create a Form with Microsoft Forms, 2023*), as follows:

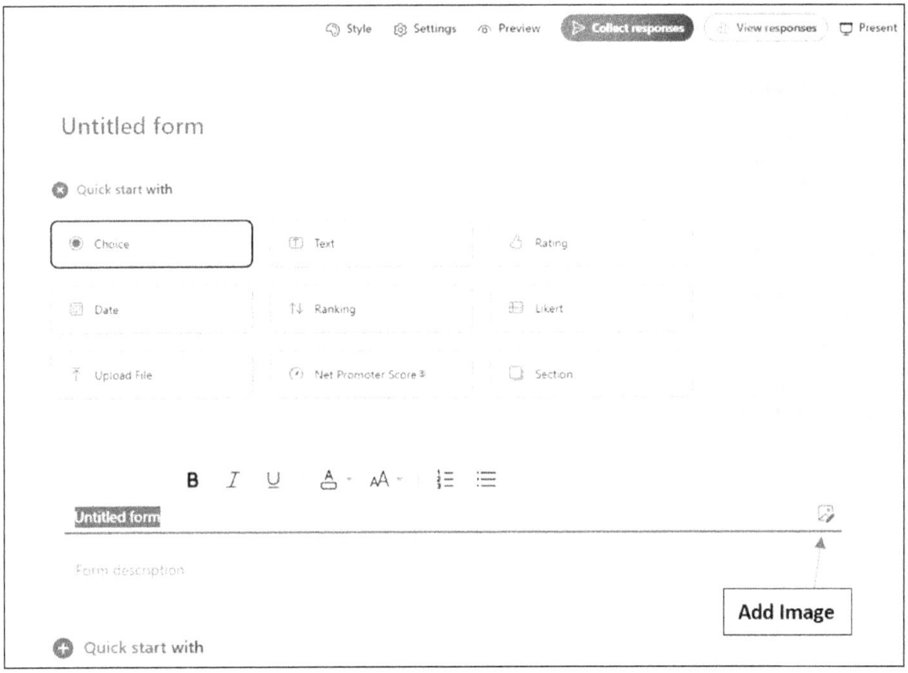

Figure 10.3: Creating Microsoft Forms from scratch

Figure 10.3 demonstrates the process by which a user can generate a form and input the required details. While adding the form name, the user can format the text, including bold, italic, and underline. Font color and size can also be changed, along with bullet and numbered lists. If necessary, add an image by selecting the **Image** icon, as shown:

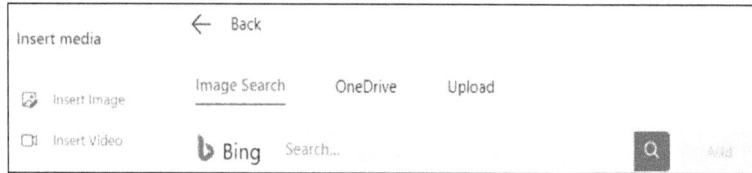

Figure 10.4: *Various sources to upload images*

Figure 10.4 demonstrates that when a user clicks on **Insert Image**, they can choose an image from Bing, OneDrive, or upload a file from their device or another location. Once an image has been added, it can be edited by selecting the pencil icon displayed next to it. Edit the image to show more or less of it, using Zoom. For screen readers, add a descriptive/alternative text using the **Envelope** icon. All edits to the form and its contents are automatically saved.

Add question in the form

Various categories of questions can be included. Each question is automatically assigned a number on the form. *Figure 10.5* illustrates various categories of questions, with a detailed description mentioned for each type, as follows:

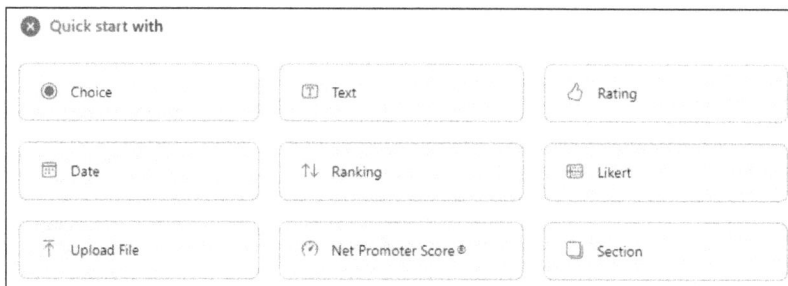

Figure 10.5: *Various type of questions*

- **Choice:** Provides a set of answers to the question.
- **Text:** Allows the answer to be free-form text.
- **Rating:** Rating questions, offer stars or numbers. There are 10 types of categories that are available. You can add a descriptive label to help the person answer the question.
- **Date:** Ensure that the answer is in a date format.

  Note: **The US date format is used in the form, which is m/d/yyyy.**

- **Ranking:** Provides set answers to be arranged in order.

Once a form is created, users can take a preview by clicking on **Preview** available at the top.

- **Preview your form:** Select **Preview** to view how your form will look. The form will open in preview mode, allowing you to see how it appears to respondents. Switch between **Computer** and **Mobile** to see how the form appears on a desktop or a mobile device, respectively.

Figure 10.6 illustrates that by clicking on **Add new question,** user can select the type of question. If required, the users can also add an image to a question, as shown:

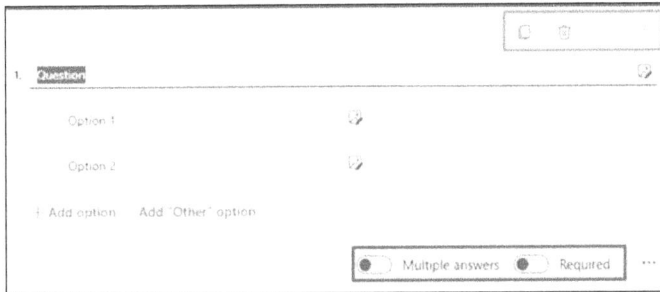

Figure 10.6: *Adding a question in the form*

While entering a **Choice** based question, it will suggest the type of answers you want to add based on the question. Forms also suggest answers if keywords are recognized. While adding answers, the users can add an image next to the answers. It will help to choose correct answers based on the pictorial images given for answers (*Anderson, 2023*). Use the toolbar in the top right corner of the question window to rearrange the question order, duplicate it for reuse, or delete it from the form.

Enable the selection (on) of more than one choice, if **answers are multiple**, and to make a question mandatory, turn on the slider control for **Required**.

Click the ellipsis (three dots) to access additional options for the question. Every question includes a **Subtitle** option.

The following are the available options for the **Choice** question type:

Shuffle options	Randomly rearrange a set of choices.
Drop-down	A list of options when clicked, allowing users to select one.
Subtitle	Add a help tip next to the question.
Add branching	Add branches in the form.

Figure 10.7: *Additional options for the questions*

Add sections to your form

If you are creating a lengthy survey, it is very helpful to organize your questions into multiple pages or sections, which can be easily rearranged. Sections will help you to orient your form responders, to consume a long survey that has been organized into smaller parts (*Add Sections to Your Survey or Questionnaire, 2023*).

To add a section, select **Add New** | Select the section by clicking on three **(...)** dots. Add a section title and description to provide more context for the questions in this section.

Note: **Once you include sections in your form, the shuffle questions feature is disabled.**

Organize sections

In the section, if you want to move, duplicate or remove, click on more settings for the section using ... in the upper right corner.

You can select any of the following options (*Writtenhouse, 2022*):

- **Duplicate section:** Allows you to make a copy of the question within that section.
- **Remove section:** Select **Just** section to remove just the section header or select **Section and questions** to remove the section and all questions within it.
- **Move section:** Use the **Move up** or **Move down** arrows to rearrange the order of your sections.

Add branching

The questions you add to the form are all numbered sequentially and will be presented in that order. The answer to a question might dictate which question is displayed next or even at the end of the form. The process is called **Branching** (*Use Branching Logic in Microsoft Forms, 2023*), as shown:

Figure 10.8: Adding branches to the form

Select a question and then select the ... (ellipses) to add branching in the form. Click a question or question option and pick the next action from the drop-down menu to the right of it. Select **End of the form** when you want to jump directly and click **Submit** to finish the form. Click **Back** when the required **Branching** has been applied.

Add a style

If you would like to change the static background color or add an animated image as a background, or any live theme in the form, or any music, simply select the **Style** option in the top right corner. A live theme is a type of animative background, which could auto-replay on its own like an endless loop. With these animative live themes, survey senders and respondents will feel a sense of engagement, connection, and inclusivity. The theme is applied immediately to the whole form.

If creating for a specific scenario, a predefined live theme is automatically advised, based on the relevancy and hopefully saves your time searching and navigating. The form will suggest a set of cover page templates based on your theme, like holiday, picnic, education, training feedback, etc. You can also upload your image from your device or *Bing.com*. Get the attention of the users by adding music to the form, as follows:

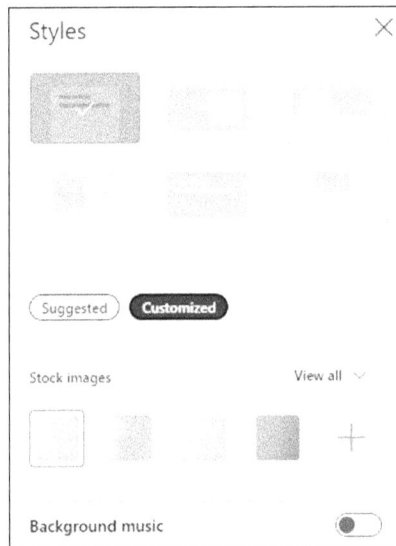

Figure 10.9: Different styles are available for forms

Form offers a variety of sound bites to amplify your message and theme. The live theme works for both quizzes and forms.

Note: **Microsoft will be rolling out mobile experiences in the coming days.**

Collect responses

Distribute to multiple channels, with an adaptive view for more responses. To provide designers with a quick and easy method of making attractive invitations available on different platforms, Microsoft has updated the distribution capability of forms. To increase response rates, users now have a variety of distribution options when sending forms/surveys to multiple channels, including Outlook, Teams, QR codes, and consumer accounts on Facebook and Twitter (*Send a Form and Collect Responses*, 2023).

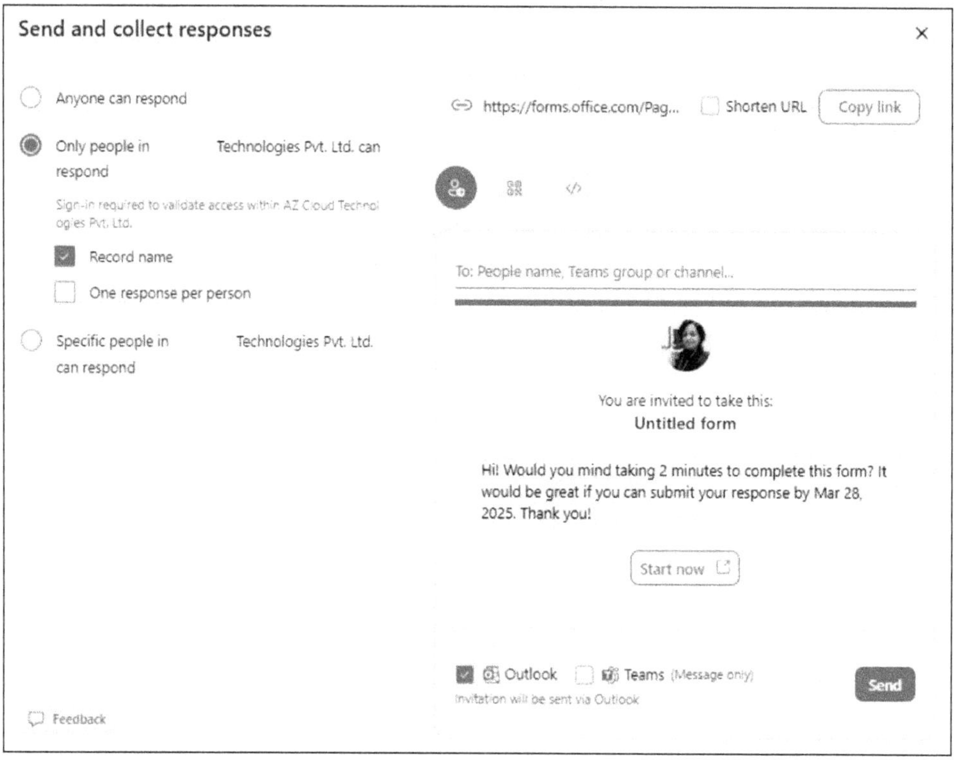

Figure 10.10: Various modes of collecting responses

There are several methods available for gathering responses. After the form has been prepared, Microsoft Forms can be distributed through the following means:

- **Link:** Users can share the form through a link. The link creates a unique address/ shortened URL for the form, which can be copied to another web page, email, document, channel or in a message. Forms are commonly published in this manner (*Check and Share Your Form Results*, 2023).

- **Invitation:** Select the **Invitation** option to send your form/survey, through Outlook and Teams (in a chat through message only). The cover page will be added automatically in the email as shown in the following figure:

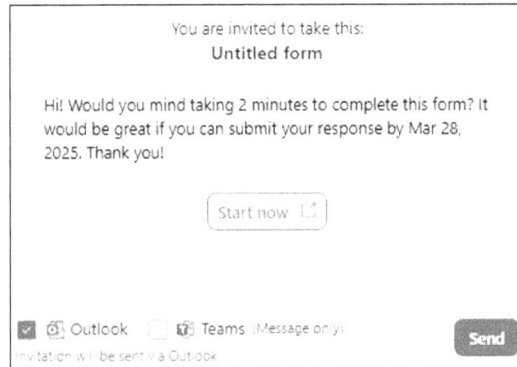

Figure 10.11: Sharing through Outlook and Teams

- **QR Code:** Share your form via QR code. When you want to share your form in an offline mode, you can generate a downloadable, unique QR code to capture more responses, as shown:

Figure 10.12: Sharing from through QR Code

- **Embed:** Use this method to physically embed the form into another application, such as Sway blogs or any other web page. The form is completed directly in Sway or the web page, without the need to navigate to another page, as shown:

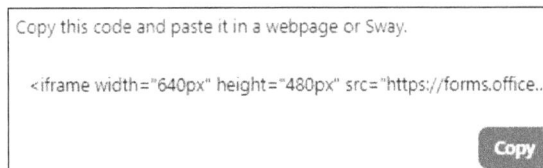

Figure 10.13: Sharing through embedding in Sway or another webpage

Present mode

Microsoft has introduced a new feature in Forms, i.e., live presentation capabilities, which offers a new way to share forms or quizzes in any online or in-person event. By simply clicking on the **Present** icon located in the top right corner, you can enter the interactive present. Once in the present mode, a QR code to vote or a short link to the survey will be displayed on the right side of your form. Using their smartphones, respondents can access the form through this gateway. All they need to do is scan the QR code with their phone's camera or a QR code scanning app, and they will be instantly directed to the form, as shown:

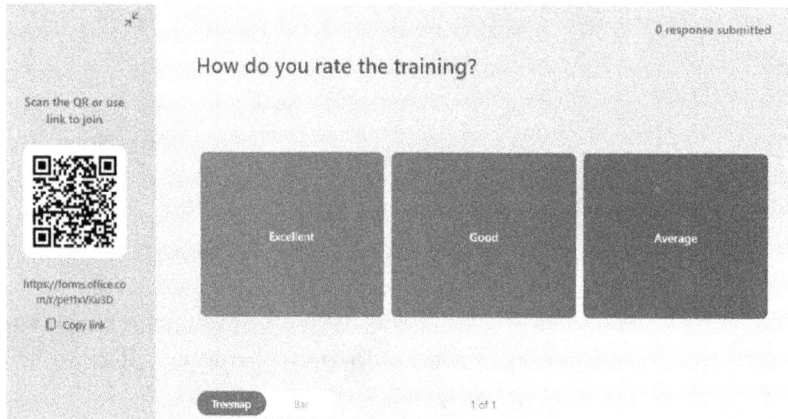

Figure 10.14: Submission through QR code

In the present mode, there is no need to navigate back to the response page to check the responses, since they are visible on the question. When new responses come in the result, they will dynamically update to reflect the latest information. All responses are saved in the **View responses** tab once you exit the present mode and enter editing mode.

Permission control

Forms and quizzes will respect the permission settings set at the form or quiz level. However, we suggest selecting **Anyone can respond,** if you have an external audience or you want to capture as much information as possible. Switching to the other two permission modes will require respondents to sign in to a Microsoft account, as shown:

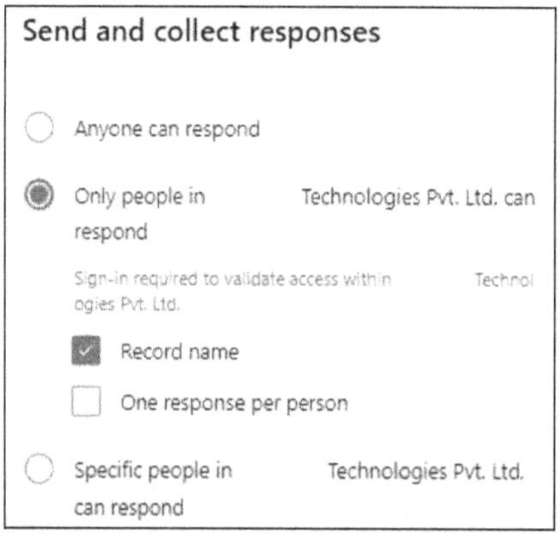

Figure 10.15: Permission for submitting form

Responses

Responses are automatically collected and displayed in real time, eliminating the need for manual compilation. The top banner provides an overview, and you can click **Check individual results** to view each submission or export the data to Excel, as follows:

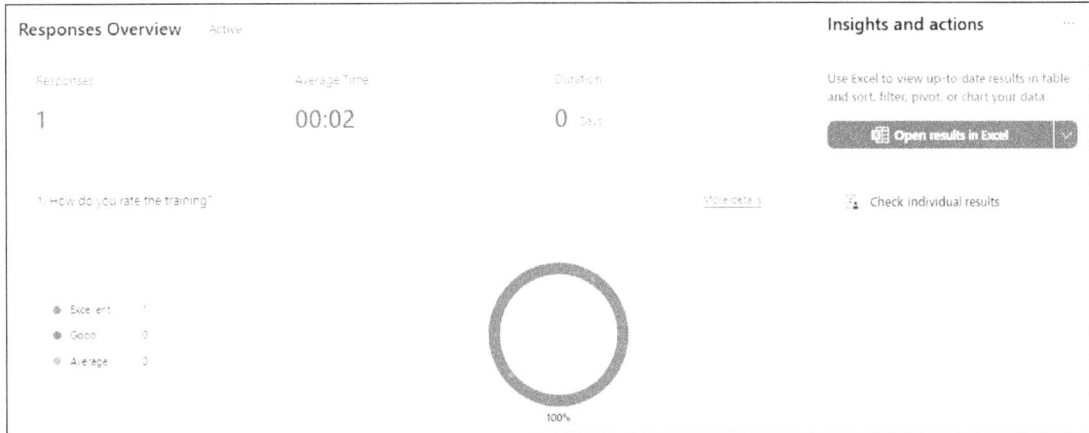

Figure 10.16: Viewing results

Each question appears sequentially below the banner, accompanied by a graphic that visually represents the responses. Most graphics are displayed as charts, while rating questions showcase the selected style (e.g., stars) along with the average rating. Selecting **More Details,** next to a question will open a separate window with a table listing all the responses to the selected question, as shown:

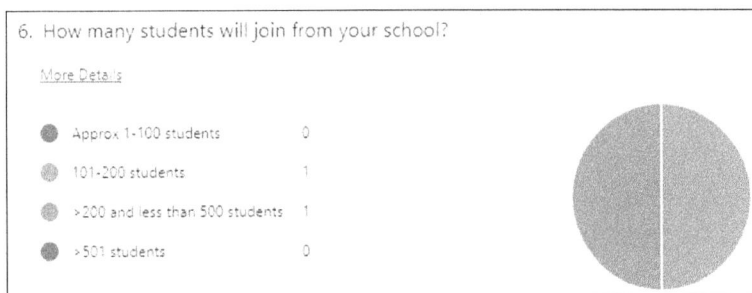

Figure 10.17: Responses are available in graph/chart

Exporting responses

Responses can be exported by printing or by opening them in Excel. All responses to all the questions can be printed by selecting the ellipses **(…)** and the **Print summary** option. This will open the print dialog box, allowing you to select an appropriate destination, e.g., OneNote, a printer, XPS, or PDF, as follows:

Figure 10.18: Insights and actions of all responses

The responses from an individual can also be printed by selecting **Check individual results.**

If there is a need to take the responses and analyze them, or use them outside of the form, select the **Open results in Excel** option. A formatted data table will be created in a new workbook.

Preview

Before you share your form, it is a good idea to test it using **Preview** option. The form will be displayed as if it has been shared and is a fully working copy. Select **Mobile** to check the preview for phones, as follows:

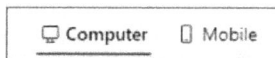

Select the ellipses **(...)** to collaborate and view the results, and to get a link to duplicate. Invite others to add or edit questions, view responses, and share with others. Allow others to use your form as a template and make it their own. Responses are not included, as follows:

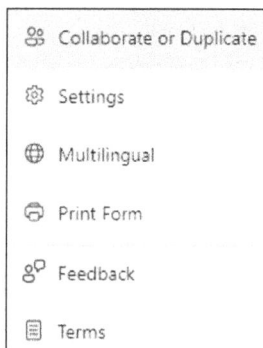

Figure 10.19: More option for collaboration and settings

Settings

Form settings can be done before the form is shared with others. The option controls **Who can fill out this form** and when it is available. Decide whether you want to limit the form just to the people who are inside the organization and whether they can only complete the form once or provide multiple responses.

Organizers can select **Accept Responses** and choose a **Start Date** and **End Date** of the form. Set the time duration so that the responder can fill out the form during the set time. Editing is not allowed after the timer ends. Their answers will be auto submitted when the timer is up.

> Note: **If names are not recorded, you cannot restrict the number of times a person submits the form. Disabling Accept responses will prompt you to enter a message for anyone attempting to access the form. This option is useful when the form is no longer active.**

Show Progress bar is only available for multi-page surveys. An option is available for **Shuffling** the questions. Having determined who can complete the form, you may wish to limit its availability and alter the order in which the questions are displayed.

You can also customize a thank you message for the sender.

Once the required options have been set, click away from the **Settings** menu to apply them. All changes are saved automatically.

Response receipts can also be set after each submission, and the organizer will get an email notification of each response, as follows:

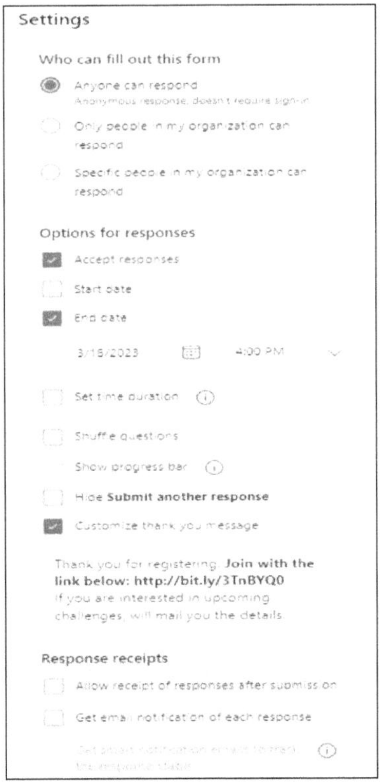

Figure 10.20: Settings for the form

Creating a quiz

Quizzes share the same authoring, reviewing, and sharing processes and features as forms. There are two differences noticeable when creating the questions. A points rating is given to the questions, and, for some questions, the correct answer is specified. Start the authoring process by selecting **New Quiz.** Enter a title and description as required and give the quiz an image, as shown:

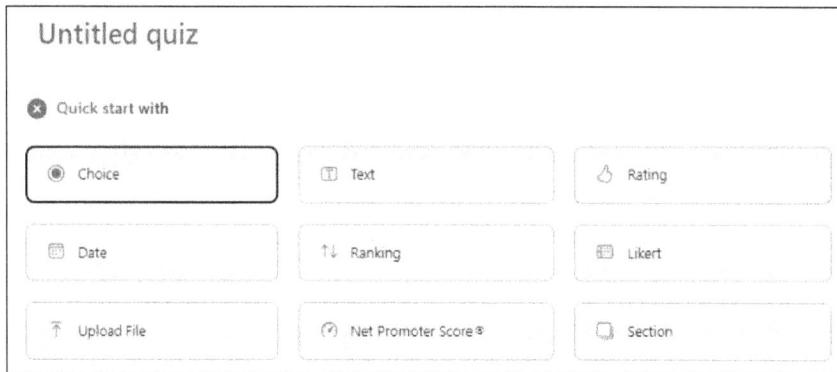

Figure 10.21: Creating a quiz

Adding questions

Questions are added just like they are on a form. The question types are the same for a quiz as they are for a form, although some of the options differ slightly. Enter the keywords and suggested answers will be displayed. Here is an **Option** question example with the correct answer being set:

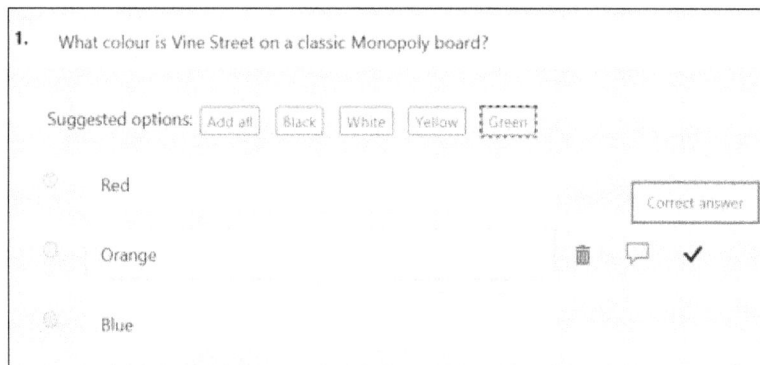

Figure 10.22: Various options can be set for the question

In this **Text** question, multiple possible answers are provided, as follows:

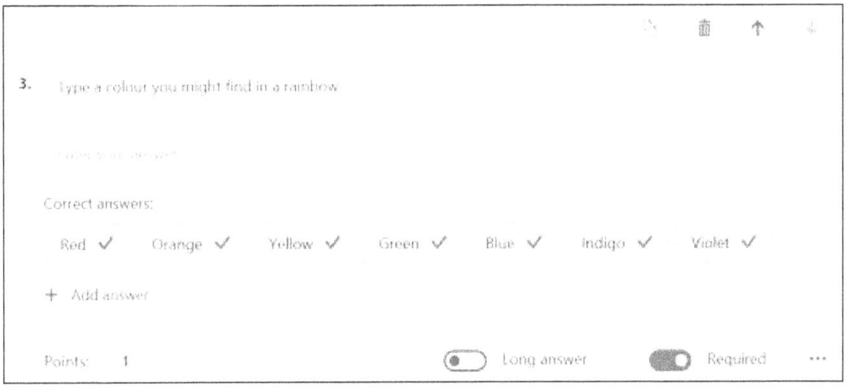

Figure 10.23 Multiple answers for a question

Here, a **Ranking** question is being created. The correct order of the answers is set by the author when the question is written.

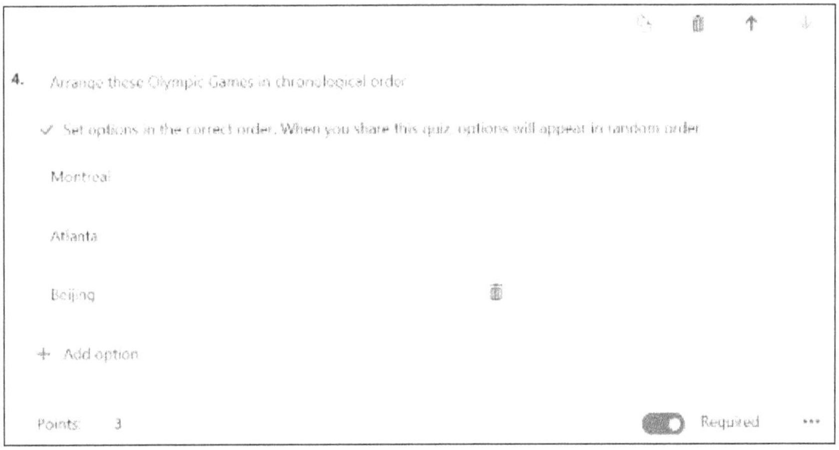

Figure 10.24: Setting correct order of ranking question

Setting question options

Most options are the same as for the forms. Set whether a question is required and add **subtitles** to provide some context or help with the question. Options specific to a quiz include setting the point value if a score is being collected.

If a quiz is being used as a test, it might be useful to have suggested options displayed in a different order each time the quiz is completed. Use **Shuffle** to turn on the feature for a question. Quiz questions can also include numbers and equations. To use numbers, classic mathematical operators such as ÷ for divide, or other symbols, use the **Math** option.

The math input panel will be displayed to select the symbols from, as follows:

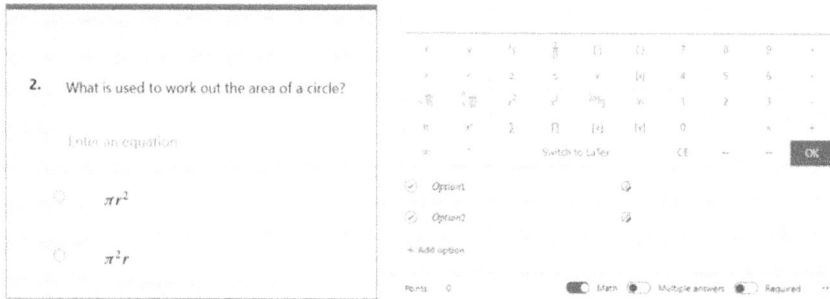

Figure 10.25: Setting Math's question in a quiz

Add a style

Styles are added by selecting **Style** in the Microsoft quiz window. The same built-in colors, animated immersive styles, pictures, and background music are used for both quizzes and forms, or you can add your own.

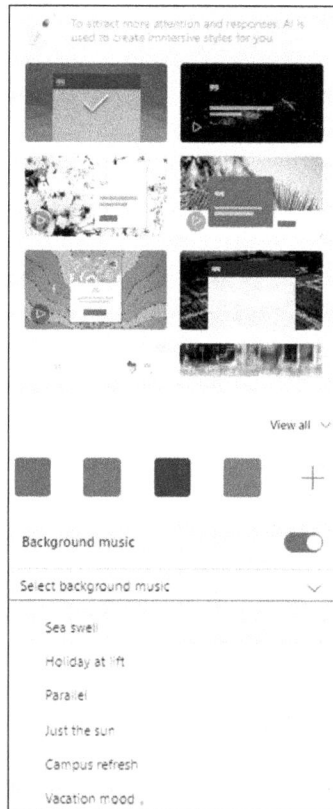

Figure 10.26: Different styles available for quiz

Preview of the quiz

Before the quiz is shared, it should be previewed to test that the questions work as required:

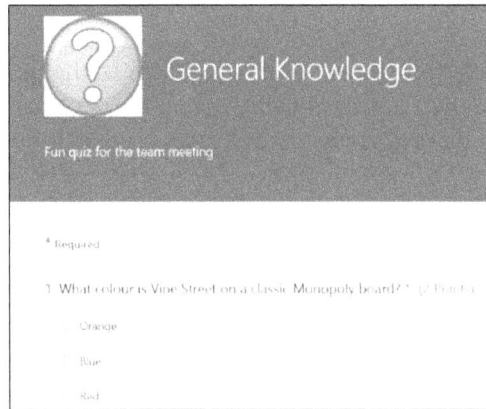

Figure 10.27: Preview of the quiz

Quizzes completed as a preview are live. The results are automatically collated under **Responses** and should be removed before sharing.

Quiz sharing

Quizzes share the form options, controlling who can complete the quiz and whether their name is collected, and date-based boundaries control when the quiz is live (*Adjust Your Form or Quiz Settings in Microsoft Forms*, 2023).

An additional option is also set for a quiz. The option controls whether the person sees their results automatically. Found under **Settings**, the slider control is used to change the option. It is set to be on as a default, as shown:

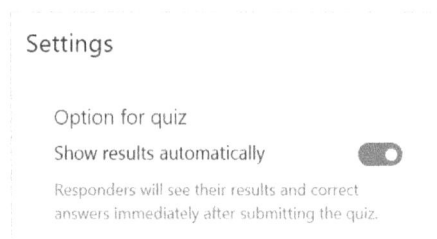

Figure 10.28: Settings for the quiz to see results automatically

Share the quiz

Once the quiz settings and questions are set, the quiz can be shared. Microsoft Forms provides multiple ways to share a quiz with respondents, making it easy to distribute and collect responses. The available sharing options are via link, invitation, QR code, and embedding in a webpage or website.

Responses

Responses can either be sent to the person who has just taken the quiz or to the author. Personal responses will, if set to be shown automatically, reveal the score achieved. The questions that were either answered correctly or incorrectly are displayed as follows:

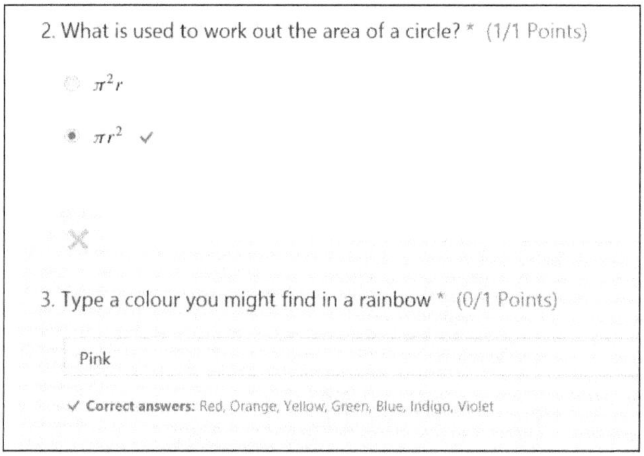

Figure 10.29: Responses of the quiz

The quiz author should navigate to **Responses** by opening the quiz directly in Microsoft Forms. Answers can be reviewed by a person, exported to Excel, and printed or deleted.

Providing feedback and posting

A quiz has an extra feature. Feedback can be provided directly to a person for an individual question, or results can be posted. Use to access the answers by people or by question. Each question or response can be viewed as follows:

Figure 10.30: Reviewing the answers of quiz

To provide feedback directly to the person who has given the answer, select the **speech bubble.** This will display a text box to write feedback into.

All responses back to individuals are sent by choosing a **Post scores** option. Scores can be posted from the main **Responses** view. Posting scores will give respondents access to view feedback and the results of their quiz. Respondents can view their results using the same link that they used to launch the quiz, as shown:

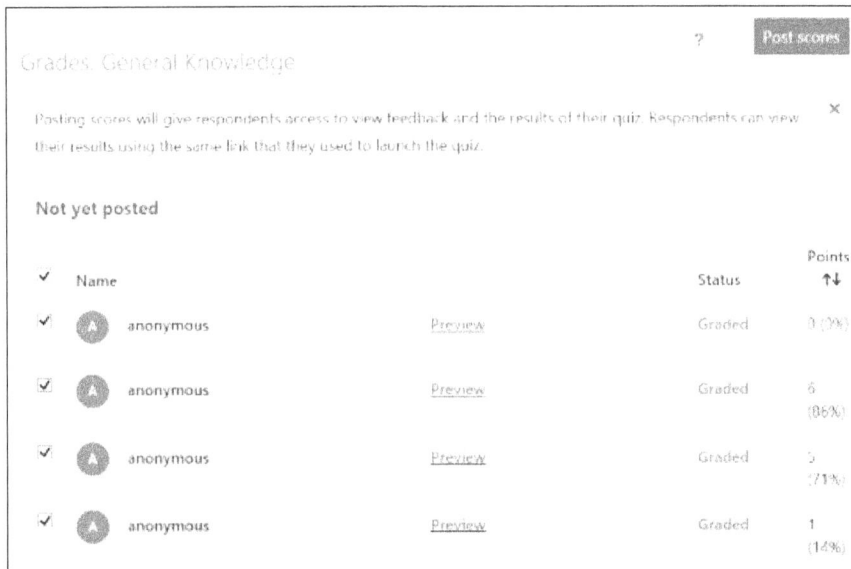

Figure 10.31: Reviewing the answers and Post scores to the respondents

People are selected in this dialog box to receive feedback and scores. Posting scores makes them available, along with individual feedback, to everyone selected. Scores and feedback are accessed by following the same link to the quiz that was shared previously.

Note: **Scores and feedback can be provided even if the quiz is still open.**

Microsoft Outlook

Outlook desktop is one of the most important prominent tools. It is used to receive emails, manage tasks and schedule meetings with ease. Here, you are going to learn different features that contribute towards saving your time and helping you boost your productivity. You will also learn tips to manage and share your mailbox and Outlook calendar. Outlook will enhance productivity and allow you to focus on the messages that matter most to you. It also allows you to share files from the cloud (OneDrive) so that the recipients always have the latest version. With Outlook, you can stay connected and productive, wherever you are. It brings you new features, intelligent assisted capabilities, as well as a modern and simplified design for your Outlook application.

Introduction of Outlook

Outlook is a productivity tool designed for sending and receiving emails, organizing messages, and managing and sharing calendars. It offers intelligent assistant capabilities and a new modern and simplified design. Outlook includes numerous functionalities that enhance daily productivity, and you will explore various features that can be beneficial for everyday tasks.

Outlook user interface

When Outlook opens, it displays the *Mail* view by default. *Figure 10.32* shows the Outlook interface which is divided into three sections: folder pane, content pane and reading pane:

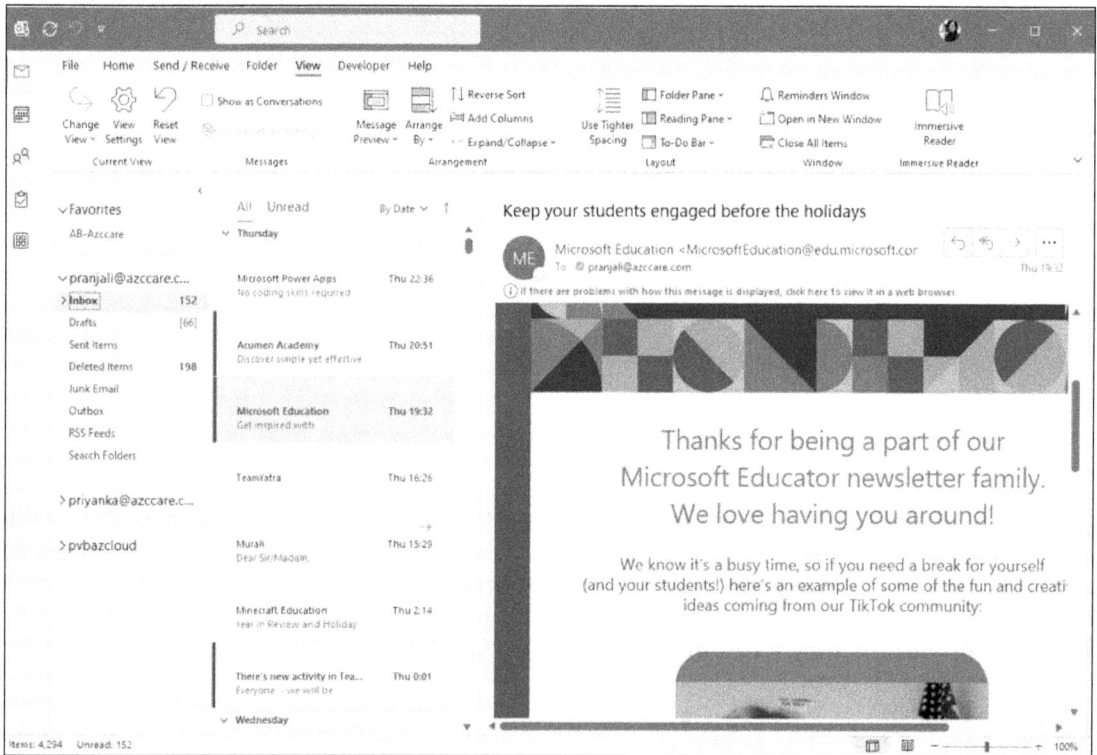

Figure 10.32: Outlook Interface

Users can change the user interface of Outlook by clicking on the **View** ribbon and locating the **Folder** pane and **Reading** pane commands. Select the options that suit you best as shown in *Figure 10.33*:

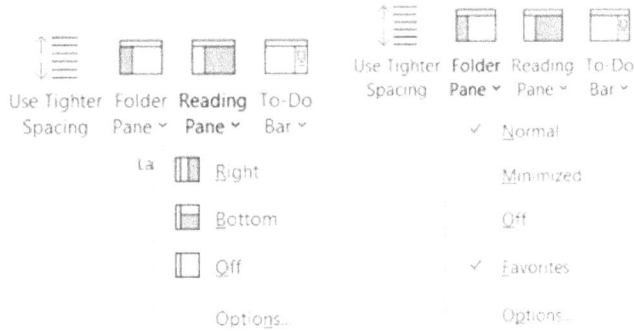

Figure 10.33: Outlook panes

You can **Minimize** the folder pane by clicking the arrow at the top of the pane. To easily switch between the different Outlook item views, i.e., mail, calendar, contacts, tasks, etc., use the **Navigation bar** in the bottom left corner of the screen given in *Figure 10.34*:

Figure 10.34 Navigation Bar for various options

Get acquainted with the ribbon

The top toolbar of the application is called a **ribbon**. In Outlook, the ribbon includes the **Home**, **Send/Receive**, **Folder** and **View** tabs.

Home tab

Home tab consists of various options. To create a new email, click on the **New Email** button in the **Home** ribbon. If you need to schedule a new appointment or Teams meeting, these options are available in the **New** sub-group. Additionally, the **Delete** sub-group provides options to **Delete** and **Archive** emails as shown in *Figure 10.35*:

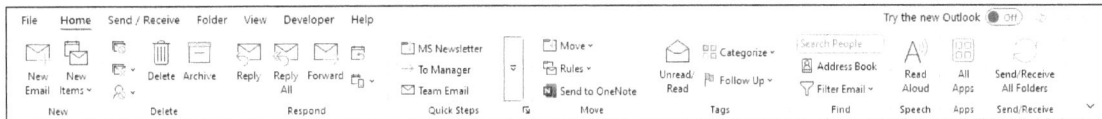

Figure 10.35: Home ribbon

The following are some of the tips:

- **Want to delete all auto-complete suggestions:** When you are typing an email address in the *To* field, and suddenly you want to change or delete that email address, you can simply click on the X icon. To enable this, go to **File | Options | Mail**, scroll down to the **Send** messages section, and click the **Empty Auto-Complete List** button or uncheck the **Use Auto-Complete** to turn it off.

- **Responding to emails:** Responding to an email can be done by either **reply** or **reply to all** options.

- **Reply**: Click the **Reply** icon to respond directly to the sender of the email only. If the original email contains attachments, these are not attached in the response.

- **Reply all:** Choose **Reply All** to respond to the sender and all email recipients included in the **To** and **CC** (but not the Bcc) fields. As with **Reply**, none of the original attachments are sent.

- **Forward**: Choose **Forward** to send the email to another user not included in the original message. Attached files from the original email are also sent.

Configuring rules and quick steps

Quick steps are shortcuts that allow you to perform repetitive actions with ease. For example, create a shortcut to forward a message to your manager.

Some existing quick steps are already set up; others will require editing before they can be used, as shown:

- **To create a custom quick step:** Select the **Quick Steps** menu from the **Home** ribbon tab and click on the **Create New** command. This opens the **Edit Quick Step** dialog box. Give the quick step a name and select the **Choose an Action** drop-down arrow. Select an action. In this example, **Move to Folder** is selected as shown in *Figure 10.36*:

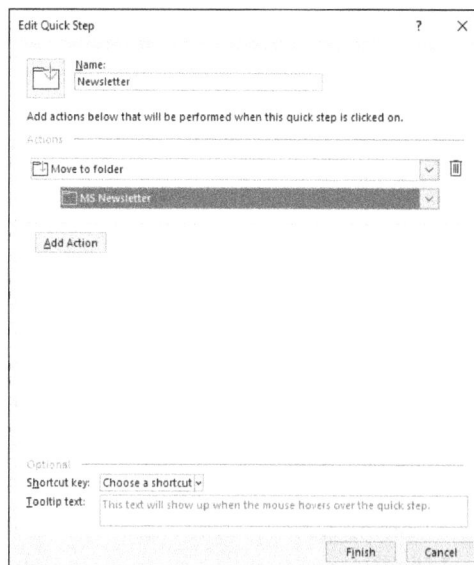

Figure 10.36: Quick Step window

You can add another action by clicking the **Add Action** button. In this example, a **Reply** action has been selected, as shown in *Figure 10.37*:

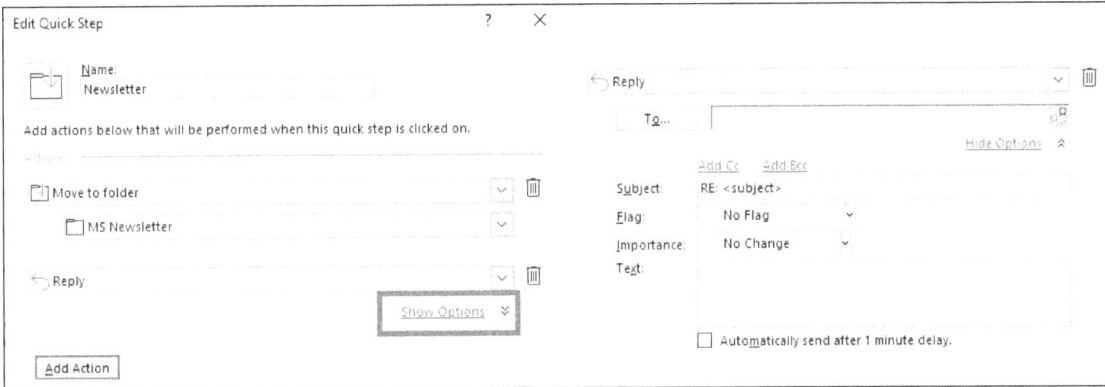

Figure 10.37: Editing quick step

This type of action requires more features. Click the **Show** Options link below the action. Here, you can add the details to create a reply email. Add further actions as needed. If you wish, add a shortcut key and Tooltip text. Click **Finish.**

Custom rules

To automate actions within Outlook, you can create a rule that is triggered when mail arrives or is sent.

Let us discuss basic vs. advanced rules.

To create a basic rule, select an email message, click the **Rules** drop-down arrow in the **Home** ribbon, and choose **Create Rule**. The **Create Rule** dialog box will then appear, as shown in *Figure 10.38*:

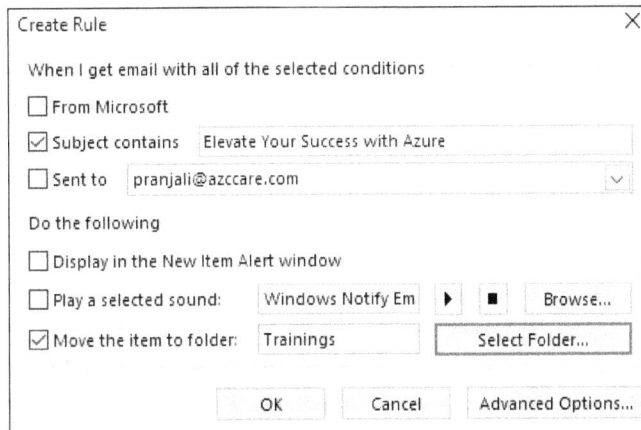

Figure 10.38: Create Rule dialog box

Fill in the rules, conditions, and actions, then click **OK.** For a more complex or advanced rule, click the **Advanced Options...** button.

The **Rules Wizard** window will open, consisting of **three screens**. The first screen sets the conditions of the rule. Tick the checkboxes to build the condition, then refine the condition's rules. The **second screen** defines the rule's actions, while the **final screen** enables you to specify exceptions. Click **Next**, assign a name to the rule, and verify that all **conditions, actions, and exceptions** are accurate.

Moving or copying items between folders

To move or copy selected items between folders, go to the **Home** tab on the ribbon and click **Move**, or right-click an existing folder and choose **Move**. Choose the **Other Folder** option to move the item or select **Copy to Folder** to duplicate it. Then, pick the desired folder and click **OK**, as shown:

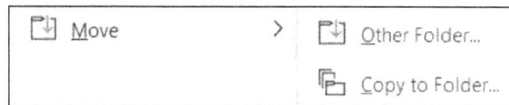

Figure 10.39: Moving and copying files

Note: **You can also create a new folder here.**

There are other options available in the Move group in the Home tab. Here are some options, along with a description given as follows:

- **Send to OneNote:** A message can be sent to an existing OneNote notebook as a new page. Select the message you want to send to OneNote. Select the **Home** tab on the ribbon and select the **Send to OneNote** option. A dialog box appears. Select the notebook section or page you wish to add the email to and click **OK**. OneNote will open to display the sent pages.

- **Attach a file while sending an email:** Once you have completed your draft email, click on the **Send** button. A copy of the email gets placed in the **Sent Items** folder. If you want to attach files or other items, then click on the **Attach** icon. Attachments can be sent as embedded documents or as links to files stored in the cloud.

- **Linking to files from web locations:** If you use a cloud-based file storage system, for example, OneDrive or SharePoint, you can add direct links to these documents. This is advantageous, as it avoids document duplication and ensures the recipient can view the most recent copy of the file. To create a link to a document, click on the **Attach File** command, and then select **Browse Web Locations**. A few options will be available to you, as follows:

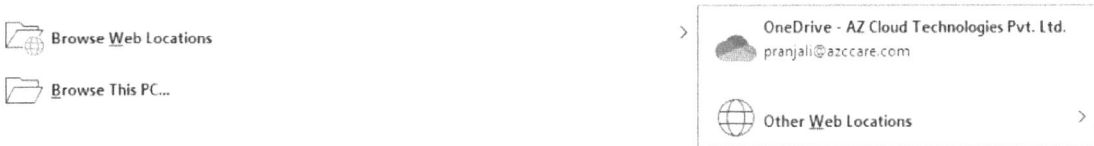

Figure 10.40: Browse location on the cloud

- o **OneDrive:** Select files from your OneDrive account. This can include files shared with you.
- o **Sites:** Browse any Office 365 SharePoint document libraries you have access to.

Choose the appropriate file location, then select the file you want to link to. This opens the following dialog box, illustrated in *Figure 10.41*:

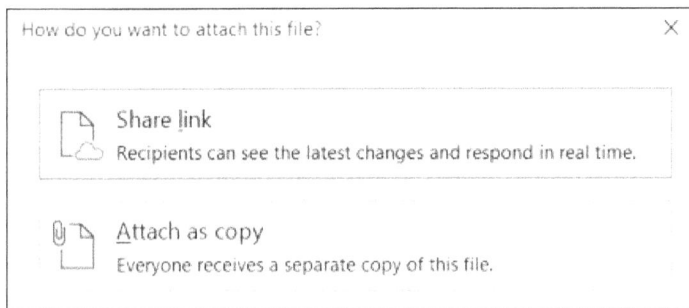

Figure 10.41: Attach files via link or attachment

Select the **Share link,** and a link to the file is added to the email. Adding a file to your email will change the permissions of the linked file. By default, all members of the organization to whom you send the link will be able to edit the document. Change this by clicking on the linked file in Outlook, selecting **Change Permissions** and choosing a permission option. Once shared from OneDrive, people will ask your permission to **View** or **Edit**.

Dictate and Read Aloud feature

The dictate feature enables speech-to-text recognition using a microphone and a reliable internet connection to compose emails effortlessly. This is an instant and easy way to draft your emails. To use this feature, create/compose a new email, click on the **Dictate** icon, and wait for the microphone button to activate. Once its listening, start speaking, and your words will appear as text on the screen.

Note: **Dictation also works with forwarded emails, calendar appointments, and meetings in Outlook.**

Make sure you speak clearly. To add punctuation, say the name of the punctuation mark you want to add. If mistakes occur, correct them manually (*Dictate Your Emails in Outlook, 2023*).

Click on the gear icon to check the available settings:

- **Spoken language:** View and change languages in the drop-down
- **Microphone:** View and change your microphone
- **Auto punctuation:** Automatically insert punctuation while dictating
- **Profanity filter:** Mask potentially sensitive phrases with ***

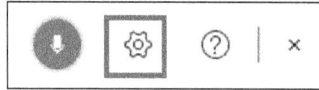

Figure 10.42: Dictate Toolbar

The **Read Aloud** feature is a **text-to-speech tool** that will read your email aloud. It will help you to proofread your emails. On the **Home** tab | select the **Read Aloud** icon. The **Read Aloud** toolbar will appear in the upper right corner as shown in *Figure 10.43*. Click on the **Play** button to start listening to the email. Use the **left and right arrows** to move between the previous and next paragraphs. The **settings** button will help you to adjust the reading speed, and under the voice selection, select the voice of either male or female, as shown:

Figure 10.43: Read Aloud toolbar

Benefits of Read Aloud in Outlook are given:

- Helps in proofreading emails before sending.
- Useful for visually impaired users or those who prefer listening.
- Allows multitasking while Outlook reads emails aloud.
- Helps in improving reading comprehension and reducing errors.

Outlook settings

You can customize the Outlook settings to best suit your way of working.

Automatic replies (out of office)

To configure your out of office messages, go to the **File** tab and select **Automatic Replies.** Once the dialog box opens, choose **Send automatic replies** option. If you want the replies to be sent only during a specific period, check the "**Only send during this time range"** box and set the start and end times. Then, enter your **out of office message** for both internal and external recipients. Finally, click ok to save your settings.

Using the calendar

The calendar is another integral component of Outlook. This is used to plan your day-to-day activities. In addition to planning your activities, it can also be used to invite colleagues to meetings. Additionally, you can share your calendar with other users to allow them to be aware of your whereabouts.

Calendar View

You can navigate to the Calendar View by clicking on the **Calenda**r button on the **Navigation** bar, on the side bar of the screen as shown:

Figure 10.44: Menu available for navigation

When you open the calendar, it will default to the **Monthly** view, with today's date highlighted:

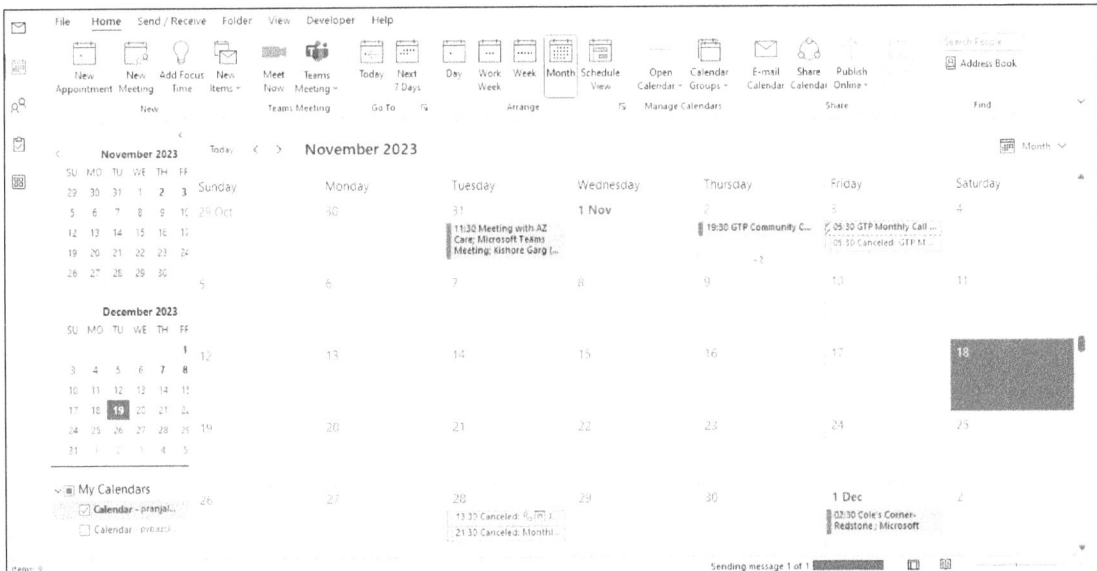

Figure 10.45 Calendar view

The folder pane on the left of the screen shows the **current and upcoming months** and highlights the calendars you have access to. The calendar view can be changed to different timescales by selecting the appropriate command on the Home or View ribbon tabs. You can navigate between months, weeks, and days (depending on your view) by using the navigation arrows at the top left-hand corner of the calendar.

You can add different types of events to your calendar as follows:

- **Appointment:** A personal calendar entry with a start and finish time.

- **Meeting:** A shared calendar entry with a start and finish time, which has other attendees.

- **Event:** A personal, all-day event with no start and finish time, for example, a party. This does not affect your free time.

- **Creating a recurring meeting:** A meeting can be scheduled to repeat at regular intervals in the future. To set a recurrence interval, click the **Make Recurring** option while you create a meeting. This opens the **Appointment Recurrence** dialog box as shown in *Figure 10.46*. Select the recurrence pattern and choose the range of occurrence, then click **OK**, as shown:

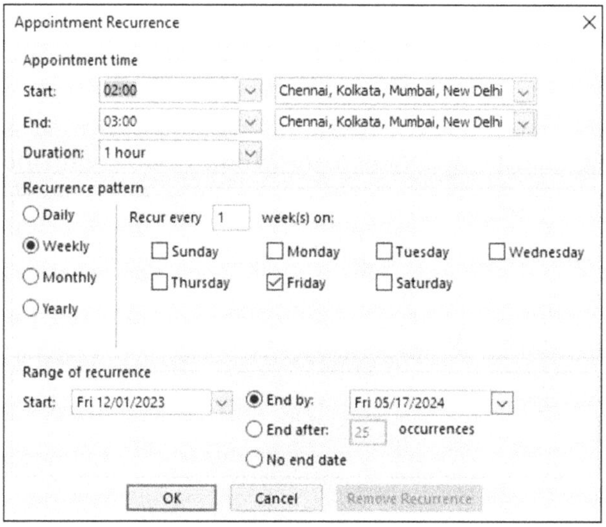

Figure 10.46: Appointment recurrence dialog box

- **Share a calendar**: Sharing your calendar is an option if you would like others to view your schedule. To share your calendar, click the **Email Calendar** or **Share Calendar** command from the **Home** tab and select the calendar you wish to share, as illustrated in *Figure 10.47*:

Figure 10.47: Sharing calendar

This opens the **Calendar properties** dialog box on the **Permissions** tab. From the permissions options, select which permission level you would like for the calendar. Click the **Add** button to open the address book and add the users you would like to view your calendar. Click **OK** to close address book and **OK** again to close the **Calendar properties** dialog box. Your calendar will be shared.

More advanced message options

There are additional email features available when sending emails, such as voting buttons, which allow recipients to provide quick responses, as illustrated in *Figure 10.48*.

- **Use of Voting buttons:** Voting buttons can be used to get a quick response in the form of a simple poll from your email recipients, as shown:

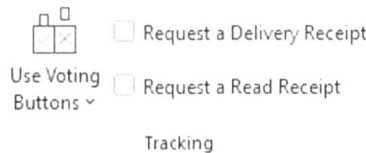

Figure 10.48 Advanced features of Outlook

While using Voting buttons, you can use options like **Approve**, **Reject**, **Yes**; **No**, **Yes**; **No**, and **Maybe**. You can also select whether you want to request a delivery receipt and a read receipt. When a user receives your email, he/she will know that the message contains a voting button, as a label is displayed at the top of the message. You can click this message to respond to the voting request.

- **Delay delivery of emails and set an email expiration date:** Based on your needs, you might wish to delay the delivery of an email until a specific date or have an email expire if it is not actioned before a particular time. An expired email will be deleted from the recipient's inbox if it is left past the expiry date.

Figure 10.49: More options for delay delivery for emails

- **Redirect emails to other recipients:** You can redirect email replies to one or more recipients. To do this, create a new email, go to the **Options** tab on the ribbon, and select **Direct Replies To**. This will open the **Properties** dialog box. Find the **Have replies sent to** field and click the **Select Names** button to open the address book. Choose the recipients who should also receive replies, then close both dialog boxes. Conditional formatting in Outlook.

You can apply conditional formatting with a view to emphasizing information. For example, highlight messages on a specific topic.

The following are some steps given:

1. On the **Home** ribbon, click on the **View Settings** command.

2. This opens the **Advanced View** settings dialog box.

3. Click on the **Conditional Formatting** button to open the **Conditional Formatting** dialog box.

4. To create a new conditional format, click the **Add** button, and give the new format a name.

5. Click the **Font…** button and choose a font style and color.

6. Click the **Condition** button to open the condition dialog box.

7. Add conditions to the messages, more choices, and advanced dialog boxes.

8. Click **OK** to close all the dialog boxes, as shown:

Advanced View Settings: Compact	✕
Description	
Columns…	Categories, Importance, Reminder, Icon, Attachment, Fro…
Group By…	None
Sort…	Received (descending)
Filter…	Off
Other Settings…	Fonts and other Table View settings
Conditional Formatting…	User defined fonts on each message
Format Columns…	Specify the display formats for each field
Reset Current View	OK Cancel

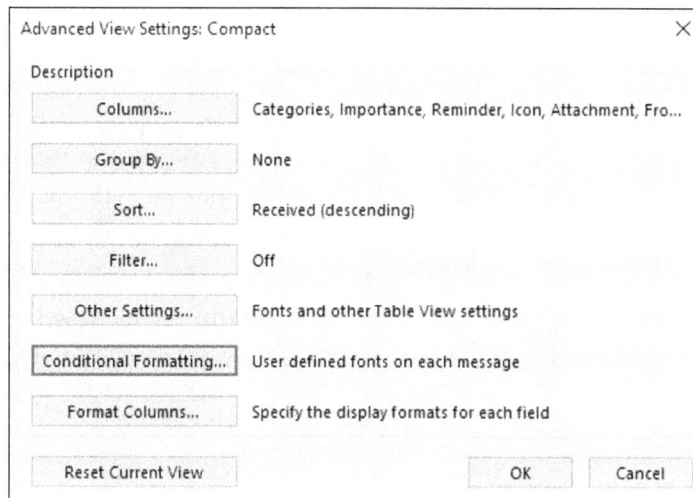

Figure 10.50: Advanced view settings

Microsoft Planner

Microsoft Planner is a task management tool and is a part of the Microsoft365 suite and is designed for team collaboration and project tracking. In the Planner Hub, plan members can view single or multiple plans, assign tasks, check progress reports, and track individual assignments, all via the Planner app.

You can go to *tasks.office.com* and sign in with your account credentials. To pin the Planner App to the top level of the app launcher, select ellipses **(…),** then select **Pin to Launcher**.

Build your plan

Microsoft Planner offers a simple and visual approach to organizing a team's tasks and collaborating on the project. It serves as a central hub where team members can create plans, assign tasks, and track progress using dashboards. Users can also store files in a centralized location, allowing the team to share and access data easily.

Microsoft Planner ties in very closely to Office 365 groups in Outlook. Creating a plan creates a group and vice versa. If you have any pre-existing groups set up, then the plans will appear on the planner hub.

Signing in to Microsoft Planner

To open the application, go to *portal.office.com* | select the **App launcher** | **All Apps** | then Planner (*Organize Your Team's Tasks in Microsoft Planner, 2023*). It will launch the application, enabling users to **create a visual plan, organize and assign tasks, share files, and track progress updates**. *Figure 10.51* shows the interface of Planner. The Planner app will provide a few templates related to various plans, like simple, project management, software development, business, and employee onboarding. If you are new to the Planner app, starting with templates is a great way to get started, as shown:

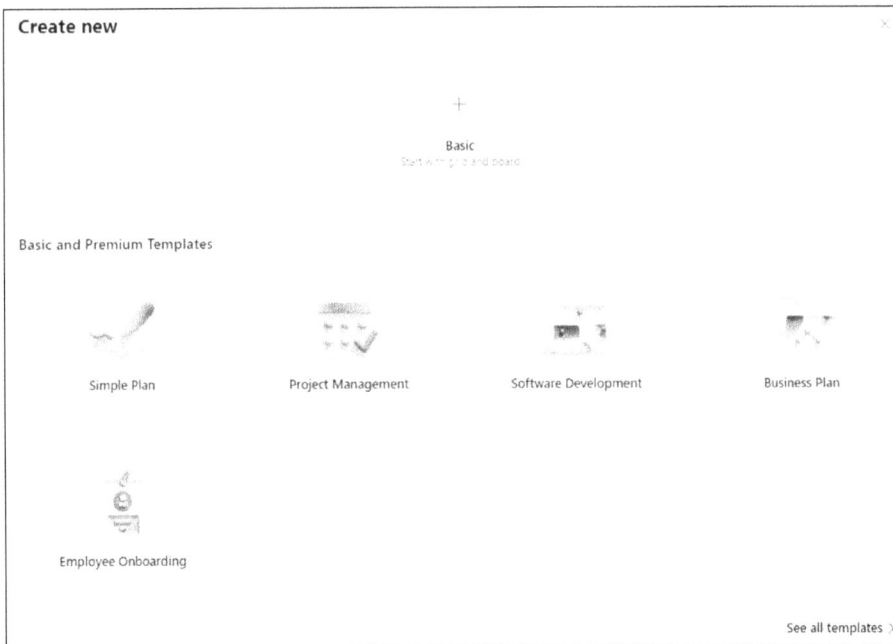

Figure 10.51: Planner Interface

The planner hub is the main page. On the left-hand side of the screen, a menu is available. Key components with details are mentioned here:

- **New Plan:** To create a new plan.
- **Planner Hub**: All plans and favorite plans are displayed here.
- **Assigned to me**: It displays the tasks assigned to you.
- **Pinned**: A quick link to your favorite plan.

Create a plan in Planner

To create your first plan, select **New Plan**. Either start with **Basic** or **Predefined Templates**. Provide a name and select **Create**. Assign Task and add members in your plan as shown in *Figure 10.52*:

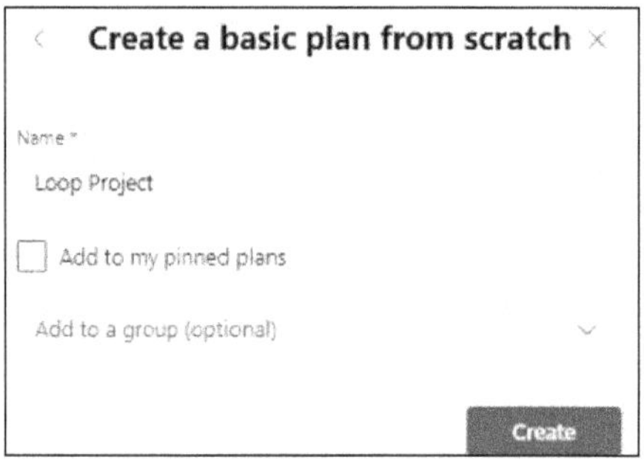

Figure 10.52: Create a plan from scratch

Creating a new plan in Microsoft Planner has created a new Office 365 group in Outlook, making it easy for you and the people you are working with to collaborate not only in Planner, but also in OneNote, Outlook, SharePoint, and other apps. Outlook shows all groups in the Groups section by default. However, a favorite plan appears in your Outlook favorites at the top. Planner also creates an email address for your plan automatically. You can use this for discussions with all the plan members. The plan email address that the Planner creates shows within the Outlook group conversations.

When anyone is added as a member to a plan, they receive a welcome email notification in their main inbox, which provides useful information to get started.

Privacy options

There are two types of privacy settings: public and private. The difference between the two are as follows:

- **Public:** Anyone in the organization can see the plan's contents.
- **Private:** Only the members of a plan can see the plan's content.

Privacy options are added when a new plan is created. This can be adjusted later, if required, by selecting the three dots on the right-hand side of the plan's name on the board and selecting **Edit Plan**.

Add people to a plan

Your colleagues, who are a part of the team working on the plan, are added as members, as follows:

1. Select **Members**.

2. Type the name of a person within your organization whom you want to add to the plan.

3. Select the person's card when it appears.

4. Now that you have members in your plan, you can go ahead and create tasks to assign them to.

You can remove a plan member if required, as follows:

1. Select **Members** and enter the person's name.

2. Select the three dots and click **Remove.**

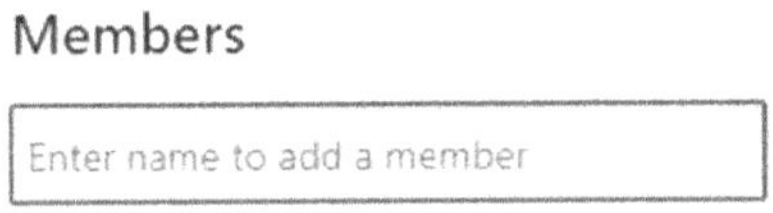

Members

```
Enter name to add a member
```

Figure 10.53: Adding members

Buckets and tasks

We have a new plan; any tasks are added to the default bucket called **To Do.** A personalized task list showing all tasks assigned to you across different plans. Each **Plan** represents a project or team workspace. Tasks within a plan are grouped into **Buckets** (e.g., *To Do In Progress, Completed*), to help break things up into phases.

It is, therefore, likely that you will set up additional buckets and perhaps rename the **To Do** bucket to a more relevant name.

To set up buckets for your tasks, follow the steps:

1. Add **new bucket** and enter a name for the bucket.

2. This can be changed at any time by simply overtyping. The buckets will be listed from left to right on the planner hub.

Creating tasks

Now that we have buckets to organize our tasks, we can start adding tasks to the relevant buckets. Creating tasks in Microsoft Planner is simple and helps teams organize work effectively.

The following are some steps to follow, as shown in *Figure 10.54*:

1. Locate the bucket where you want to add the task.

2. Select the **Add Task** button. Provide a name for the task.

3. Assign to team members who will be responsible for completing the task.

4. The tasks will appear in the selected bucket. Drag & drop tasks between buckets to change their status, as follows:

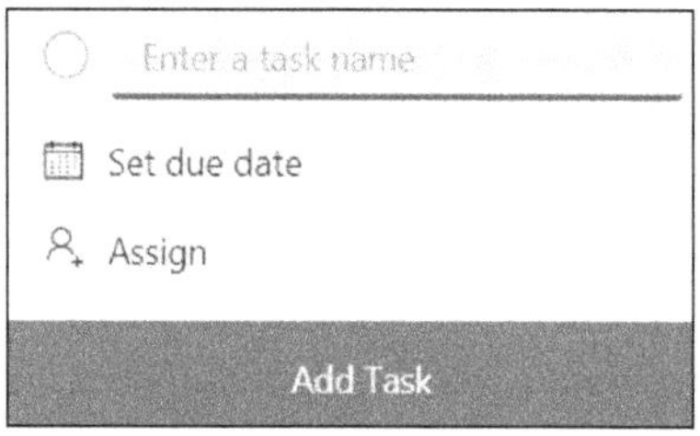

Figure 10.54 Adding tasks in bucket

Note: **You can also set a due date and assign the task to specific users here if you wish.**

Add additional task details

Once you have created a task, you can select it and add more details, if required.

Follow the steps given:

1. Select the task to open the task window.

2. Select **Start anytime** below **Start date**, and then select the start date that you want.

3. Select **Due anytime** below **Due date**, and then select the due date that you want.

Assign people to tasks

When you have decided which member(s) will work on a task, you can assign them to the relevant tasks. Assigned members are responsible for completing the task before the due date, as follows:

1. Select the task to open the task window.

2. Select **Assign** to choose a plan member from the list (You can choose more than one). You can also drag plan members from the members list down to their tasks.

An easy way to change assignments is to group by **Assigned To** and drag the tasks between your plan members. You can remove an assignment by selecting the assignment on the task, and then the X to the right of the person.

Comment on a task

Comments are a handy way of raising discussions and questions about what you are working on, as shown:

1. Select a task to bring up its details.
2. Use the **Comments** box to add your comment.
3. Click **Send** when you are ready to post the comment.

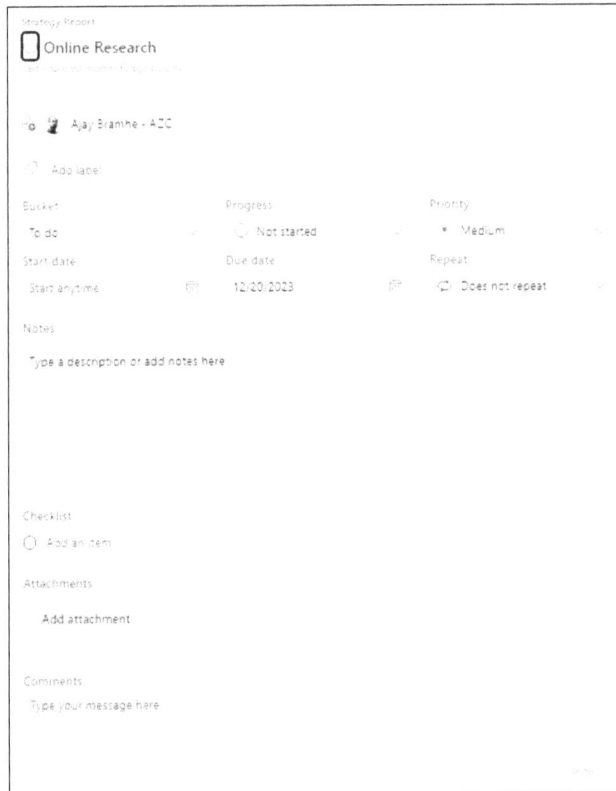

***Figure 10.55** Adding more details on the bucket*

A task will show a comment symbol against it so that the plan members are aware there is a comment to read. The most recent comment is listed at the top. Any comments can also be viewed from conversations.

Attach files or links to a task

You can attach files or links directly to a task, to help your plan members get their work done more easily.

1. Select a task to bring up its details.

2. Click **Add attachment**.

You can choose from file, link or SharePoint at this stage.

Type	Description
File	Upload a file from your local computer. Files you upload are stored in the SharePoint document library associated with your plan
Link	Fill in a URL and the text to display in Planner
SharePoint	Choose files from the SharePoint document library associated with your plan

Table 10.1 Type of files to attach in a task

3. Once attached, the file can be selected to work on in Office Online. If you need to collaborate on a document with a colleague, this can accommodate real-time co-authoring.

Note: **Files can also be attached to a conversation.**

Checklists

A checklist is a useful way of keeping on top of all the things you need to do in relation to a task, as shown:

1. Select the task to bring up its details.

2. Click **Add an item** and type your list item.

3. Press **Enter** to add another item to the list.

4. If you select the **Show on Card** option, you can see the checklist against your task on the board.

5. You can check these off as they are completed.

A checklist item can be made into a task if it gets more complicated. Select the task to bring up its details, point to a checklist item, and then choose the upward arrow symbol to promote it. If you choose the bin symbol at this point, you can delete the checklist item.

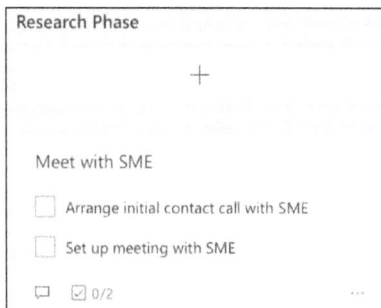

Figure 10.56: Checklist for the task

Provide labels for tasks

Microsoft Planner does not have a direct **flag** feature like Outlook, but you can prioritize your tasks using labels, priority settings, and due dates to flag important tasks as shown in *Figure 10.57*:

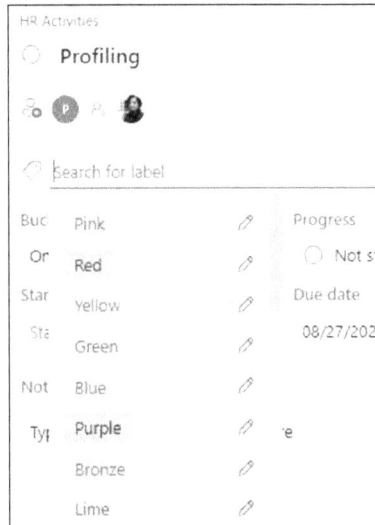

Figure 10.57: Flag tasks in MS Planner

1. Select the task to bring up its details and scroll to the **Labels** section.
2. Assign a color-coded label (e.g. Adoption, Certification etc) and customize labels by clicking on them and renaming them.
3. Once a label is defined, it is available to all tasks in a plan.

Set a preview picture for a task

In Planner, each task on the board can have a preview picture to help identify the task. A preview can be an attached photo or a checklist or you can use the task description text.

Select the **Show on card** check box to make the required item your preview. To remove, clear the **Show on card** check box.

If you use an Office file as a preview, you can select the link on the card to open it in Office Online.

Update progress on a task

The progress of a task can be set as follows:

- Not started

- In progress
- Completed

If you wish to simply mark a task **Complete**, point to the check mark on the right-hand side of the task, and it will turn green, and mark it as complete. It will have a strikethrough on the text to show that the task is completed and will disappear from the Tasks list, as follows:

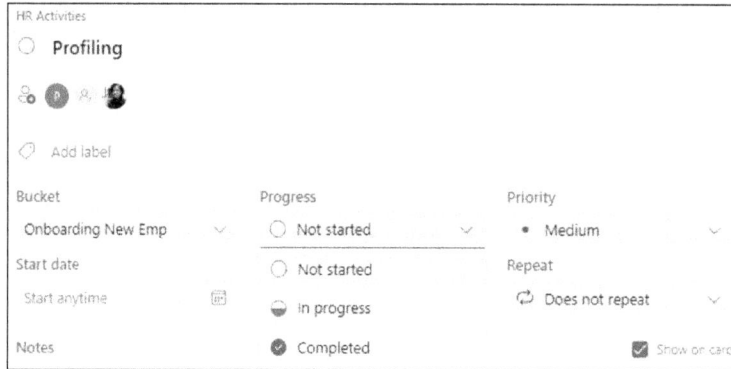

Figure 10.58: Status of Progress

If you wish to update the task to **In progress**, you can select the task itself to bring up its details and use the Progress drop-down box. If you have marked a task **Complete** by accident, click on **Show completed** and click on the **Reactivate task** checkmark on the right-hand side of the task to mark it as incomplete.

View your personal tasks

You can view only your tasks across all plans by selecting the **My tasks** view on the Planner hub, as shown:

Figure 10.59: All tasks in Microsoft Planner

Move and copy tasks

The simplest way to move tasks between buckets is to drag them into the required bucket.

Alternatively, you can click the three dots on the right-hand side of the task and select **Move task**. It brings the **Move task** dialog box onto the screen. Select the **Bucket name** you wish to move your task to, then select **Move** as shown in *Figure 10.60*:

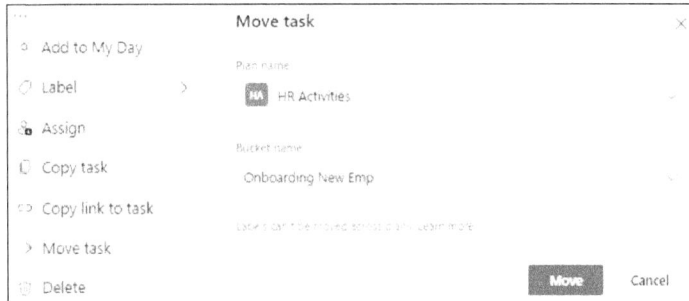

Figure 10.60: Moving tasks

Note: You cannot move a task to another plan.

Copying tasks

Tasks can be copied between buckets in the same plan or to other plans (with some limitations). Click on the three dots on the right-hand side of the task and select **Copy** task as shown in *Figure 10.61*. This opens the **Copy** dialog box. Change the task name if needed and select which Plan and Bucket you want to copy the task to, as shown in *Figure 10.61*. You can **Include** additional task information, such as the **Assignment** details and attached files.

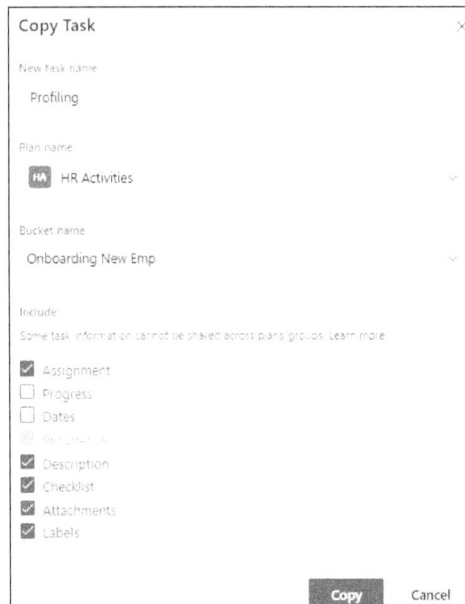

Figure 10.61: Copying tasks

Copy link to tasks

A link to a task can be copied to the clipboard. Click the three dots on the right-hand side of the task and select **Copy link to task**. A box appears, informing you that the link is copied. Paste the link into an email or other programs.

Charts view

In a planner, every plan has a Chart view in addition to a board view. The Charts view shows how your plan is progressing, with details like completed, in progress, not started, and late tasks. It is a visual summary of task progress, helping teams track workload, priorities, and deadlines immediately. To see the tasks in each category, you can click on the colored bars, and the tasks will be displayed on the right-hand panel.

You can also click on the bars, as shown:

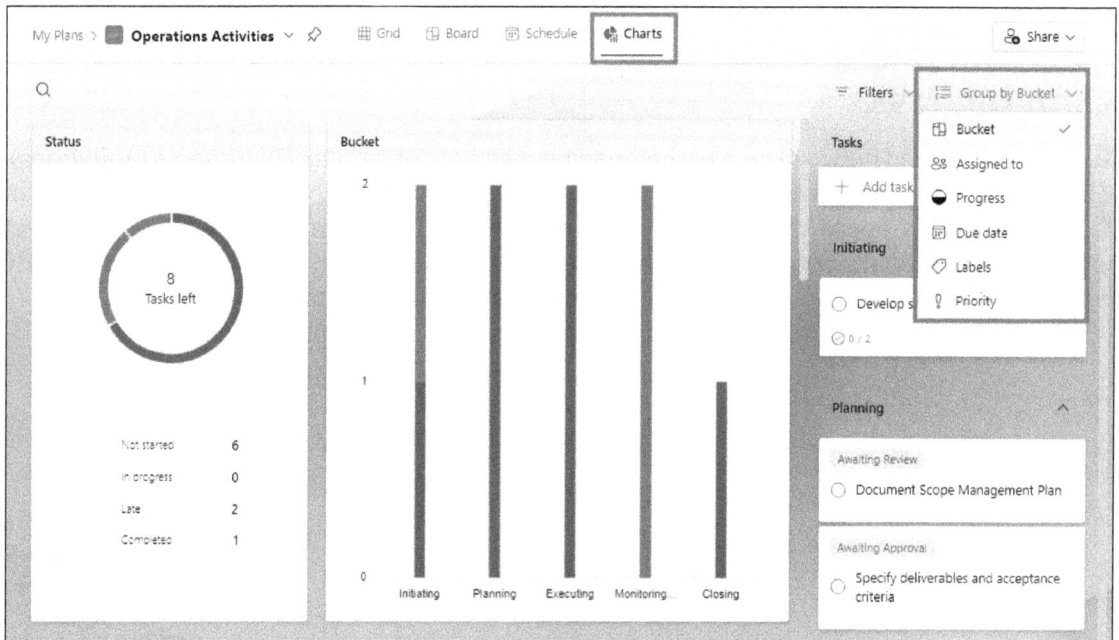

Figure 10.62: Chart view of task in Microsoft Planner

The color-coded pie chart displays task status and helps identify tasks that are overdue or pending. Tasks can also be added in this view by clicking the plus symbol displayed on the right-hand panel. To view any late tasks, the view can be grouped by **Due date.**

Chart view quickly identifies bottlenecks in project progress, tracks team workload to ensure fair task distribution, prioritizes urgent and overdue tasks, and gets a visual snapshot of the plan's overall health.

Reassign work in charts

To reassign work in this view, you can group by **Assigned To** and select the relevant bar to filter the task list. Select the task to view it and then change who it is assigned to.

Microsoft Yammer

Yammer is an enterprise social network platform that is used by organizations to connect with people, and it is a part of Microsoft 365 (formerly known as Office 365). Yammer allows users to create groups, update posts about any topic, share files, and engage people in various discussions within the organization.

Introduction to Microsoft Viva Engage

Engaging people is more critical than ever. Especially in today's increasingly distributed work environment, community engagement is crucial for bringing people and teams together and is a critical pillar of employee well-being. This is the reason Microsoft has rebranded Yammer as **Microsoft Viva Engage,** with new experiences.

By implementing this change, Viva Engage users will see a unified experience across web, mobile, and other endpoints, as well as a consistent experience across Yammer and Viva. It is a Microsoft Teams app, powered by Yammer, that connects leaders, communicators, and all employees within an organization to build communities, share knowledge, and engage everyone (*What Is Viva Engage?*, 2023).

Microsoft Viva Engage provides features like those of Yammer, which include the following:

- **Communities and groups:** Users can create communities and join groups based on shared interests, projects, or departments to collaborate and exchange ideas.

- **Posts and updates:** Employees can post updates, questions, and announcements to keep their colleagues informed and engaged.

- **File sharing and collaboration:** Viva Engage integrates with other Microsoft 365 tools, allowing users to share and collaborate on documents, spreadsheets, and presentations.

- **Employee recognition:** Managers and colleagues can recognize and appreciate the efforts and achievements of their peers through praise and badges.

- **Discover and follow topics:** Employees can follow topics and people of interest to receive relevant updates and participate in discussions related to their areas of focus.

Microsoft Viva Engage aims to create a more connected and engaged workforce, fostering a sense of community within the organization. By leveraging the power of social networking and collaboration, Viva Engage encourages employees to share knowledge, collaborate on projects, and build relationships across different teams and locations.

Interface of Viva Engage

As we know, Viva Engage builds on Yammer, integrated in Teams, and brings together Yammer's experiences with new capabilities for self-expression and sharing through storyline and stories, and upcoming innovations. Find the look of Viva Engage on desktop and mobile devices as shown in *Figure 10.63*:

Figure 10.63: *Viva Engage Interface*

Users can access the same content and features, regardless of whether they visit **https://www.yammer.com/**. Use a Yammer mobile app for iOS or Android, use the Communities app in Outlook, or use the Viva Engage app in Teams (*Get Started with Viva Engage*, 2023).

Join and create a community in Viva Engage

To open Viva Engage, go to *portal.office.com* and log in with your credentials. Then, look for **All Apps** where you can see the Engage icon (for Viva Engage), and open the **Application**.

Use the Home feed to stay on top of what matters, tap into the knowledge of others, and build on existing work. Click on **Communities in Viva Engage**, which provides a central place for all the conversations, files, events, and updates as illustrated in *Figure 10.64*:

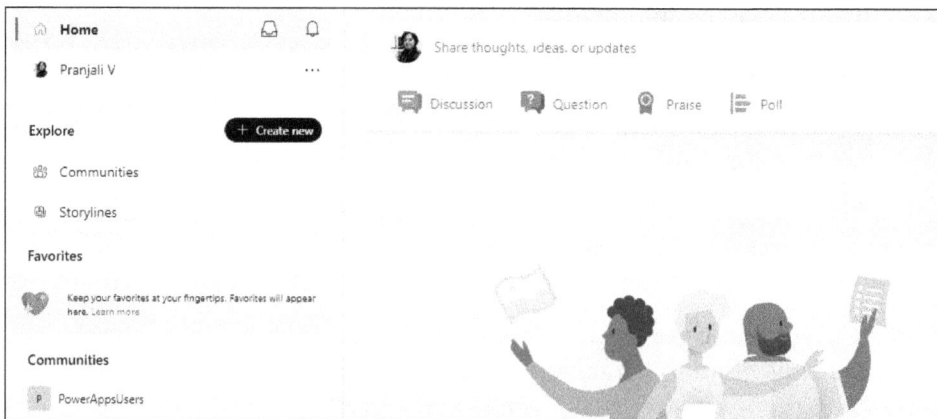

Figure 10.64: *Home page of Viva Engage*

When you create a community, you will become the owner of that community. Anyone can join the community to stay informed and connect with coworkers. If you already belong to a community, then it is listed under the **Communities** section in the left navigation pane, as follows:

- Search for experts, conversations, and files.
- Join in the conversation, react, reply to, and share posts.
- Use "@" to mention someone, to loop them in.
- Attach a file, GIF, photo, or video to enhance your post.
- Praise someone in your network to celebrate a success, or just to say thanks.
- Create a virtual event where your community can ask a question and participate in a live event or watch the recording afterwards.
- Use polls to crowd source feedback and get answers fast.
- Stay connected outside the office with the Viva Engage mobile app.
- Use Viva Engage in Microsoft Teams, SharePoint, or Outlook.

Once you click on your profile icon, it will allow you to write on Storyline. Start any discussions or ask any questions. Praise your colleagues and start with a poll to ask any questions within the community.

The following options are available in Viva Engage:

- **Storyline:** Your storyline is a place to share experiences, celebrate milestones, propose ideas, and discuss your interests. People across your organization can visit your storyline to learn more about you and your work.
- **Posts:** Create posts with photos or videos to express yourself, ask questions, share articles, and praise colleagues (*Manage Email with Viva Engage Digests*, 2023).
- **Make an announcement:** Community admins can mark any post type as an announcement to share information with the entire community and maximize the reach. Members will see a notification about the announcement within Viva Engage and Outlook.
- **People value your perspective:** People across your organization can discover your storyline posts in feeds. They can follow you and choose to get notifications when you share your storyline.
- **React and reply:** Viva Engage makes it easy to connect with your colleagues and keep the conversation going, wherever you are.
- **Grow your personal network:** Following others will help you learn more about them. As people follow each other, it will become easier to share and exchange ideas.

- **Ask a question:** Use a question to get answers fast. Upvote qualified answers and mark *Best Answer* when you have received the correct answer.

- **Create a poll:** Need to crowdsource feedback, or want to get a pulse on your company? Use polls to create a quick survey and get answers fast.

- **Reach people everywhere:** Storyline posts reach people where they work. They can read, react, and comment from Outlook, Teams, Viva Engage, and Viva Connections.

Pin Viva Engage in Microsoft Teams

Viva Engage can be pinned in Microsoft Teams. For that, open Teams | on the left pane | select the ellipsis icon ... (three dots) | right click on the Viva Engage icon, then select **Pin** to keep it always visible.

Pin Viva Engage using the mobile app

At the bottom of MS Teams, select the ellipsis icon ... (three dots) | select **Reorder,** and drag and drop the app so it is no longer in the **More** section.

Select **Done** to save your changes.

Download the Microsoft Teams in mobile app

To download Microsoft Teams on a mobile device, go to the App Store or the Play Store and search for the application, and download it. Once installed, sign in using your work email address and password.

Note: **Based on your organization's security settings, you might need to re-enter your password.**

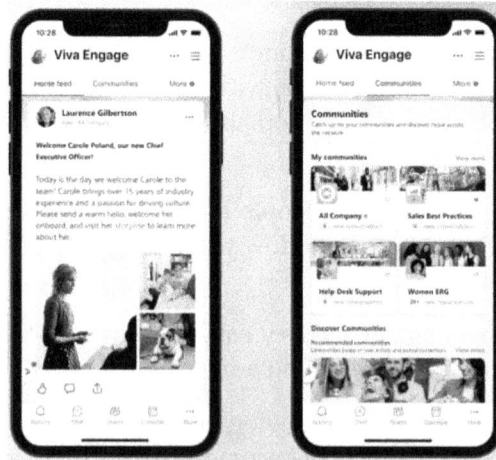

Figure 10.65: Viva Engage on Android and iOS device

Conclusion

In this chapter, we covered Microsoft Forms. In this application, M365 subscribers create forms and quizzes and share them with other users via different modes. Additionally, the Planner application will assist you in creating your plans and delegating tasks to your colleagues. Once you create a plan, groups are also formed in the backend of Outlook. Planner can also be integrated into Microsoft Teams to let the teams know about it.

In Outlook, we discussed many things like creating rules, setting out of office message, setting your calendar, changing the view of outlook, how to use **Dictate** functionality for your email or listen to an email using **Read Aloud**, using a Focused mailbox as compared to a regular mailbox, setting up folders for a clutter-free inbox, using email templates and quick parts to create, store and insert reusable pieces of content, mailbox rules and categories, and understanding the difference between an appointment, meeting and event. Additionally, we understood the best way to share the calendar with others and utilize conditional formatting for your calendar meetings to enhance ease of access. You have also learnt how to move emails to OneNote.

You have learnt about social engagement within the organization with the help of Viva Engage, where you can start a post daily, ask any questions, and anyone can respond, if your community is open to all.

In the next chapter, we will cover the OneNote application included in the Microsoft 365 suite. OneNote serves as a valuable tool for organizing ideas and managing to-do lists within your digital notebook. Additionally, we will examine Sway, a digital storytelling application that facilitates the creation of presentations, which can be easily shared via a public link. Furthermore, we will discuss Microsoft Whiteboard and the To Do application, which allow users to incorporate sticky notes and develop task lists for their daily activities, respectively.

References

1. *Add sections to your survey or questionnaire. (2023). Microsoft Support.* **https://support. microsoft.com/en-us/office/add-sections-to-your-survey-or-questionnaire-c6578df5-0343-4629-8cf6-ab3bd87475ee**

2. *Adjust your form or quiz settings in Microsoft Forms. (2023). Microsoft Support.* **https:// support.microsoft.com/en-us/office/adjust-your-form-or-quiz-settings-in-microsoft-forms-f255a4ba-e03c-4e12-b880-f7e8b62e0665**

3. *Anderson, S. (2023). How to Add Questions in Microsoft Forms. The Windows Club.* **https:// www.thewindowsclub.com/how-to-add-questions-in-microsoft-forms#google_ vignette**

4. *Check and share your form results. (2023). Microsoft Support.* **https://support.microsoft. com/en-us/office/check-and-share-your-form-results-02859424-341d-406f-b32a-9a0fbaf357af**

5. *Create a form with Microsoft Forms. (2023). Microsoft Support.* **https://support.microsoft.com/en-us/office/create-a-form-with-microsoft-forms-4ffb64cc-7d5d-402f-b82e-b1d49418fd9d**

6. *Dictate your emails in Outlook. (2023). Microsoft Support.* **https://support.microsoft.com/en-us/office/dictate-your-emails-in-outlook-4010d238-bb25-45e9-89f6-8f9b54fcc0fc**

7. *Get started with Viva Engage. (2023). Microsoft Support.* **https://support.microsoft.com/en-us/topic/get-started-with-viva-engage-729f9fce-3aa6-4478-888c-a1543918c284**

8. *Manage email with Viva Engage digests. (2023). Microsoft Support.* **https://support.microsoft.com/en-us/topic/manage-email-with-viva-engage-digests-6c309167-02b2-4f32-9374-9117ef95d186**

9. *Organize your team's tasks in Microsoft Planner. (2023). Microsoft Support.* **https://support.microsoft.com/en-us/office/organize-your-team-s-tasks-in-microsoft-planner-c931a8a8-0cbb-4410-b66e-ae13233135fb**

10. *Send a form and collect responses. (2023). Microsoft Support.* **https://support.microsoft.com/en-us/office/send-a-form-and-collect-responses-2eaf3294-0cff-492d-884d-a1dee909e845**

11. *Use branching logic in Microsoft Forms. (2023). Microsoft Support.* **https://support.microsoft.com/en-us/office/use-branching-logic-in-microsoft-forms-16634fda-eddb-44da-856d-6a8213f0d8bb**

12. *What is Viva Engage? (2023). Microsoft Support.* **https://support.microsoft.com/en-us/office/what-is-viva-engage-1b0f3b3e-89ee-4b66-aac5-30def12f287c**

13. *Writtenhouse, S. (2022, November 10). How to Use Sections in Microsoft Forms. G-Post.* **https://www.groovypost.com/howto/use-sections-in-microsoft-forms/**

Join our Discord space

Join our Discord workspace for latest updates, offers, tech happenings around the world, new releases, and sessions with the authors:

https://discord.bpbonline.com

CHAPTER 11

OneNote, Sway, Microsoft Whiteboard, and To Do

Introduction

In this chapter, you will learn about OneNote, which will help you understand how to put your thoughts, ideas, and to-dos and sync them with all your devices. You can also store and share your notebooks on OneDrive. We will additionally explore Sway, a digital storytelling application that facilitates the presentation of your data. Furthermore, we will examine Microsoft Whiteboard, a digital platform that allows users to write, take notes, engage in brainstorming, add sticky notes, and collaborate on various tasks. Indeed, we will also discuss To Do, an application that enables users to create task lists for personal organization. Notably, it integrates with other applications within the M365 suite. This chapter is structured to provide insights into note-taking applications in conjunction with various other apps.

Structure

In this chapter, we will explore the following topics:

- Getting familiar with OneNote
- Introduction to Sway
- Overview of Whiteboard
- Overview of To Do

Objectives

By the end of this chapter, you will be familiar with the OneNote digital notebook interface, including how to create, edit, organize, and enhance notes, as well as effectively search for information. You will also explore digital storytelling presentations and collaborative Whiteboard features. Additionally, you will learn how to use the To Do application to create task lists and integrate them with other Microsoft 365 applications.

Getting familiar with OneNote

OneNote is a digital notebook available under the Microsoft 365 suite of applications. It offers a single point of storage for a wide range of content, including text, images, audio, video, handwritten notes, drawings, web clipping, Office documents, links, and many more. Powerful search capabilities allow content to be located and retrieved easily. It is a versatile application. OneNote can be found in the Search Box under the **Start** button.

If it is not installed on your device, open the link given here and click on the **Download** button. **https://www.onenote.com/Download**

This application is available on Windows, Mac, iPad, iPhone, and Android.

Creating a new notebook

To create a new notebook, go to the File tab and select the **New** option. Notebooks are comprised of sections and pages. You can create sections with the flexibility to add as many pages as needed under each section. Sections can be organized by topics, months, or any other work-related categories. When you are creating a new Notebook, you will be prompted to choose a location for saving it. *Figure 11.1* illustrates the interface where the notebook name is required to fill in. The moment you provide a name to your Notebook, the **Create Notebook** button gets enabled, as shown:

Figure 11.1: Create new Notebook

Notebooks can be saved on either OneDrive or SharePoint site, to allow easy access within the team or in the local drive. It will ask whether you want to share with other people for collaboration purposes.

Figure 11.2 illustrates the dialog box to collaborate with other people:

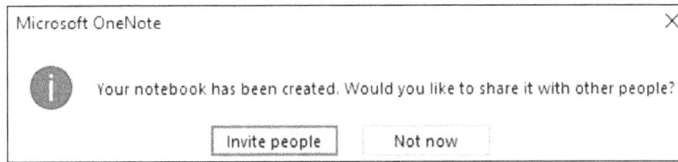

Figure 11.2: *Invite People via Notebook*

Note: Notebooks are saved automatically after they have been edited.

The new notebook will have a single section and a single Untitled Page by default. You can rename the section, either by right-clicking on it or by double-clicking on the section and adding the pages from the right-hand pane. In the page area to the right of the OneNote window, select **Add Page**. Use sections to help organize the notebook's pages and content. Adding sections is the simplest when you click or press the addition sign (+) to the right of the existing sections tab. As sections are added, a set of tabs is created above the container area. The tabs can be rearranged by dragging them left or right as required. The active section will have a taller tab. Adding pages to a section follows a similar process to creating a section.

The new page will be added to the bottom of the list of pages already in the section. It will not have a title but will have the date and time the page was created. You can add a title by typing in the area above the date. Pages in a section can be reordered by dragging them up or down the list in the page area.

Note: The date and time can be changed or deleted by clicking on them.

Each section is assigned a default color, which can be changed by right-clicking on the section. The context menu provides a **Section Color** option, allowing you to select a different color as needed, as shown in the following figure:

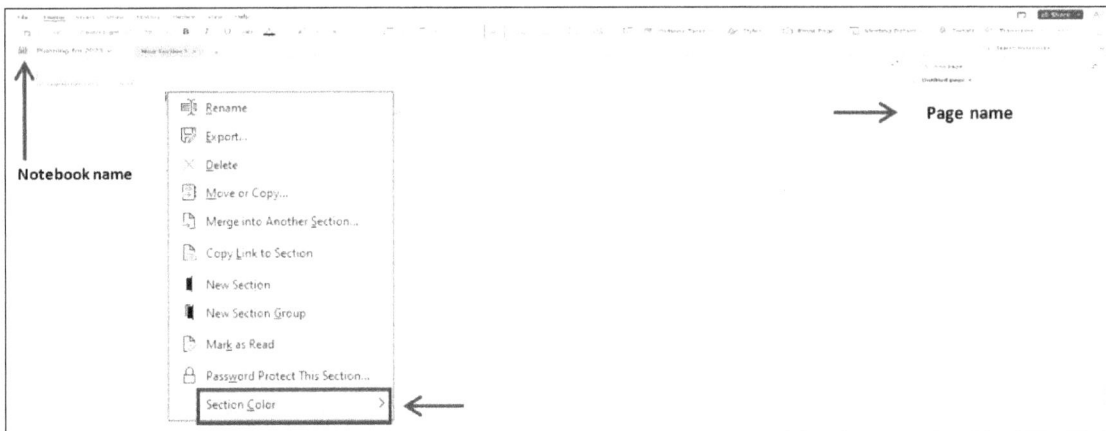

Figure 11.3: *OneNote section*

The context menu in OneNote is a shortcut menu that appears when you right-click on an element such as text, sections, pages, or notebooks. It provides quick access to relevant options and actions based on what you right-click on. The context menu has more options.

If you right-click on the section, it will provide more options that are illustrated as follows:

- **Rename:** This option will allow you to rename the section name.

- **Export:** It will provide a dialog box to export selected pages/section/notebook (which you can choose) to another place.

  Figure 11.4 shows export options as follows:

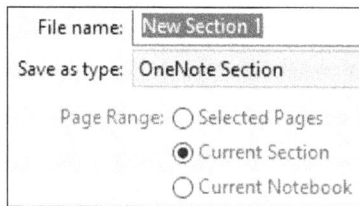

Figure 11.4: *Export OneNote section*

- **Delete:** This will allow you to delete the section.

- **Move or copy:** This will allow you to move or copy the section to a different location.

- **Merge into another section:** It allows you to merge the current section with another section.

- **Copy link to section:** It will copy the link of the current section, which you may later paste in another section or page.

- **New section:** It creates a new section.

- **New section group:** It creates a new section group, where you can create a new section.

- **Mark as read:** It shows the content as **Read**.

- **Password protect this section:** It will provide a separate window on the right hand, where you can set a password for the current section. You might not be able to view the password-protected section unless you enter the correct password.

- **Section color:** It will provide color options to apply to your section.

OneNote has various ribbons with different purposes, as follows:

Ribbon Tab	Description
File	File actions including new, open and share provide links to all open notebooks.
Home	Commonly used formatting options, tags and Outlook integration.
Insert	Objects are inserted here, including files, links and tables.

Ribbon Tab	Description
Draw	Touch screen or pen drawing and highlighting actions.
History	Edits, authors, versions and a link to the notebook recycle bin.
Review	Grammar and spellcheck tools in common with Office. Password protection for sections is available.
View	Page layout information, zoom and window controls.
Help	Links to application help and training.

Table 11.1: Ribbons available in OneNote

Adding content to a notebook

One of the key advantages of OneNote is its ability to store and display almost any type of digital content. This content can be either typed or handwritten, and it supports most file formats. You can add graphics, images, audio, video, and more. If a notebook serves as a central hub for referencing specific content, it is best to use links to external files. For example, files stored in SharePoint or Teams that are relevant to the notebook's purpose but need to remain in their original storage location. Adding text is simple, you can type anywhere on the blank page, just like writing in a physical notebook. OneNote automatically generates a text box as you start typing.

No alignment is needed to enter the text. You can do formatting and apply **Styles** from the **Home** tab, as shown:

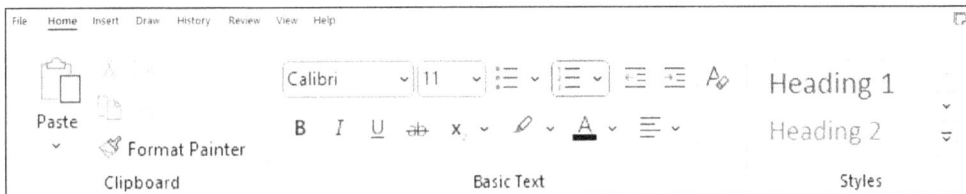

Figure 11.5: Home ribbon

Pages in notebooks are designed to be fluid. The objects added to a page can be moved around by dragging the border of the object.

There are more options which are available under the **Home** tab, as shown:

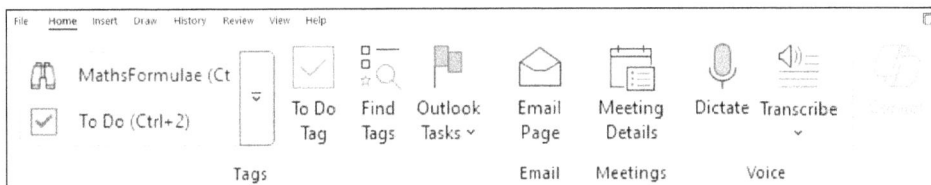

Figure 11.6: Home ribbon options

Working with tags and tasks

Working with content effectively can be difficult, especially if the content is spread across the pages of a notebook. Tags are a great way of marking and subsequently acting on content. They not only provide easy methods of marking content for action but also provide a direct link to Outlook.

Tags can be picked from the drop-down menu, and a marker can be added next to an item on a page. The choice list contains a wide range of action items and markers ranging from a simple To Do to items that involve other users. Select or click next to the item to tag and then pick the tag to use from the menu (*Apply a Tag to a Note in OneNote*, 2024).

Figure 11.7 shows the usage of a To Do tag. Tags are like digital labels or annotations that help you identify different types of information within a notebook. Tags will help you to search for a specific type of content within notes, as shown:

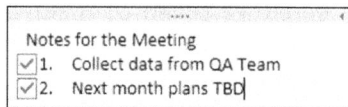

Figure 11.7: Creating tags

You can create your own custom tags. OneNote allows you to create custom tags from scratch with your own label, icons and font color or highlight color. This can be beneficial if you have specific categories or labels that are not covered by the predefined tags. You can give a unique name according to your business requirement.

You can also modify a tag using the predefined tags. Select **OK** twice and add the tag to the drop-down list, as shown:

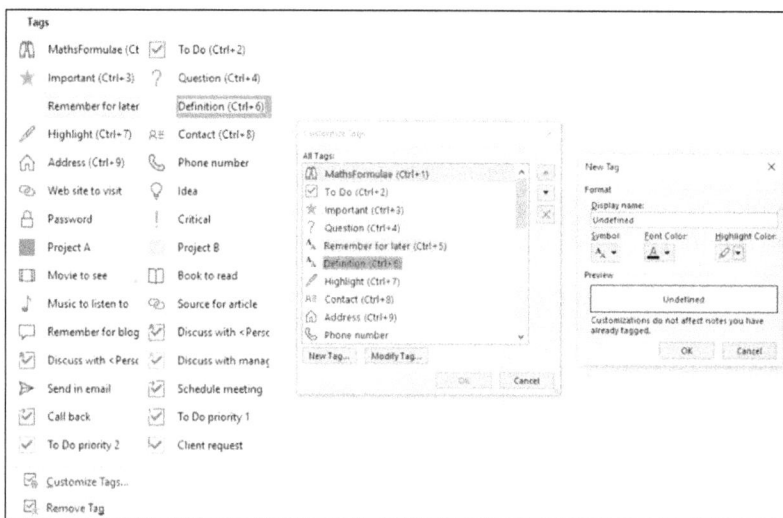

Figure 11.8: Customize tags

Creating Outlook tasks in OneNote

OneNote seamlessly integrates with Outlook, allowing you to create an Outlook task directly from OneNote. To do this, select the item you want to flag as a task in OneNote and choose the required option from the **Outlook Tasks** drop-down menu. This is useful for action items from meetings or quick notes that require follow-up.

Once assigned, the task is tagged, and an entry is created in Outlook. You can then manage the task from either **Outlook** or **OneNote**. The **Outlook Tasks** menu in OneNote provides options for handling these tasks efficiently as shown in *Figure 11.9*:

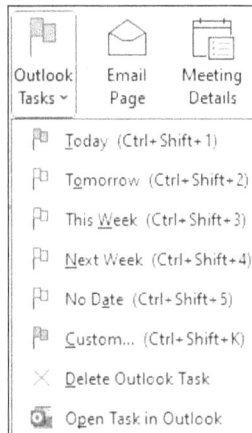

Figure 11.9: Outlook tasks

When you create an Outlook task in OneNote, you can assign a due date, and this information will be synced with your Outlook calendar. You can also set reminders that will appear in Outlook. Items marked as tasks in OneNote appear in your Outlook Tasks list, creating a unified task management system across both applications.

Managing tasks

Tasks created in OneNote are automatically synced with Outlook. Any changes made to these tasks in one application is reflected in the other. This includes completing the task, changing the due date, or updating the task description.

You can view and manage your tasks either through OneNote or Outlook. Tasks will appear in Outlook's Tasks and To Do List, with links back to the OneNote pages where they were created.

Email page

OneNote is beneficial for taking notes, adding images, videos, audios and even files. It might be possible that the page content is important for the team. In that case, start sharing your

OneNote page via **Email Page** option available under the **Home** tab. Ensure that you select the correct page. Select the **Email Page**. OneNote will redirect to Outlook and create a new email containing the page's content and include any files attached to the page.

Note: **Treat the email as if had been created in Outlook with all the same options.**

Meeting details

This option will show all the meetings directly from Outlook. User can select a meeting, and all the details related to the meeting (all email addresses along with subject line) will be added to your current page.

Select the option and it will display a menu with all lined up meetings scheduled for the day together with the option to browse for a meeting on a different date. Highlight the meeting details and insert them on the page.

Dictate and transcribe

Let us look the details as follows:

- **Dictate:** This feature is available to convert your speech into text and add in the page. You can also use keyboard shortcut *Win + H* to start dictation. Once the microphone is active, start speaking and your words will be transcribed into text. You can dictate notes, create drafts, capture ideas and make comments in your page. It also accepts punctuation marks, symbols, currency, emojis, etc. (*Dictate Your Notes in OneNote*, 2024).

- **Transcribe:** It is one of the most intelligent services available in OneNote, bringing power of the cloud to help save your time and produce better results. Transcribe converts speech-to-text transcript. Each speaker is individually separated and synced with ink strokes and audio, which you can then edit.

Draw shapes and format background

OneNote lets you draw, sketch or write notes on touch screen with stylus or even the mouse. It allows you to choose from the Shapes gallery instead of drawing freehand, as follow:

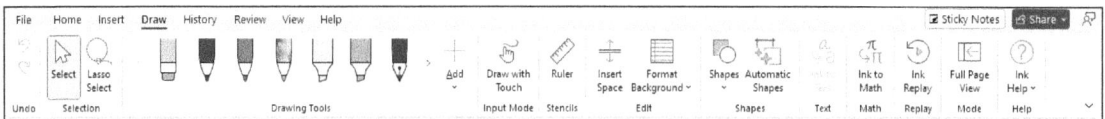

Figure 11.10: Draw ribbon

Click on the **Draw** tab. Select **Draw with Touch** option and tap on any pens or highlighters shown on the ribbon and then use either a finger, stylus or mouse to write down your notes or to draw anything. While selecting the pens, you can choose the thickness, effect and color of your pen and highlighter.

To draw a shape, select an item in the **Shapes** gallery, and then drag your mouse, stylus or finger on the page to draw the shape (*Draw and Sketch Notes on a Page*, 2024).

When the shape is selected, you can drag it to resize or move it to a different place on the page. To erase your notes or drawing, you can use Eraser.

You can use **format background** to change the color of your page from the **Draw** tab. Choose the gridline to help guide your ink.

To draw a straight line, select **Ruler** button and adjust the angle as follows:

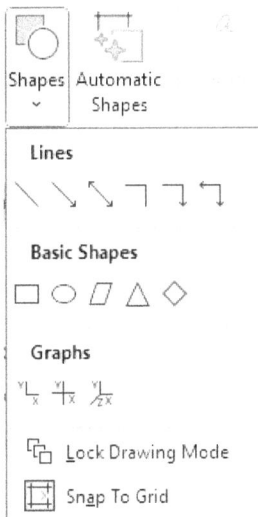

Figure 11.11: *Insert Shapes*

Insert various contents to OneNote page

The OneNote page can contain various contents, such as tables, files, images, media files (audio and video), links, recordings, timestamps, etc.

The **Insert** ribbon in Microsoft OneNote is an essential part of the interface, enabling users to enhance their notes with various types of content beyond plain text. This feature expands OneNote's functionality, making it a powerful tool for notetaking and information management.

The following is an overview of the key features and tools available under the **Insert** tab in OneNote as shown in *Figure 11.12*:

Figure 11.12: Insert ribbon

- **Tables:** Tables can be added to a page when the layout of the information needs to be controlled. Go to the **Insert** tab | Select **Tables** | specify number of rows and columns to create the table. The width and height of each row and column is adjusted automatically when the content is added to the table (*Insert a Table in OneNote for Windows 10*, 2024).

- **Files and links:** OneNote is a repository of all the types of content that includes other files or links to files. Go to the **Files** group and select **File Printout**.

- **File Printout:** Insert a printout of a file (like a PDF or Word document) that can be annotated directly in OneNote.

- **File Attachment:** It is like attaching a document to an email. Select the **Paper Clip** icon and browse for the file which you want to attach to your notes. You must select any type of file, and while pasting it offers you the following dialog box. Select **Attach Files** and OneNote will add an icon to the page for the file.

  These files can be opened directly from OneNote (*Insert or Attach Files to Notes*, 2024) as follows:

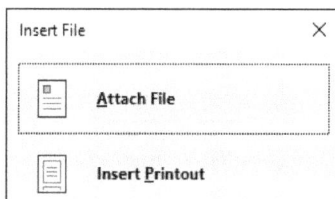

Figure 11.13: Insert File via File Attachment

- **Spreadsheet:** Insert an Excel spreadsheet, which can be a new spreadsheet or an existing file. If you select an existing file, it will give you three more options, as follows:

  o **Attach File:** It has the same result as **File Attachment** | **Attach File** command.

  o **Insert Spreadsheet:** It will open the Excel spreadsheet and add it to the page, as if it was being opened in Excel. It can be edited.

    Note: **A copy of the file is inserted. Edits do not update the original file.**

  o **Insert a Chart or Table:** It will only work correctly if the source Excel file either has a formatted table or content. If either are found by OneNote, a dialog box will display. Selecting the required choice will place the objects into the current page.

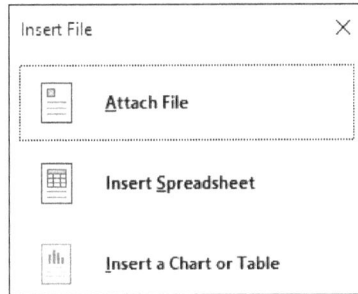

Figure 11.14: Insert file via Spreadsheet

- **Links:** It will allow you to add hyperlinks to your notes, linking to web pages, files, emails, or other sections or pages in OneNote. Images section will provide users to add images via **Screen Clipping** or **Pictures** option as follows:

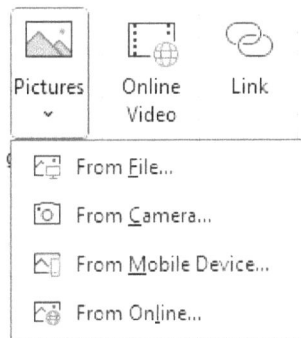

Figure 11.15: Various options to insert pictures

- **Pictures:** Insert images from your computer. Insert pictures by taking a picture from your device camera or from variety of online sources, like YouTube, directly into your notes.

- **Screen Clipping:** With this option you can take a snapshot of part of your screen and add it to the page. OneNote will hide while you capture webpages, documents, or anything else.

   Note: **OneNote can search for text in screen clipping.**

- **Links:** If the file that needs to be referenced in the notebook is stored elsewhere, you can use **Link** option to link it. This is useful where the file version needs to be controlled, its contents should remain where it is stored or perhaps if the file is very large (*Create Links to Notebooks, Sections, Pages, and Paragraphs in OneNote for Windows 10*, 2024). Select the **Link** command to display the following dialog box:

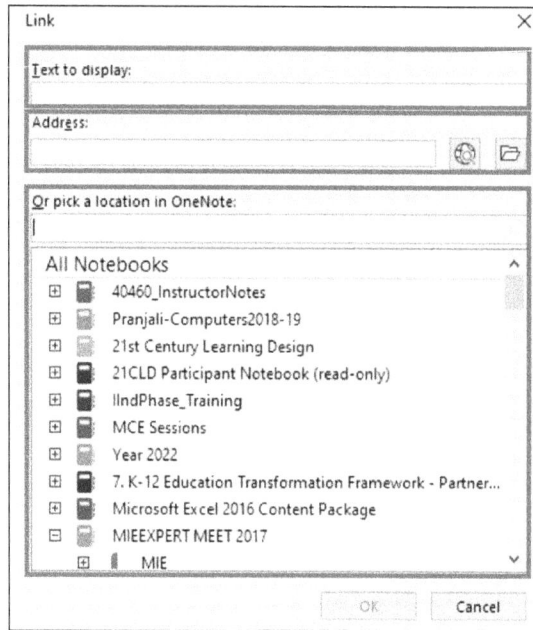

Figure 11.16: Link dialog box

In the top section, add the text that will be displayed in the page. Use the second section to browse for the file location. The lower section is used if the file to link to is already stored in a notebook you have access to.

The resulting link is added to the page in a text box and the link can be activated by selecting the text.

Note: A link can be created using the shortcut *Ctrl + K*.

- **Online Video:** This option allows you to insert a variety of online videos within OneNote. Once you capture the video, it will embed into the current page.

- **Time Stamp:** If you want to add date and time stamp in the current notebook, go to the **Insert** ribbon and use the option.

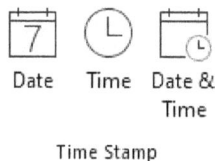

Date   Time   Date &
              Time

Time Stamp

Figure 11.17: Timestamp option

- **Page Templates:** Different page templates are available in OneNote. A template can be used to change the layout, color, add defined content and images to a page.

Templates are found in the **Insert** ribbon. There are different choices of templates. Once you select any command, a drop-down menu of template choice is available.

Selecting one of the templates will instantly apply the template to the current page. This will overwrite the color and lines previously applied. The text entries in a template can be edited and any content can be added to the page in the normal way.

Undo can be used to restore the page if the template is not appropriate.

If you want to create your own template, define color page, add tags, images or lines according to your requirement, and **save the current page as template** option, which is given below of the **Page Template** dialog box, as follows:

Note: **Using a Page Template will add a page to the notebook.**

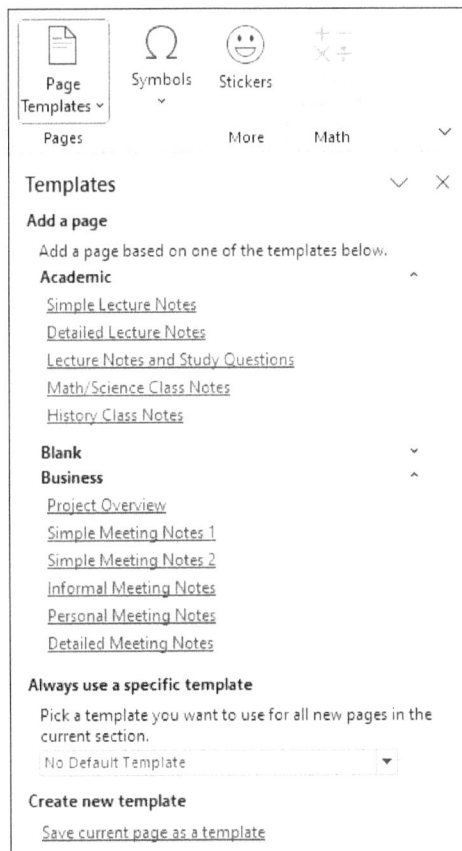

Figure 11.18: Insert Templates dialog box

For instance, if we are working on a specific project and want to create a document, ww would prefer to use the template. Templates are beneficial for implementing company brandings within the document, presentations or OneNote page.

Integrate OneNote with other applications

Microsoft OneNote and Outlook are both part of the Microsoft Office suite, and they integrate with each other in several useful ways, particularly concerning task management. The functionality of Outlook Tasks in OneNote allows you to streamline your productivity and task tracking across both applications.

We have already covered Outlook tasks integration with Outlook, and how it can be added in OneNote. If you are creating a to-do list for yourself, it integrates with the To Do application, and you can open the application and complete your to-do tasks.

In a similar way, OneNote can be used in Microsoft Teams for better team collaboration.

The following are the benefits of integration:

- **Centralized task management:** Combining OneNote's note-taking capabilities with Outlook's task management tools allows for a more centralized and efficient way of managing work.

- **Contextual task tracking:** By creating tasks directly in your notes, you maintain the context of each task, which can be essential for understanding and efficiently completing the task.

- **Accessibility:** Tasks and notes are accessible across devices, provided you are using OneNote and Outlook with an Office 365 subscription or a Microsoft account, ensuring seamless access whether you are on your computer, tablet, or smartphone.

The following are the limitations and considerations:

- **Version compatibility:** This functionality works best with the desktop versions of OneNote and Outlook, especially those that come with an Office 365 subscription.

- **Internet connectivity:** For syncing to work effectively, an active internet connection is typically required.

- **Platform availability:** The level of integration can vary, depending on whether you are using OneNote on Windows, macOS, or mobile platforms.

Collaborate feature using OneNote

Collaborating with OneNote is a very effective way to work together in real time or asynchronously on shared notebooks with colleagues. When you click on **Share** option available in OneNote at the top right-hand side, various options are available as shown in *Figure 11.19*:

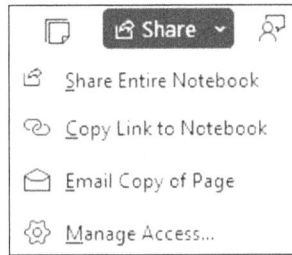

Figure 11.19: *Sharing Notebook*

Sharing a Notebook requires it to be stored in OneDrive, Teams or SharePoint Online. You need to set the sharing permissions by allowing others to either view or edit the notebook and then share the notebook by sending invitations to collaborators via email or by sharing a link to the notebook.

Collaborators can access the shared notebook and start editing the notebook. Changes will sync across all devices, and you can view the past versions of pages to see what changes were made and by whom, which is helpful for tracking edits.

To prevent edits on specific sections or pages, you can lock those areas. Users can leave comments or notes for other collaborators, making it easier to communicate the changes they have done.

Introduction to Sway

Sway is a new application for most of you. It is a free app from Microsoft Office. Although it is available under Microsoft 365 suite of applications, Office Sway is a new application in the Microsoft Office family of products that comes with the tagline, *Reimagine the way your ideas come to life*. Our mind is a canvas, and we can visualize our creations without any limit with Sway. It is a dynamic and interactive web canvas which is used to create and share interactive reports. Since it resides in the cloud, it allows any user who has Microsoft account to work across any platforms, i.e., mobile phones, tablets, desktops, laptops, etc. Sway makes sure your creation looks great on any screen. Nowadays, people need to use various types of content such as text, images, hyperlinks, etc. while sharing information or expressing ideas.

To open Sway, go to *office.com*, login with Microsoft 365 credentials and click on **Sway**, as follows:

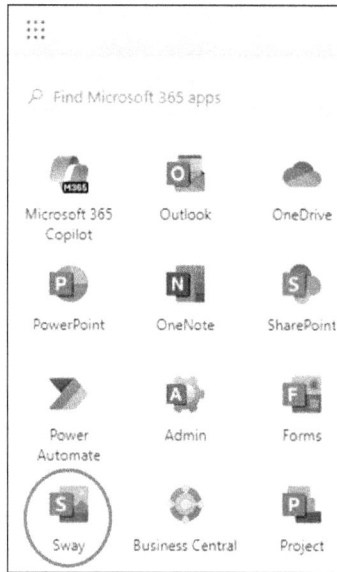

Figure 11.20: Sway application

Note: Now Sway is available through https://sway.cloud.microsoft. Your existing sway links will continue to work.

As shown in *Figure 11.21*, Sway is an easy-to-use digital storytelling application from Microsoft that makes it easy to create and share interactive reports, presentations, research stories, newsletters, personal stories, and so on. It comes with a built-in design engine to help you create professional designs quickly. Text and multimedia images flow together to enhance the story and are formatted to work on all your devices and are easy to share with anyone.

Teachers can use Sway for the creation of interactive web-based lessons, assignments, and project info that can be shared with the students, as shown:

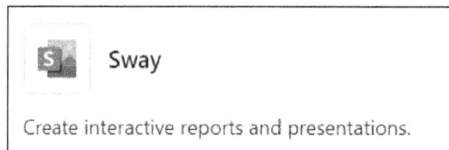

Figure 11.21: Sway application

Sway can be used for the following activities:

- View suggested search results based on your content
- Instantly transform your Sway with great designs
- Easily share by sending a link

Sway can be accessed using Hotmail, Outlook and Microsoft365 accounts.

If you are using Sway, you do not need to spend a lot of time on formatting and designing. You can always take a preview, and if it does not match your taste, then you can apply another or fully customize accordingly.

Once you open Sway, it will redirect you to the welcome page, where three broad buttons are available, as follows:

- **Create New:** You can create a blank Sway.
- **Start from a topic:** Just write a topic and sway will be created with an outline.
- **Start from a document:** You can begin to create a new Sway or import your existing work (in Word, PowerPoint, or a PDF document) as a Sway.
- **My Sways** shows the Sways you have edited recently (A bit like recent Files).
- **Viewed:** Shows the recently viewed Sways.
- **Analytics:** It gives a breakdown of how people are consuming your Sway.
- **Deleted:** It will show all the deleted Sway presentations, as shown:

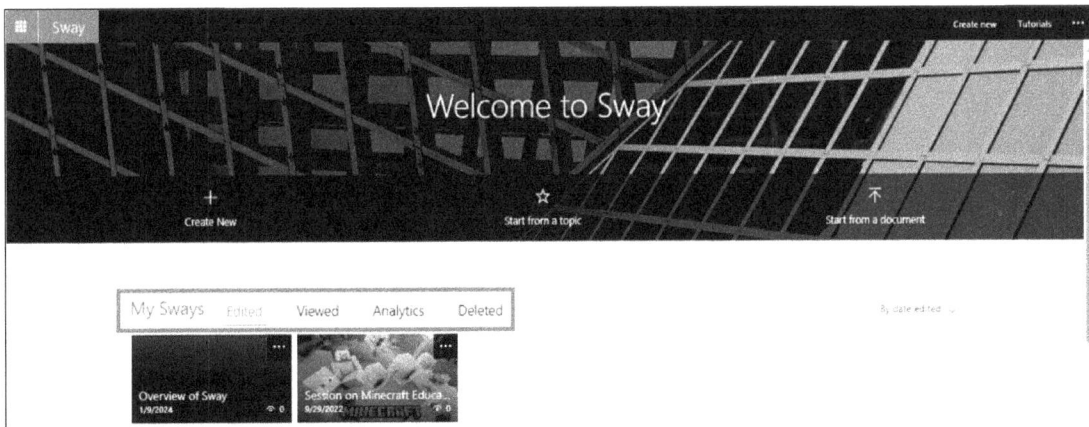

Figure 11.22: Sway home screen

To create a new sway, click on **Create New** button. Just think of what you want to create. It could be just an outline or probably an entire sway presentation.

Also, it is a good practice to collect some data and graphics to add on, as follows:

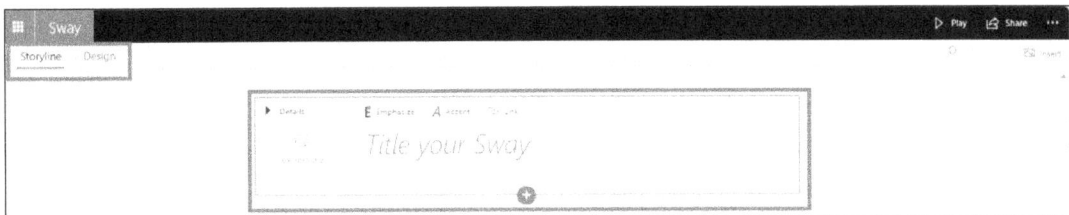

Figure 11.23: Creating Sway

Here, you will find two tabs, namely **Storyline** and **Design**.

A **Sway** card is like a PowerPoint slide where you can put information. You can add the content via Cards. When you are finished with your sway, click on the **Play** button in the top right corner to get preview your presentation.

Storyline is available for card view, where you can put the contents and add more cards to your sway.

Design tab is available for styles. Once you click on the **Design** tab, click on **Style** on the right side if you want to change style, variations, font size, background and emphasis colour. Even the themes can be changed through the **Design** tab.

Remember Sway is letting you concentrate on the content, and it is taking control of the layout or design.

In Sway, you will find seven styles, in which you can find 50 variations.

You can click on the **Remix** button available on top right corner and check the preview. Sway's built-in engine will automatically create beautiful designs for your presentation as follows:

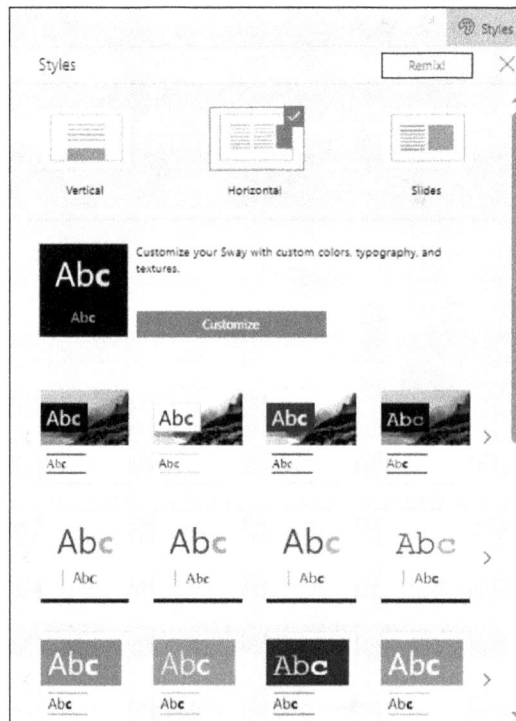

Figure 11.24: Styles available in Sway

Now we are coming to cards. You can add your own text and images, search for and import relevant content from other sources, and then let Sway handle the rest.

Adding content to Sway

The **Storyline** tab will help you to add cards, where you can type, insert, edit and format the content. It can be classified into three categories, i.e., **Text**, **Media** and **Group**. Your content can be arranged in sequence by adding more cards If you want to change the order of the cards, you can easily do by dragging them.

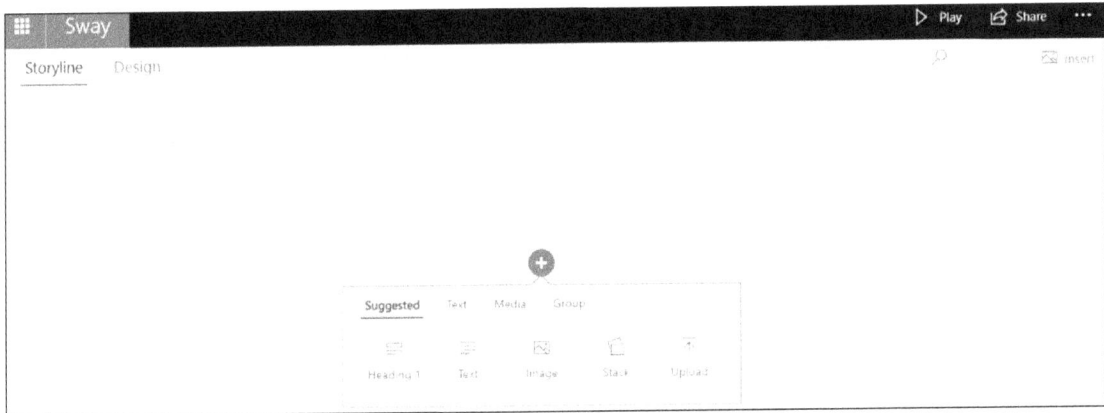

Figure 11.25: Adding content in Sway

Click on the first card to add a title or a meaningful description for your presentation. You will get a placeholder, where you can easily type, add images or upload from your device. Cards represent the various types of content that can be inserted within a Sway. Sway allows you to search from the web for the most relevant content like images and videos and you can add them in your Sway. Just click on + icon and select the **image** option to add images. It will quickly provide you with the **Suggested** dialog box on the right. You can search for videos also. Moreover, it can also suggest you search data from various sources like OneDrive, Flickr, Pickit, etc.

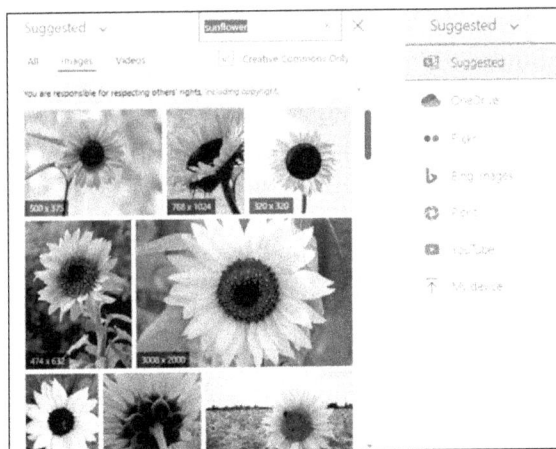

Figure 11.26: Adding images in Sway

Share your Sway

Once your sway presentation is ready, you can share it with the world. Click the **Share** button available on top right corner as shown in *Figure 11.27*. It will give you various option to share your Sway. You can then, wisely select the given options and check the rights before you share. Sways can also be embedded in PowerPoint and SharePoint.

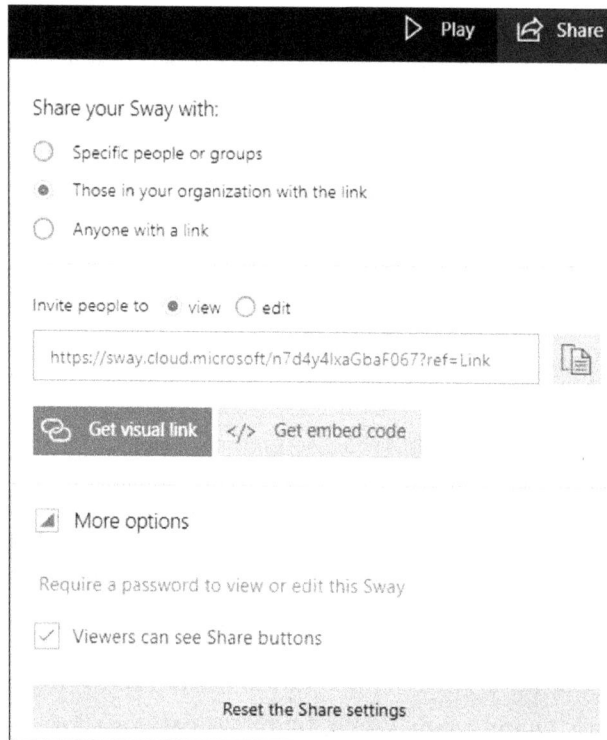

Figure 11.27: Options available for sharing Sway

Sharing options are as follows:

- **Specific people or group:** Once you choose this option, it will quickly add an option where you must enter email addresses of the people with whom you want to share your Sway.

- **Those in your organization with the link:** This option will allow you to share your sway within the organization. No one else outside of the organization can view the presentation. Also, the people who receive the link will need to enter the credentials to open/view the presentation/sway.

- **Anyone with the link:** Once you select, it will give you various options to share your Sway with the world, via Facebook, X (formerly known as Twitter), LinkedIn, and get embed code to add in the blog or website or anywhere else.

Figure 11.28: Inviting people to view or edit

You can simply select the link and share with anyone. Also, choose if people can **view** or **edit** and you will get a link accordingly.

Click on **More Options** to set a password. Once you set a password, you need to share the password with the users to open or view your Sway. It will give you an option for **Visibility of Share buttons** to the users. Users can share your sway, as shown in the following figure:

Note: **If you click on Get Visual Link, it will provide a pictorial image which you can copy and paste into an email to share your sway with others.**

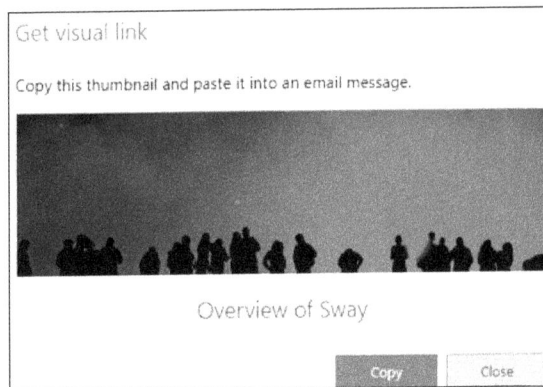

Figure 11.29: Preview of thumbnail

Managing Sway settings

Sway gives freedom to change the privacy settings to control over what the user can share after the creation of Sways. While you share your sway with others via Share button, click on the ellipsis (**...**) for more advanced settings, as follows:

- **My Sways:** It will redirect you to the home page.
- **Create New:** It allows you to create a new blank sway.
- **Duplicate this Sway:** Duplicates the Sway, with an option to rename.

- **Save as Template:** If you want to use the same Sway settings, then save the current Sway as a template.

- **Print:** It will print your Sway.

- **Export:** It will convert your Sway into Word or PDF format.

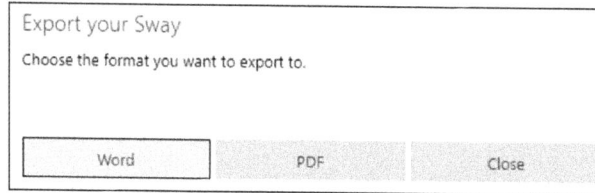

Figure 11.30: Export options in Sway

- **Accessibility Checker:** It checks your Sway for content that people with disabilities might find difficult to read.

- **Accessibility View:** It displays the Sway in a high-quality design, with full keyboard functionality and screen-reader access to all the content.

- **Help:** It will redirect to the help page.

- **Sign out:** Once you finish your work, use Sign out option to log out from the Sway application.

Settings for Sway

You can select the language for your sway and select the checkboxes for **text direction buttons,** i.e., left and right alignment and **right-to-left layout**.

View Settings: This option is available under advanced settings where you can define permissions as shown in *Figure 11.31*:

- Sway is accessible to viewers and co-authors.

- Duplication of Sway allows viewers to print and export.

- Block/unblock viewers from changing the layout.

- Block viewers from seeing the informational footer.

- Always play Sway in autoplay mode (if it is on). You can manage seconds.

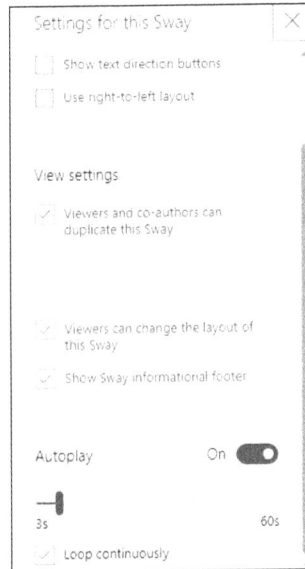

Figure 11.31: Setting options in Sway

Go mobile with Sway

Sway is compatible with all modern devices, regardless of the platform. It stands out for its user-friendly interface and ability to create visually appealing designs with minimal effort. Sway is always just a tap away.

Sway offers several key features for mobile which are given as follows:

- With Sway's mobile app, users can create, edit, and view Sways from anywhere, using their mobile device.
- Sway's interface on mobile devices is user-friendly, making it easy to add and arrange content with simple gestures.
- Users can seamlessly integrate text, images, videos, and other multimedia content into their Sways directly from their mobile device.
- Changes are saved automatically in the cloud, allowing users to start a project on one device and finish it on another.
- Sways can be shared easily, and users can collaborate on Sway in real-time, making it a versatile tool for teamwork and shared projects.

Using Sway on mobile devices

Download the Sway app from the App Store (iOS) or Google Play Store (Android). Once installed, its user-friendly interface has an intuitive design, making it easy for beginners.

Visually stunning designs are available to create professional-looking content with minimum effort and sharing is quick without needing additional software.

The following are the benefits of Microsoft Sway:

- Like traditional authoring tools, Sway allows users to create presentations without selecting a pre-made template. You can later share the Sway presentation via email, or by posting it to social media, like *Facebook*, *Twitter* or *LinkedIn*. You can also adjust the privacy settings.

- No design skills are needed for using Sway, as it has inbuilt advanced algorithms to auto-arrange the content.

- The built-in design engine makes the creation of content really fast, saving a lot of time of the users.

- It can import content from Word, PDF and PowerPoint. A great way to start a Sway is to start from an existing file. Import it into Sway at the start, and you can take it from that starting point.

- Just as an aside, you can also create a Sway from Word using the Export function. You can use Word to setup your content and then create a Sway from there.

Overview of Whiteboard

Microsoft Whiteboard, in Microsoft 365, is a free-form, digital new canvas where people, content, and ideas come together. Whiteboard lets team members collaborate in real time, wherever they are. It also gives your ideas room to grow, with an infinite canvas designed for pen, touch, and keyboard.

To open the app, login with Microsoft 365 credentials and click on the app icon or use the link **https://app.Whiteboard.microsoft.com** to open (*Getting Started with Microsoft Whiteboard*, 2024) as indicated in *Figure 11.32*:

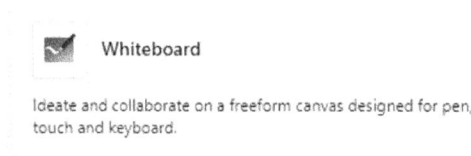

Whiteboard

Ideate and collaborate on a freeform canvas designed for pen, touch and keyboard.

Figure 11.32: Whiteboard app icon

With the help of Whiteboard, users can run effective meetings, brainstorm, collect ideas, and use them for project planning or daily stand-ups. Whiteboard is available on different platforms like your web browser, in Microsoft Teams meetings, chats, and channels, and even on mobile devices like iOS, Android, and Surface Hub devices. Microsoft Whiteboard provides an infinite canvas, where imagination can be implemented. You can draw, type, add a sticky note, or an image to move them around. It also allows you to rename your Whiteboard. It is designed to be adaptable for various audiences, whether they are beginners or advanced users.

A new Whiteboard can be created using an application within the M365 environment. Follow the steps as given here:

1. **Create a new Whiteboard:** Once you open the application, it will ask you to start a new Whiteboard to capture or ink new ideas as shown in *Figure 11.33*.

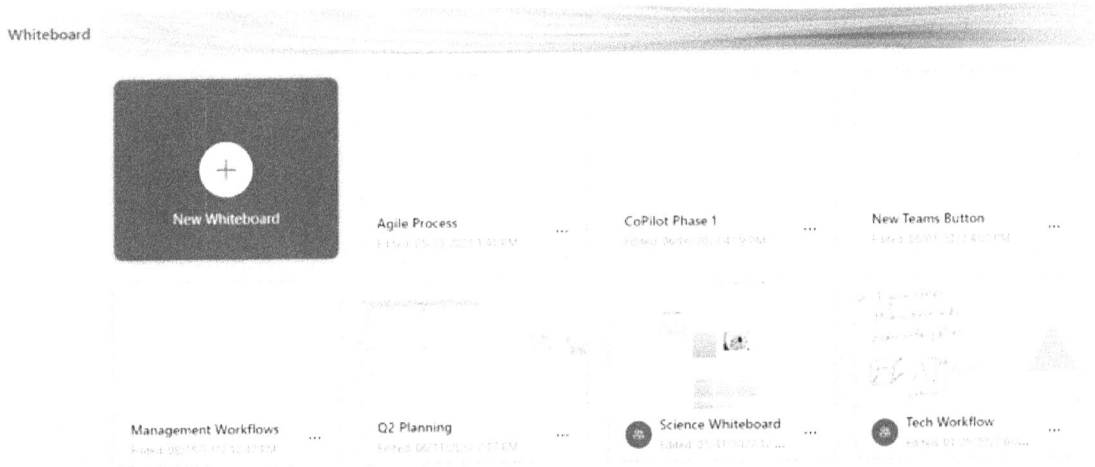

Figure 11.33: Whiteboard home page

Click on the + icon to create a **New Whiteboard**. It will prompt you to either use templates or **Start with blank canvas**, as shown:

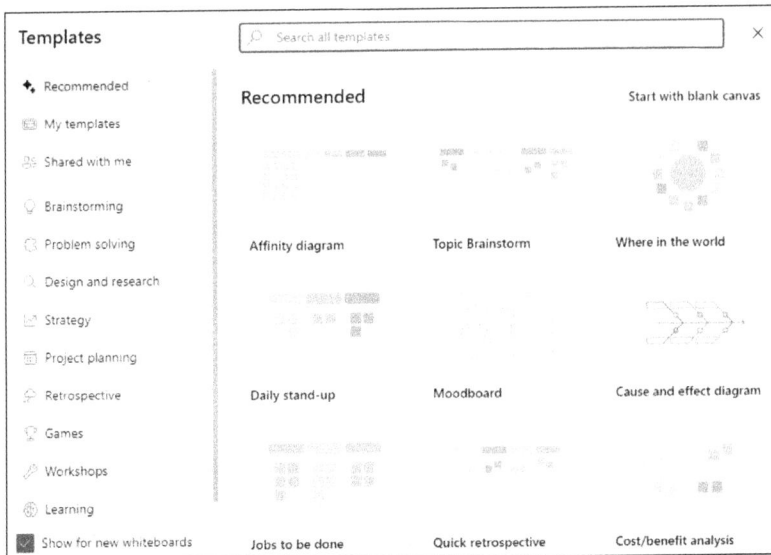

Figure 11.34: Templates available in whiteboard

2. **Basic area of Whiteboard:** Basic areas of Whiteboard consist of many things. You will find pointers or inking mode as well as expand or collapse the create panel. The **Create** panel allows you to add items to your board like sticky notes, text, images, shapes and many more. Understanding the basic area and functionalities can help users maximize its potential.

3. **Understanding the user interface:** Microsoft Whiteboard's **user interface (UI)** is crucial to maximizing its collaborative and creative potential. In addition to being intuitive and user-friendly, the UI enables users to quickly adapt and make the most of its features. The central area of Microsoft Whiteboard is known as the canvas. This is the place where users can create all the content, as shown:

Figure 11.35: Pens and ink tools

4. **Using pens and ink tools:** Pens and ink tools are available on the Whiteboard to draw and keep your ideas. Users can select the inking tool, and the shortcut to use it is *Alt +W*. Three different pens, highlighter, laser pointer, eraser (users can choose *partial stroke* or *entire stroke*), ruler, and lasso select to select the entire area.

5. **Utilizing sticky notes and integrating images and media:** Users can add sticky notes, either individually or in the notes grid format, as shown in *Figure 11.36:*

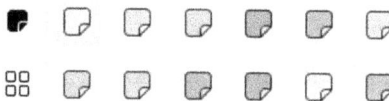

Figure 11.36: Notes and grid notes

Users have the ability to insert images and documents into their content, annotating and iterating across multiple types of content. Also, Whiteboard provides several fun reactions known as **emojis**, to share the views or feedback.

Figure 11.37: Reactions on Whiteboard

6. **Inserting and manipulating shapes:** Users can insert shapes and lines on the Whiteboard and add different types of arrows. Users can also create collaborative diagrams using shapes, lines, text, and ink.

7. **Loop components in Whiteboard:** There are various components available on a Whiteboard, such as users can add a variety of templates available for different

purposes (*Get Started with Microsoft Loop, 2024*). Whiteboard also allows you to add images, documents (as a screenshot), videos, or any important link to the current board, as shown:

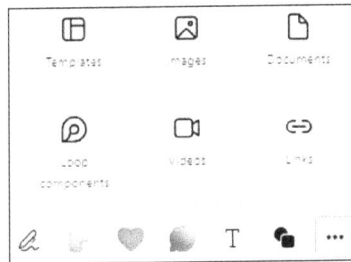

Figure 11.38: Loop components in Whiteboard

Whiteboard loop components allow creativity, collaboration, and decision-making to take place in real-time. Microsoft Loop went in public preview in March 2023, and is currently integrated with four other applications like Outlook, Teams, Word and Whiteboard.

To create a loop component, select the **…** dots from the bottom chrome menu and then select the loop components option (*Loop Components in Whiteboard, 2024*).

You can see that **Task list**, **Table**, **Voting table**, **Progress tracker,** and **Checklist** options are available, as follows:

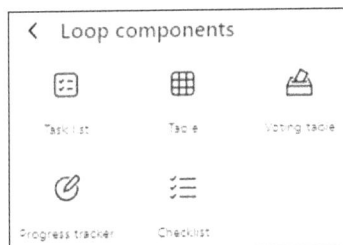

Figure 11.39: Loop components options

8. **Task list:** Task lists are portable pieces of content that stay in sync across all the places in Microsoft 365. This option lets you create tasks, set due dates, and assign to colleagues/peers. Following is the format of the task list available in the Whiteboard under loop components:

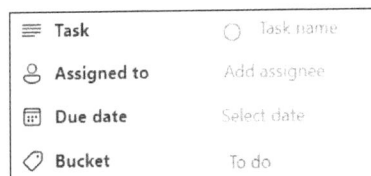

Figure 11.40: Task list, Loop components

9. **Table:** This option lets you create a table, apply filters, and condition each column. You can also change the column type (i.e., the type of data you enter in the column, such as text, number, date, person, vote, and label) and give your table a name. In fact, columns can be sorted in ascending or descending order.

10. **Voting table:** The voting table allows you to submit your ideas, mention pros and cons, and ask members to vote on your ideas.

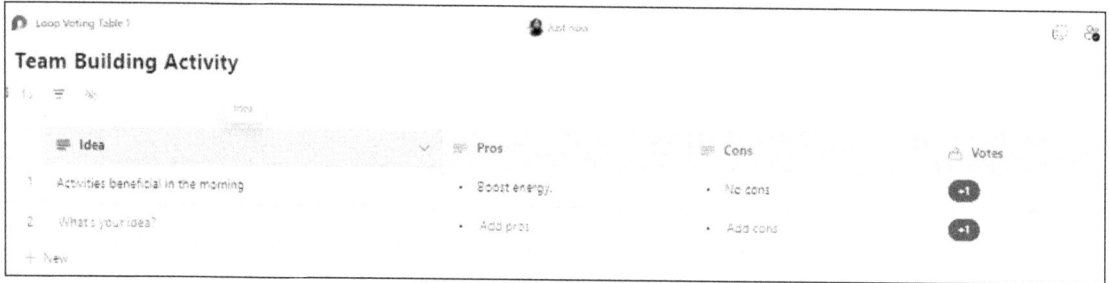

Figure 11.41: Voting table in Loop component

11. **Loop progress tracker:** This option lets you set work area, assign to colleagues, set the status along with the end date and blockers, if any.

12. **Checklist:** This option allows you to create a checklist and send it to others to start collaborating. As people edit, everyone will see the changes instantly.

13. **Collaboration in Microsoft Whiteboard:** Whiteboard allows users to collaborate with their peers. This is a new core feature that lets you see what other collaborators are doing on the Whiteboard through collaboration cursors. With the Laser Pointer, you can share your best ideas and get people's attention. Reduce distractions while guiding users through ideas with **Follow Along**. Users can collaborate across apps by bringing in fluid components like tables or task lists.

14. **Inviting participants to a Whiteboard session:** Anyone can invite their peers to collaborate on a Whiteboard. Click on the **Share** button available in the top right corner of the Whiteboard application, and you will get a dialog box where you can add a name or email address and provide editing or viewing rights. The user can click on the gear icon to choose the share settings and then click on the **Apply** button, as shown:

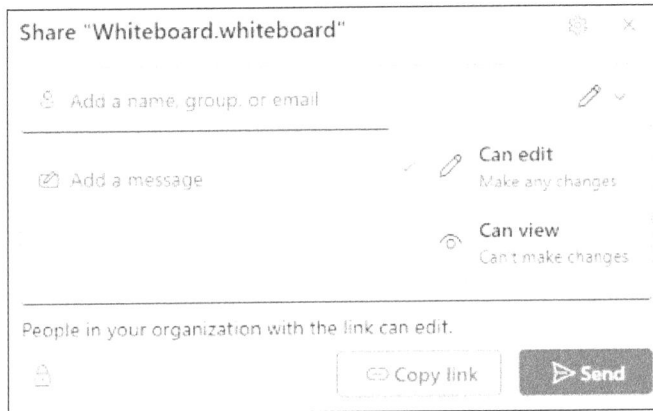

Figure 11.42: Sharing Whiteboard

Once the Whiteboard is shared with the peers, they can do real-time collaboration, and the owner can manage the participants permission like edit or view rights.

15. **Integration with other Microsoft tools:** New Whiteboard is now integrated with other Microsoft 365 tools to fit into existing workflows more seamlessly. Whiteboard is integrated with Microsoft Teams (in Channels and Chats) and allows team members to easily start collaborative work. Whiteboard can be integrated within Teams meetings, making it easier for team members to collaborate in real-time and making presentations more interactive. Multiple participants can draw, write, or add images to a Whiteboard simultaneously. Presenters can use it to illustrate points more vividly, and attendees can contribute in real-time.

Content from other Office 365 applications like Word, Excel, or PowerPoint can be easily incorporated into Whiteboard. This integration is beneficial for seamless transition between discussing ideas on the Whiteboard and documenting them in Office applications. All changes and additions to the Whiteboard are automatically saved to the cloud. This means that users can access and edit their Whiteboards from anywhere and at any time, if they have an internet connection and access to their Office 365 account.

The best part is, Whiteboard is accessible on various devices, including desktop computers, tablets, and smartphones, making it a versatile tool for all types of users.

16. **Exporting Whiteboard:** Exporting content from Whiteboard is an easy process, allowing users to work in various formats for sharing or archiving. Microsoft Whiteboard allows you to export boards as image files. The common format is **Portable Network Graphics (PNG)**, which captures the entire board in a single image.

Note: **PNG files are commonly used for web design, digital art, and storing high-quality images where clarity and transparency are important.**

To export, click on the gear icon on the right-hand side and select **Export**. It will give you another window which allows you to select the **Image** option, and then you can select the image size, either a **Standard resolution** or **High resolution**. Once you select it, click on the **Export** option.

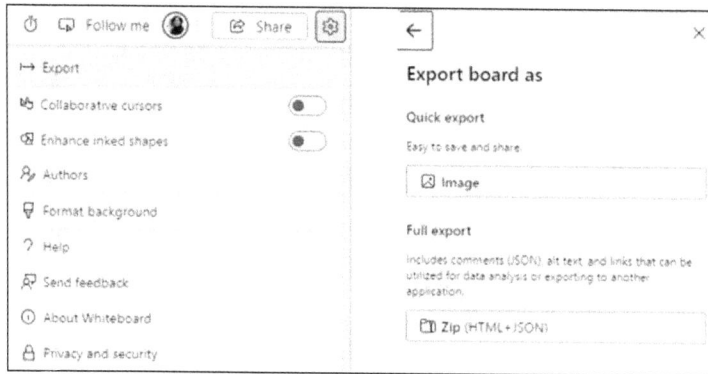

Figure 11.43: Exporting Whiteboard

If you are using Whiteboard on a mobile device, the process is similar to exporting your Whiteboards. Look for a share or export option in the app's menu. Once you choose to export, you will be prompted to choose a location to save the file. You can save it on your device or upload it directly to a cloud storage service, if the app supports this feature.

After exporting, you can share the saved image file via email, messaging apps, or through file-sharing platforms. If you have exported the file to a cloud service, you can often share a link directly to the file.

17. **More features in Whiteboard:** The timer is available in the Whiteboard. On the top right corner, click on the watch icon to start a timer. Set minutes and click on play and pause button. You can increase or decrease the time by clicking on + or – icons.

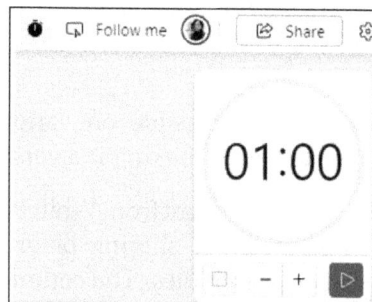

Figure 11.44: Timer in Whiteboard

18. **Format background:** Users can click on the gear icon and select the option **Format background** to give a different look to your Whiteboard.

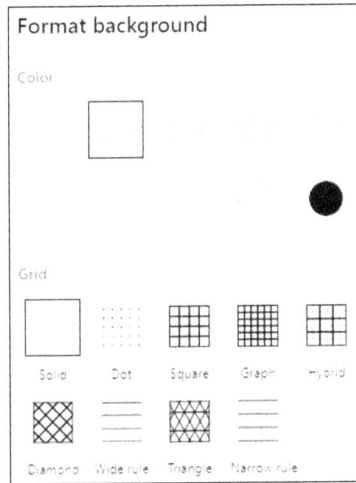

Figure 11.45: *Format background options in Whiteboard*

Best practices for digital Whiteboarding

Whether you are working remotely or in a hybrid environment, using a digital Whiteboard effectively can significantly improve communication and idea-sharing.

Here are some best practices to ensure a seamless experience, as follows:

- The canvas can be expanded infinitely, providing ample space for complex or extensive projects. Use a Whiteboard in different scenarios, e.g., meetings, brainstorming sessions, education, etc.

- If you are leading a session, make sure to prepare your Whiteboard in advance, like setting up templates, draft initial ideas or outline the session's goals. This preparation can help guide the discussion going forward and keep the session focused.

- In a collaborative setting, encourage all participants to contribute. This might involve prompting quieter team members for input or assigning specific tasks or areas of the Whiteboard to different people.

- The best part is that all your Whiteboards are saved on the cloud. Be mindful of the information you put on digital Whiteboards, especially if sensitive or proprietary data is involved. Follow your organization's policies for data security and compliance.

As a part of the Office 365 suite, Whiteboard adheres to the same security and compliance protocols, ensuring that all data and information shared on the Whiteboard is secure.

It is available to users on iOS and Android devices. Users can view and edit loop components in Whiteboard but can neither create them nor copy/paste them (*Gleave, 2023*). On Surface Hubs & Microsoft Teams room devices, users will not be able to view, edit, create, or copy/paste loop components in the Whiteboard.

Overview of To Do

It is becoming increasingly difficult to manage digital clutter. The Microsoft To Do application focuses on keeping people at the center of the task management process. Microsoft To Do is a simple and intelligent application that helps to manage and focus on work and keep track of all the important list items in one place. It acts as a smart daily planner, where you can set yourself up with intelligent and personalized suggestions to update your daily to-do list. The application is available on desktop as well as a mobile app. It is also known as a cross-platform task management application. It is integrated with Outlook Tasks, making it easier to manage all your tasks in one place.

The To Do application is used to list and manage your tasks. The icon is illustrated in *Figure 11.46*:

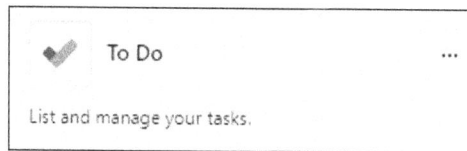

Figure 11.46: Microsoft To Do app

It consists of three key parameters:

- Displaying urgent and important tasks.
- Collecting tasks from a variety of sources.
- Assisting users in completing tasks.

Here, you will learn top tips for getting tasks under control. The interface will prompt some helpful information regarding the application as depicted in *Figure 11.47*:

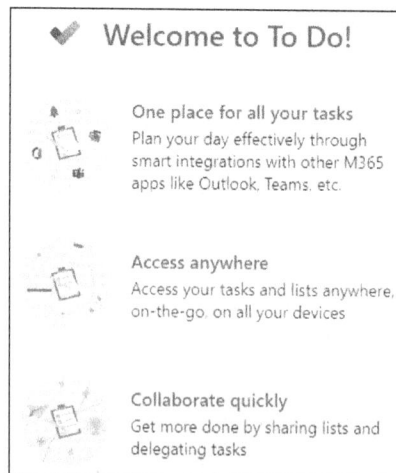

Figure 11.47: All tasks at one place

You can start your day with **My Day** by adding any number of new tasks to organize your work or choosing from **Suggestions** to plan your day. The Suggestion pane includes tasks from My Day, your other lists, and other M365 apps. You have an option to group your tasks by category.

Once you open the application, you will get a few options. Click on **My Day** and add a task. You can add a due date (for today, tomorrow, next week or pick a date from the calendar) to complete the task, reminder at a level (pick a date and time), and repeat if you need to repeat the task on daily basis, weekdays, weekly, monthly or yearly. Users can customize according to their preferences, as follows:

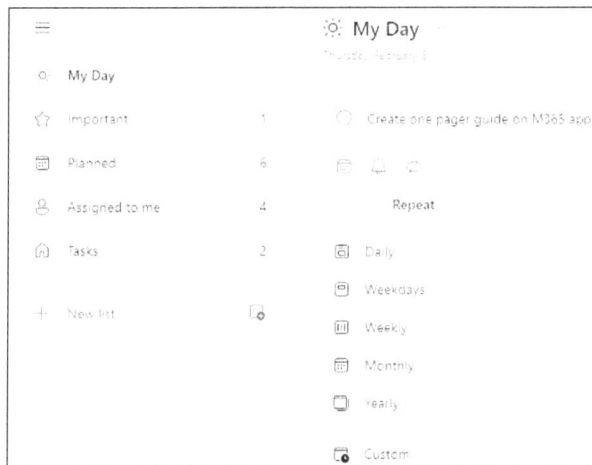

Figure 11.48: Plan your day

Prepare your own list or group of lists. In each list, you can add as many tasks as you want. You can also customize each list by selecting the background. Again, keep in mind that you can set due dates and reminders for each task and star your most important tasks. You can use small steps to break down your larger tasks into more manageable tasks and add notes to record extra details, as shown in *Figure 11.49*:

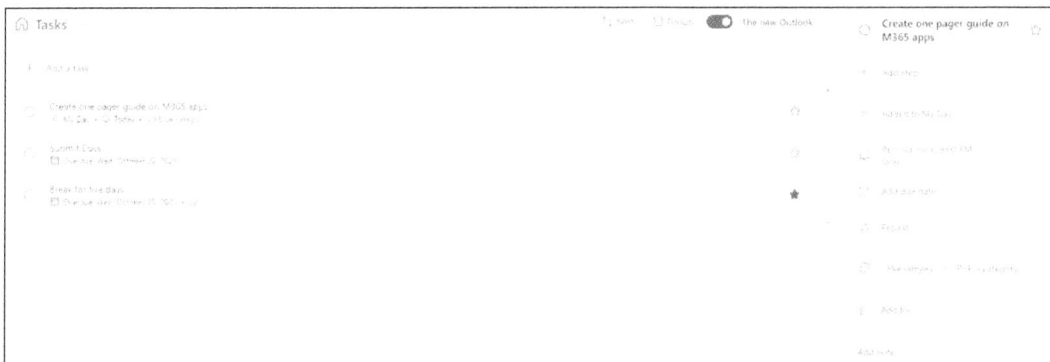

Figure 11.49: Adding more details in tasks

While adding extra information to tasks, users can also add files from mobile devices. Clicking on **Add file** will open a dialog box where you can select any file, or click on **Update from mobile**, which shows a QR code to scan and start pairing your mobile device, as shown:

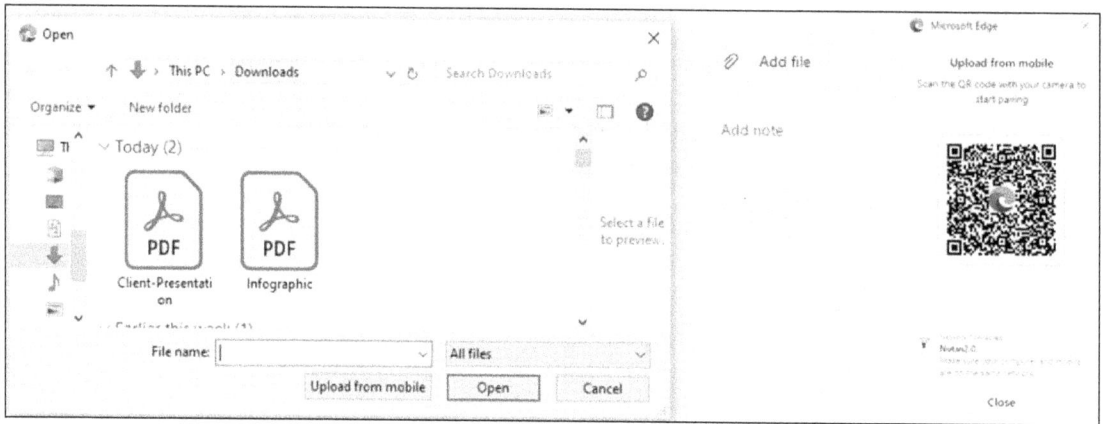

Figure 11.50: Add file from mobile to tasks

- **Edit a task:** If you want to rename a task, select the task to open its detail view. Once the task is in detail view, you can click or tap the task's title. A cursor will appear in the title field, allowing you to edit or rename the title (*Create, Edit, Delete, and Restore Tasks,* 2023).

- **Delete a task:** To delete a task, select the **trash can** icon in the bottom right corner of the task's detail view, or you can right-click and select **Delete selected task** if you are on desktop. On Android and iOS, you can swipe from right to left to delete.

- **Delete multiple tasks:** If you want to delete multiple tasks, you must be on desktop mode, then use shift key to select the tasks you want to delete and click **Delete tasks**.

- **Flagged email:** Access your flagged emails from Outlook in To Do. Visibility of these tasks can be controlled from the To Do settings. To Do is integrated with Outlook tasks. To view To Do tasks in the Outlook desktop client, use the same Microsoft account to sign in to both applications. Since all of your tasks are stored on Exchange Online servers, they automatically appear in Outlook tasks.

- **Restore a deleted task:** You can restore a deleted task, as tasks are stored in Exchange online and also visible in Outlook Tasks. Hence, you can easily recover deleted tasks in Outlook.

Create a list

Users can create a list for sorting the tasks in common projects. On the left-hand side, click on **New list** and type a name for the list, and then press *Enter*, as shown:

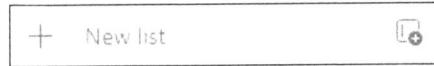

Figure 11.51: Create a list

Plan tasks in Microsoft To Do, and you can check your group tasks at the same time as you are checking your tasks using the **Assigned to you** feature in the Microsoft To Do application.

The **Assigned to you** section, which appears on the left-hand side, shows you all the tasks that are assigned to you via the Planner application. You can change the name of each task. You can add, change, or complete the checklist items, change the due date, add or change the description, or add the tasks to **My day** in To Do.

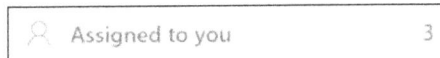

Figure 11.52: Assigned tasks via Planner

Conclusion

In this chapter, the author has outlined the features and functionalities of four Microsoft applications one by one, i.e., OneNote, Sway, Whiteboard, and To Do. In the context of OneNote, it is a digital notebook, similar to a traditional notebook, in which a professional or student can create pages and organize them in different sections, which can be maintained and synchronized across all the shared devices. Sway is an online presentation tool that is somewhat like PowerPoint, with some features that are **out of the box**. Sway has a continuous one-page layout, focuses more on templates, and requires an internet connection, whereas PowerPoint uses slides, possesses extensive customization, and can be used offline. Thus, Sway is a web-based application used to create a presentation by directly uploading a document or article. Microsoft Whiteboard is the collaborative digital canvas in Microsoft 365, for coordinating effective meetings and promoting engaging learning. The Whiteboard tool can be used to maximize outcomes with ink, sticky notes, templates, and more, which have been covered in the chapter. At last, Microsoft To Do is an application that focuses on managing tasks efficiently for scheduled meetings and whatever tasks are reflected on Planner. It can be easily navigated within the Microsoft To Do application, which enhances productivity and manages tasks efficiently. In a nutshell, all these applications are vital for information professionals, researchers, educators, teachers, and for student community to brainstorm and collate ideas, organize, present, and share them with the relevant stakeholders.

In the next chapter, we will explore the various applications within the Power Platform.

References

1. *Apply a tag to a note in OneNote.* (2024). Microsoft Support. **https://support.microsoft.com/en-us/office/apply-a-tag-to-a-note-in-onenote-908c7b92-6ed0-498d-bc7d-1b44e6827d05.**

2. *Create, edit, delete, and restore tasks.* (2023). Microsoft Support. **https://support.microsoft.com/en-us/office/create-edit-delete-and-restore-tasks-30346281-30d4-4d6b-a6fa-55beca8d38a3.**

3. *Create links to notebooks, sections, pages, and paragraphs in OneNote for Windows 10.* (2024). Microsoft Support. **https://support.microsoft.com/en-us/office/create-links-to-notebooks-sections-pages-and-paragraphs-in-onenote-for-windows-10-48dd0e82-623c-405d-b63a-df4eaf55c72a.**

4. *Dictate your notes in OneNote.* (2024). Microsoft Support. **https://support.microsoft.com/en-us/office/dictate-your-notes-in-onenote-2f5d1549-afe1-4abd-95ff-829a839e3d00.**

5. *Draw and sketch notes on a page.* (2024). Microsoft Support. **https://support.microsoft.com/en-us/office/draw-and-sketch-notes-on-a-page-e34b425a-9431-4b73-b52d-63c44a67f67a.**

6. *Get started with Microsoft Loop.* (2024). Microsoft Support. **https://support.microsoft.com/en-us/office/get-started-with-microsoft-loop-9f4d8d4f-dfc6-4518-9ef6-069408c21f0c.**

7. *Getting started with Microsoft Whiteboard.* (2024). Microsoft Support. **https://support.microsoft.com/en-us/office/getting-started-with-microsoft-Whiteboard-48cab0ee-90b3-483a-9a48-ff17fe476c6b.**

8. Gleave, J. (2023, July 26). *How Microsoft Loop integrates with Whiteboard.* Business Tech Planet. **https://businesstechplanet.com/how-microsoft-loop-integrates-with-Whiteboard/.**

9. *Insert a table in OneNote for Windows 10.* (2024). Microsoft Support. **https://support.microsoft.com/en-us/office/insert-a-table-in-onenote-for-windows-10-35052542-ca8e-42fe-be3f-bc5c748a14b1.**

10. *Insert or attach files to Notes.* (2024). Microsoft Support. **https://support.microsoft.com/en-us/office/insert-or-attach-files-to-notes-f11eac68-144d-48bd-946f-c42d9104b17e.**

11. *Loop components in Whiteboard.* (2024). Microsoft Support. **https://support.microsoft.com/en-us/office/loop-components-in-Whiteboard-c5f08f54-995e-473e-be6e-7f92555da347.**

CHAPTER 12

Microsoft Power Platform

Introduction

In this chapter, we will explore the various applications within the Power Platform, including Power BI for data visualization, PowerApps used for creating low-code solutions to address business challenges, and Power Automate for process automation.

The Microsoft Power Platform serves as a low-code environment for rapidly building customized end-to-end solutions, comprising four major components: Power BI, Power Apps, Power Automate, Power Virtual Agents, and Power Pages. Every application can function independently or together by underlying Microsoft Dataverse technology.

Structure

In this chapter, we will discuss the following topics:

- Power Platform
- Overview of Power BI
- Introduction to Power Apps
- Get started with Power Automate

Objectives

By the end of this chapter, we will have a comprehensive understanding of Power Platform and its core components, PowerBI, Power Apps, Power Automate, and Power Virtual Agents. We will also understand how these tools work together to analyze the data, automate processes, develop custom applications, and create AI-powered chatbots with minimal coding expertise.

Additionally, we will be able to explore the concepts of Dataverse for secure data storage and AI builder for integrating artificial intelligence into their solutions. After mastering the above-mentioned concepts, we will be able to leverage Power Platform to improve business efficiency, automate repetitive processes, and make data-driven decisions.

Power platform

Microsoft Power Platform is a powerful collection of applications that has the capabilities to automate daily tasks, build amazing solutions, build reports, and create virtual agents. It is an intuitive, collaborative, and extensible platform that empowers everyone in the organization to create professional and effective solutions.

It consists of major components:

- **Power BI**: A business analytics tool that allows you to **discover intelligent insights** from diverse data. You can create stunning dashboards and visualizations to support decision-making and data-driven initiatives.

- **Power Apps**: An application development platform where you can **build no code to low-code solutions** to address various business needs. Whether it is creating custom apps or automating processes, Power Apps provides a user-friendly environment for development without extensive coding knowledge.

- **Power Automate**: Formerly known as Microsoft Flow. This application will streamline your processes with **no-code automation.** It enables you to create workflows, automate repetitive tasks, and integrate different services and applications.

- **Power Virtual Agents**: Power Virtual Agents are known as intelligent virtual bots and handle routine inquiries at scale with conversational AI. It lets you create chatbots that assist users efficiently, freeing up human resources for more complex tasks.

- **Power Pages**: While not as commonly mentioned, Power Pages is another component of the Power Platform. It allows you to create and manage web pages within your organization.

As explained, Power Platform is comprised of Power BI, Power Apps, and Power Automate (formerly known as Flow). These applications are used to manage the digital world, where data is the king and the basis of any enterprise process.

Their applications are given as follows:

- Data can be displayed and analyzed using Power BI.
- Data can be acted on and modified using Power Apps.
- Data/Tasks can be automated using Power Automate.

Figure 12.1 illustrates the interrelationship among Power Platform applications that can be utilized for analysis, action, and automation:

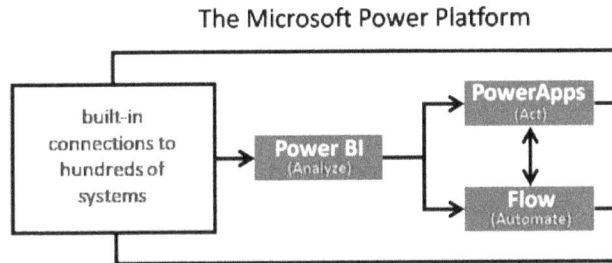

Figure 12.1: *Microsoft Power Platform applications*

Overview of Power BI

Power BI is a business analytics application that enables users to create dashboards based on data. You can interact with the real-time dashboard and get proper insights at a glance. The advantage is that you can gain insight regardless of where your data lives. Power BI has the capability to transform your visuals with advanced data analysis tools.

Microsoft Power BI comprises a suite of software services, applications, and connectors seamlessly integrated to transform disparate data sources into cohesive, visually engaging, and interactive insights. Power BI enables effortless connectivity to diverse data sources, whether stored in a basic Microsoft Excel workbook or a mix of cloud-based and on-premises hybrid data warehouses. With Power BI, you can seamlessly connect, clean, and model your data without altering the original sources, visualize crucial insights, and effortlessly share them with specific individuals or a wider audience. Fundamentally, used for data visualization that combines an intuitive user experience. It helps users make better decisions by infusing insights into the applications that you see every day.

Figure 12.2 illustrates the dashboard that integrates various data sources for the purpose of data visualization:

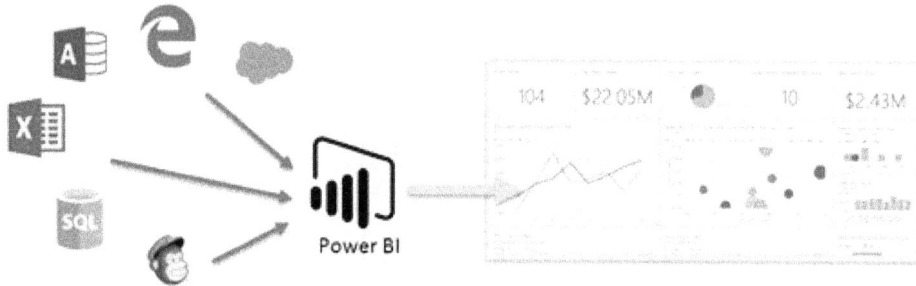

Figure 12.2: *Connecting with multiple data sources to visualize the data*
(**Source**: *Describe using Power BI to build data-driven analytics - Training | Microsoft Learn*)

Designers can create data models and build reports and dashboards to display information about any aspect of the business or the larger environment. Dashboards about sales, customer service, manufacturing, technical projects, and reports can be shared on the website in SharePoint, MS Teams, and other apps. Power BI consumers manipulate the dashboards to be able to gain additional insights into the business or about specific business units. Whilst visualizing the data in Power BI, it offers a wide range of different styles, including graphs, maps, charts, scatter plots, and many more.

Power BI consists of a Microsoft Windows desktop application known as Power BI Desktop, which is used to create reports, an online **Software as a Service (SaaS)** service known as Power BI service, used to publish the reports, and mobile Power BI apps that are available on Android/iPhones and tablets. You can embed and share reports into other Microsoft services like MS Teams, PowerPoint, Excel, and Power Platform.

Figure 12.3 illustrates the trio of components that are designed to enable individuals to generate, share, and utilize business insights in a manner that best aligns with their needs or professional roles:

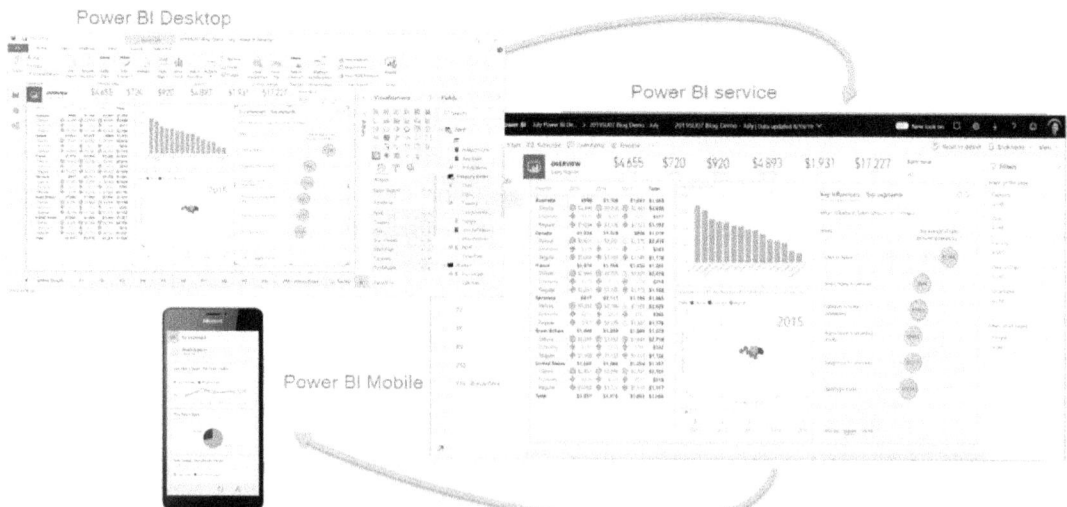

Figure 12.3: *Power BI elements*

Before installing the Power BI Desktop, ensure your system meets the following minimum requirements:

- The operating system should be Windows 10 or 11
- The processor should be 1 GHz or faster
- RAM should be 8 GB or higher for large datasets
- Enough disk space should be available

Figure 12.4 illustrates the interface when downloading Power BI Desktop. Use the link **https://powerbi.microsoft.com/en-us/downloads/**, as follows:

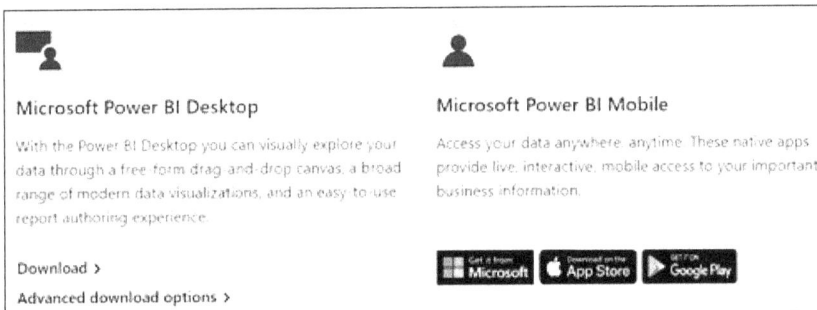

Figure 12.4: *Power BI Desktop and Mobile Application*

Building blocks of Power BI

Creating Power BI Solutions involves several key components, which play a pivotal role in determining both the data presented and its visual presentation to end-users. These components include datasets, reports, and dashboards.

These elements are structured within workspaces and are established on capacities as follows:

- **Capacities**, fundamental to Power BI, encompass a collection of resources utilized for hosting and delivering your Power BI content. These capacities are classified as either shared or dedicated. A shared capacity is available to various other Microsoft customers, while a dedicated capacity is entirely reserved for a single customer. Additionally, dedicated capacities require an active subscription. By default, workspaces are created on a shared capacity.

- **Workspaces** are containers for dashboards, datasets, reports, and dataflows in Power BI. There are two types of workspaces: My workspaces and workspaces.

  By default, the user has access to *My workspace*, which is the personal space for any individual user where dashboards and reports are saved, whereas **Workspaces** are used to share and collaborate on content with your colleagues. Colleagues can be added to your workspace and collaborate on dashboards. With one exception, all workspace members need Power BI Pro licenses.

Figure 12.5 shows the interface of the workspace area, which is available in Power BI:

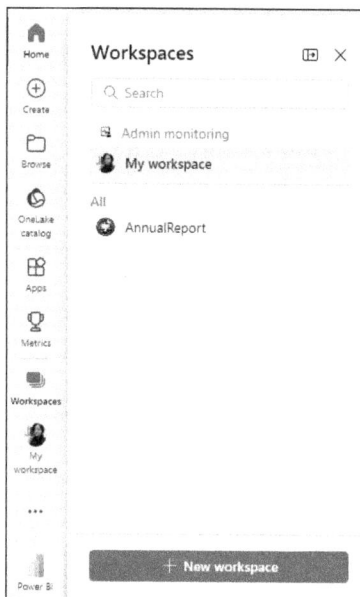

Figure 12.5: *Workspaces in Power BI*

- **Semantic models** are the source data from dataflows. Dataflows allow users to transform and clean the data they import from Excel, OneDrive, etc., before loading it into PowerBI.

- **Reports** are the place where you can get all the information about your data in the form of a dashboard. Users can visualize the data through different elements like filters, drill-throughs, slicers, charts, maps, and many more. There are two modes to view and interact with reports: reading view, which is used to display the report, and editing view, where any individual with edit permission can modify the elements on the report. A report can have one or more pages, just like an Excel file can have one or more worksheets.

- **Dashboards** are canvases that contain one or more tiles and widgets. Every tile is pinned through a report, or QnA displays a solitary visualization derived from a dataset and pinned to the dashboard. Entire report pages can also be pinned as individual tiles onto the dashboard.

Data visualization

Data visualization is the graphical presentation of information, with the goal of providing the viewer with a qualitative understanding of the information content. It is a process of using a wide range of communications methods, presentation technologies, and media formats to visually reveal the meaning of data to viewers.

Figure 12.6 illustrates the graphical presentation of raw data available in rows and columns, complex, effective, and accurate data available in various graphs:

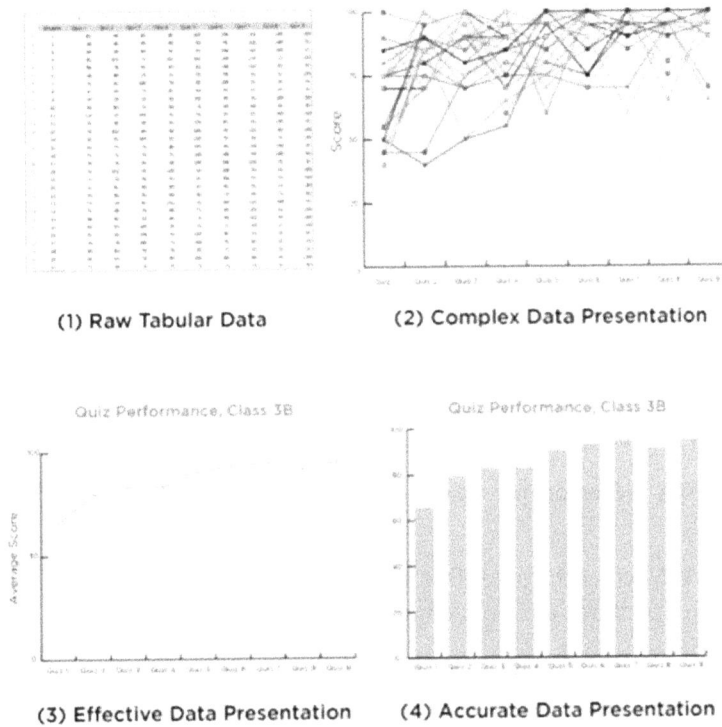

(1) Raw Tabular Data   (2) Complex Data Presentation

(3) Effective Data Presentation   (4) Accurate Data Presentation

Figure 12.6: *Data visualization*

When you download Power BI, you will be able to access free desktop applications, services, and report servers that enable you to monitor your data and create reports in a variety of different ways. With managed services, you can get the most out of these products and optimize them for better business processes.

Power BI product and its components

There are three Power BI products as follows:

- **Power BI Desktop**: The free desktop application allows businesses to test out Power BI. You can connect, transform, and visualize your data.

- **Power BI service**: Power BI service is the main product in the PBI offering and lets you send reports securely to your colleagues for collaboration.

- **Power BI report server**: This is the web portal that allows you to display and manage **Key Performance Indicators** (**KPIs**) and reports. It is very similar to the Power BI online service, but you can create paginated reports, mobile reports, and KPIs.

There is a reason that Power BI is a business intelligence tool for many companies. The different features allow for a variety of reporting and in-depth visualization.

Let us look at some of the main products that make Power BI so significant.

Microsoft Power BI components

The following are some of the components of Microsoft Power BI:

- **Power Query**: Let us transform, combine, or enhance your data for more excellent value.

- **Power Pivot**: Microsoft Power BI's memory tabular data modelling tool. Use it to create data models that highlight essential business information for the future of decision-making.

- **Power View**: The core visualization tool that allows you to create business charts, graphs, and any visualization you can think of.

- **Power Map**: A more complex data visualization tool, a power map creates geospatial maps.

- **Power Q&A**: Microsoft Power BI's very own search engine. Type in your enquiry, and Power BI will produce a report-based answer.

Power BI Desktop is a free application you install on your local computer that lets you connect to, transform, and visualize your data. With Power BI Desktop, users can connect to multiple data sources and combine them (often referred to as modeling) into a data model. This data model allows the building of visuals and collections of visuals that a user can share as reports with other people inside the organization as follows:

- **Report:** In this view, you create reports and visuals, where most of your creation time is spent.

- **Data:** In this view, you see the tables, measures, and other data used in the data model associated with your report and transform the data for best use in the report's model.

- **Model:** In this view, you see and manage the relationships among tables in your data model.

Once you have the Power BI desktop application available on your device, you will be able to view the **Report View, Data View,** and **Model View** by selecting icons available from the left side. The **Publish** button is also available on the top right-hand side to publish your data. You will also see the **Visualization** option available on the right side. You have the option to switch between available Pages.

Figure 12.7 presents the views arranged in the sequence in which they are shown. In Power BI Desktop, users can select from three available views on the left side of the canvas:

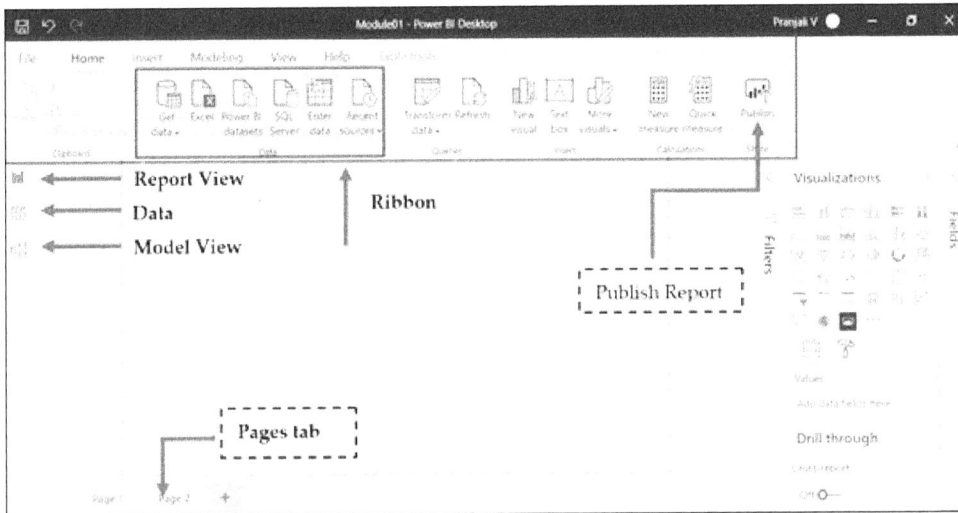

Figure 12.7: Power BI Desktop interface

- **Connect to the data**: The Power BI Desktop application facilitates connections to a wide array of data sources, encompassing local databases, worksheets, and cloud-based data services. Occasionally, the gathered data may lack the desired structure or cleanliness. To refine the data, transformation becomes imperative, enabling actions such as column splitting and renaming, data type alteration, and establishment of relationships between columns.

Figure 12.8 illustrates export data from various sources like Excel, CSV files, SQL Server, etc:

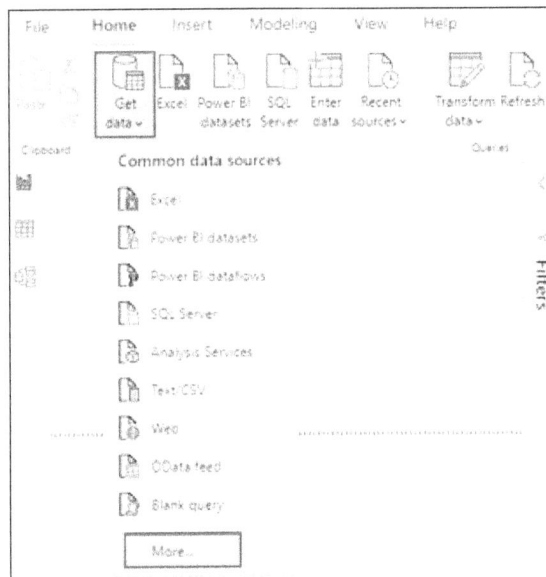

Figure 12.8: Export data from various sources

- **Create visuals in Power BI:** The visualization pane is located on the right side of the screen. Once you have a data model, you can drag fields onto the report canvas to create visuals. A visual is a graphical representation of your data in the model. You can customize colors or axes from this pane, apply filters, drag fields, and much more. If no visual is selected on the canvas, a new visual is created based on your selection. A report is a collection of visuals in one Power BI Desktop file. There are different types of visuals like heatmaps, charts, tree maps, maps, tables, slicers, decomposition trees, matrices, Q&As, paginated reports, gauges, cards, Azure maps, and so on. *Figure 12.9* illustrates the types of graphs available for visualization.

You can collapse the **Visualizations**, **Filters**, and **Data** panes to provide more space in the Report view by selecting the small arrow, as shown in the following figure:

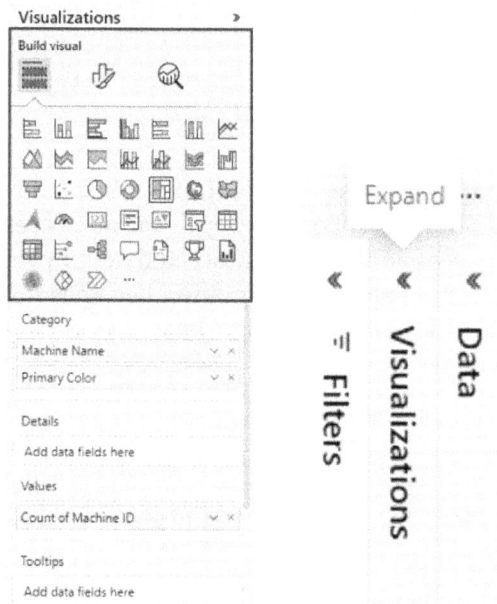

Figure 12.9: Various graphs are available for visualization

- **Report creation workflow in Power BI**: A typical workflow for report creation in Power BI follows a specific sequence. Initially, you utilize Power BI Desktop to establish connections to data sources and construct the report. Subsequently, you will publish the report on the Power BI service.

The following are the steps to create and publish the report:

1. Install Power BI Desktop.
2. Sign in, then launch the Power BI Desktop and explore the user interface.
3. Connect to data.
4. Transform and model data with Power BI Desktop.

5.   Create visualizations and reports.

6.   Publish reports to the Power BI service.

7.   Distribute and manage reports in the Power BI service.

Figure 12.10 shows the Power BI service, which assists in creating detailed dashboards that can be divided into reports:

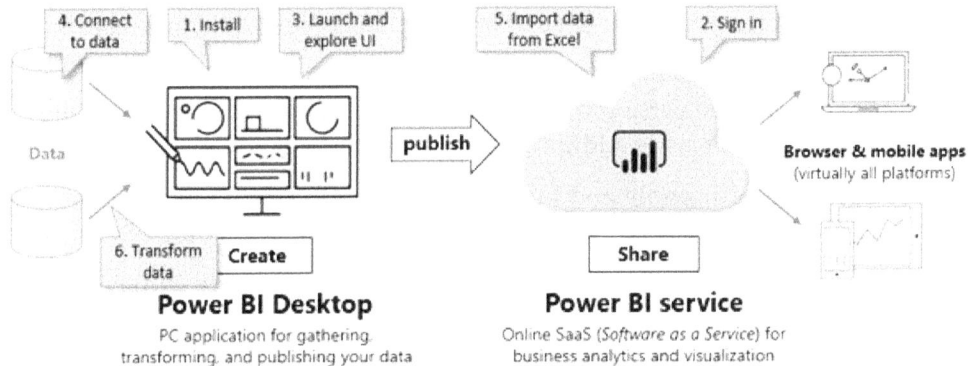

Figure 12.10: *High-level dashboard of Power BI Desktop and service*

Benefits of Power BI

Although the standard Microsoft Suite provides a basic reporting and analytics tool in Excel, it does not enhance business outcomes effectively. In contrast, Power BI is specifically designed to serve as an optimal solution for comprehensive reporting and insights. Rather than struggling with spreadsheets to interpret extensive data, users can generate intuitive reports that facilitate a clearer understanding and enhance decision-making capabilities. This tool is suitable for businesses of all sizes and across various industries that require assistance in making data-driven decisions.

Power BI is a powerful business intelligence tool that helps organizations analyze and visualize data for better decision-making. Though we work with various businesses and often find ourselves implementing Power BI solutions for insurance and manufacturing companies. The following are some of the top reasons they decided to implement Power BI in their business processes:

- With Power BI's built-in machine-learning abilities, users can quickly analyze data like year-on-year sales to track trends and predict future sales. This feature helps uncover hidden patterns and trends.

- Regardless of your subscription model, Power BI updates your information regularly, ensuring you always have the most up-to-date data. You can also set up custom alerts to display important metrics like stock levels to keep your team on their toes. Helps businesses make quick decisions based on up-to-date data insights.

- Power BI connects to multiple data sources like Excel, SQL Server, SharePoint, Azure, Salesforce, Dynamics 365, and many more. It supports cloud, on-premises, and hybrid data integration with security features.

- Power BI provides interactive and visually appealing reports with charts, graphs, and dashboards. Users can create custom visualization without needing advanced technical skills.

- It uses Microsoft's enterprise-grade security to keep your data protected in the cloud or on-premises.

- Power BI offers a free version (Power BI Desktop) for individual users, while Power BI Pro and Premium provide additional collaborations and advanced features.

- Power BI is a user-friendly and low-code platform to create reports and dashboards. Its drag-and-drop interface makes data analysis simple and intuitive.

- Power BI allows users to easily share reports and dashboards with colleagues using Power BI Service. Its integration in Microsoft 365 applications like Microsoft Teams and SharePoint enhances teamwork and collaboration.

- Power BI is easy to navigate for users familiar with Excel and has beautiful visualization templates to make your data sing.

Power BI is an adaptable and secure business intelligence platform that assists organizations in data analysis, automate reporting, and make data-driven decisions.

Introduction to Power Apps

Power Apps is a **Low-Code Application Platform** (**LCAP**) that empowers developers to develop and deploy applications more quickly and seamlessly. Power Apps is a robust suite of tools designed to empower users to create custom business applications without the need for extensive coding knowledge. It also encompasses a collection of apps, services, and connectors, enabling the creation of tailored business applications without the necessity for coding. Offering a swift development environment, Power Apps facilitates the construction of apps tailored to your specific business requirements. By leveraging Power Apps, you can build sophisticated solutions utilizing AI-driven development, preexisting templates, and connections to numerous data sources and systems. Whether addressing financial, sales and marketing, human resources, operational, or frontline worker needs, Power Apps provides the means to solve a myriad of business challenges. One of the key features of Power Apps is the integration with Microsoft's ecosystem, enabling seamless connectivity with other Microsoft applications and services such as SharePoint, Excel, and Dynamics 365.

PowerApps allow you to interact with your data on any device, and it works best in web browsers as well as on mobile devices. To use Power Apps, it is not required to have coding experience. PowerApps allow you to connect to the existing data to create apps, forms, and workflows without writing code and share your apps with your coworkers so that they can use them on any devices such as web or mobile apps. Power Apps allow you to create three types of apps, i.e., canvas, model-driven, and portal.

Power Apps building blocks

PowerApps is a collection of services, applications, and connectors that work together to let you do much more than just view your data. You can act on your data and update it anywhere and from any device. To create, share, and administer applications, users can use the following sites:

- **To make a Power App**: Go to **https://make.powerapps.com**. This link will redirect you to the Microsoft 365 platform and ask you to sign in with your work account (if you have not already signed in). You can open an application, specify the type of application you want to create, share your application, and make data connections and flows.

- **For Power Apps Studio**: Go to **https://create.powerapps.com//studio**. This link will allow you to configure **user interface** (**UI**) elements and Excel formulas. Power Apps Studio is the app designer used to build canvas apps. The app designer makes creating apps feel more like building a slide deck in Microsoft PowerPoint.

- **To manage the Power Apps admin center**: Define the environment and data policies for the organization by clicking the link **https://admin.powerplatform.microsoft.com**.

An environment is a space for storing, managing, and sharing your organization's business data, applications, and workflows. It also serves as a container to separate apps that might have different roles, security requirements, or target audiences. It is always a question of how you choose to use the environment, depending on the organization and the applications you are trying to build.

For example:

- You can choose only to build your apps in a single environment.

- You might create separate environments that group the test and production versions of your apps.

- You might create separate environments that correspond to specific teams or departments in your company, each containing the relevant data and apps for each audience.

- You might also create separate environments for different global branches of your company.

To get started, you need to sign in with a work account. Click on the waffle icon available on the top left corner and click on **All Apps** | Select **Power Apps** from the portal. To create an app, you can quickly start with **https://make.powerapps.com.** It will open the Power Apps application on the screen. A menu is available on the left-hand side. In the middle of the screen, Copilot is also available to develop any app that is built on Dataverse.

Note: **You need to have a Copilot license to use it.**

Figure 12.11 shows the interface of the Power Apps application and its available menus:

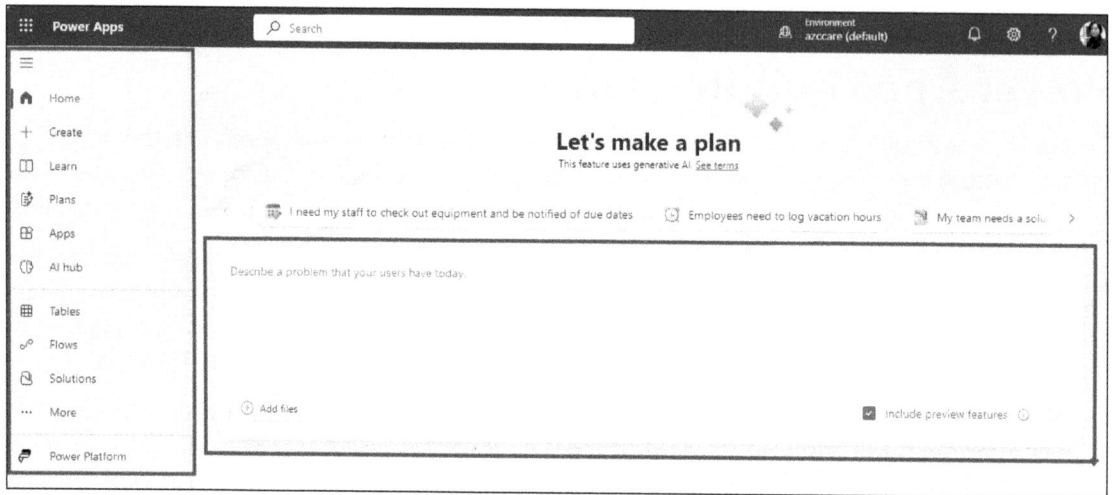

Figure 12.11: *Power Apps interface*

Initially, you will get access to the default environment. To get started with building an application on any data source, select the **Create** button from the left-hand menu. Power Apps provides various ways to start from common data sources, such as SharePoint and Excel. Dataverse and SQL are superior data sources, capable of handling large amounts of data efficiently. If you are building your own developer environment with Dataverse, there is an additional cost (license) to it.

Figure 12.12 illustrates the options for creating a blank application or starting from any other data source. You can choose the option to make your app as follows:

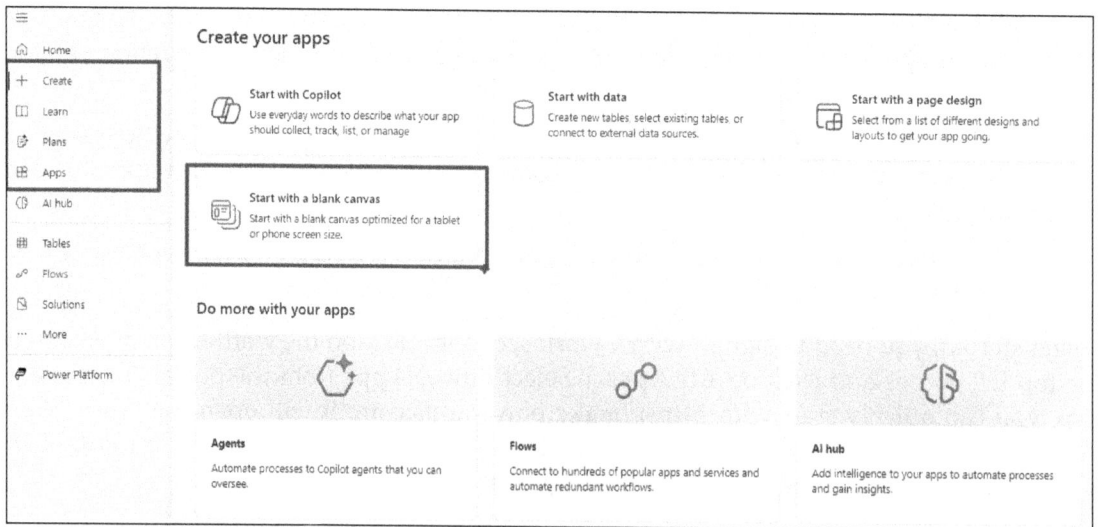

Figure 12.12: *Create an application via different data sources*

If you click on **Create**, it will display additional options. You can create a blank canvas or a blank canvas based on Dataverse, as depicted in *Figure 12.13*.

You can create no-code websites with power pages that you can customize according to the requirements, as follows:

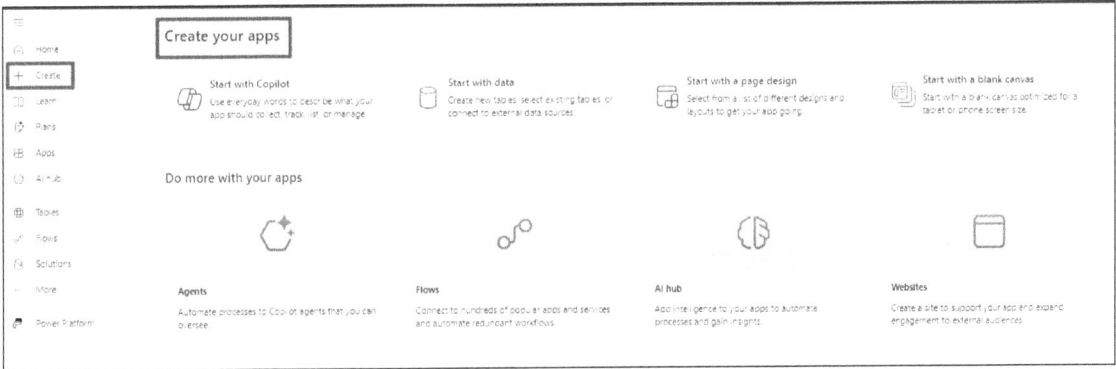

Figure 12.13: Create an application in different ways

In the **Learn** tab, as illustrated in *Figure 12.14*, you will find links to various Microsoft trainings, news, blogs, and discussion forums, along with articles and instructional videos:

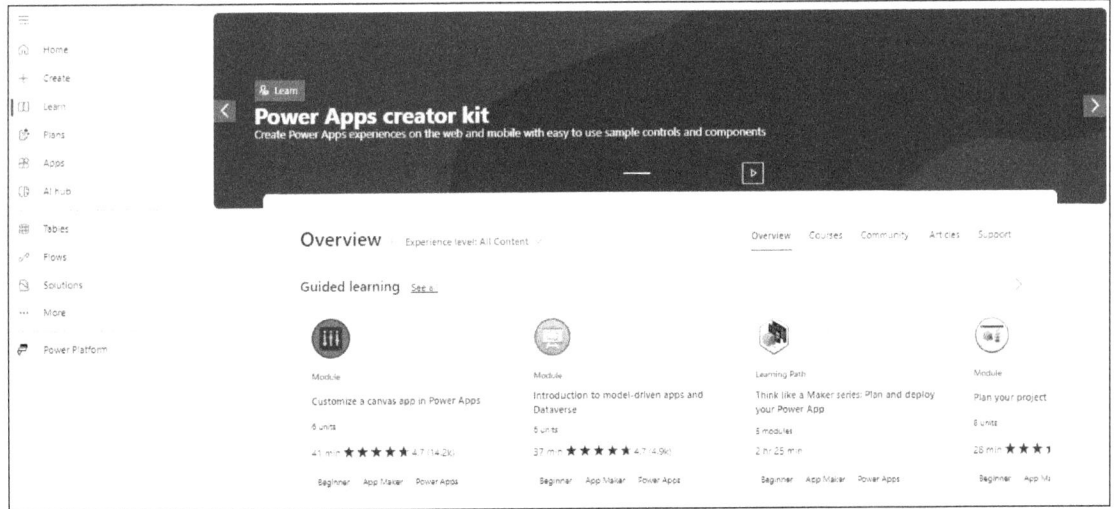

Figure 12.14: Links to Microsoft learning materials

The **Apps** tab provides a list of applications. A user wants to s*tart with Copilot* or to *start with data* where you can pick a table or existing data or to *start with a page design* or s*tart with an app template*. Templates are a great way to see how an app can behave with your data.

Figure 12.15 illustrates various options available in the **Apps** section:

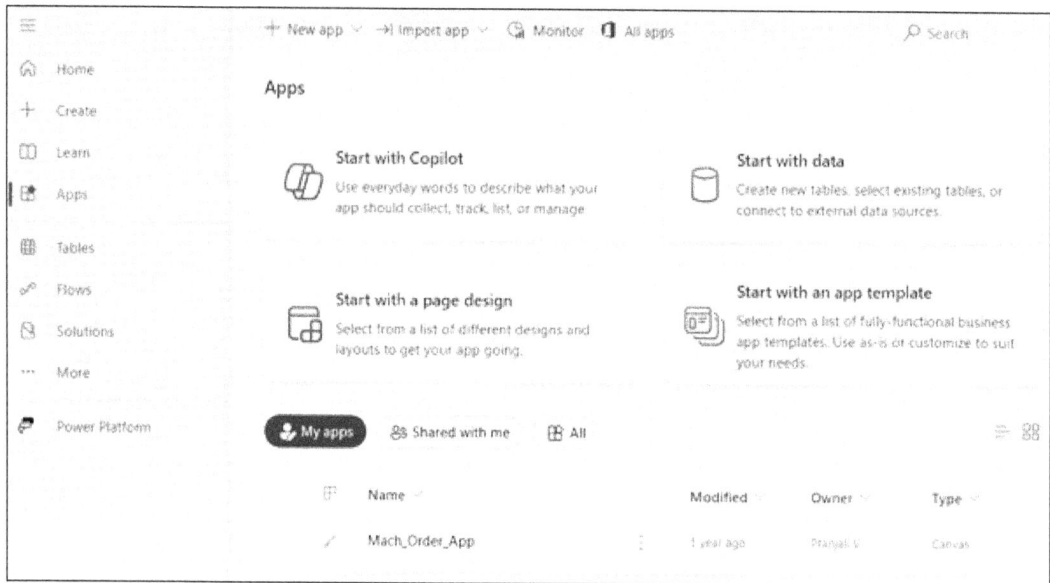

Figure 12.15: List of applications to start with

Create an application from Excel spreadsheet

In the following example, we are creating an app with an Excel table as a data source. The first and foremost thing is that you need to convert your Excel data into a table and save that file onto OneDrive, as shown in *Figure 12.16*:

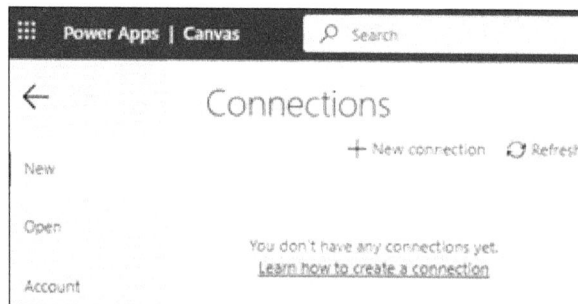

Figure 12.16: Creating connections in Power Apps

First, select the app launcher waffle box in the top left corner and select OneDrive. It will open the application in another browser tab. Here, we are clicking on **the Add new** button in the top left corner to add a file from anywhere on your device. This is the data file that is used in the application. After we create an application, it is available on mobile devices to run. For that, install Power Apps from the respective Play Store and sign in with your work account on mobile devices.

Here, we are going to create a three-screen app to understand how controls interact with each other. To get the data, open OneDrive and add new | Files upload. Select the data source file and click on **Open**. To start an application, select the **Create** tab from the left-hand side menu. Choose **Excel**.

Select the **+New Connection** button | Select **OneDrive for Business** | Select the **Create** button to create the connection. It will establish a connection with OneDrive for Business, as shown in *Figure 12.17*:

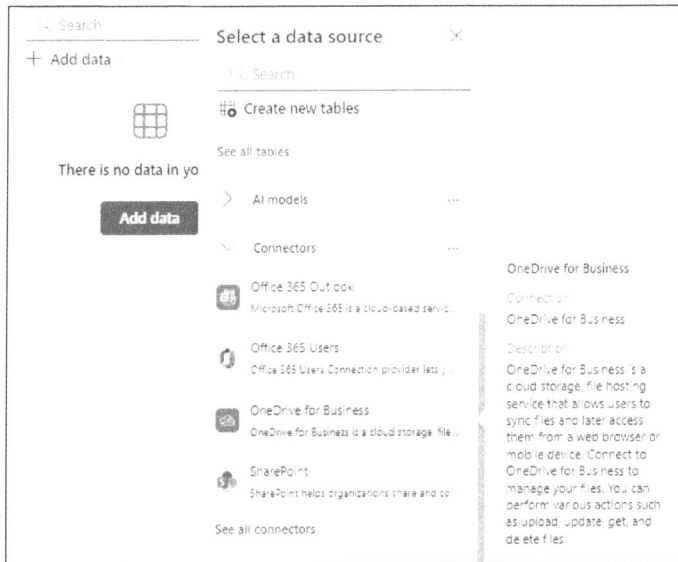

Figure 12.17: Connect with OneDrive for Business

Select the Excel file that you uploaded earlier on OneDrive for Business, and then select your Table. (The table is the area in the Excel file where your data resides, and you have saved your data by providing a name to your table.) Select the **Connect** button on the bottom right.

It will take some moments to fetch your data from the database and connect it with PowerApps. Once it is done, it will open Power Apps and build a three-screen app.

Now, you can view a fully functional app with a mobile look to it. To get a preview, use *F5* or click on the play button on the top right-hand side.

Components of Power Apps

The major components of Power Apps are listed as follows. These are useful when you are creating an application.

- **Gallery**: The gallery component in PowerApps visualizes data within the application. It is a template that allows one to view and navigate the data while reviewing all records.

Figure 12.18 shows different templates available in PowerApps:

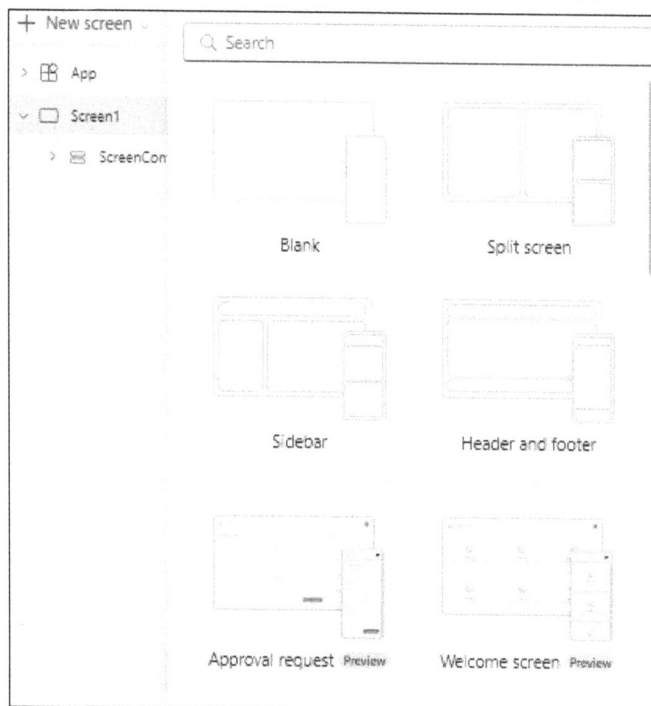

Figure 12.18: *Gallery view*

- **Screen**: A screen is a way to visualize the data set or record on a screen (mobile, iPad, or Desktop). Usually, you can view all records on one screen and edit them on another screen. Every time you create an application, you will find pre-defined templates available for you to choose from. You can always choose more screens in your application. You can rename a screen by clicking on the ellipsis. You can move up or down the screens. In fact, you can copy or duplicate the screen and use it by making a few changes. Deleting the screen is also possible if necessary. A comment can be added to the screen.

Figure 12.19 illustrates available screens while creating an application:

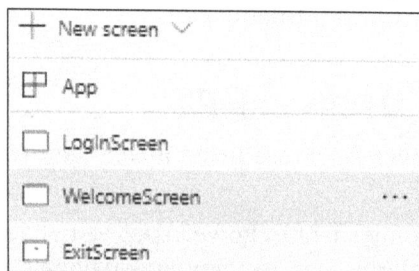

Figure 12.19: *Adding a New Screen*

- **Card**: A screen consists of cards. A card will contain all attributes related to the display of the record. A card is a placeholder that displays a specific record from a database, such as a SharePoint list or Excel table, to build an application. A card contains all different attributes and displays the record.

Figure 12.20 shows the card view:

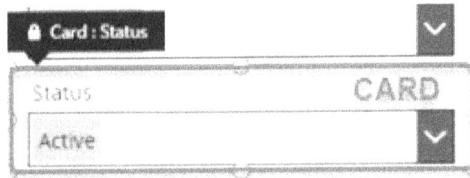

Figure 12.20: Cards View

- **Control:** It is used to visualize and interact with records. Depending on the field type, you can have different types of controls, such as buttons, drop-downs, Combo boxes, Date pickers, List boxes, Check boxes, text labels, and more.

Figure 12.21 shows different types of controls available to add to the application:

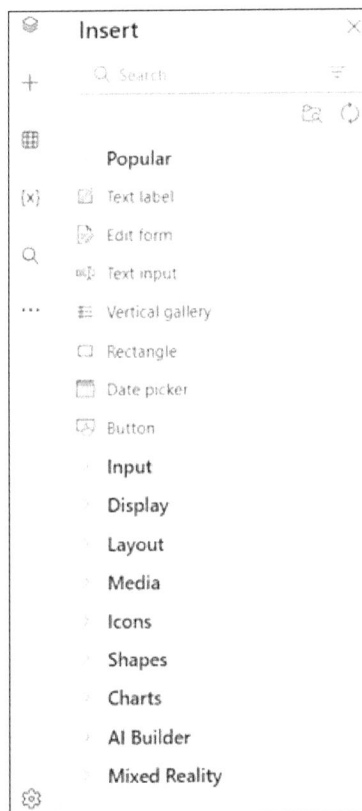

Figure 12.21: Different types of controls

- **Property**: Each control has various properties. For example, a text box has a property to change the font size, text color, text box fill color, and so on. Properties can be accessed and changed from the **Properties** panel on the right-hand side once the property is selected. If you are using a button, then properties will populate on the right side of the panel.

Figure 12.22 illustrates the properties of any selected control:

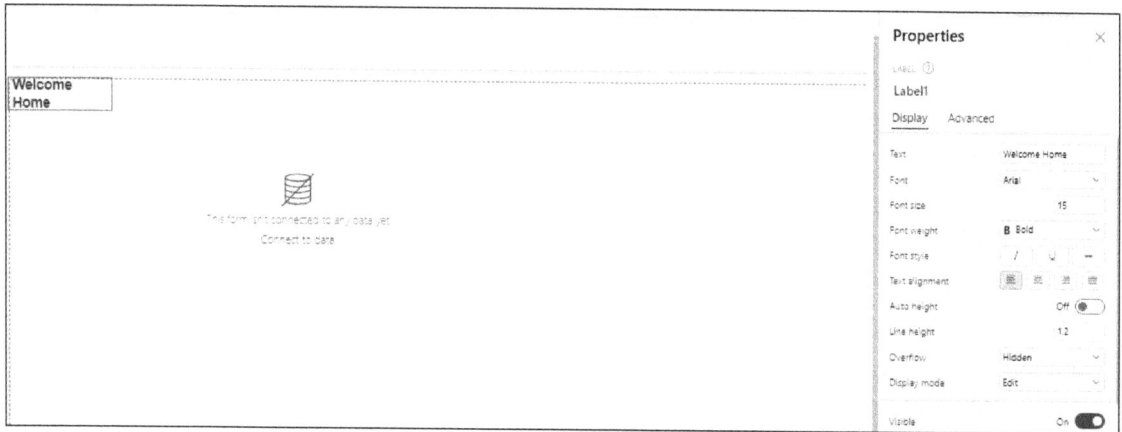

Figure 12.22: Properties of selected Label

- **Function**: Functions are predefined operations that perform specific tasks within an application. These functions allow users to manipulate data, control app behavior, and interact with various elements of the app. Functions take parameters, perform an operation, and return a value, like you are using functions in Excel. For instance, an if statement is used to change the property of a control depending on the value of the field.

  For instance: `If(ThisItem.Status.Value="Active", Red, Green)`

Difference between canvas app and model-driven app

Now you have understood the basic components of Power Apps. Once you build the application on the web-native Power Apps Platform, it will live in the cloud. These apps are easily shared and run on various platforms. By now, you know that it is a no-code or low-code platform for building applications. When an application is created, you need to connect to data with the help of various connectors. Some of the data sources include SharePoint, Dataverse, SQL Server, Office 365, and Excel, among others. You can choose any data source as Power Apps supports multiple data connections, bringing your data together from many platforms into a single app. There are two primary types of applications created in Power Apps, i.e., Canvas and model-driven apps.

Every application type offers various features and functionalities to assist in diverse scenarios, as follows:

- **Canvas apps**: The advantage of canvas apps is their ability to interact with data from more than 200 data sources. It allows your creativity and business sense to guide how you want your apps to look and feel. With Power FX formulas, developers can add desired functionality to their applications by dragging and dropping different controls. You can start to build your application from Microsoft tools where your data lives, like from a SharePoint list or from a Power BI dashboard. Moreover, Canvas can be embedded into SharePoint sites, Power BI reports, model-driven applications, or even Microsoft Teams. A canvas app would be ideal if the sales team needs a highly customizable user interface tailored to their specific needs. For instance, the sales team needs a mobile-friendly app that allows them to quickly access customer information, update sales opportunities, and collaborate with team members on the go. The Canvas app can include interactive dashboards, maps to visualize customer locations, and custom forms for entering sales data. Users can easily drag and drop components to design the app's layout according to their preferences.

- **Model-driven application**: Model-driven applications are used as management applications. It automatically generates awesome UI that is responsive across devices (a browser, a mobile phone, or a tablet). No need to worry about app size with model-driven apps. The organization typically uses a model-driven app to manage incoming requests, assist users with troubleshooting, dispatch someone to resolve them, and analyze overall operations. Managers can see overall performance using dashboards and charts, such as how many issues are reported and resolved. A model-driven app would be suitable if the sales team requires a structured and standardized interface with built-in business logic and data validation. For instance, the sales team needs a centralized platform with standardized forms, workflows, and business rules for managing customer interactions and sales processes. A model-driven app can include pre-built entities for managing accounts, contacts, opportunities, and activities. Users can leverage built-in features such as business process flows, data validation rules, and role-based security to streamline sales processes and ensure data consistency.

The following table provides a high-level comparison between the two. The choice between a canvas app and a model-driven app depends on factors such as the level of customization required, the complexity of business processes, and user preferences for user interface design and user experience, as follows:

Consider while creating an application	Canvas App	Model-driven App
Data Source	Not Dataverse-driven	Dataverse-driven
App purpose	Screen or task focused	Process focused
User Interface	Custom UI Device integration Easily embeddable	Responsive UI User personalization Data relationship navigation

Table 12.1: High-level comparison

Get started with Power Automate

Power Automate is a cloud-based service from Microsoft that allows users to automate workflows, integrate applications, and streamline repetitive tasks with minimal or no coding. It helps businesses improve efficiency by connecting different services, applications, and data sources to create automated processes.

Before we start Power Automate, let us imagine having a personal assistant who can handle all those repetitive tasks for you, like sending emails, updating spreadsheets, or even posting on social media. That is basically what Power Automate does, but in a digital form. It is a tool that helps you automate your workflow by creating **flows**, sequences of actions that are triggered by specific events. So instead of spending time on manual tasks, you can let Power Automate do the work for you, freeing up your time for more important things.

As the latest technological trends continue to evolve, the foundational tools that support new advancements are becoming increasingly intricate over time.

When we talk about automation, we (mostly tech enthusiasts or those with a background in tech) generally think about topics such as Internet of Things (connecting obsolete technology or modern appliances and giving them certain intelligence through the power of the internet), artificial intelligence, Generative AI or certain complex programs that oversee numerous complicated tasks. The concept of automation has now exceeded robotics, which can oversee industrial development on a high-end scale. However, if we talk about automation in a nutshell, it is basically defined as a procedure or process that requires minimum human effort.

Power Automate refers to automate repetitive manual work in Microsoft 365 environment. It is all about process automation. It is a service that helps you create automated workflows between your applications and services to synchronize files, get notifications, and collect data. You need to sign in with Microsoft 365 credentials, and you will find Power Automate on the web as well as in a desktop application.

Figure 12.23 illustrates the initial screen of Power Automate, as follows:

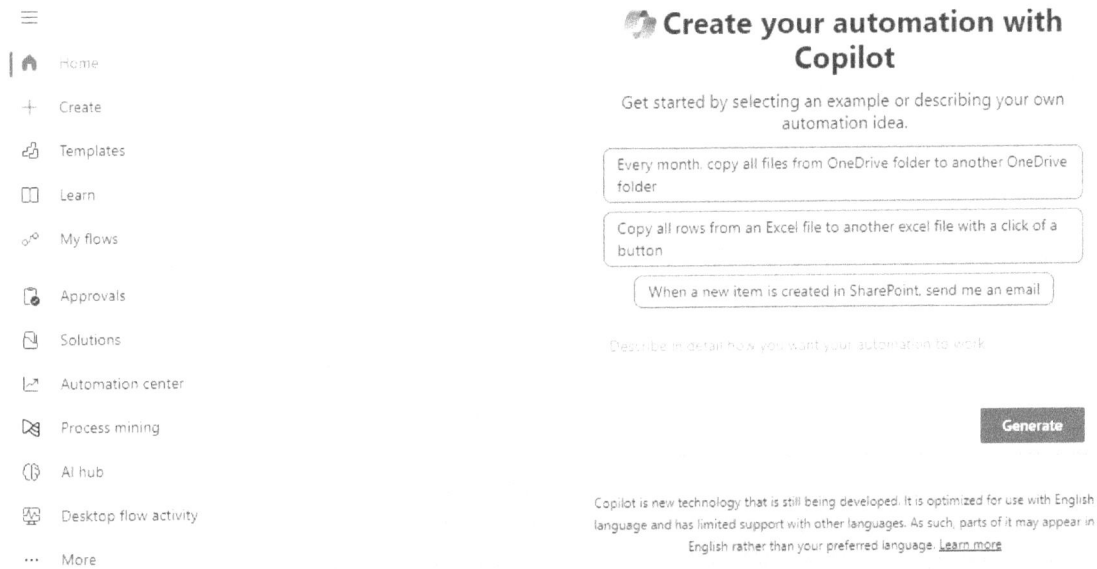

Figure 12.23: *Initial screen of Power Automate*

Power Automate offers automation capabilities for both individual users and enterprise-level process automation. Its user-friendly interface accommodates users of all technical levels, ranging from novices to experienced developers, enabling them to automate work tasks effortlessly.

Elements of Power Automate

There are a few key elements that are required to enhance the solutions you create in Power Platform. The following is the description of elements:

- **Connectors**: Connectors play an important role as you need to connect apps, data, and devices in the cloud. There are more than 1000 prebuilt connectors to enable all your data and actions to connect cohesively. A few of the connectors are Salesforce, Dropbox, Google services, Microsoft 365, etc.

- **AI Builder**: It allows users to add AI capabilities to the workflows they create and use. AI Builder is a feature within the Microsoft Power Platform that empowers users to easily incorporate **artificial intelligence** (**AI**) capabilities into their business applications. It provides a set of pre-built AI models that can be seamlessly integrated into Power Apps and Power Automate workflows without the need for extensive coding. With AI Builder, users can leverage AI functionalities such as form processing, object detection, text recognition, prediction, and sentiment analysis to enhance their applications and automate processes. It democratizes AI by making it accessible to a wider audience, enabling businesses to derive valuable insights and improve decision-making through AI-driven automation.

- **Dataverse**: Dataverse is like a digital filing cabinet where you can store and organize all your business data. It is a secure and scalable database service provided by Microsoft that allows you to store and manage your data in a structured way. With Dataverse, you can create tables to store different types of information, define relationships between tables, and set up rules to ensure data integrity. It's the backbone of many Microsoft business applications, providing a central repository for your data that can be easily accessed and utilized across various apps and services.

- **Power FX**: It is the low code programming language that is used across Power Platform.

- **Managed environments**: These are secure and isolated environments that allow organizations to build, test, and deploy applications while maintaining control over data and resources.

- **Microsoft Copilot Studio**: Copilot Studio is a low code tool and suggests pre-built templates, actions, and conditions based on the user's requirements. It can assist in creating flows to automate business processes, integrate with other applications, and handle data more efficiently.

To start, sign in with a Microsoft 365 account. When you sign up, you are going to connect with hundreds of services and can manage data either in the cloud or in on-premises sources like SharePoint and Microsoft SQL Server.

Figure 12.24 points out the place where you can sign in with a Microsoft 365 account:

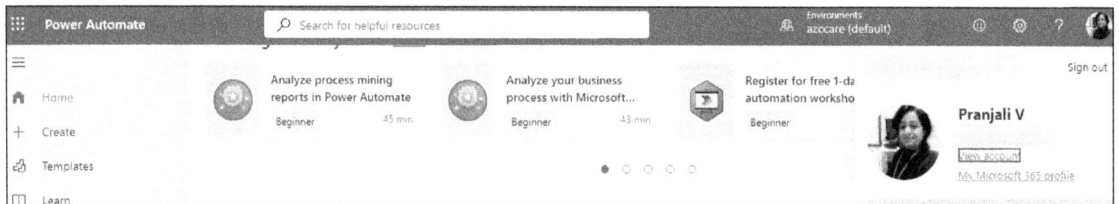

Figure 12.24: Initial screen to sign-in

You will be able to see the home screen of Power Automate where you have some learning materials linked, and Copilot to automate your workflows. For instance, you can create flows that post a message on a Microsoft Teams channel whenever a file is deleted from OneDrive.

Figure 12.25 illustrates various options available on the Power Automate home page:

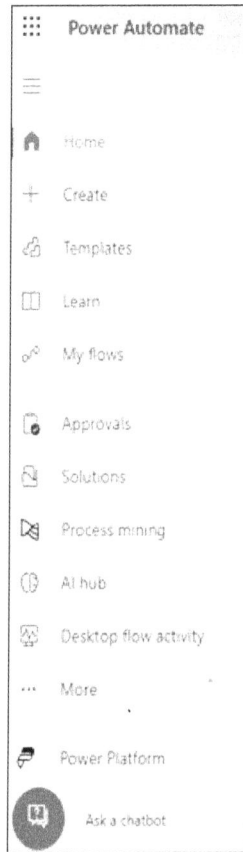

Figure 12.25: Available options

On the left-hand side, you will find the following options, as shown in the aforementioned figure:

- **Create**: By clicking, you can start a new flow.

- **Templates**: It is a place where you will find the most popular templates to start with. If you are a beginner, it is a good option to start with pre-defined templates. These templates are available for all.

- **Learn**: Clicking on this option will redirect you to the Microsoft Learn website, where you can find information that will help you quickly ramp up on Power Automate.

- **My flows**: It is a place where your existing flows reside.

- **Approvals**: where you can manage approvals and business process flows.

- **Solutions**: It will manage your solutions.

- **Process mining**: It is a place where you can create processes to help your organization better understand places to streamline workflows.

A common use of automation is to receive notifications. The best way to use Power Automate is to use templates. Templates can rapidly construct flows by making a few configuration adjustments.

As an illustration, templates enable you to effortlessly create flows for tasks like receiving weather forecasts, setting periodic reminders, or receiving phone notifications whenever your manager sends you an email.

Templates in Power Automate

You will be able to view different categories of templates that are available. Templates are pre-built automation workflows that help users quickly set up automated processes without creating flows from scratch. These templates provide ready-to-use automation for common business tasks, saving time and effort.

Figure 12.26 shows various available templates in Power Automate:

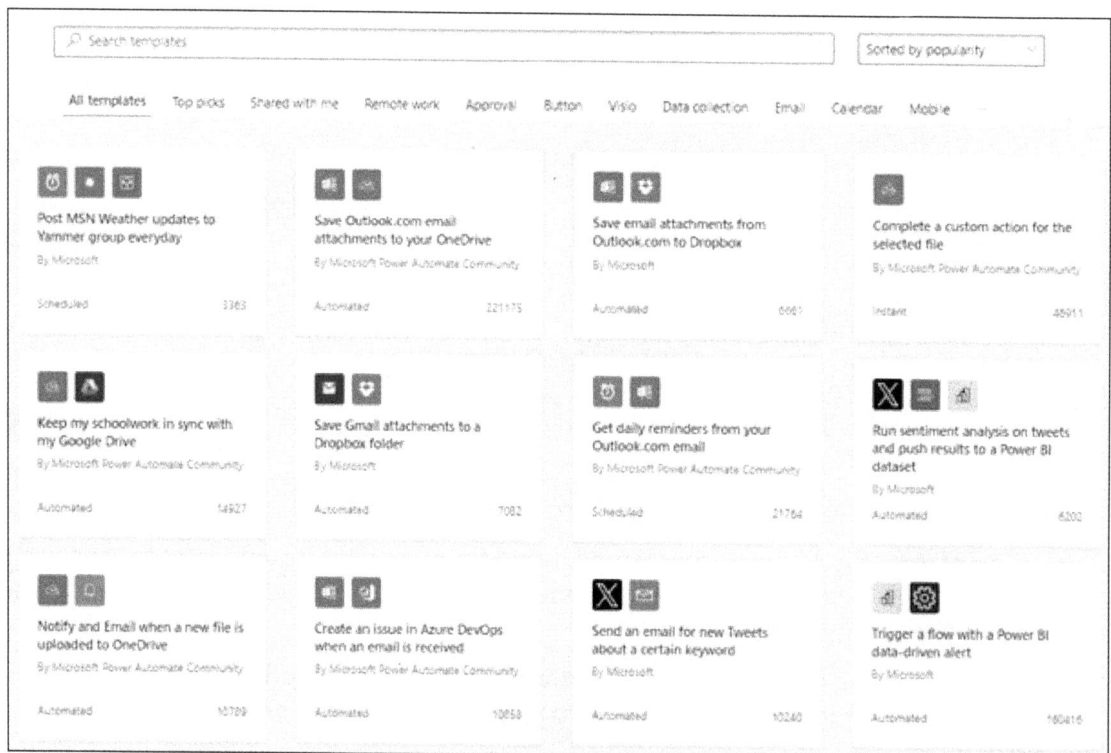

Figure 12.26: Predefined templates

Types of flows

There are different types of flows in Power Automate, each serving a specific purpose and catering to different automation needs:

- **Automated flows:** These flows are triggered by an event, such as a new email arriving in your inbox, a file being added to a folder, or a record being updated in a database. Once triggered, the flow automatically executes a series of actions based on predefined criteria.

- **Instant cloud flows:** Also known as **Button Flows**, these flows are manually triggered by a user with the click of a button. They are useful for ad-hoc tasks or processes that require human intervention to initiate.

- **Scheduled cloud flows:** These flows are triggered at specific times or intervals, such as every day at 9:00 AM or every week on Mondays. They are ideal for automating recurring tasks, such as sending out weekly reports or reminders.

- **Desktop flows:** Use this **robotic process automation (RPA)** to record actions on the desktop. Formerly known as *UI Flows (RPA)*, these flows automate repetitive manual tasks by mimicking user interactions with the user interface of desktop or web applications. They are useful for automating tasks that involve navigating through multiple screens or performing data entry in legacy systems.

- **Business process flows:** These flows guide users through a series of steps or stages to complete a specific business process, such as onboarding a new employee, processing a customer order, or handling a support ticket. They provide a structured framework for managing and tracking complex processes.

Each type of flow offers unique capabilities and is suited to different use cases, allowing users to automate a wide range of processes and tasks within their organization.

Before creating a flow, a few important things to keep in mind are as follows:

Every flow has two main parts, a trigger and an action. A trigger in the context of Microsoft Power Automate is an event that initiates the execution of a workflow or flow. It acts as the starting point for the automation process, prompting the flow to begin when a specific event occurs.

An action, on the other hand, is a step within the workflow that performs a specific operation or task. Actions can include sending an email, updating a record in a database, posting to a social media platform, or any other operation that you want the flow to perform.

For instance, you want to create a flow that sends you an email notification whenever a new lead is added to your CRM system. In this scenario, the trigger would be *when a new lead is created* in your CRM system. The action would be to *send an email* to your inbox notifying you about the new lead. So, whenever a new lead is added to your CRM system (trigger), the flow will automatically send you an email (action) to notify you about it.

Now, when you click **Create** from the left side menu, there are options to make flow. Users can create **automated cloud flow**, **Instant cloud flow**, or **Scheduled cloud flow**.

Figure 12.27 depicts various categories of flow:

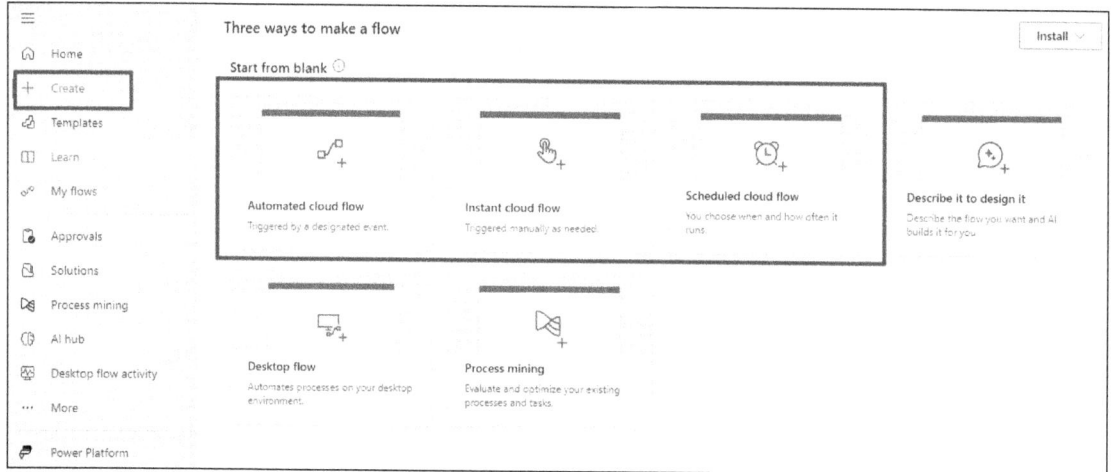

Figure 12.27: *Various types of flow*

The following exercise will help you understand how to create a flow.

Create a flow that automatically performs one or more actions after an event triggers it. In this flow, when any email comes with an attachment and with a defined subject line and email address, the flow will copy the attachment and save it to a SharePoint library.

Figure 12.28 illustrates how to build a flow. Here, we are using the SharePoint site and its default **Documents** library. Go to the home screen of Power Automate. Select **My flows** and use the drop-down list from **New flow**, as follows:

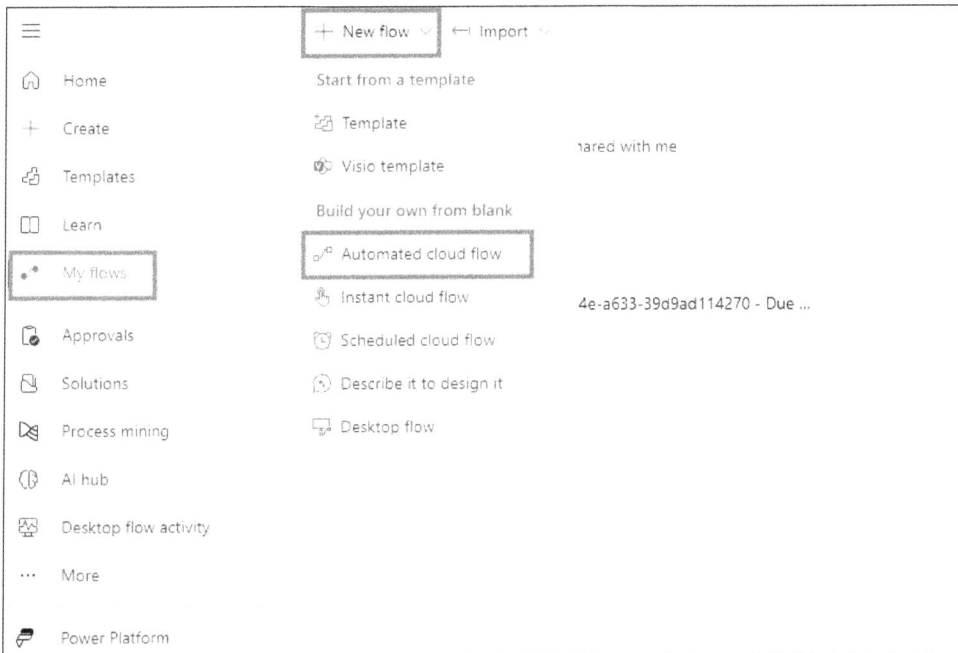

Figure 12.28: Build a flow using My flows

Under **Choose your flow's trigger**, enter **Outlook**, select the **When a new email arrives (V3)** trigger, and select **Create**, as follows:

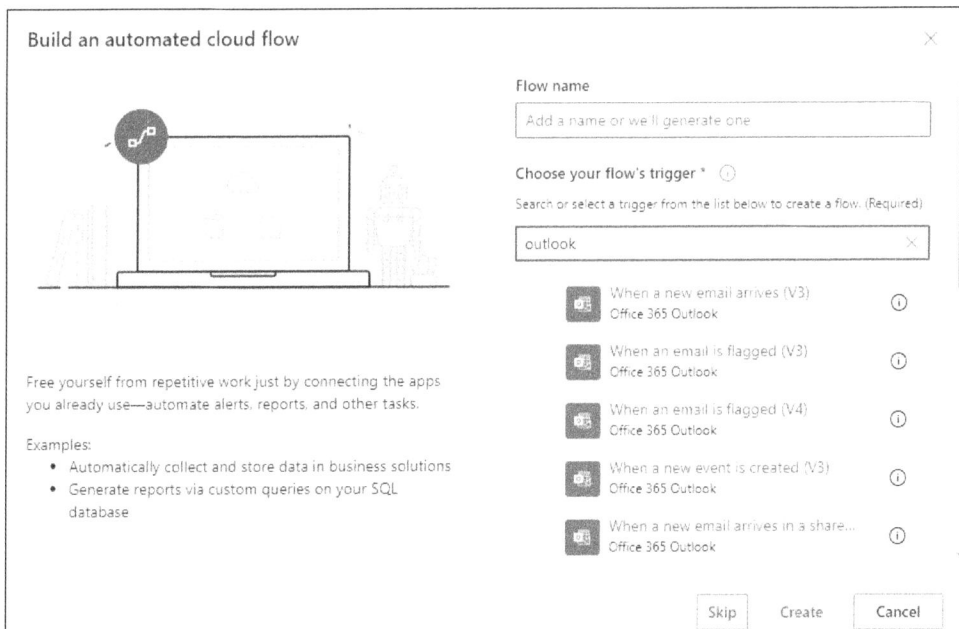

Figure 12.29: Steps to build an automated cloud flow

Select the trigger and then select the **Show all** button as follows in *Figure 12.30*:

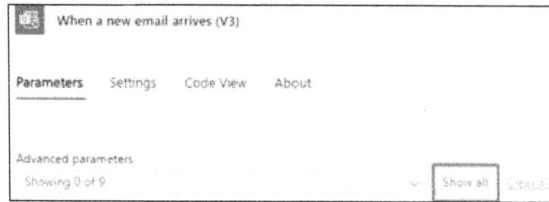

Figure 12.30: Setting parameters

Figure 12.31 illustrates how to add your organization email ID, fill in **Yes** in Include Attachments, fill in **Subject filter**, **Importance**, **Only with Attachments,** and **Folder** fields, as follows:

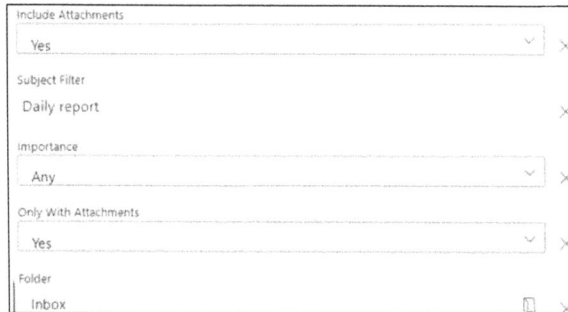

Figure 12.31: Different fields of a trigger

- Specify an action. Select **Insert a new step,** and then select **Add an action** field.
- Search for **Create file**, and then select the **SharePoint Create file** action.
- For Folder Path, select **/ShareDocuments**.
- Select the **File Name** field and select the **Enter data from previous step** button.

Then select **Attachments Name** for **Dynamic Content**, as given in *Figure 12.32*:

Figure 12.32: Connect with SharePoint database

Select the **File Content** field and select the **Enter data from the previous step** button. Then select **Attachments Content** from **Dynamic Content**, as shown:

Figure 12.33:

Once the **Attachments Name** is added, the **Create file** action is automatically added in an **Apply to each.**

This will handle scenarios when an email comes in with multiple attachments.

After performing all the steps, you will be able to successfully build a Power Automate flow, which will monitor Outlook emails and submit them to the **Documents** folder in the SharePoint library.

In this chapter, we have covered the basics of Power Automate, though we are also covering the Power Automate desktop application, where you can learn how to create desktop flows.

Power Automate for desktop

The Microsoft Power Automate for the desktop platform broadens the RPA capabilities by enabling users to automate everyday repetitive tasks. Install the Power Automate desktop application. A major benefit of using desktop flows is the ability to perform actions on desktop applications.

Figure 12.34 illustrates the welcome screen of Power automate desktop application:

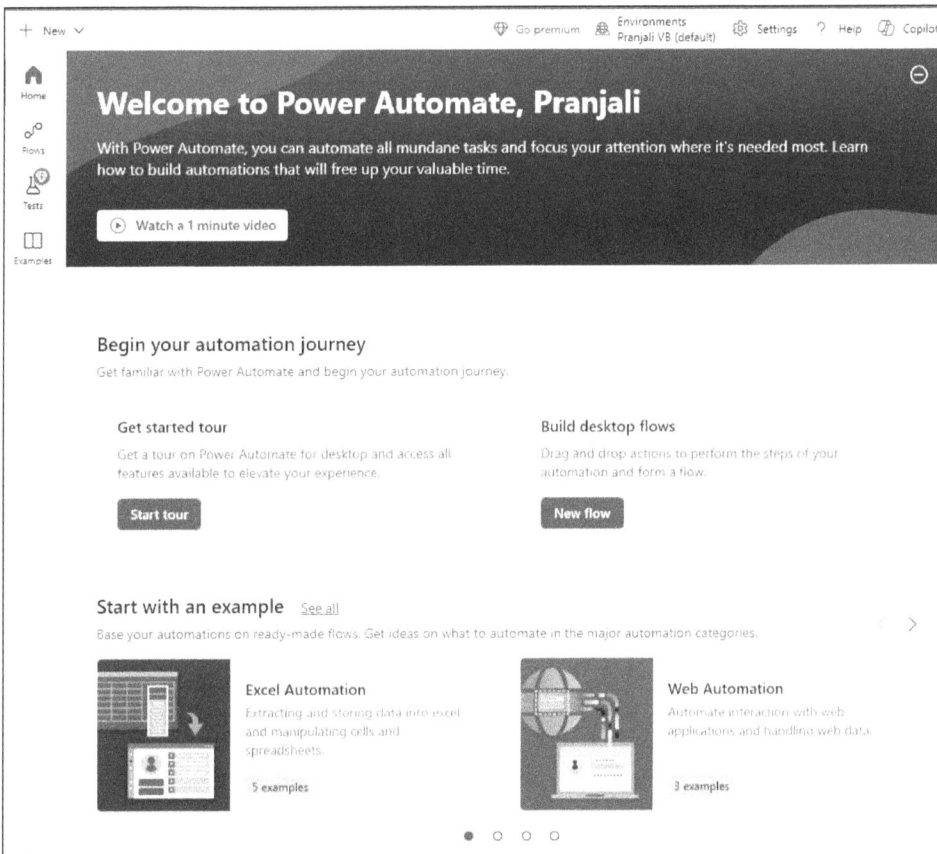

Figure 12.34: Home screen of Power Automate

Power Automate desktop consists of two main components that enable you to create and manage flows: the console and the flow designer.

The console is the main control panel of the platform from which you can launch the flow designer to create or edit flows. You can also delete, rename, and run existing flows through the console's options.

Open and explore Power Automate. Under **My Flows**, your existing desktop flows will display, where you can edit, start, or delete them. You can explore creating or editing a flow process by selecting the + **New flow** button in the upper-left corner or starting with an example with pre-defined templates, as illustrated in *Figure 12.35*:

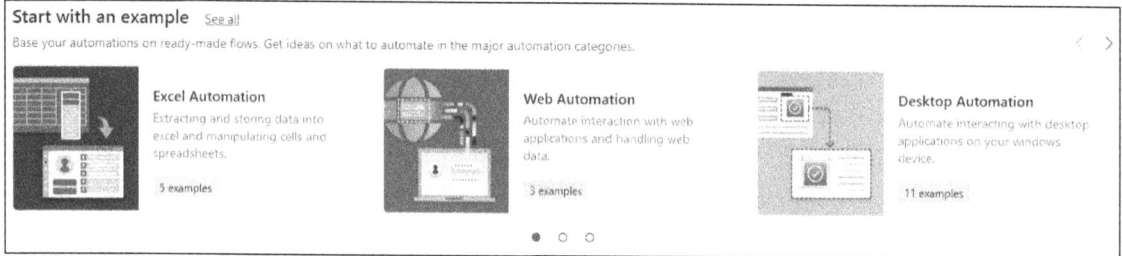

Figure 12.35: Initial screen to select pre-defined templates

Once you click on +**New** flow, it will pop up a dialog box where you are going to type the name of your flow, then click on the **Create** button, as shown in *Figure 12.36*:

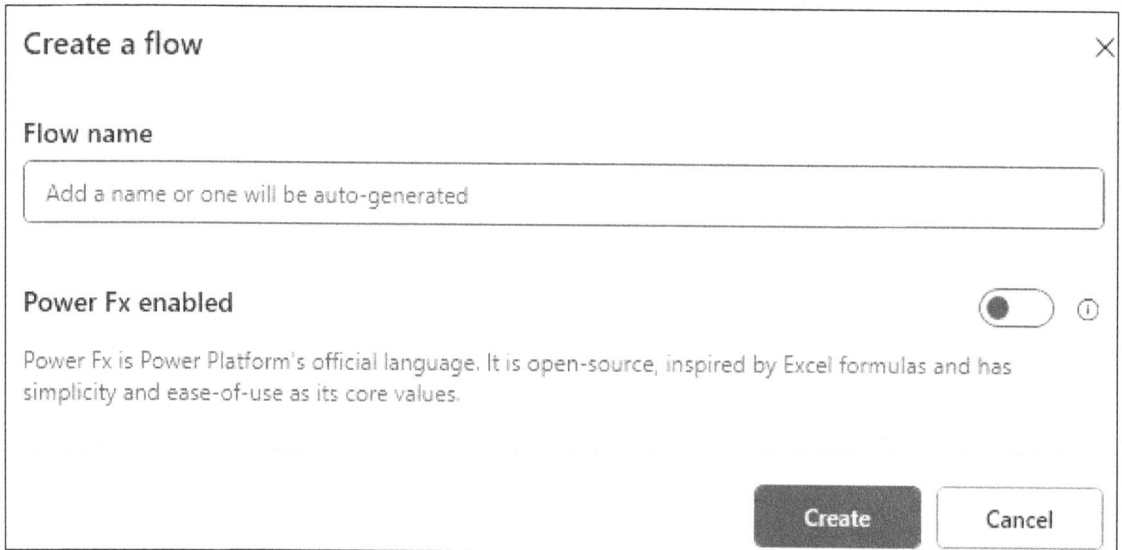

Figure 12.36: Interface for providing name to your flow

Once you click the **Create** button, the Power Automation designer page will open. *Figure 12.37* illustrates different areas that the page will contain to understand:

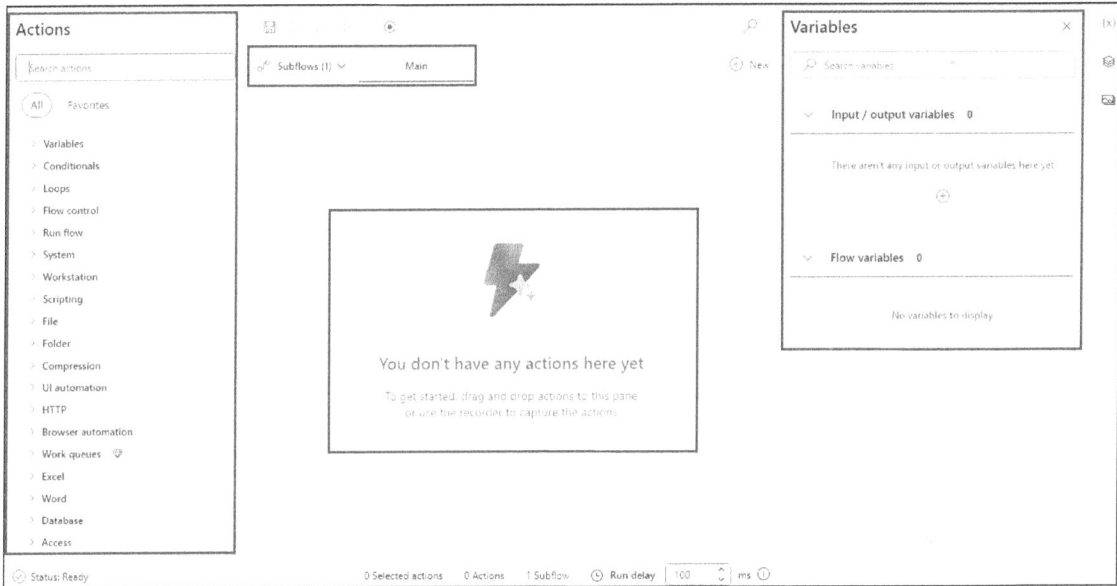

Figure 12.37: Power Automate desktop Interface

In the top left corner, different menus are available, as follows:

- **Toolbar**: It contains basic operations for use with actions (**Save**, **Undo**, **Copy**, **Debug**, and **Paste**) and buttons to start the desktop/web recorders and control the process implementation (**Start**, **Pause,** or **Stop**).

- **Subflows**: This option allows you to create subflows under your **Main** flow.

- **Actions pane**: On the left-hand side, it contains all Power Automate actions and includes a search bar that helps you find specific actions by matching the action name to the text string.

- **Workspace**: The middle area contains all actions that have been added to the process so far. Functions are separated into tabs.

- **Input or output variables**: It contains all variables that you have created in the process.

- **Flow variables**: A List of all variables that are used in the process.

You can check your flow under the **My Flows** tab. Now, we need to add the action. Desktop flows are created to mimic the actions of a user who is performing steps in a process. To add actions to your flow, select the desired action and then drag it to the Main canvas. Under the Excel dropdown menu on the **Actions** pane, select the desired action and drag it to the main canvas. Here, we will use the **Launch Excel** action. You will use this feature to launch Excel. It will open a dialog box. Select the required option from the menu. Click on the **Save** button. Click on **Play**. It will open an Excel file, as follows:

Figure 12.38 illustrates the step-by-step process that automation will run:

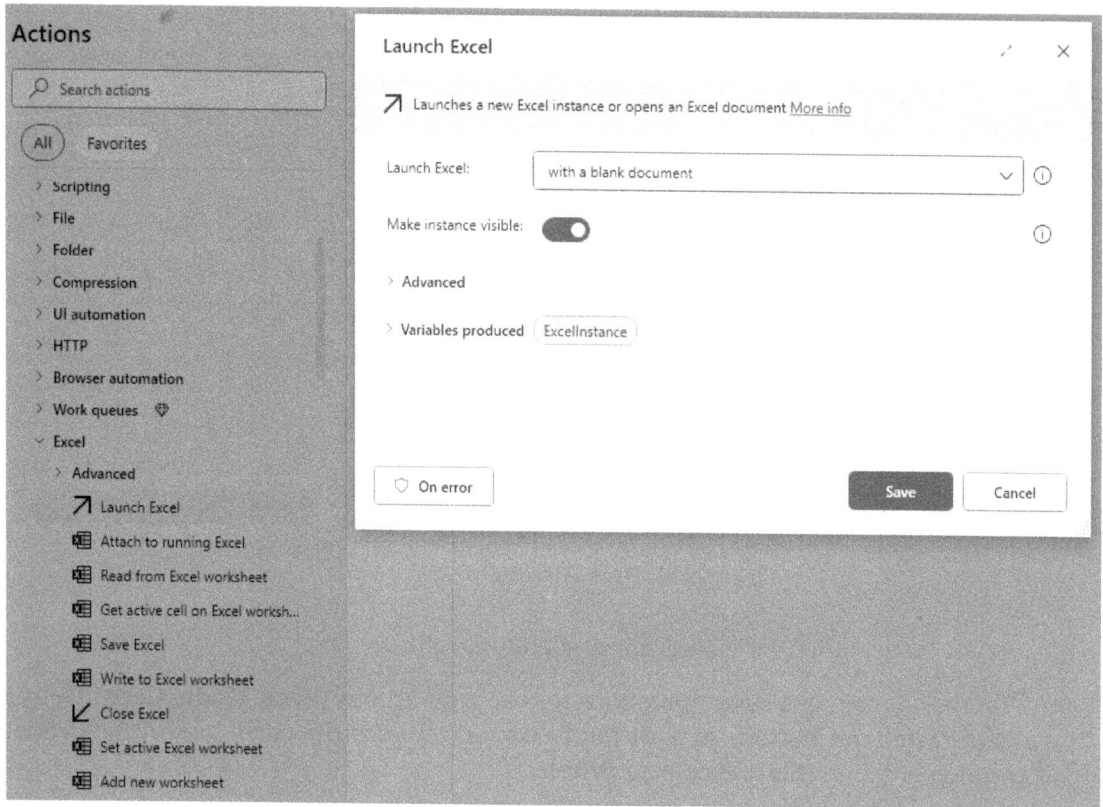

Figure 12.38: *Select actions and drag them to the right side*

When we are using Excel automation using Power Automate, there are numerous tasks that can be done. It allows users to automate tasks involving Microsoft Excel files, such as data manipulation, report generation, and data entry. *Figure 12.39* illustrates various Excel automation templates that can be used in a Power Automate desktop application.

The following are some examples:

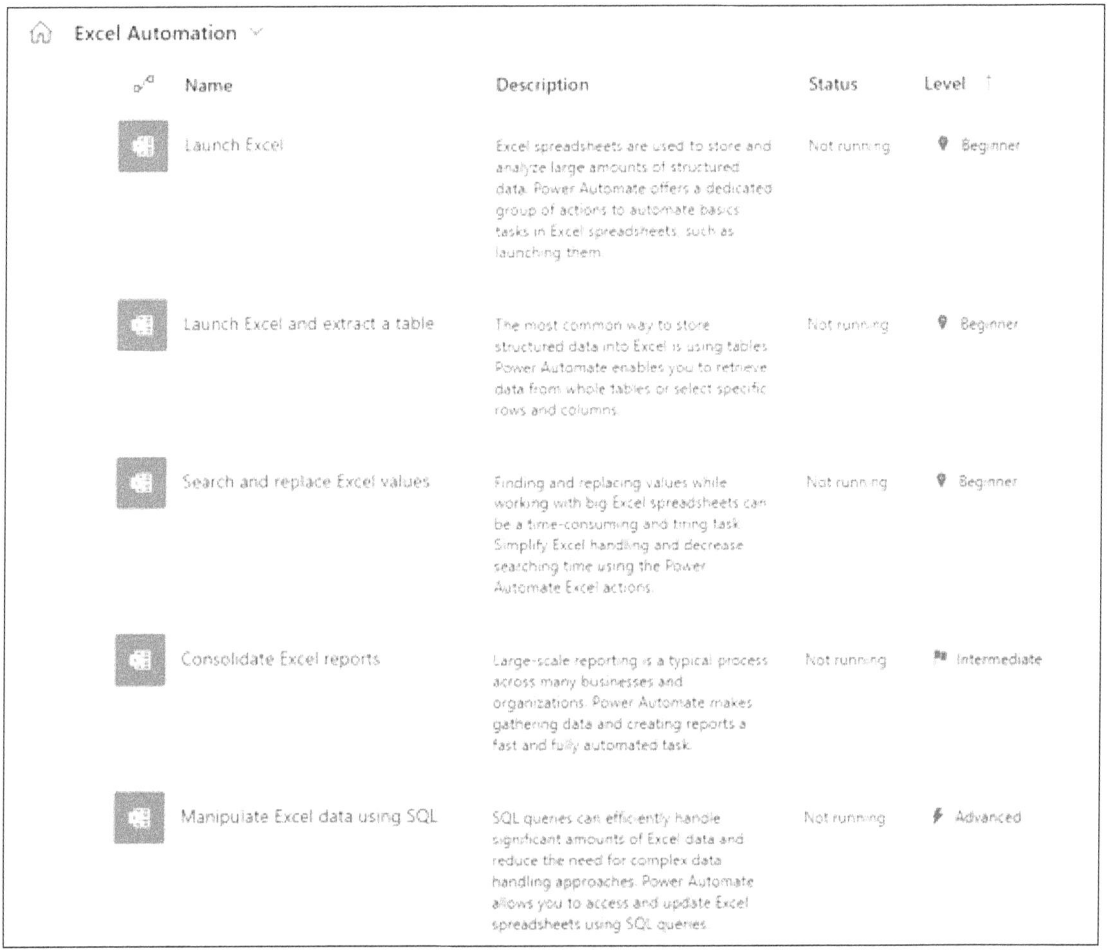

Figure 12.39: Taking actions and dragging to the right side

The advantages of Excel automation in Power Automate Desktop are as follows:

- **Time savings and accuracy**: Automating repetitive Excel tasks can save users time and effort, allowing them to focus on more strategic activities. Users can reduce the risk of errors associated with manual data entry and manipulation.

- **Scalability**: Power Automate Desktop allows users to create complex workflows that can scale to handle large volumes of data or perform intricate data transformations.

- **Integration**: Excel automation in Power Automate Desktop seamlessly integrates with other Microsoft and third-party applications, allowing users to automate end-to-end business processes involving Excel files and other systems.

- **Standardization**: By automating Excel-based reports and processes, users can ensure consistency and standardization across their organization, reducing variability and improving data quality.

PDF automation in Desktop Power Automate can be utilized to automate various tasks involving PDF files, such as extracting text, merging or splitting PDFs, filling out PDF forms, and converting files to or from PDF format, as shown in *Figure 12.40*:

Name	Description	Status	Level ∧
Create PDF from selected PDF page(s)	PDF files may have tens or hundreds of pages depending on the nature of their content. An effective way to handle specific information from these files is to gather it in a separate file. The Power Automate PDF actions enable users to extract any possible combination of pages and save them in different files for further manipulation.	Not running	♀ Beginner
Get images from PDF	Apart from text content, PDF files can contain important information in the form of images. Power Automate offers a PDF action that extracts images from PDF files and enables users to access and process these images independently of the original file.	Not running	♀ Beginner
Merge two PDFs	PDF manipulation is an ideal candidate for automation, as many scenarios, such as merging reports, require strictly standardized steps. Power Automate provides a series of PDF actions to automate these tasks and handle PDF files efficiently.	Not running	♀ Beginner
Extract table(s) from PDF	Although PDF format is typical for sharing content, directly manipulating tables inside it can be overwhelming. Power Automate enables users to extract tables from PDF files and store them in other file types, such as Excel worksheets, for easier editing.	Not running	⚑ Intermediate
Get number of pages in a PDF	While handling PDF files, users may encounter scenarios that require them to extract specific information regarding the files. The available PDF actions enable users to retrieve various details from PDF files, such as the total number of their pages.	Not running	⚑ Intermediate

Figure 12.40: PDF automation in Power Automate desktop application

It can be used as follows:

- **Table extraction:** You can create a flow that automatically extracts tables from PDF files and stores them in a cloud storage service like OneDrive or SharePoint. These extracted tables can then be used for further processing or analysis.

- **PDF merging and splitting:** You can automate the process of merging multiple PDF files into a single document or splitting a large PDF file into smaller ones. This can be useful for organizing and managing PDF files more efficiently.

- **PDF form filling:** You can create a flow that automatically fills out PDF forms with data from other sources, such as a SharePoint list or an Excel spreadsheet. This can streamline the process of completing forms and reduce manual data entry errors.

- **PDF conversion:** You can automate the conversion of files to or from PDF format, such as converting Word documents, Excel spreadsheets, or images to PDF format, or vice versa. This can make it easier to share and distribute documents in a standardized format.

Overall, PDF automation in Desktop Power Automate can help streamline document-related processes, reduce manual effort, and improve efficiency in handling PDF files within your organization.

The following are the steps to define a flow:

1. **Plan**: Outline the flow's purpose and requirements.

2. **Design**: Create and configure the workflow

3. **Make**: Save progress frequently

4. **Test**: Validate and refine the flow, monitor the variable values if any.

5. **Deploy**: Activate and monitor the flow.

Conclusion

In conclusion, Microsoft's Power Platform, comprising Power Apps, Power BI, and Power Automate, offers a comprehensive suite of tools that empower users to build custom applications, analyze data, and automate workflows with ease. Power Apps allows users to create tailored business apps without extensive coding knowledge, while Power BI enables users to derive actionable insights from their data through interactive visualizations and reports. Additionally, Power Automate streamlines business processes by automating repetitive tasks and integrating with various applications and services. Together, these components of the Power Platform empower organizations to drive innovation, increase productivity, and make data-driven decisions to achieve their business goals.

Desktop flows allow you to create custom automations; however, you will need to have access to make changes to the environment in your tenant and have the appropriate licenses and permissions. Recording your actions is as simple as pressing a button. RPA is accessible to anyone who uses the Power Automate application.

Points to remember

- **Enhanced productivity and efficiency:** Power Apps, Power BI, and Power Automate offer numerous advantages for enterprises where users utilize them daily, like increased efficiency, in which Power Apps allow users to rapidly create custom business applications tailored to their specific needs, streamlining processes and reducing manual work. Power Automate automates repetitive tasks, freeing up time for more strategic activities. Power BI provides insights into data, enabling informed decision-making and driving efficiency.

- **Enhanced collaboration:** These tools facilitate collaboration across teams by providing a centralized platform for app development, data analysis, and workflow automation. Users can easily share apps, reports, and workflows, fostering collaboration and improving productivity.

- **Improved data management:** With Power BI, organizations can consolidate and visualize data from various sources, allowing users to gain insights and make data-driven decisions. Power Automate ensures data consistency and accuracy by automating data entry and validation tasks.

- **Scalability**: As enterprise needs evolve, Power Platform solutions can scale to accommodate growing data volumes, user bases, and business requirements. Power Apps, Power BI, and Power Automate are cloud-based services that offer scalability and flexibility to adapt to changing business demands.

- **Cost savings:** By reducing manual effort, streamlining processes, and improving decision-making, Power Platform solutions can lead to cost savings for enterprises. Additionally, these tools offer flexible pricing options, allowing organizations to pay for only what they use.

- **Empowerment of citizen developers:** Power Apps empowers citizen developers—users with little or no coding experience—to create applications, democratizing app development within the organization. This enables faster innovation and reduces the reliance on IT resources.

- **Integration with Microsoft Ecosystem**: Power Apps, Power BI, and Power Automate seamlessly integrate with other Microsoft services and applications, such as Office 365, Dynamics 365, and Azure. This integration enhances interoperability and enables users to leverage existing investments in Microsoft technology.

Overall, Power Apps, Power BI, and Power Automate offer significant advantages for enterprises, including increased efficiency, enhanced collaboration, improved data management, cost savings, empowerment of citizen developers, and integration with the Microsoft ecosystem. These tools empower organizations to drive digital transformation, innovate faster, and achieve their business objectives more effectively.

References

1. https://www.encorebusiness.com/blog/what-is-the-power-platform/
2. https://powerplatform.microsoft.com/en-in/what-is-power-platform/
3. https://learn.microsoft.com/en-us/training/modules/get-started-with-powerapps/1-powerapps-introduction
4. https://learn.microsoft.com/en-us/training/modules/introduction-power-apps/3-explore-canvas-applications
5. https://www.powerbi-influential.com/solutions/azure-synapse-analytics/
6. https://learn.microsoft.com/en-us/training/modules/introduction-power-platform/4-explore-connectors-microsoft-dataverse
7. https://learn.microsoft.com/en-us/training/modules/get-started-flows/1-introduction
8. https://learn.microsoft.com/en-us/training/modules/build-first-desktop-flow/

Index

www.ingramcontent.com/pod-product-compliance
Lightning Source LLC
Chambersburg PA
CBHW061743210326
41599CB00034B/6778